A MAGNIFICENT DISASTER

A MAGNIFICENT DISASTER

*The Failure of Market Garden,
the Arnhem Operation,
September 1944*

By
DAVID BENNETT

CASEMATE
Philadelphia & Newbury

Published in the United States of America in 2008 by
CASEMATE
1016 Warrior Road, Drexel Hill, PA 19026

and in Great Britain by
CASEMATE
17 Cheap Street, Newbury RG20 5DD

Copyright 2008 © Dave Bennett

ISBN 978-1-932033-85-4

Cataloging-in-publication data is available from the Library of Congress
and the British Library.

Printed and Bound in the United States of America.

For a complete list of Casemate titles please contact:

CASEMATE PUBLISHERS
Telephone (610) 853-9131, Fax (610) 853-9146
E-mail: casemate@casematepublishing.com

CASEMATE PUBLISHERS
Telephone (01635) 231091, Fax (01635) 41619
E-mail: casemate-uk@casematepublishing.co.uk

CONTENTS

FOREWORD *by Carlo D'Este*   xi

1. THE PROSPECTS FOR THE WESTERN ALLIES   1
2. TWO WEEKS OF ALLIED PREPARATION   19
3. THE OTHER SIDE OF THE HILL   43
4. AN AMERICAN TRIUMPH   61
5. AIRBORNE HIATUS   87
6. BLACK TUESDAY   103
7. SUCCESS CLASHES WITH FAILURE   115
8. *POLONIA RESTITUTA*   137
9. STAGNATION   143
10. THE POLES' SECOND CROSSING OF THE RHINE   151
11. DITHERING AND DECEIT   157
12. THE LAST HOPE FADES   169
13. THE NIGHT OF THE CANADIANS   181
14. ASSESSMENT   191

EPILOGUE   203

Appendix 1: Chronology of Events   211
Appendix 2: The Supply Situation of 21st Army Group on
             the Eve of *Market Garden*   217
Appendix 3: The Air Forces in Operation *Market Garden*   225
Appendix 4: The Humiliation of General Sosabowski   235
Appendix 5: Brian Urquhart's Recollections of Intelligence
             at Arnhem   241
Appendix 6: Glossary of Terms and Acronyms   245

Notes on the Text
Acknowledgments
Bibliography
Index   273

In memory of three good men:

Leading Seaman Herbert Bennett, DEMS, Royal Navy, 1940–45

Willi Derkow, Berliner, labor leader, refugee, scholar, and human rights activist

Major General Stanislaw Sosabowski, the bravest of them all

The Battle

"The battle of Arnhem was a magnificent disaster."
— Major G.G. Norton, 1971

"There were no exceptions from the fighting line; all ranks were in it. Staff officers, signallers, batmen, drivers and clerks all lent a hand. We were content. Amid the din of continuous fire and crash of falling burning buildings, laughter was often heard."
— Major General John Frost, 1980

"The biggest mistake historians make is to glorify and narrow-mindedly concern themselves with Arnhem and Oosterbeek. The Allies were stopped in the south just north of Nijmegen—that is why Arnhem turned out as it did."
—SS Major-General Heinz Harmel, 1987

"The Battle of Arnhem, this magnificent feat of Arms, and the most glorious battle of the War is over."
—Major General P.R.C. Cummings, Colonel, The South Staffordshire Regiment, letter to anxious relatives of the Second Battalion, 1 October, 1944

The Guards Armoured Division

"I always thought that the Guards were the best soldiers that I saw on either side in the war—not only because of their soldierly qualities, but because of their nonchalance and style. . . . It was a remarkable division."
— Major General James Gavin, 82nd Airborne Division

"And those Guards divisions—they're good outfits. Best in the British Army. You can't get into 'em unless you've a 'Sir' in front of your name and a pedigree a yard long. But don't laugh at them. They're good fighters."
—Lt. Colonel Robert Sink, 506th PIR, 101st Airborne Division

"I was very conscious of the price we had to pay for victory—the Guards Armoured Division [in World War II] had 956 killed, 545 missing and 3,946 wounded. I have since visited their graves; in battle, it was a particularly sad sight to see a burnt out tank and four crosses beside it. I loved them all."
—Major-General Allan Adair

The American Ground Forces

"All ranks of [George S. Patton's Third Army], when they saw our red berets, would say: 'Arnhem, Aye. We'd have gotten through. Yes, sir. We'd have gotten through.' I could not help believe they would have. There was nothing slow and ponderous about them and they didn't stop for tea, or the night, for that matter."
—Lt. Colonel John Frost at his liberation from a POW camp

The British Ground Forces

"The British 5th Battalion DCLI formed up in lines of skirmishers to walk shoulder to shoulder across the open fields. It seemed a very foolish command to us. . . . Enemy artillery came in screaming and moaning. . . . Many of the British went down but they still pressed forward, closing the gaps in blown in their lines by the barrage. They marched steadily on, firing their Enfields from the hip, working the bolts and firing again. The English soldiers were brave to a fault, staying in line and moving forward through the crush of artillery, machine-gun and small arms fire. They marched unwaveringly to their deaths. This sort of attack went out with the bloody assaults of our Civil War in the 1800s."
—Pfc. Donald Burgett, on the Island after *Market Garden*

The 101st Airborne Division, the Screaming Eagles

"I don't believe any division other than one of these two Airborne Divisions could have kept the 25 kilometres of this one road open, with increasing German pressure coming in from both sides. . . . [They] were in fact the toughest troops I have ever come across in my life."
—Lt. General Sir Brian Horrocks

"You'd better hurry up, medics. They're gaining on you."
—The badly wounded Captain Melvin C. Davis, on receiving
medical aid, then being hit again

*"They are as fine fellows as we have ever worked with, or could wish
to work with, and we both would have liked to have done an
assault together."*
—Major Michael L. Tucker, 23rd Company,
Royal Canadian Engineers

The 82nd Airborne Division, the All-Americans

"Some of the finest airborne soldiers the world has known."
—Major-General Roy Urquhart

"I never saw such a gallant action."
—Lt. General Frederick Browning, on the 504th PIR crossing of the
Waal, September 20, 1944

*"I'm proud to meet the Commanding General of the finest division
in the world today."*
—Lt. General Miles Dempsey to Brig. General James Gavin,
September 23, 1944

The 1st Airborne Division, the Red Devils

*"The British 1st Airborne Division landed at Arnhem was an elite
unit. Its performance, especially at the road bridge was, in the last
analysis, acknowledged as really heroic."*
—Walther Harzer in "Fallschirme ueber Arnheim, Nach Unterlagen
von Walther Harzer"

*"In all my years as a soldier, I have never seen men
fight so hard."*
—General Wilhelm Bittrich

". . . the outstanding independent battalion action of the war."
—James Gavin, writing of the action of the
Second Parachute Battalion

The 23rd Field Company, Royal Canadian Engineers

"Thank you, mate, for what you and your comrades did for us in 1944. We could not say 'thank you' then, because you were just whispers and shadows in the night."
—British paratrooper Bill Bateman to Norman Caldwell,
a Canadian engineer, 1988

The First Polish Independent Parachute Brigade

"I have never been under the impression of such courage. You did not hear one sound of screaming or crying. These were people from hundreds of miles away waiting for a doctor to operate or amputate. A people so very earthy, so honest and with a sincerity that has always impressed us."
—Cora Balthussen

The Germans

"The German is no fool and a mighty warrior."
—Regimental Sergeant-Major J.C. Lord

"I doubt whether there was any such animal as a sub-standard German soldier."
—Private James Sims

"The German AFVs were knocked out one after another as they tried desperately to disengage or negotiate the flaming metal coffins. Black smoke belched from the leading tank, now well ablaze, but any movement from our positions still brought a stream of well-aimed machine-gun fire from the turret guns. The paratroops shouted to the SS man to come out, promising to spare his life, for they were impressed by his fanatical courage. The only reply was a further burst of fire. As the flames got to him we could hear his screams of agony, muffled by the steel turret, but none the less disturbing for that. They seemed to go on for an awfully long time before this brave soldier died for Fuehrer and Fatherland."
—Private James Sims at the Arnhem road bridge

FOREWORD

By Carlo D'Este

THE PRICE OF OVER-CONFIDENCE

*"In war more than anywhere else in the world things
happen differently from what we had expected, and look
differently when near from what they did at a distance."*
—Von Clausewitz

On September 17, 1944 the Allies launched the largest airborne and
glider operation in the history of warfare. One of the most daring
actions of World War II, its objective was to gain a vital bridgehead over
the greatest obstacle to an advance on the German Ruhr, the Rhine
River. By outflanking the heavily defended West Wall, the Allies would
have had an unimpeded route into the Ruhr. Indeed, if successful it
might well have altered not only the outcome of the war but also the
postwar map of Europe.

No military operation of World War II began with higher expectations only to disastrously fail. What made its failure all the more tragic
was that by all rights it ought to have succeeded. Instead, it not only
produced what author David Bennett has aptly titled A Magnificent
Disaster, but has generated controversy and bitterness that after more
than a half century has yet to bring closure.

With the exception of the D-Day landings in Normandy on June 6,
1944, no other battle of World War II has captured the imagination of
the public more than what was code-named Operation Market Garden.
Its purpose was for the British 1st Airborne Division to capture and

hold the vital bridge over the Rhine at Arnhem, while the U.S. 82d and 101st Airborne Divisions seized the river and canal crossings around Eindhoven, the bridges across the River Waal at Nijmegen, and the Maas at Grave—and hold them open while a ground force drove down a sixty-five mile corridor along the only direct link to Arnhem, later dubbed "Hell's Highway."

The story of Market Garden was little known until the publication in 1974 of Cornelius Ryan's best-selling account, *A Bridge Too Far.* Director Richard Attenborough's 1977 film of the same name, headed by an all-star cast, further thrust the story into the public consciousness —where it has remained.

Whereas the D-Day landings in Normandy were the result of months of planning that culminated in the best possible plan the Allies could devise, Market Garden was a military disaster thanks largely to the blunders of its architects who ignored obvious danger signals, violated established principles of offensive warfare, and failed to take note of the valuable (and sometimes costly) lessons gained from earlier airborne operations.

In Normandy, bravery and good leadership were rewarded by victory; at Arnhem valiant men were ill served and died needlessly. All but forgotten by the gallant stand of Lieutenant Colonel John Frost's parachute battalion at Arnhem's "bridge too far" is that Market Garden relied too heavily on a script for success that left no room for error or the inevitable unpredictability of war.

Market Garden brought together the key figures of the Allied coalition, each of whom played an important role in a challenging, logistically complicated, and enormously multifaceted military operation that was undertaken in haste (it was planned and carried out in a little over a week) which, in order to succeed, required a seamless meshing of ground and airborne operations. Yet, from its very inception, through its planning and execution, Market Garden contained the seeds of failure in what proved to be a lethal combination of over-confidence, inexperience, and a shocking refusal to heed the warnings and advice of more experienced officers.

That it even took place was the result of events that no one could have foreseen when the Allies invaded Normandy on June 6, 1944. Allied strategy and planning for fighting the war in Northwest Europe never envisioned the rout that followed the successful American breakout from the Cotentin Peninsula at the end of July 1944 by the First and Third U.S. Armies that broke what had become a near stalemate in Normandy. Nor could anyone foresee the entrapment of German Army Group B in the Argentan-Falaise pocket and the stunning end to the Normandy campaign at the end of August.

With the remnants of the German army in the West in full retreat toward Germany it was a time for pursuit, not consolidation. However, SHAEF (Supreme Headquarters Allied Expeditionary Force) had no plans for dealing with success on such an epic scale. When the campaign was planned earlier in 1944 such a scenario had never been envisioned. Instead, the original plan for the campaign in Northwest Europe forecast a lengthy pause at the River Seine to regroup, advance Allied logistical bases forward, and make plans to resume the offensive.

In war opportunities are fleeting. Halting to regroup at the Seine was suddenly unthinkable. British, American, Canadian, and Polish troops swept into Belgium, while Jacob L. Devers's Sixth U.S. Army Group advanced rapidly up the Rhone Valley, and Patton's Third Army thrust deep into Lorraine. The Allied advances north of the Seine saw gains of as much as fifty miles a day. In early September 1944, the Allies were only prevented from sweeping into Germany by what has been called "the tyranny of supply."

Normandy was a triumph for everyone but the Allied logisticians who faced crushing problems by early September. The transportation infrastructure in western France had been mostly destroyed in the pre-D-Day aerial campaign to isolate the Normandy battlefield and could not easily be rebuilt.

A mobile army runs on enormous quantities of fuel, and General Dwight D. Eisenhower's logisticians could only fill a small fraction of the chronic shortages of fuel and ammunition required to sustain an advance into Germany. Allied supply dumps were daily more distant from the beaches of Normandy and resupplying the rapidly advancing armies became a nightmare in what war correspondent Ernie Pyle has described as "a tactician's hell and a quartermaster's purgatory." Even stopgap measures such as the famous Red Ball Express were able to fill only a fraction of the requirements for fuel and ammunition. And while the opportunity to win it all existed for a brief time in September 1944, as the official historian of SHAEF has written, "there was not sufficient time, however vast the effort, to make the necessary readjustments in the logistical machinery which would insure speedy victory."

While the Allies grappled with the logistical nightmare, they also began focusing on the means by which they would carry out an advance to the borders of the Reich. Yet, if the initiative was to be sustained, the Ruhr encircled and the war won the war in 1944, they needed bridgeheads over the great obstacle of the mighty Rhine. Thus, the appeal of a means of rapidly breaching the Rhine grew more important with each passing day.

The victory in Normandy also produced another unintended consequence in the form of over-optimism and self-deception within the ranks of the Allied high command, producing a widely held belief the war would soon end. A "victory disease" swept unchecked, leaving in its wake myopically preconceived perceptions that failed to take into account the earlier lessons of the war. With Allied spearheads achieving astounding advances, the reasons seemed clear enough. The German army was in complete disarray – losses in 1944 were staggering: 900,000 on the Eastern Front, while another 450,000 men of Army Group B were lost in Normandy. All signs certainly pointed to an imminent Allied victory.

London Daily Mail correspondent Alexander Clifford accompanied Lt. General Miles Dempsey's Second British Army as it drove into Belgium and recorded the sense of sheer delirium. "This mad chase is getting crazier hour by hour. . . . You can't digest it in the least as you go along. It is so big and so swift that you almost feel it is out of control. . . . Our columns just press on and on and on. . . . The atmosphere is heady and intoxicating."

Eisenhower sounded one of the very few notes of caution at a press conference in London in mid-August, when he strongly condemned those "who think they can measure the end of the war 'in a matter of weeks.' Hitler and his gang have nothing to lose by enforcing prosecution of the war." Yet by September he too had succumbed to the euphoria that the end was imminent. Only Winston Churchill remained skeptical, warning, "It is at least as likely Hitler will be fighting on the 1st January [1945] as that he will collapse before then. If he does collapse before then, the reasons will be political rather than purely military."

Even Eisenhower's chief intelligence officer was blinded. "The enemy in the West has had it," he wrote on August 26. "Two and a half months of bitter fighting have brought the end of the war in Europe within sight, almost within reach."

However, someone neglected to inform Adolf Hitler of this fact. There still remained some 3.4 million troops in the German army, over a million of which were to be committed to the defense of the Reich on the Western Front. Moreover, any notion of capitulation was suicidal heresy. The war would be fought to the bitter end and anyone who suggested otherwise invited execution.

A certain sign of German intransigence was Hitler's relief of Field Marshal Gerd von Rundstedt as commander-in-chief of the German Army in the West (OB West) and his replacement by Field Marshal Walter Model, a tough-minded, veteran commander who was known as "the Fuhrer's Fireman" for his ingenuity in salvaging seemingly hopeless situations on the Eastern Front.

The miscalculation most consistently made by the Allies throughout World War II was to invariably underestimate the will and tenacity of the German army to resist against overwhelming odds, under the most appalling conditions. Sicily, Salerno, Cassino, Anzio and Normandy were all examples. In mid-September 1944 that mistake was to be repeated in Holland with Market Garden.

Normandy also spawned one of the most contentious strategic debates of the war over how the Allies would continue their advance into Germany. What has been called the broad-front, narrow-front debate pitted Eisenhower against British Field Marshal Sir Bernard Montgomery who, up to the end of the Normandy campaign, had been the acting Allied ground commander-in-chief. When Eisenhower assumed command of the ground campaign on September 1, 1944, he articulated a broad-front strategy for the Allied advance on Germany that was at odds with Montgomery's belief that the quickest way to end the war was by means of the so-called narrow-front advance on the Ruhr by his 21st Army Group. Eisenhower prevailed but while the debate raged over strategy, hasty planning went ahead for Market Garden.

The creation of Lt. General Lewis Brereton's First Allied Airborne Army in early August brought increasingly heavy pressure from Washington on Eisenhower to employ it in a major airborne operation. Numerous plans had already been scrapped after its objectives were captured before they could be implemented. The two British and three American airborne divisions in England awaiting a mission had become, as one official historian put it, "like coins burning a hole in SHAEF's pocket . . . SHAEF had decided to buy an airborne product and was shopping around." With the need to find a means of bouncing the Rhine, the launching of Market Garden was brought to a rapid fruition.

Its key players were like the three blind mice of fable: Montgomery and Brereton, had little experience of airborne operations, while the commander of British airborne forces, Lt. General F.A.M. "Boy" Browning, although appearing to possess brilliant qualifications as one of the pioneers of British airborne operations, in reality lacked battle experience. Far more detrimental was Browning's hubris when he not only ignored warnings from more experienced airborne commanders that the drop zones were too far from Arnhem Bridge, but actually concealed the fact that he'd been so advised.

All three were utterly blinded by their eagerness to make something happen, and much like Lt. General Mark Clark's decision to launch the ill-fated Rapido River crossings in Italy in January 1944, when a better option was available, the Market Garden commanders and their staffs attempted to mold their plan to fit a deeply flawed premise. Montgomery's own staff was opposed to the plan, as was his own chief of staff. Others in various commands weighed in with warnings and objections that went unheeded. Added to the virulent mix of the logistical crisis, overconfidence, and the bitter disagreement over strategy were not only an unsound plan for the airborne and glider landings, but also an equally ill-fated plan for the ground operation.

There were no rewards for the failure of the Allies to secure the vital bridgehead at Arnhem, making it yet another example of that quaint British penchant for turning military disasters such as Dunkirk into gloriously celebrated events. Sadly, it also brought out the worst in otherwise honorable men. Finger pointing and irrational excuses ranged from Montgomery's meaningless claim that the operation had achieved 90 percent of its objectives, to Winston Churchill's illogical declaration that Arnhem was "a decided victory" and his unrepentant assertion that "I have not been affected by any feeling of disappointment over this and am glad our commanders are capable of running this kind of risk." Although Eisenhower hardly mentioned the operation in his best-selling postwar memoir Crusade in Europe, in 1960 he privately admitted Market Garden had "miserably failed."

Easily its most disgraceful and unforgivable aspect was that the British contrived to pin responsibility on the Polish airborne commander, Maj. General S.F. Sosabowski, whose warnings were ignored. Sosabowski was the one commander who might have pulled British chestnuts from the fires of defeat. Instead, he was unjustly relieved of command at Browning's instigation, an act that stained the honor of one of the war's bravest soldiers and that of the exile Polish forces who fought bravely for the Allies only to be betrayed a second time by a post-war British government that denied them full citizenship.

History is of little use unless new generations embrace the past and learn from it. Those who fought at Arnhem, Nijmegen and other lesser-known places in September 1944 are now few. David Bennett's splendid, well-researched account is a welcome addition to the literature of a tragic battle that will leave the reader both informed and saddened by the chain of events that resulted in A Magnificent Disaster. Not only is this book a major contribution to the historiography of Market Garden, but it is also a lasting tribute to the valiant men and women sacrificed so much for so little.

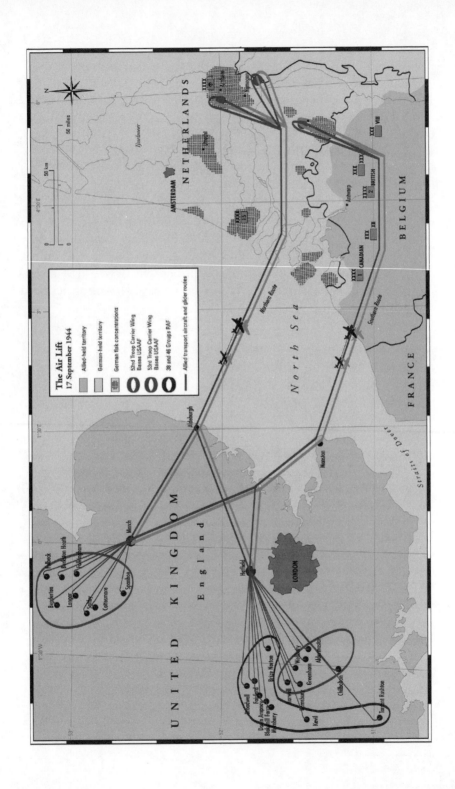

The Air Lift
17 September 1944

Allied-held territory
German-held territory
German flak concentrations

○○○ 52nd Troop Carrier Wing Bases USAAF
○○○ 53rd Troop Carrier Wing Bases USAAF
○○○ 38 and 46 Groups RAF

Allied transport aircraft and glider routes

NETHERLANDS

Nijmegen

IJsselmeer

Tungol

AMSTERDAM

XXX US

XXX VIII

XXX

XXX BRITISH

XXX 2

Antwerp

XXX XII

XXX CANADIAN 1

BELGIUM

North Sea

Northern Route

Southern Route

Aldeburgh

March

Manston

Hatfield

LONDON

UNITED KINGDOM
England

FRANCE

Straits of Dover

Bärkston
Balderton Heath
Fulbeckham
Saltby
Cottesmore
Spanhoe

Broadwell
Down Ampney
Fairford
Blackbull Farm
Membury
Harwell
Brize Norton
Tarrant
Keevil
Greenham
Welford
Aldermaston
Chilbolton

50 miles
50 km

N

1

THE PROSPECTS FOR THE WESTERN ALLIES

September 17, 1944 saw the start of the greatest airborne operation of all time. This was a combined operation of airborne troops with ground forces which would take the Western Allies over the River Rhine at Arnhem. In that Dutch city, Sunday September 17 was a bright, warm late-summer day. Most of the German forces in the area were relaxed and at ease. At Hoenderloo, ten miles to the north, the acting commander of the 9th SS Panzer Division *Hohenstaufen*, SS-Lt. Colonel Walther Harzer, had just driven down from his HQ at Beekbergen, eight miles further north. He was at Hoenderloo to decorate his Reconnaissance Battalion commander, SS-Captain Viktor-Eberhard Graebner, with the Knight's Cross for distinguished service in the Normandy campaign.

At thirty-two, Harzer had taken over command of the *Hohenstaufen* from SS-Major General Silvester Stadler, who was wounded when the divisional headquarters in Normandy had been attacked from the air. The HQ had been identified through radio messages intercepted by the top-secret Ultra decryption system. Most of Graebner's vehicles were loaded on flatcars at Beekbergen station, ready to be transported to Siegen in the Reich. Nonetheless, Graebner's mobile force was the closest armored unit of any strength to Arnhem. While in the city the SS troopers witnessed an "unearthly droning noise" of the huge armada of transports, gliders and fighters, all Harzer saw was some parachutes in the sky to the south. Having no reason to think that a major attack was underway, he sat down to lunch in the officers' mess. It was exactly one week after Operation Market Garden had been authorized.

A little later, on the Meuse-Escaut Canal at the starting-point of the ground operation, *Garden*, the Sherman tanks of the Irish Guards

1

moved forward under a rolling artillery barrage. German gunners, well hidden and camouflaged at the sides of the concrete road, let the first tanks of the leading squadron pass, then opened up, destroying three of the leading formation and six of the next. Lance Corporal James Doggart was blown out of his tank and came to in a ditch, his burning Sherman leaning over him. Nearby, one of his comrades had an arm nearly severed and another was dead. As far as he knew, the rest of his tank crew had perished. Typhoon fighter-bombers overhead pounced on the German anti-tank positions. Joe Vandaleur, the Irish Guards commander, recollected: "It was the first time I had ever seen Typhoons in action and I was amazed at the guts of those pilots. They came in, one at a time, head to tail, flying right through our own barrage. One disintegrated right above me. It was incredible—guns firing, the roar of planes, the shouts and curses of the men. In the middle of it all, Division asked how the battle was going. My second in command just held up the microphone and said, 'Listen.'"

With the Guards infantry flushing out the Germans, Doggart ran clear of the blazing tank and jumped into a slit trench across the road, followed by two Germans. He kicked one in the face and pointed his rifle at the other. Doggart sent them to join the stream of prisoners heading back towards the start-line.

To the left of the Irish Guards on the Meuse-Escaut Canal, a little-known event took place. After the start of the Guards' assault, other formations of the British XII Corps began quietly to cross the canal at Lommel. Their aim was to establish a bridgehead and second start-line for the ground troops in Operation *Garden*. There was no artillery support so the Germans would not be alerted to a major waterborne assault and so that the airborne overhead would not confuse the crossing with the Guards' advance from Neerpelt.

Above the Irish Guards, Pfc. Daniel Kenyon Webster of the US 101st Airborne Division, looked down on what he thought was the Albert Canal, partly obscured by white and orange smoke, the latter for the identification of friendly troops. This made it more likely that the waterway that Webster observed was the Meuse-Escaut Canal, the starting-point for *Garden*. Webster dropped unopposed by flak or ground troops and landed upright, contrary to the book, but intact. He encountered an injured friend and three dead paratroopers, then joined his battalion in the assault on the Son Bridge over the Wilhelmina Canal to the south.

Webster's comrade in an adjacent battalion, Pfc. Donald Burgett, had a different experience, his drop orchestrated by descending paratroopers, the smoke and crack of flak, machine-gun tracer and burning aircraft. One of these seemed to head straight toward him, spilling troops before it crashed, killing the crew. Prior to this, a perturbed Brigadier General James Gavin, the commander of the U.S. 82nd Airborne Division, had seen the 101st's fleet below him, before his own transports and fighters swung back on course for a near-perfect landing to the north of the 101st. Like Webster, Gavin landed badly, and afterward exercised his command in great pain, unaware that he had cracked two vertebrae.

While Webster read a book on his flight, the British paratroopers en route to Arnhem mostly slept, little caring that they were taking part in "the biggest airborne operation ever launched." This at least was the view of Major Anthony-Deane Drummond, the second in command of 1st Airborne Divisional Signals. Like Gavin, Deane-Drummond found the fighter escorts "comfortingly close." When he reached the drop zone, there was a sudden burst of light flak, which penetrated the fuselage of his C-47 transport and severed a wing tip. He gave the order, "Stand up, hook up and check equipment."

The whole planeload leapt into activity. Parachutes were adjusted, static lines hooked on to the wire running down the side of the fuselage, and steel helmets given a further tightening up. Some looked a bit pale, others quite unconcerned as I passed down the fuselage checking that each man was properly hooked up." After the encounter with the flak, most were anxious to get out of the aircraft. The group of fifty aircraft dropped all of their loads on open heathland west of Arnhem. Deane-Drummond, slightly concussed on landing, collected his men together, made contact with the rest of his Signals contingent who had landed by glider, and made for the Divisional HQ.

By the end of the day, the Americans, British and Poles had landed the major part of three airborne divisions in an area from north of Eindhoven to Arnhem in Operation *Market*. The aim was to hold open a corridor of sixty-four miles, while progressively relieved by the ground forces in Operation *Garden*. The aim of *Garden* was an offensive, starting from the Meuse-Escaut Canal, by the three Corps of British Second Army: XII Corps on the left, XXX Corps in the center and VIII Corps on the right. The central corps was to advance along a corridor to the Arnhem bridges over the Lower Rhine, progressively relieving the airborne forces as it went. The final objective was way beyond Arnhem: the troops were to reach an inland sea, the IJsselmeer, with bridgeheads over the River IJssel to the east.

On D-Day, September 17, a total of 4,676 aircraft and gliders took part in the fly-in, and nearly 4,000 more on D+1. By the conclusion of Market, a total of 34,878 troops had been landed—20,190 by parachute, 13,781 by glider and 907 by aircraft. A total of 5,200 tons of supplies were flown in along with 586 artillery pieces and 1,927 vehicles. The origins of this huge endeavor were partly immediate and partly the result of strategic planning that had taken place many months before.

THE ORIGINS OF OPERATION *MARKET GARDEN*: THE GERMAN RETREAT

By September 1944, the Allies had three Army Groups in France. In the north, Field-Marshal Sir Bernard Law Montgomery's 21st Army Group (21AG) contained the Canadian First Army under General Harry Crerar, along with the British Second Army, commanded by General Miles Dempsey. To their right was the American 12th Army Group headed by General Omar Bradley with the First Army under General Courtney Hodges and the Third Army under General George S. Patton. One corps of the U.S. Ninth Army was in France but not yet committed to the front line.

To the south, General Jacob Devers' U.S. 6th Army Group landed on the Mediterranean coast of France in mid-August. The U.S. 12th and 6th Army Groups linked up on September 12, forming a continuous Western Front in France. The Supreme Commander Allied Expeditionary Force (SHAEF) was the American General Dwight D. Eisenhower, who took command of the ground forces from Montgomery on September 1.

The German retreat in northwest Europe began in mid-August and it had been a long time coming. On June 6, the Allies had landed five divisions on the coast of Normandy, supported by three airborne divisions, and gained a firm foothold inside *Festung Europa*. The Germans, who fought skilfully and stubbornly against the odds held the Allies in check for six weeks. The break came at last in late July, when the American First Army on the west wing pushed the Germans back. General Patton's Third Army spilled into Brittany and invested the port cities of the peninsula. The American armies then wheeled round and dashed for Paris, the Meuse and beyond. They also, with the Canadian First Army, encircled the Germans at Falaise. The Germans lost 10,000 killed and 50,000 captured in the Battle of the Falaise Gap. The Americans captured 25,000 more in the vicinity of Mons. The remainder, abandoning their artillery, support weapons and armor, streamed back over the Seine and the Somme to the frontiers of Belgium, the Netherlands and Germany. Such was the chaos of the retreat that "scenes were witnessed which no one would ever have deemed possible in the German Army."

The German retreat reached its height on Mad Tuesday, September 5 and then slowed down, but did not stop in the northern sector until September 22, well after *Market Garden* had begun. On September 4, the British 11th Armoured Division and the Belgian Resistance together captured Antwerp, a day after the Guards Armoured Division had entered Brussels to a tremendous welcome. All told, in the June-September campaign in France, the Germans lost about 200,000 troops killed, wounded or captured as well as over 600 tanks, many guns and much equipment.

The Allied High Command was of course elated. In some quarters there was euphoria. The Chief of the Imperial General Staff, Alan Brooke, called the advance "incredible"; both Eisenhower and Montgomery wrote in the latter part of August that they were on the verge of a "great victory." In Washington, General George C. Marshall and the Combined Chiefs of Staff calculated that a total German collapse could occur before the end of the year. The Japanese Ambassador in Berlin was of the same opinion. The bombing offensive against the German oil industry was predicted to ground and paralyse the German armies in the field by the end of 1944. The Allies even had contingency plans should there be a German collapse comparable to that of 1918.

Not everyone shared this optimism, least of all Churchill and Roosevelt. Eisenhower, the Supreme Commander in the West, warned as early as August 20 that Allied supply lines were so strained that further movement, even against very weak opposition was almost impossible. Patton's intelligence chief, Colonel Oscar Koch, expressed the view on August 28 that the enemy had not collapsed, nor was there any indication that the end of the war was in sight. Still, the general atmosphere was one of confidence and optimism. Montgomery, then ground forces commander of the Allied Expeditionary Force, thought he could get to

Berlin in a matter of weeks, while the senior intelligence officer at Eisenhower's HQ thought that the end of the war was in sight.

Just how optimistic the Allies were can be gleened from the expectations of the commanders of *Market Garden*. Horrocks, the commander of British XXX Corps, which would lead the land advance, thought that *Market Garden* "could end the war." Roy Urquhart, commander of the British 1st Airborne Division, the Red Devils, at Arnhem, thought that failure would have a tremendous significance for the duration of the war and that the Allies would lose the opportunity to "race across the north German plain!" General Gavin, commander of the 82nd Airborne, saw the operation as an opportunity to end the war in the *autumn* of 1944, and for Maj. Gen. Stanislaw Sosabowski, commander of the First Polish Parachute Brigade, by the end of the year.

The leaders of the U.S. 101st Airborne had been told by Lt. General Lewis H. Brereton, commander of the First Allied Airborne Army, "On the success of your mission rests the difference between a quick decision in the west and a long drawn-out battle." When we come to the limited objectives of the operation as authorized by Eisenhower, it is fair that he should have written, "A general impression grew up that the battle was really a full-out attempt to begin, immediately, a drive into the heart of Germany."

In retrospect, the euphoria over the German retreat is remarkable. Despite the hard fighting and slow progress experienced by the Second Army from September 6 onwards, the euphoria persisted, no where better represented than in the excessive optimism on the part of Montgomery, an optimism not shared by his immediate subordinates and which Eisenhower and his senior commanders at SHAEF passed over lightly.

THE ORIGINS OF OPERATION *MARKET GARDEN*: ALLIED STRATEGIC PLANNING, MAY 1944

During May 1944, the SHAEF planners had made two decisions that were to determine the conduct of the war in Europe until its end a year later. The first was that the economic objective of the *Ruhrindustriegebiet* was to be taken en route to Berlin. This would starve Germany of the means to continue the war, particularly in terms of coal and steel production. The second was that there would be two thrusts to Germany, a major one toward the Ruhr north of the

Ardennes, and a subsidiary thrust toward Metz and the Saar, to the south. The aim of the southern thrust was to envelop the Ruhr from the south, via Frankfurt, meeting the northern offensive, after which the Allied armies would advance deep into Germany. This twin-thrust strategy was characterized by Eisenhower as an "advance on a broad front." On September 12, the Combined Chiefs of Staff in Washington signalled Eisenhower, confirming that the northern thrust was of greater importance and stressing the need to open up the northwestern ports, particularly Antwerp and Rotterdam, before winter weather set in.

The use of the term "broad front" caused much confusion and tarnished Eisenhower's reputation as a strategist among his British military critics. Whether it vitiated Allied strategy in practice is far less certain. The trouble was that "broad front" sometimes meant the double thrust and sometimes an advance along a *wide* front. In author Ralph Bennett's view, the optimism generated by the German retreat in late August produced a "dulling effect on thought," which was "plainly traceable in most of the pronouncements in the 'broad front' controversy, which so lacked verbal precision that it is often hard to see what they were intended to mean."

The ambiguity of the meaning of "broad front" resulted in the British conflating the two meanings during and after the pursuit of the Germans in August-September. Montgomery complained of Eisenhower adopting "a broad front strategy, with the whole line advancing and everyone fighting all the time," which would result in the advance petering out and German recovery into 1945. In his diary, Alan Brooke accused Eisenhower of dispersing his effort, using "broad front" as a term of abuse to be applied variously and indifferently to the double thrust *and* attacking all along the front, which were very different things.

Montgomery's 21AG was to make the main thrust to the north and Bradley's armies the thrust to the south. When it became clear in mid-August that the Allies were on the verge of a great victory, Montgomery began to challenge the planning decisions made in May. He did this in two ways. First he argued that the aim should be Berlin, not the Ruhr. Second, he thought there should be a single offensive in the northern sector, not two. The single thrust was rejected by Eisenhower because it was contrary to the SHAEF policy that had been endorsed by the Combined Chiefs. Eisenhower was prepared to give priority to the northern thrust, though Montgomery's conception of priority was often presented as *complete* priority, tantamount again to the single thrust. Accordingly, on September 4 Montgomery was given the First Allied Airborne Army (1AAA), consisting of three American airborne divisions under XVIII Corps, commanded by Lt. General Matthew Ridgeway, as well as two British airborne divisions and the First Polish Independent Parachute Brigade under the British First Airborne Corps headed by Lt. General Frederick Browning. He was also promised the "attachment" of the U.S. First Army to 21AG for the northern thrust although this fell short of full operational control.

As to the thrust toward Berlin rather than the Ruhr, this was rejected partly because Montgomery presented the idea as a single thrust and partly because Eisenhower thought that there would never be enough troops to get to Berlin and protect the flanks at the same time. On the matter of supply, Eisenhower signalled Montgomery on September 5: "No re-allocation of our present resources would be adequate to sustain a thrust to Berlin." Montgomery persisted with the Berlin idea forcefully but intermittently; it was not an issue during the planning of *Market Garden*.

Ultimately, the Ruhr-Berlin controversy had no dire consequences. The reason was that the opening operation in the north could be used either as a springboard to Berlin or to the Ruhr. Muenster was the first city on the North German Plain and strategists on both sides regarded it as the key to the heart of Germany. The aim of occupying the triangle of Rhine-Osnabrueck-Muenster could lead equally to an invasion of the Ruhr via Hamm or an advance toward Berlin, across the North German Plain in the region of Muenster. What the Ruhr-Berlin controversy did was to contribute to what was arguably a strategic mistake or misconception on Eisenhower's part. Instead of the argument being about the Ruhr versus Berlin, the argument should have been the Rhine bridgeheads, one or two, versus the Ruhr. Thus, when *Market Garden* was envisaged, there was no deliberation about the aims of the operation— whether it was a preliminary to the capture of the Ruhr or merely to achieve a bridgehead over the Lower Rhine.

In endorsing *Market Garden,* Eisenhower was authorizing a strategic offensive aimed at "threatening the Ruhr" rather than a limited tactical venture that would obtain a foothold over the Rhine while not compromising other operations such as the opening of the ports of Antwerp and Rotterdam. Yet, despite Eisenhower's authorization of a strategic offensive, he was still thinking in tactical terms of seizing bridgeheads over the Rhine and the exploitation as far as feasible of the German retreat. Montgomery, however, was thinking in terms of reaching the IJsselmeer and bridgeheads over the IJssel, and a concentration of effort for the next round. He saw the "broad front" not as a general pursuit but as a betrayal of the single thrust.

All the while, the preoccupation was supply. Everyone was advancing, everyone was short, and everyone laid claim to the increasingly scarce supplies of gasoline, ammunition and stores. Army accused army of commandeering its resources, while the pillaging of supplies was developed into a fine art. Spotter planes from the American armies observed supply trains, while transport companies disguised as the troops of other armies carried off matériel from depots. Freddie De Guingand, Montgomery's Chief of Staff, reckoned that if Eisenhower had in August diverted all administrative resources to a northern thrust, the Allies might, at most, have gotten a bridgehead over the Rhine before the onset of winter.

THE O'ERWEENING AMBITION OF FIELD-MARSHAL SIR BERNARD LAW MONTGOMERY

When Montgomery gave the order for *Market Garden* on September 10, there was no consultation with his staff, nor did he give any specific instructions to the two armies under his command. The absence of detailed instructions was uncharacteristic of the man, as was the dearth of interventions over the following week and during the battle itself. Montgomery was of course answerable to Eisenhower, the Supreme Commander. But while he had handed command of the land forces in northwestern Europe to Eisenhower on September 1, he retained authority, as yet undefined, over the Northern Group of Armies, which included the American First Army. Above all, he basked in the credit of an indubitable success, the seaborne invasion of Normandy on June 6 and the subsequent campaign, an achievement which he shared, or should have shared, with Eisenhower's naval commander, Admiral Sir Bertram Ramsay.

Montgomery was a man in a hurry. He wanted the British to be the first into Berlin. The prospects were, however, declining by the week. His armies were suffering from severe shortages of supplies and transport. The British also had a continuing manpower crisis and, at the senior levels in London, were reluctant to risk a new round of heavy casualties after the bloody victory in Normandy. Montgomery did win from Eisenhower the promise of supplies, including that delivered by an American truck column known as the "Red Lion Express," as well as a special airborne delivery of petrol by the RAF. These promises were kept, but there were no reserves. As Montgomery failed to request additional transport, some of his divisions stood immobile on the Seine when the front line was on the Albert Canal in Belgium. Of the three corps of Second Army, only the central XXX Corps was fully deployed on D-Day, September 17. Operations against the Channel ports, the Scheldt Estuary in the Antwerp sector, and against the western end of the Albert Canal would tie down resources for an offensive by the British Second Army further east.

Nor was the First Allied Airborne Army, over which Montgomery was given control on September 4, as ready as its size indicated. The veteran British 6th Airborne Division had just returned from Normandy on August 25, while the green U.S. 17th Airborne Division had only arrived in England a few days later. There was a sufficient number of transport aircraft to lift six divisions, including the British 52nd (Air-Portable), to an extensive bridgehead over the course of a week or so, in a full-scale strategic operation. This was the kind of big airborne operation for which the Airborne Army had been designed; yet such a venture would require weeks of planning, time not available if the German retreat was to be fully exploited. Further, the British 1st Airborne had not seen action as a whole division and the constant cancellation of airborne operations was leading to a serious morale problem. The division could not tolerate more weeks of uncertainty and immobility.

Therefore, any imminent operation would have to begin sooner, be smaller, and be shorter in duration than the big one previously envisaged. Even so, a smaller operation still presented problems. Even with two "lifts" (sorties), there were not enough aircraft to transport four divisions and one brigade in the single day Montgomery preferred. The need to use the aircraft for supply and airborne reinforcements meant that the 52nd Air-Portable Division could not be transported until the sixth day of *Market Garden*, D+5. The disruption resulting from an operation like *Market* would mean the reorganization and refurbishment of the Airborne Army and a delay in the realization of its prime purpose: the six-division operation. Eisenhower and Brereton, the commander of the 1AAA, knew this. Montgomery did not care. His concern was the here and now.

As a strategic airborne operation, *Market Garden* was the largest ever, but still relatively modest. The Germans expected something bigger and the penetration to be deeper. Yet Montgomery's aspirations were ambitious. In addition to four airlifted divisions with one brigade and the British Second Army on the ground, he also planned for the U.S. First Army to seize a second bridgehead over the Rhine in the Cologne-Bonn area. Thus the Ruhr could later be enveloped, with the southern arm extending not from the Saar region according to the SHAEF plan, but further north from Cologne-Bonn. Montgomery's thinking was ahead of SHAEF's. His superiors were too preoccupied with the exploitation of the German retreat to be concerned with a grand strategic offensive, which would in any case take weeks to prepare and laying in adequate supplies of ammunition and stores. The tendency to give supplies and priority to Patton's Third Army, as well as tolerating his "misinterpretations" of orders, was in Montgomery's view a strategic betrayal. For Eisenhower, Bradley and SHAEF, supporting Patton meant exploitation as far as possible of the German retreat, as well as establishing a precursor to the strategy of the dual thrust.

When Montgomery proposed *Market Garden* to Eisenhower on September 10, the Supreme Commander had no prior warning of the plan. Communications between the two headquarters had been scandalously poor. Eisenhower seems to have accepted Montgomery's plan casually, on the nod, in spite of the consequences for the First Allied Airborne Army. After all, Montgomery had been given control of the Airborne Army on September 4 with no stipulation that it must be deployed in its entirety. Nor did Eisenhower appreciate the seriousness of Montgomery's supply situation, an issue that was only addressed two days later. Eisenhower did not query the fact that *Market Garden* was to take place within a couple of weeks, which was unusual for an operation on such a scale. The aim of a bridgehead over the Rhine had been a practical possibility for the past week or more; the lure of a second bridgehead caused Eisenhower's ready assent.

Though it went unnoticed at the time, the scale of *Market Garden* had dire consequences for a more important project, the clearing of the Scheldt Estuary and the opening of the port of Antwerp. At the time there seemed to be a real possibility of capturing the port of Rotterdam as an alternative to Antwerp. All the communications between SHAEF and the Combined Chiefs of Staff in Washington, as well as between SHAEF and the Army Group commanders in the first half of September refer both to Rotterdam and to Antwerp, as is true of Montgomery's instructions to Crerar of the First Canadian Army. As late as 17 September (D-Day), a memo that circulated in 21st Army Group among Montgomery's officers stated that success in *Market Garden* would place the Second Army within easy reach of Utrecht, thence to Rotterdam or Amsterdam, preferably the latter. Second Army was to plan on advancing on an axis of Utrecht-Amsterdam-IJmuiden and the First Allied Airborne Amy was approached to examine the feasibility of an air drop at IJmuiden. Furthermore, Eisenhower did not at the time want Antwerp as a supply port for immediate operations, only for the great, final push into Germany. Montgomery seems to have thought that the war might well end before there was any real need to open Antwerp.

Those critics who allege a conflict between the need to clear the Scheldt Estuary and the demands of the Arnhem operation fail to appreciate that none of the Allied leadership perceived any such conflict in the first half of September. It was only in the second half of the month that Eisenhower became acutely aware of the need to open Antwerp, but there was no pressure on Montgomery to do so until the second week in October. By then the Canadian and British forces were starved of resources for the campaign, which had begun on 12 September with attacks on the Breskens Pocket on the south bank of the Scheldt Estuary. No troops from Second Army on the continent could be spared, as they themselves needed reinforcing from the American 104th "Timberwolf" Division.

Lieutenant General Browning's part in planning the Arnhem project is obscure. Browning was a Guardsman with a good combat record in the Great War. With Polish help, unacknowledged, he was responsible for the raising and training of the British I Airborne Corps, of which he was commander, as well as Deputy Commander of the Airborne Army. *Market* was to be his first and only operational command in this war and he was anxious to get into action before it ended. His character and ability are hard to estimate. The intelligence officer of the British Airborne Corps, Major Brian Urquhart, who had reason to resent his treatment by Browning, described him as a sympathetic and tolerant character. After the war, Urquhart initially blamed Browning for what he regarded as an appallingly risky venture, only later realizing that the driving force had been the egotistical ambition of Montgomery, not Browning. The plan for *Market* was developed hastily, as it had to be.

For all that, Browning's planning was sketchy and rigid; he lacked the imagination and the practical ability to modify the plan as the operation developed.

The American paratroop commanders, for their part, regarded Browning as a devious manipulator and a poor planner, while Browning's attitude toward the Americans was alas typical of many senior British commanders. He treated them with a patronizing condescension, citing their lack of combat experience as proof of inadequacy. It was fortunate that the two British commanders closest to the American airborne officers, Dempsey of Second Army and Horrocks of XXX Corps, had none of this preposterous military snobbery, and both regarded the two American airborne divisions rightly as among the very best formations that the Allies produced.

As Montgomery's brainchild, *Market Garden* intrigued the Americans. At the time, Montgomery's relations with the Americans had not yet soured and they regarded him as the master of the meticulously planned set-piece battle, such as El Alamein in November 1942 or the Normandy invasion. They saw *Market Garden* as imaginative and out of character, as did the Germans. Montgomery's usual ploy was to lay down a detailed plan, which would unfold naturally, without additional intervention, into the success it was designed to be. In practice, he was more flexible than his style indicated and his "hands off" approach in *Market Garden* was not typical. When an operation developed in a way different from that originally envisaged, Montgomery insisted that this was part of the original plan and claimed credit for the fortuitous success that ensued, reinforcing his reputation as a rigid, methodical planner.

Though he was not an attractive personality, Montgomery in his defense had suffered tragedy in his personal life and could on occasion exhibit sympathy and understanding. Yet he was a deeply self-centerd character, having no conception of a reciprocal personal relationship, a man to whom others were merely the instruments of a self-regarding military purpose. Ascetic, humourless and ungenerous in spirit, he was a strange maverick, arrogant and domineering in public, a solitary loner in his personal world. Like his famous American counterpart, Patton, he had a flair for publicity, grasping correctly that the troops' confidence in a leader lay in the way they won wars.

Montgomery had no sense of diplomacy; he always had to dominate. He despised the Canadian General Crerar, the head of one of his two armies. The Poles, who as soldiers were at least as good as the British, he treated with contempt. In the case of both the Canadians and the Poles, he saw them not as allies but simply as troops to be ordered about as he thought fit. He regarded the Americans as naïve and ignorant amateurs, including Eisenhower at their head. The Supreme Commander he treated like a schoolboy, to be lectured and cajoled into right thinking. Eisenhower, to his eternal credit, responded to such insults with a bemused tolerance, aware not only that he had to keep the coalition together but that he was dealing with a highly competent professional soldier. Patton, the brilliant but equally difficult commander of the U.S. Third Army, invented a rivalry with Montgomery in a public bluster that concealed private respect. Montgomery was a paradox, whose character and demeanour pointed to failure in military cooperation yet whose professionalism invited success.

Montgomery's army commander was General Dempsey, whose principal asset was his grasp of terrain as a requisite for successful warfare. As a soldier Dempsey was more efficient than brilliant, with a modest, self-effacing character that endeared him to the Americans. Yet he did not direct the Arnhem battle, any more than Montgomery. Dempsey met almost daily with his corps commanders from D-3 onwards but, save one important order to the troops on the flanks, his influence on operations was not apparent. Twice he recorded in his diary in the early stages of the battle that progress on the flanks was satisfactory. Though concerned about the slow progress and German pressure on the two flanking corps, he did little to vary his initial orders. He was also out of radio contact with 1st Airborne Division in Arnhem until D+3.

Dempsey was well enough served by his corps commanders. Lt. Gen. Neil Ritchie of XII Corps was a soldier of no particular distinction. He had been fired as commander of the Eighth Army in the Western Desert, and was given a division back in England, then a corps command for the Normandy campaign. Horrocks of XXX Corps cultivated the image of a dashing and aggressive commander, which was good public relations and on balance an asset, since the image usually reflected the reality. But he had one handicap. He had been severely wounded in an air attack in North Africa in 1942 and from then on his health was not good. He fell ill for a spell in August and it is quite possible that his poor performance in the last stages of *Market Garden* was due to poor health. Montgomery sent him on leave in December, ostensibly for medical reasons but actually because his mental state was leading to poor command decisions.

Lt. Gen. Sir Richard O'Connor of VIII Corps was one of Britain's outstanding soldiers. His colorful career included the great victory over the Italians at Sidi Barrani in the Western Desert and a long spell in an Italian POW camp, from which he escaped. Though regarded by his peers as past his best, his corps made the greatest territorial gains in *Market Garden,* for which the troops and his three commanders, Whistler of the 3rd Division, Roberts of 11th Armoured, and Piron of 1st Belgian Brigade, share the credit.

Horrocks' own divisional commanders were not the best. Major General Allan Adair led a great fighting division, the Guards Armoured, which the Americans admired. But between engagements he was a plodder. The excuse that Adair simply did not understand the nature of *Market Garden* is plausible only if we were confident that he would have behaved differently had he so understood. The commander of the 43rd Division, Major General Ivor Thomas, was thoroughly detested by all those who came into contact with him. Even the great-hearted and generous commander of the 1st Airborne, Major General Roy Urquhart, could hardly restrain himself when writing of Thomas's boorish arrogance in his failure to relieve 1st Airborne across the Rhine in Arnhem-Oosterbeek. Known affectionately to the troops as "Butcher Thomas," he was a poor tactician.

He also clashed with the outstanding commander in the British airborne, Major General Sosabowski, who considered Thomas' plans for the relief of the paratroopers feeble. Roy Urquhart wrote: "A very highly trained soldier, Sosabowski was also a character with a vengeance. Like most of the Poles, he had a natural courtesy which contrasted violently with the sudden outbursts in speech and temper which positively withered any erring individual of whose behaviour or methods he did not approve. Nevertheless, when during the months of training I visited his brigade several times, I soon found that he not only had the affection of his men, but was tremendously well respected by all those who served with him—two attitudes to a commander which in my experience have not always gone hand-in-hand together."

By 10 September, Montgomery's armies had been fighting in Western Europe for three months. Among those troops who had also fought for four years in the Western Desert and Italy there were signs of burn-out. These were, however, a minority. For the most part, the soldiery performed as well as ever. The real problem was not the quality of the troops; rather, the need for bold and imaginative tactics which would not subject the men to the wearing battles of attrition that had characterized much of the Normandy campaign. The move to relieve the paratroopers in *Market Garden* required a lightning advance of both infantry and tanks. Yet the British ground forces moved forward slowly and ponderously, with methodical preparations that were the hallmark of Montgomery's leadership.

The American airborne, from top to bottom, came to have a high opinion of the British paratroopers, artillery and infantry as fighters, but they considered British tankers to be slow and inept, brave but stupid. Like the master German tank tactician, Erwin Rommel, they thought the British just didn't understand armored warfare. Their views reflected experience, not prejudice, yet they were still one-sided. When the breakout from Normandy occurred, the British armored divisions pursued the Germans as spectacularly as Patton's. As it happened, the two principal units were the Guards Armoured and the 11th Armoured Divisions. The latter under VIII Corps in *Market Garden* performed admirably and was largely responsible for the territorial gains made. The former displayed all the faults detected by the American airborne—an inexcusable sluggishness between engagements.

The American criticisms came from two of the best divisions in the U.S. Army. They were volunteer units, recognized by the British commanders, including Roy Urquhart of 1st Airborne, as elite, and in many respects superior to their own. There is remarkable contrast here. Few of the American paratroopers had any love for the army and few elected to stay in it after the war's end. They were temporary "citizen soldiers," most of immense practical ability through their upbringing in the plains, mountains and woodlands of the continental United States. This made them masters of fieldcraft and the immediate technologies of war as developed to date, in vehicles, weapons and equipment. These technologies had not yet outstripped the capacity of the troops to work, service and repair them. The Americans had assets that the British, for all their aggressive fighting ability, lacked.

The American rank and file respected their officers to the extent that they performed in ways that reflected the values of the working class cultures from which they came. Major General Maxwell Taylor, the commander of the 101st Airborne, was an intellectual, a fervent believer in his division. The paratroopers respected him for his leadership in action but did not warm to him the way they did to Brigadier General James Gavin, the young commander of the 82nd Airborne. Gavin mixed among the troops in a way that Taylor did not, earning him the nickname, "The Two-Star Platoon Leader." Major Brian Urquhart remarked that these commanders were "in a different world," which the British could emulate but never imitate.

The 101st reserved their affection for the likes of Lt. Colonel Robert Sink, the commander of the 506th Parachute Infantry Regiment (PIR). A hard-driving regular soldier, he was also humane, relaxed and full of good humor, appreciating the predicament and the mentality of the troops far better than did Taylor. No one in the regiment resented the fact that, out of the line, Sink lived in comfort and even luxury and that the best time to catch him was after dinner, when "Bourbon Bob" had mellowed. The counterpart to the 506th PIR in the 82nd Airborne was the 504th, known in the press as the "Anzio Roughnecks." The 504th "looked down on the 506th as upstarts," referring to them as the "Walky Talky" regiment. It was elements of the 504th that crossed the River Waal at Nijmegen under fire, paddling in assault boats, directed by a regimental commander as distinguished as Sink, Lt. Colonel Reuben Tucker. The British were both astonished and moved at the achievement.

Though he did not know it, the American airborne were Montgomery's ace card, a crucial factor for success. As Horrocks came to appreciate, without the American paratroopers, the operation would have gone nowhere. Considering the dearth of supplies and transport, and that the Second Army was not properly deployed, Montgomery's ambitions were rescued from disaster at the outset by those naïve and ignorant Americans.

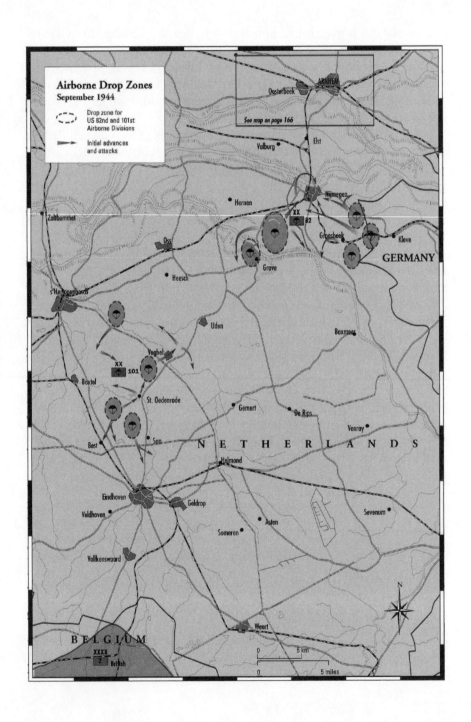

Airborne Drop Zones
September 1944

Drop zone for
US 82nd and 101st
Airborne Divisions

Initial advances
and attacks

ARNHEM

Oosterbeek

See map on page 166

Valburg   Elst

Nijmegen

Zaltbommel   Hernen   XX 82

Groesbeek   Kleve

Oss

Grave   **GERMANY**

s'Hertogenbosch   Heesch

Uden   Boxmeer

Veghel

XX 101

Boxtel   St. Oedenrode

Gemert   De Rips

Venray

Best   Son   N E T H E R L A N D S

Helmond

Eindhoven

Veldhoven   Geldrop   Sevenum

Someren   Asten

Valkenswaard

Weert

N

B E L G I U M

XXXX
2 British

0   5 km

0   5 miles

2

TWO WEEKS OF ALLIED PREPARATION

THE GENESIS OF OPERATION *MARKET*

The immediate precursor of *Market* was the proposed Operation *Comet*, which was first planned on 2 September (originally codenamed *Fifteen*). No operational order was ever issued for *Comet*, nor were there any outline plans for a link-up with ground forces. The aim of *Comet* was to use airborne troops to seize and hold bridges over the Maas, the Maas-Waal Canal, the Waal and the Lower Rhine. As was to be the case in the orders for *Market*, no unit was assigned to the Maas-Waal bridges, which were mentioned only in the summary objectives at the beginning of the order. The warning order from U.S. Major General Paul L. Williams of IX Troop Carrier Command lists the airborne units as the British 1st Airborne Division, the 52nd (Air-Portable) Division and the U.S. 878th Aviation Engineer Battalion; the First Polish Independent Parachute Brigade is not mentioned.

Comet was to proceed in two lifts and three phases. In the first phase, three *coup de main* parties of company strength were to be landed before first light in the immediate vicinity of Arnhem, Nijmegen and Grave. In the second phase, three airborne brigades would secure the Arnhem road bridge, the Maas bridge at Grave and the two bridges over the Waal at Nijmegen. In phase three, the balance of the glider element and the First Polish Brigade Group would land, the latter to relieve the airborne brigade at Grave. Unlike *Market*, the airborne forces were to link up with each other rather than with ground forces.

Without any airborne forces landing between Grave and the ground troops' start-line, the *Comet* formations would have been strung out on their own. This invited certain failure, including the probable loss of all the airborne forces involved. With the strengthening of German formations in the Arnhem-Eindhoven area, this failure was foreseen and was one reason why *Comet* was finally cancelled. In some other respects however, the *Comet* plan was superior to *Market*. Airborne *coup de main* forces would land on both sides of, and close to, the objectives. There is no hint of objection from the RAF that the ground south of the Arnhem bridge was unsuitable for gliders. Secondly, it is quite clear from the Warning Order that the Drop Zone/Landing Zone (DZ/LZ) for the 1st Parachute Brigade was to be five miles northwest of Arnhem, not the six to eight miles in *Market*; with no apparent objection from the air forces. Third, again unlike *Market,* there were to be two operational sorties (lifts) in one day, carried out by some, but not all, of the British and American aircraft involved.

Brigadier "Shan" Hackett, whose 4th Parachute Brigade was slated to seize the Grave Bridge over the Maas, thought that the Germans, however weak, would react instantly and violently, and insisted that more airborne troops be committed. Major General Sosabowski too tried to persuade Airborne Corps Commander Browning to employ two airborne divisions for *Comet*. In this, he anticipated the view of Gavin's Chief of Staff in regard to a similar predicament of the 82nd Airborne in *Market Garden,* where the divisional frontage was far in excess of the normal maximum of 15,000 yards. Although Browning agreed that more paratroopers were needed, he said his hands were tied. From the time that Urquhart received and issued orders on 6 September, the ground advance of British Second Army stalled. This led to a postponement of *Comet,* first to the night of 9/10 September, then to the night of 11/12. On the evening of the 9th, Dempsey recorded in his diary that Second Army would not be ready to fight a "real battle" for ten to fourteen days.

Like any competent military plan, *Comet* was shaped by the tactical realities present at the time of its creation. The initial planning of *Comet* took place when the German retreat was in full swing and the Allies were looking for opportunities to exploit their success and keep the Germans on the run. In this sense, *Comet* was only one of a series of small tactical operations. But on 3 September, the situation changed. Instead of pursuing the retreat in a fluid series of operations, Montgomery halted the armored forces in the Antwerp sector and ordered an all-out effort to "bounce the Rhine" from positions south of the Albert Canal further east. *Comet* was then to take its place in support of a planned ground operation, not simply in support of the continuing pursuit of the Germans.

The first inkling of *Market Garden* occurred on 6 September, when Prince Bernhardt of the Netherlands visited Montgomery at his HQ outside Brussels. Montgomery revealed that he was planning a major operation into the Netherlands with a parachute drop on a grand scale. This was clearly over and above the forces committed for *Comet,* which was envisaged before Montgomery got control of the entire Allied Airborne Army on 4 September. The plan was proposed to Eisenhower when Montgomery met him on 10 September. Dempsey was likely privy to the plans as he had met with Montgomery on 7 September, the day on which he recorded in his diary that he could get as far as Arnhem with one ground corps and the airborne in *Comet,* but, without ports and extra supplies, no further. Dempsey again met Montgomery, in the company of Crerar of Canadian First Army and Hodges of U.S. First Army on 9 September, when *Comet* was again postponed. By then, it was known that *Waffen-SS* training units had arrived in Nijmegen from Amsterdam.

Dempsey met Montgomery yet again at 0900 hours on 10 September. The airborne operation was bumped up from one to three divisions, quite probably on Dempsey's own suggestion; presumably, too, all three corps of Second Army were to be committed in Dempsey's "real battle." The reason for the stronger airborne component was not that opposition had stiffened on the Albert Canal, the rationale for the earlier postponement of *Comet.* Now the reason Dempsey gave was the increasing German strength in the Arnhem-Nijmegen area; we can surmise that this was mainly from Dutch intelligence reports, since *Ultra,* the top secret Allied radio decryption system, had not yet built up a picture of the state of II SS *Panzer* Corps in the vicinity of Arnhem. By 10 September, Dempsey was well enough acquainted with the plan to outline the operation and issue orders to Browning at 1100 hours to take back to England.

While the concept and outline plan were Montgomery's, he and his staff had thereafter little to do with the planning of *Market Garden* or the conduct of the operation. The 21AG had no liaison staff at the First Allied Airborne Army. Montgomery intervened only once, to try to get Brereton to reverse the decision to drop the troops in one lift on D-Day. Montgomery no doubt knew that the Americans disliked the plan to drop the 101st Airborne in seven places on D-Day; in the event, it was Dempsey who handled the issue to the Americans' satisfaction.

It was, presumably, on the 10th of September that Browning made his celebrated remark that, while he could hold the Arnhem Bridge for four days, "I think we might be going a bridge too far." Urquhart is the sole source for this remark and it is somewhat dubious because he attributed the response to a contention of Montgomery, not Dempsey. Montgomery had allegedly said that the ground forces could reach Arnhem in two days, while Browning had said that the airborne troops could hold on for four. Furthermore, there is no indication that Browning met with Montgomery.

There is also doubt as to what Browning meant by the remark. Urquhart thought that he was worried about the distance between Arnhem and the Second Army start-line. Most commentators have taken the remark to mean that the operation should not have tried to aim for the Arnhem bridges, notwithstanding Hackett's contention that without the Arnhem road bridge the operation was pointless. A more plausible explanation is not that Browning thought that the Arnhem Bridge was too far, but that it was too ambitious to land troops north of the Lower Rhine. This had indeed been the aim in *Comet*, so perhaps Browning had second thoughts. Author William F. Buckingham has alleged that he made the remark for posterity, which would have required exceptional powers of divination on Browning's part.

THE GROUND FORCES AND OPERATION *GARDEN*

Dempsey noted in his diary on 5 September that his task was to prevent the Germans from escaping from the Breskens Pocket, a province of the Netherlands isolated from the rest of the country, with the south bank of the Scheldt estuary as its northern boundary. The pocket resulted from the capture of Antwerp, cutting off German forces from their front line on the Albert Canal. Dempsey also had to capture a bridgehead over the Rhine. To implement the Rhine operations, Montgomery met with Dempsey and his corps commanders, Ritchie and Horrocks, on 5 September and authorized the use of the British Airborne Corps of the First Airborne Division, the Polish Parachute Brigade and the 52nd (Air-Portable) Division.

The aim of both the airborne and ground operations was to cross the Lower Rhine and achieve a bridgehead. Second Army was to mount a two-pronged attack. The 15th Division was to advance through Turnhout and Tilburg, cross the Rhine east of Arnhem and head for Ede. The Guards Armoured was to advance through Eindhoven and Nijmegen, cross the Rhine at Arnhem, and aim for Apeldoorn. The offensive came to be known as the First Arnhem Plan: the left prong of the offensive anticipated the XII Corps plan in *Garden* to advance toward Turnhout, while the right prong in both ground and airborne components squarely anticipated *Market Garden*.

A brigade of the 50th Division forced a crossing of the Albert Canal at Gheel on 7 September. On the 12th, XII Corps took over from XXX Corps, freeing the 50th, a division with a superb fighting record, for *Market Garden*. On the 7th, the Guards Armoured crossed the Albert Canal at Beeringen and was subjected to repeated counterattacks in the triangle between the Meuse-Escaut and Albert canals. During the 12th, the Irish Guards captured a bridge at the De Groote Barrier on the Meuse-Escaut Canal which was damaged but usable; the British engineers constructed a bridge overnight. This became the Neerpelt bridgehead and the launching point for *Garden*. The Neerpelt bridgehead was also counterattacked in strength before September 17. O'Connor's VIII Corps to the east had no bridgeheads over the Meuse-Escaut Canal nor, yet, did XII Corps to the west.

Originally, the position in the XII Corps sector around Gheel was to form the basis of the left prong of the ground advance, over the Rhine to Ede. When the offensive planned on 6 September was replaced by *Garden*, the Gheel bridgehead was then to become the starting point for XII Corps, to the left of the XXX Corps. The Fiftieth Division was driven out of the town of Gheel before it was transferred to XXX Corps. In some extremely heavy fighting on the part of the Scots of 15th Division, the troops recaptured Gheel and secured a small bridgehead over the Meuse-Escaut Canal at Aart. However, this was so tenuous that it was decided to abandon the idea of an advance from Aart and to force a crossing at Lommel by the 53rd Division further east, which would become the new starting point for XII Corps operations in *Garden*. The Aart bridgehead was itself abandoned on D+3 and the plans to advance from Gheel, as a further route north, became academic.

Overall, Second Army had improved its tactical position only at Neerpelt since the Aart bridgehead was unusable. The counterattacks had indicated that the "thin crust" of German defenses was too thick to envisage an easy advance northwards over the canals. Two crossings of the Meuse-Escaut Canal, one by XII Corps and the other by VIII Corps, would have to be made before there could be any advance by these flanking corps. Neither corps could do this by the time of the XXX Corps advance at 1400 hours on 17 September. Far from being ready to deliver a quick hammer blow on D-Day, only XXX Corps of Second Army was properly deployed. Nor was there any reason at all to believe that there could be a rapid and immediate advance in the sectors of any of the three corps involved.

Of the three, VIII Corps was in the worst position. On D-Day, O'Connor had only the 11th Armoured and 1st Belgian Brigade Group in place, with his Advance HQ established a mere two days before. On D-Day, the bulk of 3rd Division was still on the move from the Seine, with many gaps in the column, some three miles long. By the evening of D+1, the infantry battalions were "still not completely in" and there was yet no bridgehead over the Meuse-Escaut Canal. The last VIII Corps troops, the 91st Anti-Tank Regiment, left the Seine as late as D+8! Of the three divisions of XII Corps, the 7th Armoured (Desert Rats) had only one of three regiments in place. The bulk of the division was still at Herenthals, defending the Antwerp area and the XII Corps left flank. On D+3, Dempsey was still worrying that his position would not be satisfactory until the Canadian army took over responsibility for the Albert Canal in the Herenthals sector.

The Market Garden plan was to bring responsibility for the flanks of XXX Corps under a separate command. Yet this was not to be the only task of the two flanking corps, since both were given a further task in addition to protecting the XXX Corps advance. The XII Corps was to advance on Turnhout, then move north to the Maas and "possibly beyond." But Turnhout would take it away from the XXX Corps axis of advance instead of protcting its flanks; this task recalled the earlier plan to advance on Turnhout and Tilburg from Gheel. The second task of VIII Corps made the divergence even geater; the corps was to oper-ate on the right flank of XXX Corps, broaden the base of Second Army for its advance into Holland, and move northeast, away from XXX Corps, to the line of the Maas.

The best explanation for this dispersal of effort is that Dempsey did not see the main aim as a XXX Corps thrust to Arnhem but as a grand Second Army advance all along the line with the result that his entire army would be poised to descend on the Ruhr. With the exception of one brigade of XII Corps, Dempsey never ordered either of the two corps to close in with strong forces to the XXX Corps flanks. Even on D+8, when the Corridor remained cut, Dempsey directed XII Corps on Schijndel and VIII Corps on Cuyt, both north, when the action was on an east-west lateral.

The flanking corps have never been given their due in *Market Garden,* considering the achievements of VIII Corps and the severe casualties incurred by XII Corps. Ritchie's 15th Division alone suffered more casualties (1,356) than the three divisions of XXX Corps (1,333). Nor was the terrain in which they had to operate favourable for a rapid advance. Marshy ground and streams permeated the XII Corps front, though the going was better in some areas north of Eindhoven and much easier north of the Best-Tilburg lateral, where many of the small waterways ran south-north. For VIII Corps the terrain was worse, the marshy conditions reaching north almost to Nijmegen and spreading east to the Meuse (Maas). In the areas immediately north of the start-line, small lakes added to wetlands and minor waterways; definitely not tank country. There were no good north-south roads, only a road in the VIII Corps sector along the Zuid-Willemsvaart Canal from Weert, through Helmond and Veghel to 's-Hertogenbosch. The Germans, the terrain, minimal air support and no airborne component conspired to make the tasks of the flanking corps very difficult. If the aim of "progressively" relieving XXX Corps of responsibility for protecting the flanks meant keeping up with the central corps, only a day or so behind, then VIII and XII Corps were given an impossible task.

Once it had secured its bridgehead over the Meuse-Escaut Canal, VIII Corps had to contend with the Zuid-Willemsvaart Canal, over which they eventually constructed four forty-ton bridges. Their task was not nearly as formidable as that of XXX Corps and the airborne troops, which had six major transverse waterways to cross and hold, as well as a number of smaller rivers and brooks. The six crossings were over the Wilhelmina Canal, the Zuid-Willemsvaart Canal, the Maas, the Maas-Waal Canal, the mighty Waal at Nijmegen, and the Lower Rhine at Arnhem.

If the Germans destroyed the bridges, they would have to be replaced by engineers or crossed by the infantry in assault boats, either a hazardous and potentially time-consuming endeavour. On the face of it, the idea of a massive airborne operation in such a waterlogged area was too risky to contemplate. Montgomery explained his decision as due to three overriding considerations: Second Army would outflank the Siegfried Line; the enemy would be least likely to expect an attack in the area; and the distance from supporting air bases would be the most advantageous.

The terrain in the XXX Corps sector was otherwise less difficult than that of the flanking corps. The most challenging area was north of the Waal, where the land was marshy and intersected by deep, sodden ditches. Vehicles had to stick to narrow, often muddy roads, with the danger of driving off and little prospect for recovery. The wedge of land between the Waal, the Lower Rhine and the Pannerden Canal connecting the two rivers was called the Betuwe by the Dutch, and by the Allies after the battle, "the Island." The area north of Arnhem, the Veluve, is a mixture of parkland, open meadows and woods; the going would have been better had the Allies struck north of the city.

In one respect, Horrocks exaggerated the difficulties of his corps. He said that he was limited by having to use a single road to Arnhem. In fact, his main axis was called the Club Route and a subsidiary way forward known as the Heart Route. The Heart Route ran east around Eindhoven to Grave. Since there were several routes from Grave to Nijmegen and since two routes were exploited from Nijmegen to Arnhem, the belief that there was only a single road to Arnhem was more the result of operational difficulty or a variation of the operational plan, as happened between Nijmegen and the Lower Rhine.

One single-road bottleneck was at the Grave bridge over the Maas, since there were no plans to use the rail crossing at Mook. Sosabowski alone saw the importance of the Mook rail bridge, both for *Comet* and for *Market Garden*. Commentators have ignored the bridge ever since, not even noting that it had long been destroyed by the Germans when VIII Corps units crossed the Maas into the 82nd Airborne sector on D+12. The bridge was in fact blown by the Germans as elements of the 82nd approached to capture it on D-Day.

THE PLAN FOR *MARKET GARDEN* UNFOLDS

One plausible explanation for the replacement of *Comet* with *Market Garden* is that Montgomery wanted to present Eisenhower with a *fait accompli*, a major airborne operation that would force him to support a northern offensive, with the supplies to carry it out. Montgomery had signalled to Eisenhower on 7 September that, without additional supplies, he could not reach the Ruhr, and on the 9th he requested a face-to-face meeting with a staff member of SHAEF to discuss the priority of the northern advance over the Saar offensive. The question of supply was not discussed at the meeting with Eisenhower at the Brussels airport on 10 September, even though the supply chiefs of both Eisenhower and Montgomery had been summoned to attend. Supply issues were resolved to Montgomery's satisfaction at the meeting with Eisenhower's Chief of Staff on the 12th, after *Market Garden* had been approved in principle two days before.

The intent of *Market Garden* was not to capture the Ruhr, only to "threaten" it from the north, with the practical effect of cutting off communications between Germany and the Low Countries, including of course the German Fifteenth Army around the Scheldt Estuary and the V2 rocket sites in the western Netherlands. These sites had been identified by *Ultra* and by 8 September were launching rockets against London and Norwich. That there were misconceptions about the operation is clear from the Second Army Intelligence Summaries which repeatedly refer to the aim of the operation as the invasion of Holland.

Air Marshal Sir Arthur Tedder, present at the meeting on 10 September, recorded that Montgomery was probably unhappy that he had not entirely got his way in that *Market Garden* was not to be the entire and single-minded focus of SHAEF's strategy. Eisenhower told author Cornelius Ryan long after the war that Montgomery had grumbled about half-measures. Nor did Montgomery get any form of control over U.S. First Army, which had a role parallel to that of Second Army. He had, however, gotten much of what he wanted.

Montgomery issued Operational Directive M525 on 14 September, which called for two thrusts over the Rhine: one by Second Army in the north and the other by the U.S. First Army to the south. Second Army was to establish itself on the line of Zwolle-Deventer-Arnhem with "deep bridgeheads" over the IJssel to the east. The objective of the IJsselmeer, the lake formed by a causeway across the Zuyder Zee, is not mentioned in the order; this occurs only in the subsequent orders for XXX Corps. Montgomery did not direct an advance on the Ruhr, only to be prepared to advance on the Muenster Triangle with the weight of the advance toward Hamm. The task of the First Army was to establish a deep bridgehead, some ten miles in depth, through the capture of Bonn and Cologne, so as to be prepared to join up with Second Army in an envelopment of the *Ruhrindustriegebiet*.

Eisenhower warmly endorsed the directive, with a copy to Bradley, on 16 September. M525 made it very clear that *Market Garden* was to be one wing of a strategic operation involving three armies, one of them airborne. Eisenhower assured Montgomery that Bradley would do everything needed to conform to the plan. In his two memoirs, Bradley claimed that he was opposed from the beginning to *Market Garden* on the grounds that it would divert resources from the opening of Antwerp. In doing so, he is silent on the role assigned to his First Army, claiming, quite wrongly, that its proposed engagement in the Rhine operations was a result of Eisenhower's strategy meeting with his senior commanders at Versailles on 22 September. The "business of Antwerp," as Montgomery called it, was not an issue for the senior commanders in the first half of September.

When we ask "why *Market Garden?*" the most convincing answer was that it was the closest thing to a northern offensive that Montgomery was able to attain, interest in which dated back to a proposal to Bradley in mid-August that they advance together on the northern route to the *Reich* with no less than forty divisions.

Dempsey's heart was never in the Arnhem operation. Early in September, his preference was for an airborne operation aimed at Wesel on the edge of the Ruhr. The approaches were far better tank country than the Albert Canal-Arnhem axis, and Wesel was itself on the northern doorstep of the *Ruhrindustriegebiet*. It is unlikely that the airmen would have agreed to such an operation, as the aircraft would have run into the strong enemy air defenses of the Ruhr, both flak and night fighters.

As soon as Browning landed back in England at 1430 hours on 10 September, he went directly to Brereton, who formally gave him command of *Market* on the following day. He also told Brig. General Floyd Parks, Brereton's Chief of Staff, that, as with *Comet*, the operation was to be in the Arnhem-Nijmegen-Grave area but extending further south, with the same airborne force as the previously proposed *Linnet I* and *II*. More precisely, Browning was given command of the "initial phase," which would conclude with the flying in of the 52nd (Air-Portable) on D+5. At that time, the HQ of U.S. XVIII Corps (Airborne) would be flown in to join Browning's own corps HQ.

In addition to the British 1st Airborne Division and the First Polish Independent Parachute Brigade from his own corps, Browning was given the American 82nd and 101st Airborne Divisions from Ridgeway's XVIII Airborne Corps, as well as the 52nd Division. That he should have been given command of American troops was not a surprise, as the two American divisions would have been part of the British First Airborne Corps in *Linnet I* and *Linnet II*, operations planned for late August or early September. An equally important consideration was that Browning had been given command of *Comet* from its outset and it was natural enough that he should have been assigned to its successor. Ridgeway was, however, deeply disappointed that he had not been given the command.

The British 1st Airborne Division, with the Polish Parachute Brigade under command, was to capture the Arnhem bridges. The U.S. 82nd Airborne ("All American Division") was to be responsible for the Nijmegen, Grave and Maas-Waal Canal bridges and to secure the high ground between Nijmegen and Groesbeek to the east. The U.S. 101st Airborne (the "Screaming Eagles") was to capture the bridges and the land route, precarious in places, between Grave and Eindhoven, including the bridge at Son en Breughel, the bridges over the Zuid-Willemsvaart Canal near Veghel, and the Dommel River bridges in Eindhoven itself.

The 101st would be the first to link up with British XXX Corps, advancing north from the Neerpelt bridgehead on the Meuse-Escaut Canal. XXX Corps would subsequently link up with the 82nd and the 1st Airborne, then advance deep and wide into the Rhine bridgehead. The van of the XXX Corps advance was to be the Guards Armoured Division, followed by the 43rd (Wessex) and the 50th (Northumbrian) Infantry Divisions. The Guards were to reach the IJsselmeer in the region of Nunspeet while 43rd Division was to establish bridgeheads over the IJssel at Zutphen and Deventer, the 50th further south at Doesburg. The 1st Airborne was to reinforce XXX Corps in the moves out of the Arnhem bridgehead, and there is circumstantial evidence that Montgomery intended the two American airborne divisions to do the same. The 52nd Division was to be flown in on D+5 to a captured airfield at Deelen. Also under XXX Corps command was the Dutch Princess Irene Brigade, headed by Colonel de Ruyter van Steveninck. The Guards Armoured was to bypass Apeldoorn, which was to be liberated and occupied by the Dutch brigade.

The operation was scheduled to be complete by D+6. The XXX Corps also had assignments in the Corridor. The prime role of 50th Division was to protect the Corridor in conjunction with the American airborne divisions. Should any of the bridges be down, the armor would fan out and the 43rd, in conjunction with airborne troops, would undertake bridging operations to secure alternative crossings. The Eighth Armoured Brigade of XXX Corps was attached to the 43rd Division. All three of the armored battalions of this brigade fought in the Nijmegen area, one south of the Waal with the 82nd Airborne and the others in the Nijmegen bridgehead north of the river. XII and VIII Corps, protecting the flanks, would take divisions in the Corridor under command for this purpose. In fact, 50th Division came under VIII Corps command on D+1, before that corps had even secured its bridgehead over the Meuse-Escaut Canal.

A key part in the bigger plan was to be played by the engineers. Dempsey had assembled about 2,300 vehicles with 9,000 engineers and pioneers in the vicinity of Bourg Leopold. The engineers would be needed if any major bridge were down as well as to carry the advance beyond the Rhine and over the IJssel. The Army Group's Bridge Column consisted of four bridge company HQs with bridging equipment and rafts. These four engineer companies later conducted the evacuation of 1st Airborne across the Lower Rhine. Strangely, the plan did not call for any immediate advances by these engineers in support of XXX Corps, since bridging was the responsibility of 43rd Division. Small units of the engineer component were attached only to the Guards Armoured as corps troops. According to Montgomery, these were to be "sufficient to bridge small obstacles on the route and to provide assault boats and rafts to get troops and tanks across the major obstacles should the bridges be blown but held by our own Airborne Troops."

Yet when the 43rd reached the Rhine at Driel, they were crying out for heavy bridging equipment, rafts and assault boats in great numbers, since their own engineers were ill-equipped to navigate the swift current and cross the 300-foot width of the Lower Rhine. The 21AG Report acknowledged that it was on September 25 (D+8) that the 1st Airborne bridgehead was found to be unsuitable for XXX Corps since it was impossible to build and maintain a bridge in the area.

At 1030 hours on 16 September, Horrocks held his Orders Group meeting in the cinema of the drab mining town of Bourg Leopold, a scene well depicted in the movie *A Bridge Too Far*. By this time the Seaborne Echelon or "sea tail"—the land-borne infrastructure, administrative and supply units of the 1st Airborne—had arrived in the area. Horrocks spoke for over an hour in front of a large map, rarely consulting notes. He radiated confidence, a self-conscious ploy to encourage the troops. Inwardly, he had doubts about breaking out of the bridgehead "reasonably quickly." The private responses of the gathered leaders, dressed as they were in strange combinations of uniform and casual gear, varied widely. Like Sosabowski, the Dutch thought the British overconfident and too offhand about a highly risky operation.

Zero hour for the ground operation was expected to be at 1400 hours the next day, as soon as Horrocks was sure the paratroopers were down. The barrels of 350 guns would lay down a rolling barrage before the Guards, preceded on the route by rocket-firing Typhoon fighter-bombers. Montgomery's prescription was for the advance "to be rapid and violent, without regard to the flanks." Horrocks underscored this by informing the audience that "most of the available resources have been allotted to XXX Corps, [so the flanks] will not be able to advance so rapidly and we shall be out on our own, possibly for quite a long period."

Much of the remaining presentation was taken up with administrative minutiae. For the 20,000 vehicles involved, there would be a Traffic Control HQ which would allot a schedule for every column of more than five vehicles. Horrocks established the principle of "day movement only"; night moves were allowed only in the event of operational necessity or if the movement could be completed within two hours of darkness. Except for these two reservations, no units were allowed to pass those up ahead. No rearward traffic was permitted unless ordered and there was to be "no turn-about." Speed was vital as the 1st Airborne would have to be reached "if possible within forty-eight hours." If a bridge was reported down, the road would be cleared of all traffic and the Royal Engineers earmarked for that bridge rushed up. General Horrocks gave two reasons for the short notice of the operation: first that the preparations had all been made, including that for the engineers; and that security concerns required that orders to be given as late as possible.

After the briefing, the commanders of the units involved—three divisions along with the Dutch and 8th Armoured Brigades—dispersed for their respective O (Orders) Groups. The Guards Armoured was divided, as before, into four groups of the Irish, Welsh, Grenadier and Coldstream Guards. The Irish Guards Group was to take the lead; the commander of the Second (Armoured) Battalion, Lt. Col. J.O.E. (Joe) Vandaleur also led the group under the command of Norman Gwatkin of the Fifth Guards Armoured Brigade. The O Group of the 43rd

Division included the commanders of the 8th Armoured Brigade, the 147th Field Regiment and the 64th Medium Regiment, Royal Artillery and the Royal Netherlands Brigade Group. The division was allotted rations for four days and petrol for 250 miles.

THE PLANS FOR THE AIRBORNE ASSAULT

British Airborne Song (Tune: "Bless 'em all")

> *They say there's a Whitley*
> *leaving Ringway*
> *Bound for old Tatton Park,*
> *heavily laden with parachute troops,*
> *Bound for the drop that's no lark,*
> *There's many a paratrooper just*
> *finishing his jumps,*
> *There's many a twerp starting his,*
> *but he'll get no promotion if*
> *his chute doesn't open,*
> *so cheer up my lads bless 'em all.*
>
> *Bless 'em all, Bless 'em all,*
> *The parachute packers and all,*
> *We'll get no promotion if our*
> *chutes do not open.*
> *So cheer up my lads, bless 'em all.*

"These airmen were heroes."
—General Hanns Albin Rauter, SS Higher Security and Police Chief
for the Netherlands.

On 10 September, the headquarters of the First Allied Airborne Army was barely a month old. Its commander, U.S. Lt. General Lewis Brereton, had moved to the Allied Airborne after leading the Ninth Air Force in Normandy. Earlier, in December 1941, Brereton had lost most of his aircraft on the ground when the Japanese invaded the Philippines soon after the Pearl Harbor attack. His reputation never recovered despite Ninth Air Force successes in the Normandy campaign. Major Urquhart found him a querulous and somewhat bewildered character, saved from floundering only by the competence of his senior staff. The

British were not convinced that an air force commander was suitable to lead paratroopers and they blamed Brereton for what they perceived as mistakes made in the planning of *Market Garden.*

Part of Brereton's problem was that he did not have full command of the forces at his disposal. His air commander, Major General Paul L. Williams, was also commander of the IX Troop Carrier Command. The three troop carrier wings consisted entirely of C-47 Dakota "Skytrain" transport aircraft, used both as glider tugs and for paratroop drops. For *Market Garden,* 38 and 46 Group of RAF Transport Command were attached to 1AAA.

Brereton delegated to Air Vice-Marshal Leslie Hollinghurst of 38 Group the decisions over the deployment of the RAF transports in the British airborne operation. Brereton was also obliged to use his transport aircraft for supplying his troops. The situation was satisfactory in the case of supplying the American airborne, which were assigned an additional 252 B-24 Liberator bombers. Supplies could be ordered directly by the airborne divisions from units stationed on the continent. But the British were at a disadvantage over the use of their transport aircraft for supply, which led to the decision to land the 52nd Division only on D+5. For the rest, they could only ask Eisenhower's Air-Commander-in-Chief, Trafford Leigh-Mallory, for additional supply aircraft, as he retained control over the two British Air Groups. His role in curtailing supply operations to the 1st Airborne Division became contentious.

Leigh-Mallory also retained control over the air forces that were to support *Market Garden.* These were the fighters and bombers of the U.S. Eighth Air Force; fighters and tactical bombers of the U.S. Ninth Air Force; fighters of the Air Defence of Great Britain (previously and later known as Fighter Command); the Spitfire fighters and Typhoon fighter-bombers of 83 Group, British Second Tactical Air Force (RAF) and Bomber Command. The task of the U.S. Eighth Air Force was to escort the transports, attack flak batteries and engage in resupply, at least on D+1. The U.S. Ninth Air Force and the British Second Tactical Air Force were to provide air support after the drop. The Air Defence of Great Britain was to provide escort and anti-flak operations.

As soon as *Market Garden* had been authorized, planning of the air component began immediately and in great haste. The first planning meeting was at 1830 hours on 10 September. Brereton laid down a fundamental rule that decisions, once made, could not be changed. With the support of all the division commanders he decided on a daytime operation. Two routes would be taken in order not to present enemy flak gunners with too large a stream of aircraft to target. The 1st and 82nd Airborne Divisions would take a northern route over the Scheldt islands while the 101st would follow a southern route, mostly over territory occupied by the Allies.

A third decision concerned the number of sorties on the first day. The decision over a day versus a night landing and the decision over the number of lifts involved overlapping considerations, particularly the experience and training of the air crews. The division commanders all requested a second lift on D-Day because of the need to take key tactical objectives quickly, the traditional function of airborne operations. But Brereton's air commander, Major General Williams, dissented, pointing out the risk of heavy losses, the inexperience of some of the pilots, and the fact that the need for repairs and crew fatigue would lead to unacceptable casualties on the second run.

The use of 1AAA aircraft for supply missions had disrupted training and there had been no night assembly training for three months. For these reasons, Williams considered the air crews not skilled enough in navigation or formation keeping to safely fly the pre-dawn or evening runs that a two-lift plan would require. A shortage of ground crews was also cited as a reason for denying a second lift on D-Day. The decision as to the number of first day lifts was postponed untill the following morning, 11 September, wherein Brereton went along with his air commander in support of a single lift.

It was acknowledged by all parties that it would take three days to transport all elements of the three divisions and the Polish Brigade; this was later extended to four days. The plan for D-Day called for two brigades, artillery and specialized units of the 1st Airborne to be flown in; each of the two U.S. airborne divisions would land three parachute regiments and support troops. Airborne Corps HQ would be flown in on thirty-eight gliders. In the second lift on D+1, 1st Airborne would receive the rest of its complement, the 82nd its artillery, the 101st its glider infantry regiment, and each division another contingent of supporting troops.

On D+2, the First Polish Parachute Brigade would arrive, as would the glider infantry of the 82nd and the artillery of the 101st. The "sea tails" of each division were scheduled to arrive by road on D+4. On D+5, the British 52nd Lowland (Air Portable) Division would be flown in to a captured airfield, likely Deelen. The U.S. 878th Engineer

Battalion was scheduled to be flown in with the 1st Airborne, to prepare an airfield for the 52nd. The flight of the American engineers was postponed and then cancelled, when there was no ground advance north from Arnhem.

The 101st Airborne

Of the three divisional landings, the closest to the XXX Corps startline was the 101st Airborne. The division was assigned a thin, sixteen mile stretch of highway from Son, north through St. Oedenrode and Veghel to Uden. The responsibility of the 101st Airborne was to seize and hold this section of "the Corridor," which came to be known to the Americans as "Hell's Highway." On the road were a number of river and canal crossings: the Dommel River bridges in Eindhoven, the bridge over the Wilhelmina Canal at Son en Breughel, the Dommel River bridge in St. Oedenrode, the road and rail bridges over the Zuid-Willemsvaart Canal southwest of Veghel, and the road and rail bridges over the Aa River north of the town.

The 101st would link up with XXX Corps on the southern outskirts of Eindhoven by 2000 hours on the first day, while it was still light. The commander of the 101st, Major General Taylor, also decided to attempt to capture the road and rail bridges over the Wilhelmina Canal at Best, west of Son, in order to gain an alternative route north, should the Son bridge not be taken intact. This proved to be a wise move, though not for the reasons intended.

Browning had originally called for seven drops from a point south of Eindhoven to an area north of Uden, a thirty-mile stretch. According to Brereton, this original plan came from Montgomery's HQ and Browning had "virtually agreed" to it. Using sources inside 1AAA HQ, the late author Clay Blair contended that Brereton was, in the beginning, strongly in favor of the British plan. He then allowed himself to be overruled by his division commanders and by his own staff, who were concerned that the division would be too broken up to be commanded effectively. General Taylor was dissatisfied with Browning's plan, partly because of the likelihood of dispersion. There was also the difficulty of pinpointing small areas. In Normandy only 25 percent of the paratroopers had landed in the right place.

This controversy was the reason why no decision was made about the 101st DZ at the 1AAA planning meeting on 11 September. Taylor, whose dissatisfaction was then echoed by Brereton, protested to

Browning. Browning gave Taylor permission to see Dempsey at Second Army. Dempsey, who had the most profound respect for the American paratroopers, readily agreed with Taylor; the drop was limited to two principal areas, one of which comprised the airhead or base of operations, and one subsidiary. Eindhoven was relegated to a secondary objective. Dempsey showed no interest in Taylor's plan to strike out west toward Best to capture the road and rail bridges over the Wilhelmina Canal.

Because of these complications, the drop plan for the 101st was not settled until 13 September at the earliest. Brereton recorded in his diary that his Chief of Staff, Maj. Gen. Floyd Parks, went with Taylor to 21AG; Dempsey recorded a meeting at his HQ with representatives of the First Allied Airborne Army only on 14 September. Later that day the troopers of the 101st were given an unusually cursory briefing on the plan. The perception among the paratroopers that the operation was thrown together with great haste extended to their equipment as new parachute harnesses with quick-release buckles were only issued to the paratroopers on D-Day, just prior to take off. The result of the final plan was that there would be no troops landed south of the Son bridge.

The 82nd Airborne

North of the 101st, the 82nd Airborne was responsible for securing a broad and roughly circular area of operations, bounded in the south by the Grave Bridge over the Maas and the two Nijmegen bridges over the Waal to the north. Browning made it "imperative" and a condition of further operations that the Groesbeek Heights should be secured as an airhead or base of operations for subsequent drops.

The Heights were an open and fairly flat plateau of about 300 feet, the highest point in the Netherlands, reaching almost to the German border in the east, the Waal to the north, the Maas to the south and, at their foot, the Grave-Heumen-Nijmegen road to the west. On this face, the Heights were approached by a steep and heavily wooded ascent. The occupation of the Groesbeek Heights was also a defense against counterattacks from the *Reichswald,* a small forest inside Germany to the southeast, where the Dutch Resistance had reported a concentration of enemy tanks. The great Nijmegen road bridge was not to be assaulted until the Groesbeek Heights *and* the Maas and Maas-Waal bridges had been secured. The result was that the Nijmegen road bridge was relegated to a tertiary objective.

Gavin had no criticism of the assault plan assigned to his division; he said that the clear decision to give priority to the Groesbeek Heights was "most helpful," and that it "seemed imperative." He did, however, say later that, with hindsight, it would have been better to have moved on the Nijmegen road bridge with his regiment near the Maas-Waal Canal, not with the one on the Groesbeek Heights. One formidable authority, Lt. Col. John Frost, the hero of the Arnhem bridge, went further and questioned whether the Groesbeek Heights should have been an objective at all.

In the 82nd's landing, two regiments were to drop on the Groesbeek Heights. Further west, a third regiment would drop north of the River Maas near Overasselt. A vital part of the plan was that one company of this regiment would drop west of the Grave Bridge and south of the Maas. The goal of the regiment was to capture the Grave Bridge over the Maas and at least one bridge over the Maas-Waal Canal.

On the Groesbeek Heights, the 508th PIR would move out north and west to the southeastern suburbs of Nijmegen, a town of 90,000. At the same time, the 505th PIR would move west to link up with the 508th, while fanning out south to block the main road up to Groesbeek and the rail crossing over the Maas at Mook. Here the river turns sharply from a south-north to an east-west direction. This would form a perimeter, held only at key points, in an arc from Mook, along the Dutch-German border adjacent to Wyler and Beek, thence to the edge of Nijmegen. The two regiments would then strike west to the crossings over the Maas-Waal Canal.

For the 504th PIR, the closest of the Maas-Waal Canal crossings was the Molenhoek sluice bridge at Heumen, which would bring XXX Corps through the heart of the 82nd's operational area. Next further north was a smaller bridge at Malden, then another at Hatert. The northernmost was a large twin road and rail bridge at Honinghutie. This was another promising route for XXX Corps since there was no question that the bridges were sturdy enough to carry tanks. On the debit side, this alternative route to Nijmegen was more vulnerable to counterattack on the western flank.

The 1st Airborne
The northernmost airborne landing was that of 1st Airborne, northwest of the Arnhem road bridge. In the words of Roy Urquhart, it was the fruit of a complex plan which was not finalized until 12 September:

I decided to put the First Parachute Brigade and the bulk of the First Airlanding Brigade down with the first lift, which would also include my own HQ and some divisional troops. Before the main force, the [Twenty-first] Independent Parachute Company would drop in order to mark the arrival areas. The Company had twelve pathfinder aircraft, and there were 143 Dakotas from the 9th U.S. Troop Carrier Command for the parachutists of the First Parachute Brigade, and 358 tugs and their equivalent for the rest. In the second lift, which would arrive 24 hours later, the main body of the 4th Parachute Brigade would jump from 126 Dakotas while the remainder of the First Airlanding Brigade and other divisional units would land in 301 gliders. On the third day, I intended to bring in the main body of the First Polish Parachute Brigade in 114 Dakotas and thirty-five gliders.

On the first day, First Parachute Brigade would move immediately to the Arnhem bridges: the rail crossing, a pontoon bridge and the road bridge. In each case, the brigade was to occupy both the northern and southern approaches, forming the beginning of a deep bridgehead in which to accommodate the leading elements of XXX Corps when they arrived. The First Airlanding Brigade was to hold the DZ/LZ until after the second lift on D+1, then move toward Arnhem. The 1st Airborne Division would occupy a "box-shaped bridgehead" running anti-clockwise from the area of the Driel-Heveadorp ferry, south over the railway bridge to a point along the Lower Rhine about a mile and a half southeast of the road bridge. From there, the perimeter would run east to a bridgehead over the IJssel at the rail bridge where the perimeter would curve in a northern arc back to the Driel-Heaveadorp ferry.

First Airlanding Brigade would hold the western sector, First Parachute Brigade both sides of the Lower Rhine in the south, the Polish parachute brigade would hold the east, and the Fourth Parachute Brigade, the north. The supply DZ for missions beyond D+1 would be within the perimeter. Smaller units would be stationed near the Divisional HQ established in the center of the city, near St. Elizabeth's Hospital, including the artillery, the Independent Parachute Company, the reconnaissance squadron and the glider pilots, now fighting as infantry. The Driel-Heveadorp ferry, which could carry eight small vehicles, was not mentioned in the operational instruction and Urquhart did not appreciate its importance. Frost, whose battalion passed by the ferry en route to Arnhem, was unaware of its existence. The rail bridge was also not mentioned.

The route from the DZ/LZ to the Arnhem road bridge could be held open for twenty-four hours or more on the assumption of minimal German opposition. The only two strong voices to challenge this assumption were Brigadier John W. Hackett of the Fourth Parachute Brigade and Sosabowski, the commander of the Poles. In Hackett's view, his brigade would have to fight every inch of the way to Arnhem.

Like the other divisional commanders, Urquhart lost the battle for two airborne lifts on D-Day. He questioned the number of aircraft assigned to his division, including the need for thirty-eight gliders that Browning had commandeered for his Corps HQ on the Groesbeek Heights. Urquhart's further concern was that at least some of his division should be dropped onto the north side of the Arnhem road bridge and that a substantial force, though not an entire brigade, should be dropped on the south side. Here, the issue was not directly with Browning but with Hollinghurst, the more senior of the two RAF commanders, to whom Brereton and Williams had delegated the detailed planning of the Arnhem lift. The issue became contentious as it was not until the final planning meeting on 14 September that the American paratroop leaders learned, to their amazement, that the entirety of Urquhart's force was to be landed six to eight miles away from the bridge.

In view of the fact that units in the 82nd Airborne were to be dropped nearly five miles from the Nijmegen road bridge, the Americans' reaction may seem misplaced. But there was one fundamental difference: to the Americans, the 1st Airborne on D-Day had essentially one objective requiring only one direction of advance. The Americans subsequently made great play of the idea that airborne troops should advance in only one direction at any given time. Hollinghurst, for his part, reasoned that enemy flak was very heavy over the bridge. In addition, after the drop, incoming aircraft would have to turn north, running into the airfield defenses of Deelen, or turn south, in which there was a danger of colliding with the 82nd's drop, whose operations were not under Hollinghurst's control.

As for landing of troops south of the Arnhem Bridge, Hollinghurst was of the opinion that the soft *polder* (reclaimed land) south of the bridge, strewn with deep drainage ditches, was unsuitable for glider landings, though this of course was not an objection to a paratroop drop. The only vindication for this view was a vague reference to Dutch intelligence sources. The result was that no British troops were dropped south of the Lower Rhine. Given the fact that Browning had proposed seven separate drop zones for the 101st, it is sadly ironic that the crude assault plan for the 1st Airborne called for essentially a single drop/landing zone, no less than six miles from the main objective.

Hollinghurst's concerns about Deelen were largely misplaced. On the night of 2/3 September, 103 Lancasters, led by four Mosquitos, dropped 580 tons of bombs on Deelen airfield. Reconnaissance flights the next day showed that most of the flak guns had been previously removed. The nightfighters of *Nacht Jagdgeschwader 1* had also been withdrawn and the base was being used as the fighter command center for northwest Germany and the Netherlands (though Model later had specialized troops and equipment such as flame throwers flown into Deelen). It is therefore implausible to suppose that Hollinghurst was ignorant of the state of Deelen. Though the British knew that they had rendered Deelen unusable for the time being, they did not know that they had destroyed a sophisticated nightfighter control center.

Had Urquhart pushed harder and sooner, he could have got his way on both of his concerns about the assault plan. Browning had consulted Major General Richard Gale of the British 6th Airborne (the paratroop veterans of Normandy) who is reported to have said that at least one parachute brigade, should be dropped adjacent to the road bridge and that he would have pressed for this condition "to the point of resignation." But Browning did not act on Gale's advice and Urquhart remained ignorant of the deliberations that took place in his name. Gavin, in *Airborne Warfare,* said that the staff of another experienced airborne division had asserted that the plan was such that they would be "reluctant to accept it," doubtless referring to 6th Airborne. Why Browning did not address Urquhart's concerns is not known; all the explanations are speculative.

The controversy over the distance of the paratroop landings from the road bridge went deeper. With the British, the principle was that the military force, in author Martin Middlebrook's words, "states its requirements" but that the air plan was made by the air force in the light of what it perceived to be possible. The Americans did things differently, with the airborne laying down what it wanted and the air force delivering the goods. Whatever the theory, there was a more harmonious co-operation among the Americans than there was among the British, where the formalities of responsibility took precedence over the need to get the job done in the most effective way.

A further weakness in the British assault plan was that the Poles were not to be dropped on the south side of the river until D+2, when both the road bridge and the flak positions would have been taken. Nor, of course, were there to be any glider landings on the *polder*. Instead, the plan was to land the Poles' artillery, transport, ammunition and brigade troops in forty-six gliders on the northern landing zone on D+2 and to drop the paratroopers close to the rail bridge on the south side. Should the paratroopers fail to cross to the north side, they would rapidly become short of supplies and ammunition.

Their situation was made worse by the fact that Sosabowski's artillery (twelve 75mm guns) was deleted from his glider lift and from the Poles' sea tail. They were to arrive separately, via Normandy. The paratroopers on the south side of the Rhine would cross the road bridge, meet the rest of the brigade, and take up positions on the northeast face of the bridgehead. Urquhart told Sosabowski that if the bridge were not already taken, he was expected to take it, without of course his artillery. In the event that XXX Corps arrived first, as planned, the Poles would reinforce 1st Airborne in the bridgehead. It is hard to avoid the conclusion that the Poles were to be used merely as extra ground troops in the push to the IJsselmeer.

There was yet another irregularity in the plan for the Poles. The Polish glider landings on LZL would be outside the perimeter, while the divisional area would encompass only a small corner of DZK, south of the Lower Rhine, where the three parachute battalions were to land on D+2. The First Parachute Brigade was given the task of "covering" the Polish drop south of the Rhine, and First Airlanding Brigade of "protecting" the glider landings. The implication is that the perimeter would have to remain extended until after the Poles landed on D+2. In the event, LZL was held, but very insecurely, by Fourth Parachute Brigade, only because of the failure to move off the DZ/LZ and into Arnhem. The Poles' DZ on the south bank of the Rhine never was occupied by British troops and had to be changed during the operation.

In Browning's *Operational Instruction No. 1* of 13 September, Urquhart was given the primary task of capturing one or more of the Arnhem bridges. His secondary task was to establish a "sufficient bridgehead" for XXX Corps troops to deploy north of the Lower Rhine. Third, he was to make every effort to destroy the flak in the area of the DZ/LZ and Arnhem to ensure the safe passage of subsequent lifts. The first three days of the operation betrayed a tension between the primary and secondary objectives of 1st Airborne. At their worst, the two tasks were conflated and confused, a commentary on Urquhart's leadership and tactics.

Urquhart was to set up a liaison party to meet XXX Corps with the possibility of the junction taking place north of the Lower Rhine should the Arnhem bridges not be taken. Browning's corps HQ would notify Urquhart when to expect the leading troops of XXX Corps, "some time after you have landed." A common expectation among 1st Airborne officers was that XXX Corps would arrive within twenty-four hours of landing. A warning was put out that the sea tails of 1st Airborne and the Polish Brigade could possibly arrive as early as twenty-eight hours after landing.

Urquhart directed his reconnaissance squadron to reconnoitre Apeldoorn, Zutphen, Zevenaar, Nijmegen and Wageningen, and to enter Ede, proof again that minimal opposition was expected. Only one troop of eight jeeps was initially assigned to the brigade advancing on the Arnhem bridges, accompanied by engineers equipped to destroy any demolition charges placed by the Germans.

3

THE OTHER SIDE OF
THE HILL

"But the Germans, General, the Germans!"
—Major General Sosabowski, at the briefing for Operation *Comet*

THE END OF THE GERMAN RETREAT

By early September 1944, Germany had survived its greatest crisis in the war to date. While the fighting against the Western Allies in Normandy had raged, the Russians had launched Operation *Bagration*, an offensive of stupendous proportions on 22 June, the third anniversary of the German invasion of the Soviet Union. The battle is known to history as the Destruction of Army Group Center. By the beginning of September the Russians were at the gates of Warsaw, with bridgeheads over the Vistula.

By then, too, the offensive in the East had run its course, as Russian supply lines were over-extended and the Germans regrouped to put up an effective resistance marked by sharp counterattacks. The worst being over for Army Group Center, Hitler was able to transfer its most recent commander, Field Marshal Walther Model, "the *Fuehrer's* Fireman," to command both the western theatre of operations in France and Army Group B in the northern sector of the Western Front. Model took up his new command on 17 August. In Model, the Germans had an ideal commander who had built his reputation on rescuing difficult defensive situations from disaster. Trusted by Hitler, he was comparable to Patton in his ability to galvanize troops into action. He also had confidence in the senior officers of II SS *Panzer* Corps, who had served under him on the Eastern Front.

On 5 September, Field Marshal Gerd von Rundstedt was reappointed *Oberbefehlshafer,* Commander-in-Chief West. Model was neither surprised nor disappointed when he retained command of Army Group B. The most urgent issue was the defense of the West Wall, or Siegfried Line, which terminated just north of the River Roer on the Netherlands border and behind the German city of Aachen. The aim was to extend the West Wall through Nijmegen to the IJsselmeer. Commander of the Netherlands Armed Forces, *Luftwaffe* General Friedrich Christiansen, was made responsible for military endeavors in the area, under Nazi Party direction. At the same time, Hitler ordered a "defensive position" further forward, by extending the Siegfried Line defenses through Maastricht, along the line of the Albert Canal.

On 4 September, Antwerp fell. Immediately, Hitler ordered the defense of the channel fortresses and the manning of the Albert Canal from Maastricht to Antwerp. *Luftwaffe* Colonel-General Kurt Student was ordered to form and mobilize the First Parachute Army for the defense of the Canal.

Fifteenth Army

On the day that von Rundstedt was reappointed, the German retreat was at its height. In the sectors covered by the British 21AG and the U.S. First Army to the south, three German armies were moving east: Fifteenth Army, Fifth *Panzer* Army and Seventh Army. Of the three armies, the northernmost, the Fifteenth under Lt. General Gustav von Zangen, was the most intact. Composed entirely of infantry, the Fifteenth had six full divisions along with the remnants of five others. Zangen was entrusted with defending the coastal fortresses, including the Scheldt Estuary and the western end of the Albert Canal. The fall of Antwerp came as a shock and von Zangen, much of his army marooned in the Breskens Pocket south of the Scheldt Estuary, had the choice of evacuation by sea or breaking out to the northeast. He chose the latter, only to have the order countermanded by Rundstedt.

The alternative was evacuating through the Dutch ports of Breskens and Terneuzen across to Walcheren, thence over South Beveland to the mainland at Woensdrecht. Using two large freighters, three motorized rafts and sixteen barges, the Germans got 65,000 men, 225 guns, 750 trucks and a thousand horses across between 5 and 21 September. Some of von Zangen's units were already outside the Breskens Pocket when Antwerp was captured, including the bulk of 346th Division on the

Albert Canal. The way over the canal to the Lower Rhine was by no means clear of the Germans.

That von Zangen made good his escape to the mainland was, it is commonly said, due to an enormous Allied mistake. The British 11th Armoured Division, after night marches and with the crucial help of the Belgian Resistance, burst into Antwerp on 4 September. While the vast area of the docklands was far from completely secure, much of the port with its heavy cranes, gantries, dry docks and electrically-operated sluices was captured intact. Shortly afterward, an order came from Second Army to the armored divisions to refit, refuel and rest.

The first aspect of the alleged mistake took place when Major General Philip Roberts of the 11th Armoured, in the absence of orders, neglected to seize two bridges over the Albert Canal; the Germans blew one and recaptured the other from the Belgian Resistance. Roberts, in his defense, contended that the reason for not capturing the bridges was that there were no plans to advance to the Rhine from Antwerp, which at the time was true. In fact, the British armor could still cross to the north bank of the Albert Canal in the area of the dry docks. A second aspect was the failure to advance north to the isthmus of South Beveland at Woensdrecht, which, if it were held, would have bottled up the German Fifteenth Army and prevented its escape to the mainland. Though the fighting on the north bank of the Scheldt and the Albert Canal was heavy, it might have been possible to detach a mobile formation north to Woensdrecht, thence further to the Lower Rhine. At least the attempt should have been made. The Resistance held that the British should have advanced to the Belgian-Dutch frontier, just south of Woensdrecht.

Fifteenth Army could still have escaped to Rotterdam via Schouen Island, though this route was not amenable to the transport of heavy equipment. Yet historians have been almost unanimous in contending that the Allies made a deplorable mistake in allowing Fifteenth Army to escape through Woensdrecht. On this, the whole debate is skewed. The causeway at Woensdrecht was potentially just as important to the Germans for supporting Fifteenth Army as it was for its escape. If the military aim was to first weaken the German defense, then to clear the Scheldt Estuary to open Antwerp, the last thing that was needed was to lock the Germans in at Woensdrecht.

When it came to that point in October, the Canadians had enough trouble dealing with the German 70th Division, never mind a whole army. The 70th, the "White Bread Division," was suffering a pandemic of stomach ailments, yet it fought surprisingly well. Indeed, only two divisions of Fifteenth Army attacked the western side of the Arnhem Corridor, the 59th and the 245th. The 245th successfully opposed the XII Corps advance, allowing the veteran 59th to take part in operations that severed the Corridor on three occasions. But author Alistair Horne's idea that Fifteenth Army "tilted the balance" at Arnhem is absurd. The failure of *Market Garden* was not due to the action of two German divisions in action on the western side of the Corridor but to the formations that blunted the Allied advance north of Nijmegen. Here again, the debate has become distorted.

Allied propaganda at the time claimed that the Fifteenth Army was trying desperately to escape to the *Reich* and was blocked along the Arnhem Corridor by Second Army forces. Some historians echoed this propaganda even in the 1990s. In fact, the only troops that attempted to return to Germany were a formation from 712th Division; this blundered into XII Corps on the western flank, unaware that the British were operating as far north as Arnhem.

At the same time that the evacuation began, von Zangen had the 719th Coastal Division brought down from the northern Netherlands to guard the exit from South Beveland to the mainland. These troops were soon brought to the defense of the western end of the Albert Canal. Of the battered Fifth *Panzer* Army and Seventh Army, most formations were ordered back to the *Reich*. But the elderly, energetic commander of the 85th Infantry, Lt. General Kurt Chill, defied orders and halted on the Albert Canal, little knowing that the High Command had already decided to establish there a defensive position forward of the extended West Wall. He took two other divisions under his command, the 89th from Fifth *Panzer* Army and from the Seventh, the 84th Division, whose commander had been captured.

Chill blew some bridges and posted guards on others to recruit all stragglers, irrespective of command or mission. When Kurt Student, the new commander of the embryo First Parachute Army, drove along the canal from Maastricht on 5 September, he was gratified to find small groups of soldiers constructing defenses. Further along toward Antwerp, the 719th Coastal was taking up positions. If there was a major flaw in British operations, it was the failure to advance immediately from Brussels to the Albert Canal, after the capture of the city on 3 September and before the German defense of the canal was organized.

The II SS Panzer Corps

The formation that played the critical role in defeating the Allies in *Market Garden* was II SS *Panzer* Corps, consisting of the 9th *Waffen-SS* Division *Hohenstaufen* and the 10th *Waffen-SS* Division *Frundsberg*. These two elite divisions had played a leading part in freeing the First *Panzer* Army from encirclement by the Russians in April. They then took part in the Normandy battles from the beginning of July onward. By early September, the corps had been reduced to about 6,500–7,000, of whom a small majority were *Frundsberg* men. Both divisions were officially down to *Kampfgruppe* (Battle Group) strength, but their fighting quality was high and their leadership exemplary.

The corps commander was SS-Lt. General Wilhelm Bittrich, whom Roy Urquhart described as a leader of "tremendous professional ability." The acting head of *Hohenstaufen* was SS-Colonel Walter Harzer, who was young, articulate, able and ambitious. Both Bittrich and Harzer were Anglophiles, which accounts in part for the healthy respect which both sides held for each other. The commander of *Frundsberg* was SS-Maj. General Heinz Harmel, whom the historian of the *Waffen-SS*, Col. General of the SS Paul Hausser, referred to as a leader of "proven ability." He was known to the troops with warmth as *Der alte Frundsberg* (Old Frundsberg Himself).

During the retreat of II SS *Panzer* Corps from the Falaise pocket on 21 August, command and control of Army Group B broke down completely. Model rarely knew where his units were or what shape they were in, receiving information that was either out of date or otherwise unreliable. Hausser, the commander of II SS *Panzer* Corps before he was promoted to head Seventh Army, was carried out of the Falaise Pocket, badly wounded, on the hull of one of the last remaining tanks from 1st SS *Panzer* Division.

During this chaotic period, Bittrich, who had taken over from Hausser, still found time to demand 111 new tanks on 26 August. On 3 September, Model had ordered all SS armored divisions to refit north of Namur in Belgium; this order was apparently never received by Bittrich. By 4 September, Bittrich had been out of touch with Army Group B for three days. He made his way on foot to Model's HQ near Liege and received verbal orders to disengage and move north into Holland for rest and refitting. Both the 9th and 10th SS divisions began withdrawing on 5–6 September, advanced units of the former reaching the Arnhem area by the evening of the 6th.

Bittrich then discovered to his chagrin that in refitting his two divisions they were to be split up; *Frundsberg* remaining in the Arnhem area and *Hohenstaufen* entraining for Siegen in the *Reich,* just east of the *Ruhrindustriegebiet. Hohenstaufen* was ordered to hand over its remaining armor and vehicles to *Frundsberg,* but these were still with the division on D-Day, when only technical and administrative units had left for Germany. Despite the corps order, both divisions were prepared for imminent action.

Hohenstaufen was divided into nineteen *Alarmheiten,* each of about company strength, comprising about 2,500 men in total. Most of these "alarm companies" were stationed 10–15 km northeast of Arnhem so that they could be brought to bear against any landing west of the city as well as north and east. Particularly crucial was the location of the 9th SS Reconnaissance Battalion at Beekbergen. In defiance of the order to hand over their vehicles to *Frundsberg,* the *Hohenstaufen* men disabled them in various, reversible ways such as having the tracks removed. While most of the vehicles were already loaded onto flatcars ready to move to Siegen, the battalion was otherwise poised to descend on Arnhem and points south.

Most of the corps had been thoroughly trained in anti-paratroop operations in France in 1943. Where the corps was deficient was in transport; the alarm units having to travel, for the most part, on foot or by bicycle. Communications with Harzer's HQ at Beekbergen outside Apeldoorn and between the companies were also so poor that the resulting siege of Frost's battalion at the Arnhem bridge was achieved as much by luck as by design.

Frundsberg's Harmel, with more men and heavy weapons than *Hohenstaufen*'s Harzer, also reorganized his division so that by 17 September he could call upon three battalions of *Panzergrenadiere* motorized infantry, a tank group of *Panzerkampfwagen* (*Panzer*) IVs in Vorden, and a flak (anti-aircraft) regiment in Dieren. *Panzergrenadier* Regiment 21, with a complement of 12 anti-tank guns, was stationed at Deventer.

The dispositions of *Frundsberg* are essential to an understanding of the German reaction on D-Day. The division's reconnaissance battalion under SS-Major Brinkmann was at Borculo and Eibergen, east of Harmel's HQ at Ruurlo, and the furthest of all the *Panzer* Corps units from Arnhem. The units at Vorden, Dieren and Deventer were also further from Arnhem than those of *Hohenstaufen.* The only units close to

Arnhem were Battalion Euling at Rheden and the battery of artillery at Dieren commanded by SS-Lt. Colonel Ludwig Spindler. The reason they were there was that they had been transferred to *Frundsberg* from *Hohenstaufen;* after the airborne landings, Spindler took charge of all *Hohenstaufen* units that were put into the fight against the First Parachute Brigade.

Frundsberg, most of it further away from Arnhem than *Hohenstaufen,* was directed on to Nijmegen, including Euling's battalion. There, *Frundsberg* barred the way to Arnhem, which was even more important than the success of *Hohenstaufen* and SS Training Battalion Krafft in checking the British at Arnhem-Oosterbeek. The actions of *Frundsberg* were the death-knell of *Market Garden.*

On 17 September, *Frundsberg* was without its commander. During the Normandy battles, there had been rumblings of dissent among the *Waffen-SS* leadership. Discontent with the military direction of the war had reached such a pitch that Rommel, the commander of Army Group B, hatched a plan to end the war on the Western Front. He sounded out several of his commanders, including those of the *Waffen-SS.* Hausser, Bittrich, even Sepp Dietrich, an old Nazi and the longest-serving of the senior SS commanders, all expressed support.

The plan was that Hitler would be arrested but not killed and Rommel would direct an orderly withdrawal to the Siegfried Line and invite the Western Allies to occupy France. But then Rommel was wounded in an air attack on 17 July and Army Group B was without a commander until Model took over on 17 August. The attempt on Hitler's life on 20 July caught these western conspirators by surprise and Rommel later killed himself, not because his plot had been discovered but because his name was on a list of senior figures designated by the 20 July conspirators to take over from Hitler.

Bittrich's diatribes against the military leadership during the Battle of Normandy had reached the ears of the *Reichsfuehrer SS,* Heinrich Himmler. The last straw came when Bittrich heard that Col. General Erich Hoeppner, his former commander on the Eastern Front, had been condemned to death by hanging. Bittrich exploded in fury, saying that such a disgraceful fate meant the end of the German Army. Himmler dismissed Bittrich although his senior officer, General Hans Eberbach of the Fifth *Panzer* Army, refused to let him go. Himmler tried again during the Arnhem battle but Model again refused to release Bittrich, quite possibly saving his life.

Unfortunately, Bittrich still needed to plead the case for more heavy weapons and equipment from the *SS-Fuehrungshauptampt* (Operational Department). Since *Frundsberg* was in the most immediate need of heavy weapons, it was Harmel who was sent to Berlin, unbeknownst to Model. The fact that he left his division shows that Bittrich had no inkling at all of the massive attack that was to fall on the Germans from Eindhoven to Arnhem. Harmel left Ruurlo by car on the evening of 16 September and met with *SS-Obergruppenfuehrer* Hans Juettner, the head of one of the two vast military bureaucracies governing the *Waffen-SS*, and Himmler's military Chief of Staff. Juettner promised 1,500 recruits but was noncommittal about heavy weapons. Negotiations were overtaken by events and Harmel was summoned by teletype back to Arnhem on the afternoon of the 17th.

ANTICIPATING ATTACK

The Germans certainly anticipated Allied paratroop landings in offensive actions to follow up their retreat. In general, they expected the landings to be larger than those in *Market* and much deeper behind the German lines. The only inkling that the Allies had of the Germans anticipating *Market Garden* were *Ultra* decrypts of 14 and 15 September, showing the Germans expected large-scale air landings in Holland and a thrust by ground forces on both sides of Eindhoven to Arnhem.

The decrypt of 15 September is particularly revealing. The message was decoded at a time when, apart from the military situation at Brest, most of the decrypted messages concerned the Aegean, the Adriatic and the Mediterranean. The Germans correctly identified XXX Corps and speculated that a further corps would be brought up to the front line. They also projected that 800 to 900 tanks would be available, which was an overestimate. However, the Germans were correct in their speculation that a ground offensive would take place, moving up on both sides of Eindhoven to Arnhem, with the aim of cutting off German forces in the western Netherlands. These projections were not passed on to the lower commands. A warning by a German agent in neutral Sweden that something quite close to this scenario was about to take place reached Berlin only on D-Day.

Lower down the chain of command, the greatest likelihood was thought to be a ground offensive from Neerpelt in support of the Americans to the south. Model's staff speculated that the Allies would advance from the Neerpelt bridgehead, concentrate between the Maas and the Waal, then move east toward that part of the *Ruhrindustriegebiet* east of the Rhine. Any parachute landings would be in the Ruhr area.

When the blow fell, both Bittrich and the *Oberkommando der Wehrmacht* (OKW) thought that the aim was to prevent reinforcement at the northern end of the West Wall by Fifteenth Army in an Allied attempt to open the way to Muenster. Hitler refused to allow reinforcements from Fifteenth Army toward Eindhoven that would weaken the approaches to the Scheldt. His grasp of military reality at this point was greater than that of subsequent military historians.

At the time of *Market Garden*, Hitler was already planning what became the Ardennes offensive in December. He received the news of the landings with great calm, possibly because of his confidence in Model and the preparations he had made. Hitler's military situation conference, of which only parts of the record have survived, began at midday and continued until 0207 hours the next morning. The conference was typical in that it was rambling and unstructured, switching back and forth from one general topic to the other, without systematic reports from the Army Groups or theaters. The flow was interrupted by reports on the military situation in the Netherlands, which started at around 1700 and continued until the small hours.

Hitler linked the paratroop landings with a coastal invasion. He also expected further landings on the following day and mused that the capture of his headquarters was worth the risk of two parachute divisions. He later "used strong language" about the folly of allowing bridges to fall intact into the hands of the enemy.

One officer at the conference speculated with great prescience that the offensive was aimed at the Zuyder Zee, more accurately at the IJsselmeer to the south. The officer was Lieutenant Colonel Waizenegger, adjutant to General Jodl, chief of the operations staff of the OKW. Waizenegger connected the ground assault from the Neerpelt bridgehead with the airborne operation. Though the picture was incomplete, Hitler's HQ got a fair indication of the forces that could be brought to bear, including the 107th *Panzer* Brigade to the east of the Corridor, Poppe's 59th Division from Fifteenth Army, and the 406th Division from *Wehrkreis* VI, the German military district on the Dutch border. There was much uncertainty and discussion about the strength and deployment of the First Parachute Army. II SS *Panzer* Corps was not mentioned, except for the battalion already detached to counter any advance from Neerpelt.

Bittrich's reaction was both rapid and pertinent. He ordered *Hohenstaufen*, the closest to Arnhem of his two divisions, to secure the Arnhem bridge and destroy the British formations that had landed at Oosterbeek to the west. A top priority was to keep the British away from the bridge.

Equally important was Nijmegen. He ordered *Frundsberg* to proceed immediately south to defend the Nijmegen bridge from the south bank of the Waal, seeing that Second Army would move through Nijmegen to Arnhem. At the same time, he ordered a reconnaissance in the direction of Emmerich and Wesel; the Allies learned from an *Ultra* decrypt early on D+2 that the Germans thought there had been paratroop landings in the vicinity of Emmerich as well as Nijmegen and Arnhem.

Bittrich also ordered a reconnaissance toward Nijmegen, to precede the move south by *Frundsberg*. Since the *Hohenstaufen* reconnaissance battalion at Beekbergen was far closer to Arnhem than that of *Frundsberg*, he transferred it to the command of *Frundsberg* and sent it south, over the Arnhem road bridge. The *Frundsberg* reconnaissance battalion was later ordered to secure the Arnhem bridge for the division's move south.

Model's reaction was different from that of Hitler. Early on, he ordered the bridges not to be blown, as they would be needed for a counterattack. This instinct for a counterattack while fighting a major defensive battle was typical of Model. His personal reaction was less typical: the sight of parachutists caused the hurried evacuation of his HQ and departure with unseemly haste to Bittrich's HQ at Doetinchem, east of Arnhem. By the time of Model's arrival, Bittrich had already issued orders to his corps; Model, known for meddling in the lower orders of command, could only confirm what Bittrich had already undertaken. He later received a description of the entire battle plan, taken from a downed American glider which had crashed near Student's HQ at Vaught on the outskirts of 's-Hertogenbosch.

Student sent the plans by radio to Model, who had received them before the end of D-Day. Model was sceptical about the plan but it indicated no action different from what was already under way. Even the next day, Model considered that the aim of the Allied operation was to capture him and his headquarters; he marveled repeatedly at his own escape. He was no doubt influenced by the warnings of landings near his headquarters that he had received previously from his SS and *Luftwaffe* colleagues.

Model's handling of the battle was perhaps his best military moment. He took II SS *Panzer* Corps under direct command and confirmed the order that Bittrich sent to his troops at 1730 hours. Beyond that, Model divided the defense into three sectors. The First Parachute Army was to halt the British ground offensive and eliminate the 101st Airborne Division on the Son-Veghel road. *Kampfgruppe Chill* was already in place to oppose the ground offensive, the 59th Infantry Division in transit west of Tilburg was to engage the 101st, and the 107th *Panzer* Brigade was diverted from its move to the Aachen sector to oppose the 101st from the east. Second, *Wehrkreis VI* was ordered to nuetralize Allied paratroopers on the Groesbeek Heights, to defend or retake the road and rail bridges over the Waal, and to prepare for offensive operations toward the south. Lastly, the Netherlands Command was called on to undertake operations against the British in Arnhem-Oosterbeek, under Christiansen's operations and training officer, Major General Baron Hans von Tettau. These orders were in place before midnight on D-Day.

A premise of Allied strategic thinking for *Market Garden* was that it would take many weeks for a limited number of German divisions, between six and twelve, to arrive by train from Denmark and the *Reich*. The SHAEF Intelligence Summary of 13 September said that the German "CiC West can expect no more than a dozen divisions within the next two months to come from outside sources to the rescue." Instead, the Germans pulled together, with astonishing speed and efficiency, a large number of disparate units already in the vicinity, though the myth that the German cupboard was bare persisted long after the war's end.

The Defense

Along the Albert Canal were stationed the remnants of Fifteenth Army and the 219th Coastal Division, which comprised LXXXVIII Corps under General Hans Reinhard, the German Army Commander in the Netherlands since July 1942. These Fifteenth Army remnants, likely from the 346th and the 711th Divisions, were formidable: they forced the evacuation of a British bridgehead over the Albert Canal north of Antwerp on 6 September. The 719th Coastal, which began to occupy the north bank of the Albert Canal on 4 September, was so thinly spread toward the eastern end of the canal that they could not prevent the British crossing at Beeringen. It fell to General Chill's 85th Division, which came under LXXXVIII Corps on 6 September, to contain the bridgehead and defend the eastern end of the canal. There the defense was taken over by the 716th Division, which also absorbed two *Luftwaffe* penal battalions.

All the while, from 6 September, the units of the First Parachute Army were arriving. By D-Day Student had up to 20,000 troops under command, but their equipment and state of training varied widely. Among the first units to arrive was the 6th Parachute Regiment under Lt. Colonel Baron von der Heydte, who also took a *Luftwaffe* penal battalion under command. Before that date, the troops defending the Neerpelt area were organized as *Kampfgruppe Walther,* numbering about 3,000 men. The three remaining regiments of the First Parachute Army were unified as Parachute Training Division Erdmann, under Student's chief of staff. From Fifteenth Army, the 59th was in transit to Student's sector when *Market Garden* commenced. The division had about a thousand veteran troops, a replacement battalion, eighteen anti-tank guns and about thirty medium and heavy artillery pieces. This small but powerful formation was put under the command of First Parachute Army, LXXXVIII Corps on 12 September. That corps also took the 245th from Fifteenth Army under command, placing it behind *Kampfgruppe Chill.* Zangen later paid the price when, in the absence of the 245th, the 70th Division was forced to defend South Beveland as well as Walcheren.

East of what became the "Corridor" were the troops of *Wehrkreis VI,* which were under Model's tactical control. The main unit was the 406th Infantry, a training and replacement division, comprising a number of low-grade formations. All came under the command of General Kurt Feldt as *Korps Feldt,* with a strength of about 3,400 men. An *Ultra* decrypt added a zero to a similar figure. On D-Day, the 107th *Panzer* Brigade under Major Baron von Maltzahn was diverted from a march toward the Aachen battlefront and was expected to arrive by train through Roermond or Venlo. It later fought in the area of Son against the 101st and XXX Corps.

The Nijmegen Defense Force on or before 17 September consisted of *Kampfgruppe Henke,* with a strength of about two battalions, under the command of Colonel Henke's parachute training regiment. There were also *Luftwaffe* companies, trainees from *Wehrkreis VI*, an NCO School and various railway troops and police reservists. While this was a force insufficient to defend the two Nijmegen bridges from the south, it was evidently enough to persuade the commander of the Ninth SS Reconnaissance Battalion that Nijmegen was adequately defended, since he left no troops on the south side of the road bridge before returning to Arnhem.

North of the Rhine, the Netherlands Command could call upon a hodgepodge of units, organized soon after the landings as Division von Tettau. Prior to D-Day, Lt. General Baron von Tettau had commanded the equivalent of seven weak battalions, most on the north bank of the Waal and none close enough to engage the British on D-Day. Tettau has received bad press owing to disparaging remarks by SS-Colonel Lippert and by Colonel Fullriede of the *Luftwaffe;* in fact he was, for over three years the commander of the 24th Infantry Division, which played a distinguished part in battles on the Russian front until the end of the war. Both Bittrich and von Tettau were officially commended by von Rundstedt and Model on 27 September.

Of von Tettau's formations, one of the most valuable was the SS Lippert NCO Training School *Arnheim*. This comprised two companies each of three platoons of infantry and a support platoon equipped with mortars and 20mm cannon. The trainee NCOs had a year's military service, usually on the Russian front. Lippert, seconded from *Hohenstaufen*, had previously organized 3,000 stragglers into "March Battalions" in much the same way as Chill on the Albert Canal. He was known as a good soldier without any particular Nazi traits and a fatherly figure, more interested in getting demoralized troops back into the line than in recrimination and retribution.

There was also a naval battalion comprising administrative troops and gunners which had been under the command of the *Kriegsmarine*. Next, Artillery Regiment 184 was of battalion strength; its guns had been shipped west to be used for training purposes. *Luftwaffe* stragglers in the retreat—from abandoned airfields or flak installations, were organized into *Fliegerhorst* battalions and one of these fought at Arnhem. SS *Wach* Battalion 3 in the Amersfoort area was up to strength with about 600 men; its ranks included Dutch citizens who had joined the *Waffen-SS* mainly to avoid forced labor service in the *Reich*. Their military value was minimal. Their commanding officer was SS-Captain Paul Anton Helle, who compensated for his lack of combat experience by relying on SS-Lieutenant Albert Naumann, a disabled veteran of the Russian front.

Finally, under von Tettau's authority in Oosterbeek was the SS *Panzer* Grenadier Depot and Reserve Battalion 16, with a HQ and three companies, two of which were infantry and the third a heavy weapons company with a strong complement of mortars and anti-tank guns. The battalion was commanded by SS-Captain Sepp Krafft, in whose report it is easy to distinguish the self-serving remarks of a committed Nazi from those of a highly competent professional soldier. Krafft had twelve officers, sixty-five NCOs and 229 soldiers, the majority in an advanced state of training. His mission was to reconnoitre that area between the Waal and the Lower Rhine, to prepare for and attack airborne landings, to defend the bridges and ferries over the Rhine, and to prepare them for demolition.

It is likely that Krafft had demolition teams at the road and rail bridges but no guards at the Driel-Heveadorp ferry, as this was still being used as late as D+3 by British troops who had landed south of the Lower Rhine. The presence of Krafft's battalion was known to the Allies from *Ultra,* and to the German Town Commandant of Arnhem, Major General Friedrich Kussin, but not to Bittrich. By the end of the 17th, the battalion came under the command of II SS *Panzer* Corps. In Arnhem were bridge guards and a small number of local defense forces.

Krafft's battalion was well deployed to meet the British assault. When the massive air raid on Arnhem took place on the morning of the 17th, Krafft moved one company out of the city and into the woods to the east, to continue training until the air raid was over. This put the company directly in the path of the First Parachute Brigade. Von Tettau's own HQ was well sited at Grebbeburg, about ten miles west of Arnhem and north of the Lower Rhine. Some of the companies of Helle's Dutch SS battalion were in the Arnhem area, northwest of the city, and there were three naval detachments as well as Artillery Regiment 184 just east of the British landing zones along the north bank of the Rhine. Lippert's NCO School was, however, engaged in building defenses along the Waal, way to the west around Gorinchem.

With the start of the airborne landings, Christiansen ordered Lippert to report to von Tettau at Grebbeburg to form the west wing of the "reception screen." But he received no orders to move until 1900 hours. The reason was that Tettau had reports of landings at Utrecht,

Veenendaal, Dortrecht and Tiel but not, it seems, at Arnhem. Dummy paratroopers had in fact been dropped southeast of Utrecht. Lippert, his force now expanded to regimental strength through absorbing some of the March Battalions, moved off through Leerdam, Rhenen, and Wageningen to Oosterbeek. In the lead was a battalion commanded by an SS-Captain Schulz; the two others, commanded by SS-Captains Mattusch and Oelkers, were to follow as soon as they had assembled. The march was chaotic, the NCOs commandeering any mode of transport they could get their hands on, including fire engines, wood-burning *gazogen,* bicycles and farm carts. When Lippert arrived at Grebbeburg, he found von Tettau's stop-gap HQ in a panic, possibly because the rumors of widely scattered airborne landings had not yet been dispelled. Plans were made for a coordinated counterattack to take place at dawn.

At 1620 hours on D-Day, von Tettau contacted Krafft on the radio to tell him there had been landings at Driel and Nijmegen, with no mention of those at Arnhem, of which, naturally, Krafft was well aware. Tettau was promised more troops from the Netherlands Command at 0400 hours on D+1. Among them was the small *Waffen-SS Kampfgruppe Eberwein*, of which little has been recorded; the Training and Replacement Regiment Hermann Goering; and a police training school to be supplied by Hanns Albin Rauter's SS security command. Of these, the Training and Replacement Regiment was moving by bicycle at night from positions on the coast at Katwick an Zee. One of the battalions of Security Regiment 26 had been detained to counter the phantom landings at Veenendaal, halfway between Arnhem and Utrecht.

Von Tettau was also assigned more naval units, more infantry for Artillery Regiment 184, army defense units and a company of tanks. Eberwein's *Kampfgruppe,* one battalion of Lippert's NCO School, a *Fliegerhorst* battalion, the naval troops and the artillery battalion fighting as infantry would go into action early on D+1.

WHAT THE ALLIES KNEW

The smallest irrigation ditches are 5–6 feet wide, and can easily be jumped by an infantryman; those that finish at a road are normally of this size. The others are usually about 12 feet wide, and the secret of cross-country movement is routing so as to cross only the narrower

*ditches. The wider ditches may be vaulted with a 12-foot pole which is
the practice in the Royal Dutch Army.*
——1st Airborne Division, Planning Intelligence Summary No. 2,
7 September 1944, Sec. 5, Topography

Major Brian Urquhart, the intelligence officer (G-2) of the British I
Airborne Corps was a worried man. In the days before 14 September he
had been receiving the Intelligence Summaries of 21AG and Second
Army, based on the interrogations of German prisoners and reports
from the Dutch Resistance. They indicated that the 9th SS *Panzer*
Division was in the Arnhem area and that the presence there of the II SS
Panzer Corps was suspected, especially as small elements of both the
9th and 10th SS had been identified further south.

When the reports were shown to Browning and to the Corps Chief
of Staff, Gordon Walch, neither man was impressed; they followed the
line of the Second Army summaries to the effect that the "battered
Panzer formations" were not a threat. Urquhart who, like Hackett, was
dismayed at the prospect of the Arnhem operation, decided to go further. An expert in photographic interpretation, he secured on 12
September the services of a Spitfire reconnaissance squadron based at
RAF Benson in Oxfordshire. This squadron was currently engaged in
photographing German positions and V-2 sites on the Dutch coast.

Aerial photos taken three days later by a single Spitfire clearly
showed tanks and armored vehicles parked under trees close to the drop
zone of the 1st Airborne. Browning told Urquhart that the tanks were
probably not serviceable, echoing Second Army speculation that if tanks
were refitting, they would not be available for action. Urquhart was told
that he was suffering from stress and exhaustion and sent on sick leave,
mortified as much at missing the operation as by the fact that his intelligence had been discounted and that the operation was heading for certain disaster.

On 5 September, an *Ultra* decrypt revealed that the II SS *Panzer*
Corps was to take two further armored divisions under command and
move to the area Venlo-Arnhem-s'Hertogenbosch. These two *Wehrmacht* divisions, the 2nd and the 116th, never arrived in the Arnhem
area. From 6 to 15 September, II SS *Panzer* Corps disappeared from the
Utra communications. Then on the 16th, a SHAEF intelligence summary stated that the 9th and presumably the 10th SS were withdrawing to
the Arnhem area to be equipped with new tanks from a depot at Cleves.

Eisenhower ordered his Chief of Staff, Walter Bedell Smith, to fly to Montgomery's HQ the same day.

Smith's proposals to counter the German armor at this late stage—an extra airborne division or a shift north of the drop zone of the 82nd Airborne—were hardly feasible, nor would they have solved the problem of countering the German armor. More important was Montgomery's reaction. He waved the proposals "airily aside," repeating Second Army's appreciation that the tanks were not battleworthy.

Evidently, another authority was rebuffed. Brereton's distinguished Air Intelligence Officer, Wing Commander Asher Lee, dug further into the *Ultra* sources. After the war, he told authors Ronald Lewin and Richard Lamb that he had found conclusive evidence of enemy armor at Arnhem. With Brereton's knowledge, he flew to 21AG in Brussels, where he was only able to see junior staff officers and his warning fell on deaf ears.

So it came about that nothing was done to counter the threat of German armor, nor were any warnings conveyed to the airborne commanders. Brian Urquhart knew nothing of the *Ultra* decrypt that had confirmed his own findings and, since *Ultra* information was not distributed below army staff level except in disguise, it is unlikely that Browning knew either. Nor did Roy Urquhart receive the vital information decrypted on 16 September that Model's HQ was at Oosterbeek, *between* the landing zones and the Arnhem bridge! The more senior officers of 1st Airborne were made aware only of the contents of Second Army intelligence summaries.

Roy Urquhart took this information seriously. When his deputy, Brigadier Charles Mackenzie, told him on 15 September that his lift on the first day would be reduced, no doubt because gliders were needed to transport I Airborne Corps HQ, he responded that his anti-tank gun complement must not be cut and that he was taking no chances with the German armor. During the battle, Urquhart received reports from the Dutch Resistance that a large body of German tanks was approaching the landing zone. Later in his life, Urquhart wrote how "Mackenzie now recalled those vague and unconfirmed stories about the re-fitting *Panzer* Corps about which we had been given so little information by Second Army."

As with the questions of supply, transport and the deployment of Second Army, that of the dissemination of intelligence verged on professional irresponsibility. It was not that the operation should have been cancelled or postponed, but rather the stubborn failure to even consider modifying the assault plan that was so tragic.

Although the Allies knew there was a large proportion of poorly trained *Luftwaffe* ground troops throughout the defended areas, they underestimated the role that such troops were to play and the importance of other troops in the operational area of Second Army, particularly the training schools and formations. However, the intelligence summaries up to D+13 show that the *Ultra* information still had not filtered down to Urquhart's division and the relief troops on the south bank of the Rhine.

Lieutenant Colonel Frost at the Arnhem bridge had reported to Urquhart that he was up against the *Waffen-SS;* Frost was more perturbed by the fact that he faced first-class troops than the prospect of German tanks. Neither Frost nor Urquhart was aware that they faced the *Hohenstaufen* and the *Frundsberg.*

4

AN AMERICAN TRIUMPH

The 101st Airborne Division

After dark on D-Day, a depleted platoon of Company H, 2nd Battalion, 502nd Parachute Infantry Regiment, dug in on the north bank of the Wilhelmina Canal, east of the road bridge. This was the conclusion of the first attempt to seize the four bridges—two rail and two road—at Best, in order to secure a further route north for XXX Corps.

From the DZ, the plan called for the company to advance west and slightly south toward the two road bridges, one carrying the Eindhoven-Boxtel road over the canal and the other over that road to the north. Parallel to the road and further west was a pair of rail bridges, with the town of Best between the northern road and rail bridges. The initial advance was over open meadows, then the party assigned to the southern bridges would proceed through the western edge of the Sonsche Forest and emerge into a clearing in the area of the road bridge. The area on the south bank of the bridge was also open; the forest otherwise continued along the south bank toward Son.

The party assigned to the two northern bridges, first road, then rail, would emerge from two small woods to a clear area south of the road bridge. Company H assembled and set out, accompanied by a section of light machine guns from Battalion HQ and a platoon of engineers. But the company commander, Captain Robert E. Jones, lost his bearings and emerged within 400 yards of the Best crossroads. Small groups of Germans, soon reinforced by lorried infantry from the 59th Division, opened fire on them and, in attempting to get close to the road bridge, the company became dispersed.

As this was happening, the battalion commander, Lt. Colonel Robert G. Cole, radioed Captain Jones, telling him to get the machine gunners, engineers and his second platoon down to the southern road bridge immediately. Without these troopers, Jones' position became untenable, so he pulled his company back into the Sonsche Forest and established a defensive line. Jones then sent a platoon under Lt. Edward L. Wierzbowski off to the south. Wierzbowski's men were delayed by machine gun fire along a series of firebreaks, the Germans having infiltrated across the canal and into the Son woods. By the time they reached the canal it was dark. Wierzbowski and his leading scout, Pfc. Joe E. Mann, reckoned they were still 500 yards east of the southern road bridge. Following his scout along the canal, they arrived at the bridge and waited for the rest.

Back at the starting point, the remainder of the platoon took fire from the other side of the waterway. Wierzbowski and Mann ran back to the platoon, gathered the scattered men and dug in yet further east along the canal, German artillery now having joined the small arms fire. Wierzbowski had three officers and fifteen men, along with a machine gun and 500 rounds, a mortar with six rounds and a bazooka with five rounds. German fire died down at 0300; rain fell almost till dawn.

Captain Jones sent his third platoon to find Wierzbowski's party but this relief was stopped in its tracks. Overnight, Company H suffered thirty-nine more casualties. Lt. Col. John H. "Iron Mike" Michaelis realized when Company H was originally checked that the whole of 2nd Battalion was needed at Best, but the remainder of the battalion was halted by artillery and mortar fire a mile from the town. The only contact with Company H was by radio. Lt. Col. Cole's attack on Best had not succeeded, but it did keep German forces away from the airhead and the St. Oedenrode-Son road.

The advance on Best was something that Lt. General Browning had not required of the 101st Airborne. Major General Taylor realized that he could not hold the entire stretch of Hell's Highway in strength and elected to hold key centers and rush troops back and forth to threatened points as needed, a move reminiscent on a small scale of Manstein's campaign in the Crimea in 1942. Equally and in view of the narrowness of the highway, he could not afford simply to sit and wait for a German attack. At the same time, Taylor could not exploit any offensive advantage too far from his allotted sector for fear of excessively thinning out his own forces. His options were therefore limited to either driving the

Germans away from Hell's Highway or attempting a pincer movement to envelope the German attackers.

The fact that Taylor's mission was the least risky of the three divisional landings in no way qualifies his outstanding success, the more so because VIII and XII Corps, with responsibility for protecting the flanks, did not keep pace with XXX Corps. Taylor's contact with the flanking corps was solely by radio and telephone until he met up with units of XII Corps in the vicinity of Best on D+7. There was no physical contact with VIII Corps until after *Market Garden* was officially concluded. Taylor came under the command of XII Corps on D+6.

The first lift of the 101st Airborne was carried by no less than 590 C-47 Dakota aircraft acting as both troop carriers and glider tugs. Gliders carried 16–22 troops or a jeep, trailer and ammunition. Earlier, four pathfinder aircraft had dropped a handful of paratroopers to lay out the DZ/LZ, though one of the planes was shot down. The main DZ/LZ (for two parachute regiments) was west of the Son-St. Oedenrode road, which also landed the subsequent glider lift. The smaller drop zone "A" was reserved for a further regiment and positioned in a corner southwest of the Zuid-Willemsvaart Canal and the St. Oedenrode-Veghel Road. A battalion of the 501st PIR was to drop west of Veghel at drop zone "A2" between the Aa River and the Canal. This battalion was to converge on Veghel with the remainder of the regiment moving north. Perhaps because of the loss of the pathfinder aircraft, the battalion was in fact dropped three miles to the northwest and north of the Aa River.

Between 1300 and 1330 hours, 6,769 men of the 101st were dropped with minimal casualties and loss of equipment. One in four of the C-47 transports were damaged, however, and sixteen were lost with their crews. The glider landings, which took place an hour after the end of the airborne drops were less successful. Only fifty-three of the seventy gliders arrived intact on the LZ, although they succeeded in landing 80 percent of the men and 75 percent of the jeeps and trailers. However, none of corps signals units arrived, cutting off communication with both Browning's HQ and with XXX Corps coming up from the south.

Two battalions of the 506th PIR began to move off toward the Son bridge forty-five minutes after landing on parallel routes. Since the gliders could not carry a whole platoon, many of the troops made for Son by the glider load, each commanded by an officer. While suppressing opposition from the far bank, the leading elements were within fifty yards of the bridge when it blew up, raining debris onto the paratroopers. Two smaller bridges over the canal, which were also part of the 506th's objectives, were later found to have been blown prior to D-Day.

Fortunately, the center span of the Son bridge was intact. Using this segment, the parachute engineers swiftly constructed a bridge of ropes and black market lumber commandeered by the Dutch Resistance. The two leading battalions got across in single file, followed by the third battalion and the regimental HQ. The engineers also built a raft to carry the regimental jeeps. The destruction of the Son bridge was certainly a setback but it did not prove fatal to the operation.

With the regiment assembled on the south side of the canal and the light fading and no word of XXX Corps, Colonel Robert Sink decided to halt for the night near the village of Bokt. It started to rain, the first of many soakings the 506th was to get in the seventy-two days it spent on the road to Arnhem. Eindhoven, a city of over 100,000 was to be assaulted the following day. The plan to meet up with the Guards at 2000 hours on the southern outskirts of Eindhoven did not succeed and this would prove to be the 101st's only major failure on D-Day. Yet the Guards too, coming up from the south, had not reached the rendezvous point.

The 501st PIR's mission of securing the four road and rail bridges over the Zuid-Willemsvaart Canal and the Aa River at Veghel was speedily done. The engineers immediately began the construction of a second road bridge over the canal at Veghel to provide a route for returning traffic. The only event marring this success was the German capture of forty-six paratroopers from Captain W.S. Burd's company, and eight jump-related injuries who were left behind on 1st Battalion's DZ. Lt. Col. Patrick Cassidy's 502nd PIR was tasked with securing the DZ and advancing to St. Oedenrode. The 502nd's 1st Battalion advanced to take a foot bridge and road bridge over the Dommel River on the southern outskirts of St. Oedenrode. All told, both Veghel and St. Oedenrode were taken without difficulty, in spite of the sweltering heat of the day.

The main German response was from the west. There were several thousand paratroopers in training units in 's-Hertogenbosch from which two "march battalions" were formed, one sent toward Veghel and the other, Battalion Ewald, toward St. Oedenrode, where they captured the forty-six airborne troops at Kameren. Reinforcements of artillery and infantry (which the 502nd observed) came from Poppe's 59th Division.

This accounts for the strength of the German defenses and counterattacks along the Wilhelmina Canal, a foretaste of things to come. A report from General Chill of the 85th Infantry Division in the early evening shows that the Germans were still confused as to Allied intentions and it was not until 2330 hours on D-Day that Model shared information gleened from the captured Allied battle plan.

The Guards Move Forward

Throughout D-Day and the following night there was no radio contact between the 101st and XXX Corps, nor any word of progress. XXX Corps had no inkling of the location of the 101st Airborne, nor whether the Corridor was held from Eindhoven to Nijmegen and points beyond. By 17 September, D-Day, the Germans had positioned an arc of troops to counter a breakout from the Neerpelt bridgehead, organized as the *Divisionsverband Walter.* On the right, at the western end, was the veteran 6th Parachute Regiment under Lt. Colonel Baron von der Heydte, who had fought the 101st Airborne in Normandy. Von der Heydte had four battalions under command, perhaps a thousand men. Next in line were the three battalions of the Parachute Training Regiment von Hoffman, of which only the 1st Battalion, under Major Kerutt, was of high quality (Hoffman himself was sent by Student to become the Town Commandant of Eindhoven). Regiment von Hoffman was joined at the center with *Luftwaffe* Penal Battalion Six, which the Germans placed astride the Valkenswaard road, no doubt because the airmen were considered good only for static, defensive fighting.

East of the Valkenswaard road was *Kampfgruppe Henke* with two depleted battalions from the II SS *Panzer* Corps that had been detached from the march to Arnhem. The *Kampfgruppe* consisted of one battalion from *Hohenstaufen* under SS-Captain Dr. Segler, and the other, *Battalion Richter,* from *Frundsberg.* Both took up positions east of the bridgehead along with a motorized artillery detachment of six 105mm guns. Also in place was *Panzerjaegergruppe Roestel,* originally a tank destroyer unit from *Frundsberg.* This formation had been brought around to the northwest of the bridgehead to reinforce Major Kerutt's battalion on 13 September, after which perhaps three of Roestel's tanks were destroyed in action. Kerutt also had eight or nine captured Russian guns placed near the road behind the *Luftwaffe* troops.

All told, Colonel Walther, an experienced paratrooper, had the equivalent of ten weak infantry battalions, some armor in the form of

Roestel's tank destroyers, and quite a lot of artillery, though most of this was immobile. On Walther's right was Chill's 85th Infantry Division and on his left the Parachute Division Erdmann.

While numerically the German defenses were thin, the British thoroughly underestimated the German talent for improvisation, rapid reaction and the use of veteran troops to stiffen poorly trained and inexperienced units. The 21AG report on *Market Garden* stated that, in the break-out, the enemy was in "considerably greater strength than expected." Yet at the time, few doubted that Eindhoven could be reached by dark on D-Day.

Looking down the concrete road ahead of him, Lt. General Horrocks waited until he was satisfied that the 101st Airborne drop was under way, arguably later than was needed, and launched his attack at 1415 hours. A Wing of 83 Group Typhoons plastered the axis of his advance with rockets while another Typhoon Wing subsequently made seventy-six sorties, mainly south of, and on, Valkenswaard, guided on the radio by "contact cars." These attacks destroyed all of the eight or nine German anti-tank guns sited to the rear of the defense emplacements.

At the same time as the air attacks, 350 guns put down a rolling barrage. The Germans destroyed nine tanks and set two scout cars on fire. Guards commander Joe Vandaleur called in Typhoons and deployed infantry on both sides of the road, some of whom had been riding the tanks Russian-style. The British also neutralized at least two more of Roestel's precious tanks; he was by now down to eight *Jagdpanzer* IVs.

Major Kerutt's battalion bore the brunt of the British attack, which took prisoners from the Luftwaffe Penal Battalion, the *Waffen-SS* on the eastern flank, *Division Erdmann,* and, in the west, from the 6th Parachute Regiment. However, that regiment made little contact with the British, von der Heydte being out of touch with the other formations of Walther's *Divisionsverband* and its HQ.

Seething with frustration, von der Heydte took the 2nd Battalion of the former *Kampfgruppe Hoffman* and the *Luftwaffe* battalion under command, his solution to the fact that the Valkenswaard road was the dividing line between the responsibilities of the various formations of Walther's division. Yet his other actions severed the links with Kerutt and the *Waffen-SS* east of the road. He pulled his regiment back with his left flank "in the air," his right still anchored on the Meuse-Escaut Canal. When contact with his own command resumed on D+l, he was placed under Chill's 85th Division and received some belated but characteristic remarks from LXXXVIII Corps that no commander, including von der Heydte, should be allowed to withdraw without permission. Corps HQ also insisted that contact be maintained with *Division Erdmann* on the German left.

With the resumption of the artillery barrage, the British reached the edge of Valkenswaard by 1700 hours and entered the town, unopposed, by 1930, having covered seven of the thirteen miles to Eindhoven. According to the Irish Guards' account, they arrived at the southern end of the town at 1730 and entered the town cautiously, after dark, no earlier than 1930. After much confusion, some shooting and some prisoners taken (along with one half-track) the Germans still had Roestel's tanks, possibly up to sixteen 20mm cannons, and a number of 88mm guns.

The Guards halted in Valkenswaard for the night, to the perplexity of some of the troops. Why the Guards halted is not certain. Brigadier Gwatkin visited Vandaleur in Valkenswaard. In Vandaleur's 1967 account, he did not mention any orders given by Gwatkin. Vandaleur said that his main problem was to clear the road behind him "to enable bridging to be moved forward to span the Son Canal." Vandaleur was ordered to capture Eindhoven, but there was no need for haste, "as bridging could not take place over the Son until nightfall." In the 1967 account, Gwatkin visited Vandaleur during daylight and the Guards entered Valkenswaard "in darkness." The "nightfall" clearly refers to the following night, D+1, a most curious thing to say. In his second version, Vandaleur, "as he remembered," was told by Brigadier Gwatkin that the Son bridge had been destroyed and that bridging equipment would have to be brought up before the advance could be resumed beyond the canal. Gwatkin said, "Push on to Eindhoven tomorrow, old boy, but take your time. We've lost a bridge."

Gwatkin actually gave the order to halt at 2200 hours, about five hours after the arrival of the Guards at the southern edge of Valkenswaard. As Colonel Powell has commented, the account is suspect, because the Guards needed to be at the bridge as soon as possible so that "preparations for the repairs could be started." Since it is not at all clear that the Guards knew about the destruction of the Son bridge, it is possible that Gwatkin gave the order to halt because of the non-arrival of supporting infantry.

As for the Guards' knowledge of the destruction of the Son bridge, there are three accounts. This was known to XXX Corps when the 506th PIR made contact through the 101st's dedicated radio network, Orange Net, on the morning of D+1 at 1130 hours, which was also the first news of the dispositions of the 101st Airborne. The Guards knew of the destruction of the Son bridge en route to Eindhoven on D+1. The elderly director of the Phillips works told the Guards in Aalst that they could phone a doctor's house in Son, where they got information about the blown bridge and an idea of the materials needed to repair it. The history of the Second Household Cavalry (Armoured Car) Regiment is more specific. One troop led by Lt. R.M.A. Palmer, with an American sergeant and a radio on board, met Brigadier General Higgins north of Eindhoven, who told Palmer that bridging materials were needed.

The situation becomes if anything murkier in the third account, that of Cornelius Ryan, in which the two armored cars of the Household Cavalry made contact on D+1 with the 506th PIR at Best. This was Lt. Wierzbowski's platoon. According to Ryan, Palmer's patrol contacted the Irish Guards Group on the radio, who in turn contacted the 506th at the Son bridge through the civilian phone system. Again, according to Ryan's sources, sappers were already moving up alongside the leading Guards tanks but needed "vital information" to bring up the proper bridging equipment. This sounds a bit too dramatic to be true, a confounding of the second account with an apocryphal third.

The Guards' own version is that Major F.E.B.Wignall's squadron, actually Palmer's troop, returned from Best with the news that the Son bridge was down. This would by then have been old news. The result, in any event, is that the Irish Guards did not go forward on D-Day evening. Had the Guards grasped the urgency of the situation, they would have advanced to the edge of Eindhoven to await further instructions. It looks very much as though the players used later information on the destruction of the Son bridge as justification for the halt in Valkenswaard, when it is not at all clear that they had received such information by the early evening of D-Day.

In view of a similar pattern of inactivity at the Nijmegen bridge, it appears that the Guards' leadership at some level simply did not grasp the nature of *Market Garden*. If the sights were set on Nunspeet and the IJsselmeer, it is easy to see that a few hours of delay was neither here nor there. By the next morning, the Germans had established two sets of blocking lines on the Eindhoven road, although this was not known to the higher commands. The poor state of German communications forced LXXXVIII Corps to conclude that the enemy had indeed broken through.

The timetable for the Guards' advance north comes only from the American side. When Taylor met with Dempsey on September 13, he told him that he could reach Eindhoven by 1800 and rendezvous with XXX Corps on the southern outskirts of the city by 2000 hours. At the very least, the urgency of the situation was not conveyed to the Guards, and more likely, no information as to the link-up with the 101st Airborne was given to them at all. The Fifth Armoured Brigade Operational Order No. 1, of 16 September, is vague. It states that the 101st Airborne will be dropped "in an area to include Eindhoven," which was to be reached on D-Day, preparatory to an advance to the area of Nunspeet on D+1. The Guards were to capture Valkenswaard on the afternoon of D-Day. The 231st Brigade was ordered to pause on the Judas Boundary until ordered forward by the Fifth Armoured Brigade. Judas was an east-west line running through Aalst, between Valkenswaard and Eindhoven. From there, the 231st was to contact the 101st Airborne in the area of Eindhoven. No deadlines were laid down and there is no explanation as to how 231st Brigade was to take over the lead from the Guards' tanks.

The Irish Guards' history was published in 1949, before the halt became controversial, and there is no mention of any possible or alleged delay in advancing from Valkenswaard. It seems likely that no instructions as to the link-up with the 101st were ever given to the Guards, and there are positive indications that the Irish Guards did not know that the Son bridge was down. The Guards received a radio message at 2100 from division saying that, as of 1500 hours, all the bridges were intact. The Son bridge was in fact destroyed at about that time. The little news that was received later said that the Airborne had "captured all objectives between Eindhoven and Grave," with no mention of the Son.

If any more explanation is needed for the delays, beyond the loss of the Son bridge and the hiatus at Valkenswaard, it must be that poor communications prevented good liaison between the British and the Americans. But from what we know of the Guards' conduct on the evening of D-Day, knowledge that the Americans were not in Eindhoven would have only confirmed them in the decision to halt in Valkenswaard.

The 82nd Airborne Division

On September 16, in the evening before the operation, James Gavin held a final briefing of his regimental and battalion commanders, as he had done before the Normandy drop. Each commander had to explain his mission and plan of operation, as well as his plans for contact with other units and what he proposed to do if his unit landed in the wrong place. On D-Day, 482 C-47s took off from their bases in Lincolnshire and assembled for an uneventful crossing in bright sunlight. All but three of the 82nd's gliders landed safely, along with 7,467 troops.

Both the Grave and Molenhoek bridges were captured in small unit actions as accomplished as any in *Market Garden*. A company of the 504th PIR dropped west of the Grave Bridge, but the aircraft carrying sixteen troopers of Lt. John S. Thompson's platoon overshot the DZ, dropping the troops closer to the bridge than had been planned. Thompson did not wait for the rest of his company and proceeded by stealth toward the bridge, wading through deep waters in drainage ditches and small dykes. They drove off two truckloads of Germans coming up from Grave, then shot three Germans on the bridge which they found defended at each end by makeshift flak towers equipped with 20mm light AA guns.

As the platoon approached, the south tower gunners were unable to depress their flak piece low enough to fire on the Americans, who silenced the gun with three bazooka rounds. The Americans promptly destroyed electrical equipment they thought was used for demolition charges, then turned the still functioning gun toward the north flak tower and fired away. With the rest of the company coming up from behind and a battalion arriving from the east, both Grave and the bridge were secured by the late afternoon.

The assault on the Moelenhoek bridge over the Maas-Waal Canal was equally successful. Lt. Colonel William Harrison's battalion advanced toward the bridge and felled a German running toward the control building for the demolition charges. Harrison, twice a winner of the DSO, ordered his men to keep the Germans under fire to prevent them from setting off any charges. The Americans then drove the Germans back onto a small island between the central sluice gates and got onto the bridge, removing as many charges as they could find. After that, the divisional reconnaissance platoon drove up from the DZ to the east and captured the bridge intact.

The two canal bridges to the north, Malden and Hatert, were

destroyed as the Americans came up; the 508th PIR did not approach the final road-rail bridges at Honinghutie until the early hours of D+1. The 508th PIR linked up with the 505th and formed a six-mile cordon from the vicinity of Wyler, along the base of the Heights to the outskirts of Nijmegen.

Gavin had every reason to be satisfied with the progress of his division. He was not required to advance on the Nijmegen bridges until the divisional perimeter and the Groesbeek Heights had been secured. He knew, however, that he could never achieve success without the Nijmegen bridges over the Waal. If these were lost, an infantry assault across the river would be extremely hazardous and the land advance could not resume without a forty-ton bridge over the widest river obstacle of them all. Every hour increased the chances of the Germans successfully demolishing the bridges. Whatever Browning's orders, the bridges had to be taken as a matter of utmost urgency.

The task of the 508th PIR was to link with the 505th, then to advance east on the Hatert and Honinghutie bridges over the Maas-Waal Canal. But Lt. Colonel Lindquist moved first toward the Nijmegen road bridge. He sent one platoon of Lt. Colonel Shields Warren's battalion to determine enemy strength at the bridge. The radio failed and there was no word of this patrol until the next morning. On orders from Gavin to Lindquist as the light faded, Warren moved two companies of his battalion to the bridge, beginning at 2200 hours. The Dutch welcomed them in the streets along the route. They were stopped short of a traffic circle below the road bidge by SS troops. One ptarol was sent northwest and destroyed a "control tower" thought to house the controls for demolishing the bridge, but was then cut off for three days with the commander of Company A and some Dutch civilians. Gavin saw that the prospects of capturing the bridge and at the same time defending the airhead were not good, and at 1030 hours on D+1 ordered Warren back to the LZ.

This was not Lindquist's only move. He had told the commander of the 3rd Battalion, Lt. Colonel Louis Mendez, to be prepared to move through the eastern approaches to the bridge. Mendez sent a platoon of Company G under Lt. Howard A. Greenawalt to reconnoitre toward the bridge soon after dark. Meanwhile, Greenawalt's company commander, Captain Wilde, had decided to move the rest of his troops forward, to the right of Greenawalt's advance. They killed seven Germans who were constructing a roadblock and reached the eastern side of the traffic circle, reabsorbing Greenawalt's platoon in the advance. They then found themselves on Hill 64, little more than a mile from the south end of the highway bridge. Here, like the 1st Battalion, they came under heavy fire from small arms, mortars, 88s and self-propelled guns. Greenawalt's platoon suffered five killed and the company made no further progress by daylight. At least some of Mendez' battalion was then withdrawn to counter the threat to the DZ/LZ at Beek.

Gavin described his divisional responsibility as a "staggering task," which indeed it was, yet his several accounts of the moves on the Nijmegen bridge are incomplete and contradictory over who was ordered to do what, and when. Publicly, he said that Lindquist's orders were "a bit ambiguous"; that he had the hardest task of all and that the bridge episode was controversial. But in his diary, he said that Lindquist had handled the task neither intelligently nor aggressively.

In one account, he said that Lindquist had been told just before take-off to go for the Nijmegen bridge, which does not square with his insistence that the regimental and battalion commanders should be utterly clear about each others' missions. In another account, Gavin said that moves should be made on the Nijmegen bridge "without delay after landing," while both Lindquist and Warren recollected that they should first secure the regimental cordon. The uncertainties of the initial attacks on the Nijmegen bridge suggest that Gavin was less firm in meeting the challenge than his reputation has indicated.

Gavin had landed heavily, injured so badly after his parachute drop that he had trouble rising from a prone position. On landing, he nevertheless made his way to the site of his command post, accompanied by his Dutch liaison officer, Captain "Harry" Bestebreurtje, killing Germans on the way. Bestebreurtje was able to get through to Nijmegen and to Arnhem on the civilian phone, where the operation seemed to be going well. It was not until the next day that Gavin made contact with his artillery battalion. The purpose of the artillery had been to scare off the low-quality troops that were expected to oppose them, which they certainly did. The parachute-delivered artillery was in action an hour after landing, despite the fact that each of the twelve guns came in seven pieces. The battalion fired 315 rounds in the first twenty-four hours and captured over 400 German troops.

When it became clear to Field Marshal Model that the Allies had landed south of the Nijmegen bridges, he ordered *Wehrkreis VI* to attack the paratroopers southeast of Nijmegen and on the Groesbeek Heights, as well as defend the bridges. Remarkably, Model began planning a counterattack south toward Eindhoven using reinforcements from *II Fallschirmjeager Korps* under General Eugen Meindl. The counterattack would commence once the 10th SS had arrived from Arnhem.

In Nijmegen, the defense force under Colonel Henke numbered 750 men. Henke focused his resistance on two traffic circles south of the bridges, ordering his flak guns to be depressed for use as artillery support. He also fortified the village of Lent located north of the city, which overlooked the bridges. The rest of his forces were distributed among a series of outposts around the city's southern edge. Captain Wilde's company overwhelmed one of these outposts when heading for the road bridge. Henke's troops were jittery. One battalion radioed *Wehrkreis VI* which, in view of the strength of the American landings, wrote off three companies of the defense force as lost.

The *Frundsberg* forces, ordered by Bittrich to move south, were initially organized as *Kampfgruppe Reinhold,* which included the 10th SS Engineer Battalion and the motorized Battalion *Euling.* The *Frundsberg* troops attempted to cross the Arnhem Bridge and became embroiled with Frost's battalion, which had occupied its north end. Euling disengaged, aiming to cross the Lower Rhine and reach Nijmegen by another route as it is fairly clear that he knew of the Pannerden ferry and the tortuous route to it.

The 9th SS Reconnaissance Battalion under Captain Viktor-Eberhard Graebner had already crossed the Arnhem bridge prior to the arrival of Frost's battalion. Graebner was ordered to report the presence of any Allied paratroopers in the Betuwe area, the triangle of land between the Waal/Lower Rhine confluence, Nijmegen and Arnhem, and to destroy them if encountered. Graebner reached Elst and patrolled the area, reporting from a point two kilometers south of the Arnhem Bridge that the region was clear. He reformed his column, which included motorized infantry, and made for Nijmegen, where he found Henke's *Kampfgruppe* already in place defending the two bridges.

One account says that Graebner had placed several self-propelled guns at the southern end of the Arnhem bridge; but British accounts, including that of Frost himself, state that the British were opposed by a lone armored car and by panzer grenadiers, the SS motorized infantry. In any event, Graebner got the news that *Frundsberg* units were fighting at the north end of the bridge while his own troops were engaged at the southern end. Graebner thought that the opposition was slight and that Henke could deal with it. So with fighting on both sides of the Arnhem bridge and a crisis evidently developing in his rear, Graebner placed a few self-propelled guns on the south side of the Nijmegen bridge, two flak guns at the north end, and headed back to Arnhem. Graebner, who was both bold and impetuous, defied his orders to remain in Nijmegen.

At the HQ of the 406th Division in *Wehrkreis VI*, Lieutenant General Scherbening met with his staff at 0200 on D+1. He was to assemble a force to attack the Americans early in the morning, while moving his HQ to Geldern. General Feldt then ordered the 406th to set up a tactical HQ at Kreugers-Gut on the Kranenberg-Nijmegen Road. Forces starting from Kranenberg later became one arm of a pincer movement to cut off the American troops on the Groesbeek Heights. The 406th at the time had only headquarters troops and the cadres of a number of training units so it was not clear to the divisional adjutant, Major Rasch, what they were to attack the Americans with. Meanwhile, the 505th and 508th Parachute Infantry Regiments had established their cordon and secured the Groesbeek Heights on D-Day with only light opposition.

The 1st Airborne Division

"A lone figure came running down the ramp, shouting 'Stretcher-bearer, stretcher-bearer!' Colonel Frost stepped out onto the road and said to him, 'Stop that noise.' The man came to a halt in front of him and said in a perfectly moderate voice, 'Excuse me, sir, but I'm fucking well wounded.'"

—Signalman Bill Jukes

The first lift of the 1st Airborne Division on D-Day was highly successful; no aircraft were lost over the drop and landing zones. The gliders landed first, followed by the paratroop drops. Thirty-six gliders failed to arrive, which led to a severe depletion in the number of fighting troops. These included the complement of five gliders that ditched in the sea, to be picked up by the highly efficient air-sea rescue service. All fifteen of the 75mm pack howitzers made it to the LZ. All told, a total of 5,191 troops were landed, about half the division, which was smaller than the American airborne divisions and in turn much smaller than an infantry division. Correspondingly, the parachute battalions, too, were smaller with complements of 550 to 600 men; Frost's battalion had only 48l.

By 1410 hours the parachute drop was complete and the First Parachute Brigade assembled for the move to Arnhem. First away were the Second and 3rd Battalions at 1500 hours. Of these, the task of 3rd Battalion under Lt. Colonel J.A.C. Fitch was to assist the Second headed by Lt. Colonel J.D. Frost in securing the Arnhem road bridge by taking the middle or "Tiger" route along the Heelsum-Arnhem Road. The instructions for Frost's battalion, on the lower river route, were more complex.

There were three bridges over the Lower Rhine, the road bridge in the east, a pontoon bridge close to it, and a rail bridge to the west. The main prize was the Arnhem road bridge. Frost instructed Major Digby Tatham-Warter's A Company to go straight for the bridge and to pass a platoon across to the other side. Major Victor Dover's C Company was to take the rail bridge, cross it and proceed to the south end of the road bridge. Major Douglas Crawley's B Company was held in reserve. Just before take-off, Frost learned that the pontoon bridge had been dismantled but he supposed "it might be possible to make some use of it."

The plan for 1st Airborne, such as it was, began to unravel almost immediately. What transpired was that the airborne commanders conflated the primary task of securing the Arnhem bridges with the secondary task of establishing the bridgehead for XXX Corps. This was an ongoing theme until the end of D+2. If, on D-Day, sufficient progress toward the road bridge was made by two battalions of the First Parachute Brigade, the third, held in reserve, was not to join the move to the Arnhem bridge but to take the northernmost route to Arnhem in order to secure some high ground north of the city and hold until relieved by the Fourth Parachute Brigade. In practice, First Parachute Battalion actually moved off north before the progress of the other two had been ascertained.

Frost's battalion had the most success on D-Day. Two of his three companies had reached the northern end of the Arnhem road bridge soon after dark and by the morning, Frost had about 750 men at the bridge. The trouble was with the other two battalions of First Parachute Brigade. Dobie's 1st Battalion crossed the railway embankment and "ambled along" the railway, "like a crocodile." There Dobie met Major Gough of the Reconnaissance Squadron returning from the point, who told him that the troop of the squadron assigned to Lathbury's brigade had been halted by German armor and infantry. As a result, Dobie turned north on a straight road to the Amsterdamseweg, intending to outflank the opposition. This move led the Germans to believe that some of the British were heading for Deelen, not Arnhem.

Dobie continued until he received a radio message from Frost from the road bridge. So, reverting to his role as the reserve battalion, Dobie decided to disengage, to "help Johnnie at the bridge." The battalion recrossed under the railway embankment and headed for the Utrechtseweg (Heelsum-Arnhem) assuming that 3rd Battalion had already taken this middle route. At the crossing of the rail line that ran south to the rail bridge over the Lower Rhine, Dobie ran into opposition, so he again sidestepped to the south, to take Frost's route to the bridge, which he knew to have been successful. This was as late as 0530 on D+1.

Until then, Dobie had made no contact of any sort with 3rd Battalion, in whose area he was operating. Radio contact had ceased. This was critical in Dobie's failure to reach the Arnhem bridge. Had he known of 3rd Battalion's stalled advance, he most likely would have proceeded directly along Frost's route since his tactics, quite proper for the airborne, were to infiltrate rather than overcome the opposition. The 3rd Battalion ran into Germans about two hours after leaving the DZ. B Company fired on a staff car, killing the Town Commandant of Arnhem, Major General Friedrich Kussin, who was later buried with his troops in the German cemetery at IJsselstein.

By 1730 hours, 3rd Battalion had encountered its first serious opposition when Brigadier Lathbury arrived from 2nd Battalion HQ to the south and urged 3rd Battalion onward. Lieutenant Colonel Fitch decided to detach C Company, under Major R.P.C. "Pongo" Lewis, and send it off toward the bridge by a side route to the left. Lewis and about forty-five of his men eventually reached the bridge. At about this time, Major General Urquhart moved up from the rear of the column and conferred with Lathbury.

After some violent action at about 1830 hours, 3rd Battalion reconnoitered C Company's route but otherwise halted, neither moving forward into the built-up area of Oosterbeek, nor following C Company, nor sidestepping to the south, along Frost's route. Fitch did not resume the advance until 0430 on D+1, in the absence of any prompting from Urquhart or Lathbury; on the contrary, it seems he was ordered to halt. Why Lathbury did not push 3rd Battalion forward is inexplicable as he had earlier urged greater speed on Frost as Urquhart had done with Tony Hibbert, the Brigade Major. One speculation is that Lathbury thought the going would be relatively easy, without any need for urgency, a version of the German theme that the British suffered from overconfidence.

The plan for First Parachute Brigade was not the only thing to go wrong. The divisional reconnaissance squadron under Major Freddie Gough comprised thirty-one jeeps to be landed by glider, their crews dropping by parachute. The Squadron was organized into a HQ, a Support Troop and three troops with eight jeeps each. When Brigadier Lathbury found that there was to be no coup de main force, he got control of two of the three troops under Major Gough. This formation was to rush ahead of the three battalions, along with two detachments of engineers in four jeeps. The engineers were to destroy demolition charges at the bridges. Gough, realizing that this was not a reconnaissance, asked for the landing of a troop of Tetrach light tanks, which had been used by the airborne in Normandy. This was refused, as was his suggestion that a troop precede each of the three battalions instead of two troops proceeding along a single route. Of the three routes to Arnhem planned for the brigade, Gough was assigned the northernmost, where 1st Battalion was not directed to an immediate assault on the Arnhem bridge! This was also where, as it transpired, the German defenses were the strongest.

The majority of the jeeps (twenty-eight) were landed, but it was widely thought at the time that the bulk of the squadron had failed to arrive. The engineers' jeeps had landed on the other LZ. After a delay of an hour and a half, the equivalent of one troop set off ahead of Dobie's battalion, minus the engineers, with Gough in the middle of the column. Ten minutes later, the column was halted by heavy German fire, and two jeeps and most of their crews were lost. Gough with two jeeps finally caught up with Frost at the Arnhem bridge. The remainder of the column was withdrawn from Wolfheze at 1830 hours after being relieved by a unit of glider pilots, and returned to the Squadron Rear HQ.

In Frost's battalion, Major Tatham-Warter's A Company took the lead and reached the road bridge at around 2000 hours, in the fading light. En route, the company ambushed a German column, probably a reconnaissance squadron from Krafft's battalion, killing or capturing over thirty Germans. Frost was behind A Company when Lathbury appeared, conferred briefly with him, and departed for 3rd Battalion. By his own account, Lathbury was dissatisfied with the pace of Frost's advance, even urging him to have C Company bypass Tatham-Warter.

In Oosterbeek, C Company with engineers moved south toward the rail bridge, which blew when they were fifty yards away. Frost, who had seen the explosion, recalled Major Dover for the march to Arnhem. Most of C Company was eventually captured by the Germans. B Company was first called from reserve to prevent the Germans from impeding A Company's advance, at a shallow rise known as Den Brink. It then proceeded to the pontoon bridge, where it found that the center span had been drawn up on to the north bank, a standard German air raid precaution. B Company, minus its rearguard, a platoon, eventually reached the bridge.

Frost arrived at the bridge with A Company. Tatham-Warter placed Lt. Jack Grayburn's platoon at the northern end, where the bridge embankment descended to road level. The two other platoons were placed in buildings at either side of the bridge footings, while Frost sited his HQ in a residence on the west side, overlooking the bridge and the surrounding area. The vehicles and anti-tank guns were placed in a parking lot, out of sight from the bridge ramp.

The scene was eerily calm. The bridge seemed to be undefended. According to some accounts, a group of about twenty-five guards, very young or very old, deserted their posts on seeing the airborne landings. Such that remained were ensconced at the northern end of the bridge, some in a pillbox, unaware that they were about to be attacked.

The Brigade HQ under Tony Hibbert, the Brigade Major, arrived at the bridge about forty minutes after A Company, having been delayed for half an hour by the action at Den Brink. The contingent was a large one, perhaps 110 men, with the Brigade Defence Platoon, much of the First Parachute Squadron of Engineers, a Royal Army Service Corps (RASC) platoon, which had been commandeered by Frost when that unit's assignment had gone awry, and several men from other specialized units. Of particular value were two jeeps and four trailers of the Service Corps, loaded with ammunition. Freddie Gough of the reconnaissance squadron and two jeeps arrived somewhat before 2200 hours, as did Major Munford of the Light Regiment, RA, with several signallers.

Hibbert set up his HQ with Munford, adjacent to that of Frost, detaching as many men as he could spare to bolster Frost's battalion, still limited to A Company at the bridge. A further arrival, from the action at the rail bridge, was Captain Eric Mackay with a party of engineers from First Parachute Squadron, who took up positions on the eastern side of the bridge, very close to the superstructure.

The achievement of the engineers in defending Frost's positions from the evening of D-Day to the afternoon of D+3 is legendary, and yet their performance and even their identity remain unclear and steeped in controversy. The most detailed accounts of the action are from participants: Lieutenant Peter Stainforth, in *Wings of the Wind* and from Captain Eric Mackay in *The Battle of Arnhem Bridge*, a work more often noted than read. Mackay was the commander of A Troop; he took command of all the engineers in the positions at the east of the bridgehead and, it seems, handed command of his own A Troop to Lieutenant Paul Mason, who in turn took command of those of B Troop already in position when A Troop arrived. Mackay also took command of a party of Third Parachute Battalion under Major Lewis, his senior.

Despite Martin Middlebrook's negative comments about Mackay, this was not controversial at the time. Frost wrote that Mackay and Lewis "shared a building" and that he visited the troops in the sector under Mackay's "staunch leadership"; he was also in radio contact with Mackay. Stainforth did not mention either Lewis or Mackay, nor is there any implication of their presence. While there are many points in common between Stainforth and Mackay, there are also some puzzling discrepancies. What is certain is that there were around fifty engineers in the position in and around the school on the eastern face of the bridgehead. They initially defended the school, an office building to the north of it (adjacent to what turned out of be a local German HQ), and two houses to the south of it. The school was U-shaped, the two wings facing the bridge ramp. What Middlebrook seems to have done is to mistake the troops' backbiting and grumbling about their officers, which is common enough, for historical truth.

There were three forays to capture the southern end of the bridge. In the final attempt, at about 2200 hours, the British used a flamethrower, likely from Mackay's detachment, to neutralize the pillbox blocking the way across. Instead the liquid jet of flame set fire to a nearby wooden hut containing fuel and ammunition. A huge explosion followed, causing the bridge paintwork to catch fire. This burned fiercely all night long, making an assault from the northern end very difficult. Frost's engineers advised him that the fires on the bridge had likely destroyed demolition cables.

During the night a column of two to four trucks approached the bridge from the south and were destroyed by British fire. The trucks were likely transporting panzer grenadiers from the SS reconnaissance battalion. Another attack from the northeast faltered as Euling's battalion from the *Frundsberg* disengaged to take the road to Pannerden. Still, the German cordon around the bridge was preventing reinforcements from getting through, including Frost's C Company. Indeed, the last party to arrive at the bridge was only a platoon of the 9th Field Company RE. The 16th Parachute Field Ambulance made directly to St. Elizabeth Hospital and was up and running by 2200 hours, by which time some 2nd Battalion casualties were already being treated.

At the bridge, Major Dennis Munford found that his artillery link was not working, nor were the links to division from Gough or Hibbert. Assuming his radios were at fault, Munford made an expedition back to the divisional area and returned with two more radio sets. Unbeknownst to Munford, in his absence one of his signallers succeeded in making contact with artillery HQ and on Munford's return, the artillery link was firmly established. His driver, Lance-Bombardier Bill Crook, deserved a write-up for braving enemy fire unarmed in a hair-raising fourteen-mile round trip.

On the landing zone, the First Airlanding Brigade carried out its mission with little difficulty. The battalion of the South Staffordshires remained in the vicinity of Wolfheze, while the battalion of the Border Regiment moved south to a new landing zone for D+1, one company reaching as far south as Renkum. There it overlooked the Driel-Heaveadorp ferry and the approaches from the west, both possible routes for a German counterattack.

The reason for the new DZ/LZ was that the two existing zones would be clogged with gliders from the first lift. The battalion of the King's Own Scottish Borderers (KOSB) moved northeast to protect the other D+1 DZ/LZ. This was, in Martin Middlebrook's words, "a good illustration of the weakness of the landing plan. At a time when every effort should have been directed eastward, toward Arnhem, the KOSB companies had all moved nearly three miles in the opposite direction." The furthest, B Company, was almost ten miles from the Arnhem road bridge.

While Brigadier Lathbury was at the DZ, he was informed that most of the reconnaissance squadron jeeps had failed to arrive. Urquhart too, by his own account, had heard the same rumor and wanted to contact Gough to change the plan for the coup de main; but the reconnaissance squadron could not be reached on the divisional radio net. Also out of radio contact with Lathbury, he chafed at the bit in his HQ until he could stand it no longer.

Urquhart left a message for Gough and took off to find Lathbury in his jeep, with his driver, signaller and, quite bewilderingly, Lieutenant Colonel Loder-Symonds, his artillery commander. He found the Brigade HQ toward the back of the 2nd Battalion column, but not Lathbury, who had moved on to 3rd Battalion. Like his Brigadier, Urquhart was dissatisfied with the progress, giving Tony Hibbert, the Brigade Major a "ballocking" (dressing down) as he moved off to 3rd Battalion. Lathbury in his diary wrote that he heard from Urquhart on the radio at 1700 hours, though it was probably later than this, when Urquhart expressed his displeasure at the slow progress.

Sometime afterward, Urquhart ordered his signaller to get off the divisional net in order to contact Gough; not only did this fail, but he thus lost contact with his HQ until his signaller was badly wounded and the set damaged beyond repair. Gough, for his part, was engaged, if not in a tragedy of errors, then certainly a tragicomedy. Unable to contact Lathbury, Gough returned with three jeeps from the 1st Battalion's area to find Urquhart, first at the Airlanding Brigade HQ, then Divisional HQ, which Urquhart had just left. He then set off for 2nd Battalion, whose area Urquhart had again just left, then decided to head for his original objective, the road bridge, without his squadron and without any pretence that he was still engaged in the coup de main.

In his decision to leave his HQ, Urquhart has had his defenders; but most critics contend that he made a bad mistake. The net result was that the 1st Airborne had no commander for the first 40 hours and no clear devolution of responsibility. Urquhart made no attempt to send runners back to the divisional HQ; when Lt. Leo Heaps in a Bren Carrier located him at 3rd Battalion on the morning of D+1, all Urquhart did was tell him to take a message to divisional HQ instead of delivering supplies to Frost at the bridge. Soon after Heaps left, Urquhart seems to have decided that it was a good idea after all to get back to his HQ. Loder-Symonds became separated fom Urquhart and returned to his HQ, where he properly belonged, in the evening of D-Day.

D-Day 1300 hours found Bittrich at Doetinchem; Harmel at Bad Saarow, thirty miles southeast of Berlin; his Chief of Staff, SS-Colonel

Otto Paetsch in Ruurlo; and Harzer at Hoenderloo near his HQ at Beekbergen, with his Chief of Staff in Siegen, awaiting the arrival of the bulk of *Hohenstaufen* by rail from Arnhem. Bittrich received the first reports of the landings at 1330 hours and sent out his first warning order by civilian phone at 1340. Further orders followed, again by phone, at 1600 and 1630 hours, with a general corps order at 1730. Harzer ordered Graebner to commission his reconnaissance battalion and within two hours the forty vehicles were ready to move, principally personnel carriers and armored cars. By 1440, most of *Hohenstaufen's* alarm companies had been alerted by phone from Doetinchem and had reported that they were ready for action. In the order of 1630 hours, Graebner's battalion was to reconnoiter the area between Arnhem and Nijmegen.

Under observation by the British, Graebner's thirty vehicles crossed south over the bridge at 1800 hours, and in some accounts, an hour later than that. A sub-unit was to reconnoiter toward Oosterbeek and cover the remainder of *Hohenstaufen's* move to Arnhem. This convoy of ten half-tracks along the Amsterdamseweg later helped block the advance of First Parachute Battalion. In the more detailed Corps Order of 1730, *Hohenstaufen's* Reconnaissance Battalion was replaced by that of *Frundsberg,* re-designated as *Kampfgruppe Brinkmann,* along with a detachment of towed *Nebelwerfer* (multiple rocket launchers). *Kampfgruppe Brinkmann* then came under the command of *Hohenstaufen.* The task of this group was to secure a passage across the Arnhem bridge for *Frundsberg.*

Most of the *Frundsberg* was many miles northeast of Arnhem and even with efficient movement control, it would take much time for them to cross to the south bank of the Lower Rhine. The order also put *Hohenstaufen's* alarm companies under the command of SS-Lt. Colonel Spindler, formerly of the *Frundsberg* Artillery Regiment, as *Kampfgruppe Spindler,* now under the *Hohenstaufen.* Bittrich, who by this time knew of the presence of Krafft's battalion, ordered Spindler to advance through Arnhem toward Oosterbeek, forming a blocking line in the sector between Krafft and the Lower Rhine.

The one salient fact concerning *Hohenstaufen* is that no unit ever secured the north end of the Arnhem road bridge. The only evidence that this was *Hohenstaufen's* job comes from the reconstruction of the first telephone order of 1340 hours; it is not mentioned in the three subsequent orders. According to author Wilhelm Tieke, *Hohenstaufen* never was charged with defending the Arnhem bridge. Rather, the division was fully preoccupied with the British advance from Oosterbeek. The one unit which was in a position to secure the north end of the bridge was Graebner's Reconnaissance Battalion; but he had no orders to do so, nor was he then under command of *Hohenstaufen*.

The alarm companies of *Hohenstaufen* were not always given precise orders and given that they were expected to respond to battlefield emergencies, were trained to march toward the sound of gunfire. This was a severe limitation since the main threats to the bridge occurred where there was little shooting. In author Robert Kershaw's view, "The responsible unit commanders . . . believed it was either someone else's task to secure the Arnhem road bridge, or there was already somebody there who could be relieved in time."

Such misunderstanding seems to have characterized *Kampfgruppe Brinkmann*. Brinkmann, substituting for Graebner, was much further away from Arnhem at Borcolo and Eibergen than *Hohenstaufen's* Reconnaissance Battalion at Beekbergen. According to accounts recorded by Kershaw, orders for Brinkmann were received from SS-Colonel Paetsch of the *Frundsberg* in Harmel's absence, when Brinkmann now actually came under *Hohenstaufen*.

Paetsch, apparently oblivious of Brinkmann's mission, split the battalion. One unit was to reconnoiter along the Lower Rhine as far as Emmerich and Wesel, the former being about as far from their bases as Arnhem. The Germans had received reports of landings at Emmerich as well as Arnhem and Nijmegen, something known to the British through *Ultra*. A company supported by armored cars set off toward Arnhem and arrived at the bridge at around 2000 hours and took fire from Frost's A Company. "Uncertain what was going on, they returned fire, withdrew, and radioed Paetsch on what they had seen."

Spindler's *Kampfgruppen* made their way to the southern extension of Krafft's blocking line, too late to prevent the bulk of Frost's troops from reaching the bridge. The line was still partly a matter of strong points since other formations passed through it, though it was largely solid by the time that Lathbury's 3rd Battalion resumed its advance at 0430 hours. By then, the *Kampfgruppen* or *Alarmheiten* of Spindler, Moeller and Gropp were in place with, quite possibly, *Kampfgruppe Harder* forming a second blocking line behind them. *Kampfgruppe von Allworden*, with Graebner's half-tracks, blocked First Parachute Battalion along the Amsterdamscheweg.

Between Allworden and Spindler's other groups, Krafft's well-armed trainees blocked the progress of First and Third Parachute Battalions. Krafft, believing that he was being outflanked, withdrew at 2130 hours, meeting Spindler's incoming troops an hour later and coming under *Hohenstaufen's* command at 2245. Despite his exaggerated claims, his battalion was largely responsible for checking the advance of First Parachute Brigade toward the Arnhem bridge.

Though the reaction of the *Hohenstaufen* units was haphazard and sometimes delayed, all units eventually arrived at the proper place, too late to prevent the occupation of the north end of the Arnhem road bridge but in time to prevent its further reinforcement. The situation with *Frundsberg* was different, the units arriving to fight in Arnhem instead of assembling to move south. Fifty men from a company of SS *Panzer* Grenadier Regiment 21 moved from Deventer to Arnhem on commandeered bicycles. This unit dismounted north of the bridge, proceeded on foot, and found itself moving behind a British unit advancing on the bridge. The Battalion Euling was surprised to find itself engaged with the British north of the bridge, until it was withdrawn to take the road to Pannerden. They first had to cross the IJssel, then move cross-country instead of proceeding along the side of the Pannerden Canal, which joins the IJssel to form the Lower Rhine. The task of *Kampfgruppe Brinkmann* turned from securing passage over the Arnhem bridge for *Frundsberg* to the siege of Frost's troops on the eastern face of the British position.

By 1700 hours, Harzer was in Arnhem, coordinating the defense of the bridge with Major Shliefenbaum, Kussin's Chief of Staff. After giving out his corps order at 1730 hours, Bittrich, for his part, visited SS-Captain Hans Moeller at his command post in the Den Brink area. According to Bauer's account, Bittrich did not know of the presence of the British troops at the road bridge until the "late evening" when two female *Luftwaffe* phone operators told him that the bridge was in British hands. The women were later decorated for staying at their posts throughout the battle.

Bittrich had also visited Harzer at his new HQ in Velp. He found the situation obscure. At some time in the evening, Bittrich requested reinforcements from Model, including infantry skilled in house-to-house fighting, artillery, flak and tanks. Author Christopher Hibbert wrote: "By dawn on September 18th, Model had acceded to all Bittrich's requests and orders had gone out, not only to the 191st

Regiment of Artillery, two infantry battalions (Knaust and Bruhns) and *Panzer* Abteilung 503 [actually 506] equipped with [15] *Koenigstiger* tanks; but also to *I Brigade Flakartillerie*, several smaller units of the Field Police, *Landsturmbatallons, Heeresbatallons,* and a *Pionier-lehrbatallon* skilled in the use of flame-throwers. As the sun rose on Monday morning all these units had either left or were preparing to leave for Arnhem." The first of these reinforcements arrived early the next day "in makeshift transport."

The airborne landings on D-Day were a qualified success. The 101st Airborne had taken all of its objectives except for Eindhoven, and the Son bridge was down. The 82nd Airborne too had achieved all of its vital objectives, including a bridge across the Maas-Waal Canal and the Grave Bridge. By any standard the American achievement was spectacular. Yet the great Nijmegen road bridge still stood, fiercely defended by SS troops, with every prospect of being blown before it could be captured.

The 1st Airborne's success was the most qualified. It had not taken any of its three bridges across the Lower Rhine, the primary objective of the assault plan, nor did it pass any troops over to the south bank. The division occupied the north end of the Arnhem road bridge, which was still intact, but could not move into its bridgehead unless there was a continuous link between the airhead and Frost's battalion at the Arnhem bridge. That link had been severed by the morning of D+1. Nor was there, apart from the limited forces at the bridge, even the beginning of the bridgehead for XXX Corps, which was the division's secondary objective. Urquhart, too, was cut off from the rest of the *Market Garden* forces. Dempsey, Browning and Horrocks were out of radio contact, ignorant of the state of Urquhart's division, and whether the route from Nijmegen to Nunspeet was open.

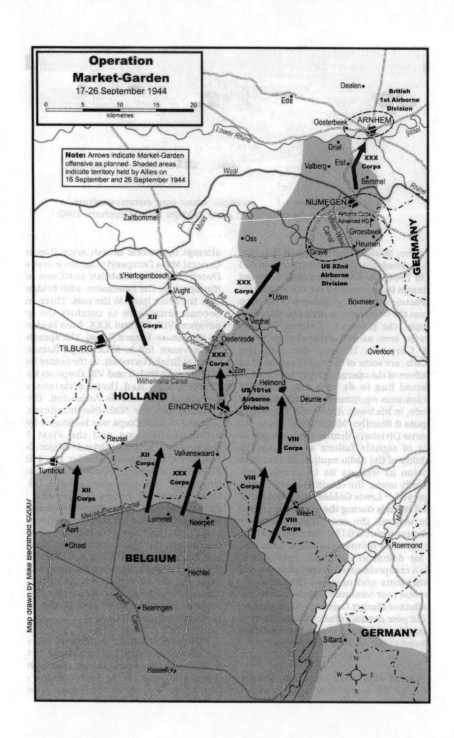

Operation Market-Garden
17-26 September 1944

0   5   10   15   20
kilometres

Note: Arrows indicate Market-Garden offensive as planned. Shaded areas indicate territory held by Allies on 16 September and 26 September 1944

Deelen

Ede

British 1st Airborne Division

Oosterbeek   ARNHEM   IJssel

Lower Rhine

Driel

Waal   Valberg   Elst   XXX Corps

Bemmel

Zaltbommel   NIJMEGEN

Rhine

GERMANY

Maas   Airborne Corps Advanced HQ

Oss   Groesbeek

Heumen

s'Hertogenbosch   Grave

US 82nd Airborne Division

Vught   XXX Corps   Uden

Aa   Willems Canal   Boxmeer

Veghel

XII Corps   Dommel   St. Oedenrode

TILBURG   XXX Corps   Zon   Overloon

Best

Wilhelmina Canal   Helmond

HOLLAND   US 101st Airborne Division   Deurne

EINDHOVEN

Reusel   VIII Corps

XII Corps   Valkenswaard

Turnhout   XXX Corps

XII Corps   VIII Corps

Meuse-Escaut Canal   Weert

Aart   Lommel   Neerpelt   VIII Corps

Gheel   Roermond

BELGIUM

Hechtel   Maas

Albert Canal

Beeringen   GERMANY

Sittard   N

W   E

S

Hasselt

Map drawn by Mike Bechthold ©2004

5

AIRBORNE HIATUS

The early morning of D+1 found the 2nd Battalion of the 502nd PIR pinned down in an area bounded by the Wilhelmina Canal to the south and the Eindhoven-Boxtel road to the west. The battalion had made contact with H Company, but heavy fire had driven the company back into the woods all along its perimeter. Lt. Colonel Cole had given up Wierzbowski's platoon for lost. Colonel Michaelis ordered the 3rd Battalion to the area, to make contact with the right flank of Cole's battalion, then advance on the bridges at Best. However, the German 59th Division had been reinforced during the night, possibly to its full core strength of a thousand veterans.

The Germans saturated the two American battalions with punishing artillery, mortar and small arms fire from the western side of the Boxtel road. While observing an air strike by P-47 Thunderbolts, Cole was killed by a bullet to the head. He had been awarded the Congressional Medal of Honor, the highest American decoration, for leading a bayonet charge at Carentan during the Battle of Normandy. Despite continued enemy fire, Major John P. Stopka was able to send patrols forward and establish defensive positions on the Boxtel road. Unbeknown to the regiment, the canal road bridge had been blown at 1100 hours.

As the day dawned, Lieutenant Wierzbowski saw that the guards on the north side of the canal bridge had been withdrawn. The south end of the bridge and the Boxtel road remained well guarded by troops dug into prepared positions. A group of Germans, survivors from the battalion attacks, made their way westward, along the north bank of the canal. Wierzbowski ambushed them, killing around thirty five. Private Mann and another soldier pushed forward, blowing up an ammunition dump with a bazooka and firing on six more Germans approaching from the north, before being hit twice by return fire. His companion then destroyed an 88mm cannon on the south side of the canal before they were strafed by P-47s from the air strike Cole had called in. Gunfire from the north gave them hope that they would be relieved.

Lieutenant Palmer's armoured car patrol from the Household Cavalry then appeared on the other side of the canal. They blasted away at the enemy with their machine guns and two-pounder anti-tank gun. A corporal rowed across to the British, who assured him that the paratroopers would soon be relieved. On seeing what seemed to be reinforcements arriving on the north bank, the British patrol departed as ordered.

In the early evening, a patrol from Company E passed by, taking news back to 3rd Battalion that the canal bridge had been destroyed, but failed to report on the plight of Wierzbowski's group, now getting assistance from three captured German medics. They later were joined by a stray platoon from Company D, who were attacked from the north by *Kampfgruppe Rink* and driven across to the south side of the canal. This platoon re-crossed further east and rejoined 2nd Battalion two days later. At dawn on D+2, not fully aware that the departure of the platoon had left their left flank open, Wierzbowski and his paratroopers were subjected to a German grenade attack.

This engagement saw the Americans at their best. One German grenade blinded Private Laino, who groped for another grenade he heard land next to him, found it and tossed it back just before it exploded—one of at least three dealt with in this way. Joe Mann, wounded four times, his arms in bandages, yelled "Grenade!" and fell on his back, covering the bomb. After the explosion he said quietly to Wierzbowski, "My back is gone," and in a minute or two he died. Out of ammunition and with all but three men wounded or dead, Wierzbowski surrendered. The group was freed later in the day in the 2nd Battalion attack. Private Mann was awarded a posthumous Congressional Medal of Honor and where he died a monument was built in his name.

At dawn on D+1, formations of the 101st Airborne were at Bokt, en route to Eindhoven, and on the approaches to Best, as well as in Son, St. Oedenrode, Eerde and Veghel. There were no troops in Uden to the north. The backbone of the German reinforcements arriving from the west consisted of Poppe's 59th Division and, later, von der Heydte's 6th Parachute Regiment. On the eastern side of Hell's Highway, *Kampf-gruppe Walther* had not so far reassembled in the Son area, nor yet had the 107th *Panzer* Brigade, a "pocket tank division," arrived from the direction of Helmond.

At dawn, the 506th PIR resumed its march from Bokt to Eindhoven, encountering 88s, mortars and some infantry on the route. The city was declared free of the enemy at 1700 hours.

It is likely that the troops under Hoffman's command had left for Best during the morning; one report has Hoffman himself killed in the fighting. At 1230, two British vehicles on patrol had entered the city from the north; this was the 506th's first contact with the British, who met up with Wierzbowski's platoon later in the afternoon. By the time General Taylor arrived in Eindhoven, the 506th PIR had contacted XXX Corps on the radio and reported to the divisional commander that they had taken the town and the four bridges over the Dommel River. Reconnaissance units of XXX Corps rolled into Eindhoven at 1830 hours.

The Guards resumed the advance from Valkenswaard at 0645 hours with great enterprise. The Second Household Cavalry Regiment led off at 0530 hours on the central Club Route, followed by the Grenadier Guards Group. The follow-up force, a battalion from 50th Division, completed its arrival in Valkenswaard by 0900 hours. The 50th Division itself came under the command of VIII Corps at 1200 hours on D+1, as did the Seventh Medium Regiment, Royal Artillery. This was in accordance with the task of VIII Corps to protect the flanks; the order was given before VIII Corps operations began.

The Irish Guards began their march at 1000 hours. The Thirty-second Guards Brigade, with the Welsh Guards Group leading, pushed the flanks out east in order to take the Heart Route. They were heavily engaged by the enemy (possibly with Roestel's panzers) and lost one tank. When they were informed by Dutch civilians that Geldrop and Helmond were strongly defended, they abandoned the Heart Route around Eindhoven and rejoined the main axis of advance. To the west, the Second Household Cavalry crossed the Dommel River but found that the bridges were not strong enough for the following Grenadier Guards tanks, a fact noted by Dempsey in his diary. At least one tank became bogged down at the crossing.

On the main route north, the Irish Guards, now leading, were held up by a mixed force south of Aalst, then again on the Dommel River. The latter hold-up lasted two hours and required yet further artillery support. No air support could be expected as the Typhoons were grounded on their Belgian airfields by fog. A patrol of the Household Cavalry worked round behind the Germans and reported that the enemy was withdrawing, having observed six abandoned 88s. By 1930 hours, they had reached the Son bridge, followed by the Fourteenth Field Squadron, Royal Engineers, who built on the work of the American engineers and constructed a forty-ton bridge by dawn. The liaison officer of the Forty-fourth Battalion, Royal Tank Regiment contacted the 101st Airborne in Son for orders for the defense of Hell's Highway between Eindhoven and Grave. It was the beginning of a good relationship that lasted for twelve days of hard fighting, costing the battalion a third of its tank strength.

At 0645 hours on D+2 the Guards, rolling north from the Son bridge, could see the Grave bridge many miles away. By the time they left Son, they were about thirty hours behind schedule, the delay equally due to the destruction of the Son bridge and to the halt at Valkenswaard, though it is impossible to say how much time would have been saved by an immediate advance north. For its part, the 101st Airborne had arrived in Eindhoven well over twelve hours behind schedule.

With VIII Corps in no position to protect the flanks of Horrocks' advance, the job fell to 50th Division inside the Corridor. In the XII Corps sector, the crossing of the Meuse-Escaut Canal at Lommel had not been strongly opposed and the engineers were able to build a nine-ton bridge by 0630 hours on D+1. The advantage of the Lommel bridgehead over Gheel-Aart was that it brought XII Corps closer to XXX Corps, about the same distance as the VIII Corps starting point at Lille St. Hubert to the east. That crossing began at midnight.

The line of advance of XII Corps remained via Tunhout to Boxtel and 's-Hertogenbosch, away from the XXX Corps axis. There were even plans to cross the Turnhout Canal and advance west to Rethie, Arendonk and Kasterlee. Subsequently, the 53rd Division was to move in a more northerly direction to capture Reusel and to dominate the Poppel-Esebeck-Diessen area. Though this was described as a screen for "protection and control," there was no plan to close with the XXX Corps axis. By the end of D+1, XII Corps had consolidated its bridgehead in preparation for 15th Division's move toward Turnhout and Kasterlee.

In the Nijmegen area, the outlook for the Germans by the morning of D+1 was poor. Their actions on D-Day had failed to keep the 82nd Airborne from establishing a 25-mile perimeter, held at various key points, nor from attaining its main D-Day objectives: the Groesbeek Heights, the Grave bridge and a bridge over the Maas-Waal Canal. There, the Molenhoek-Heumen bridge had fallen intact to the Americans and another (Honinghutie) was about to be captured. Graebner's reconnaissance battalion had, with the aid of troops from Henke's *Kampfgruppe*, stopped the dual American advance to the Nijmegen road bridge. But now Graebner had left for Arnhem and the leading formations of *Frundsberg* were yet to arrive from their crossing point at Pannerden.

Around the perimeter, the German situation was worse. There were no troops at all to oppose the Americans from the western side, which was fortunate for the Americans as they were unable to rely on British XII Corps to protect this flank for the duration of *Market Garden*. The situation on the eastern side on D+1 was little better. At his HQ in Kruegers-Gut on the Kranenburg-Nijmegen road, General Scherbening was being supplied with several *Alarmheiten* from various units in the vicinity, including an NCO school, *Luftwaffe* formations and battalions of infirmary cases suffering from stomach and ear ailments. Most were untrained infantry equipped only with rifles. From D+1 on, the Germans scraped the barrel, commandeering vehicles, guns and troops wherever they could find them and whatever their official assignment, often enough at checkpoints along the roads leading to the frontier. Press gangs invaded the local villages and towns, rooting out soldiers on leave and assigning them to the front, ignoring the protests from their families.

Three more *Luftwaffe* battalions arrived early in the morning along with artillery formations, some with captured Russian guns. By the time of the German attacks against the 82nd Airborne, scheduled for 0630 hours, the Germans had assembled four *Kampfgruppen* of about battalion strength, with 130 machine guns, 24 mortars and three detachments of howitzers and flak. The total was around 2,300 men. Three *Kampfgruppen*—"*Stargaard*," "*Fuerstenberg*," and "*Greschick*"—were to attack along the front from Beek, through Wyler to Groesbeek. A fourth, *Kampfgruppe Goebel*, with 350 men joined the battalion already placed southeast of Mook and was tasked with heading north-west to converge with the forces advancing from Kranenburg-Zyfflich.

James Gavin's first act at dawn on D+1 was to visit the 508th PIR HQ, where he learned that the road bridge had not yet been taken. His "heart sank." He had invested more hope in the possibilities of taking the Nijmegen bridge than the battle plan had called for. He also learned that the Germans had begun attacks on the LZ which was due to receive gliders at midday. Gavin also knew that there were gaps in the line held by 505th and 508th regiments. He was now paying the price of going for the Nijmegen bridge while breaking the proviso that the perimeter should be protected first. What saved him was his own prompt action, good soldiering on the part of the 82nd, the poor quality of the German troops that opposed him, and, most providentially, the delay in the arrival of the second lift.

Gavin moved rapidly from threat to threat, checking in periodically at his own HQ to get a comprehensive picture of events in his division. On one occasion, he encountered Captain Bestebreurtje and his troops all wearing orange armbands. Gavin warned them of the perils of fight-ing out of uniform and told them that their most vital job was to pre-vent the Germans from blowing the road bridge—no easy task, since his own troops had been unable to get near it. Two regiments with artillery were holding off the Germans and, to Gavin's relief, no tanks had emerged from the *Reichswald*. Nevertheless, he accompanied his reserve, two companies of his engineer battalion, to the Groesbeek area, to be sure that the LZ was cleared for the gliders.

The Germans had already faltered when the 450 gliders and tugs came in at 1400 hours, two hours late on account of the weather. Even then, parts of the LZ were still not clear of Germans. The Americans killed fifty Germans and captured 149, along with sixteen large-calibre guns. Most of the 82nd's artillery, anti-tank guns and jeeps arrived intact, along with medical, signals and engineer units. This was fol-lowed by a supply drop from 135 B-24s, 80 percent of which was recov-ered, mostly after dark and some beyond the perimeter.

Gavin had succeeded in protecting the DZ/LZ, but it had come at a cost: no further assaults on the Nijmegen bridges, thus allowing the *Waffen-SS* to fortify their defenses. The 82nd spent the day consolidat-ing the gains already made, including the capture of the Honinghutie bridges. A platoon of the 508th PIR and another stormed the crossing at Honinghutie. Unfortunately they captured the bridges only after the

Germans had set off demolition charges, destroying one bridge and leaving the other so badly damaged that it was at first deemed unsafe for armor to cross. That evening Gavin got word that the Guards Armoured would arrive at Grave at 0830 hours on D+2, his first news of XXX Corps since leaving England.

The German attacks on D+1 fizzled out. After the glider landings, Feldt drove to Emmerich to check on the progress of the reinforcements. There he found to his dismay that of the two divisions of II Parachute Corps, there were only two weak battalions available, comprising logistical troops who had retreated from Normandy. His Chief of Staff, Major Rasch, disengaged from the battle on the Groesbeek Heights to meet with Model, with Meindl, the commander of the II Parachute Corps, and Feldt, returning from Emmerich. Model put on his usual performance, galvanizing the commanders, insisting on an attack the next day and sweeping out as rapidly as he appeared. This time he did not get his way. Feldt stood up to him, expressing astonishment at the paltry state of II Parachute Corps and declaring that there was no way an attack could be mounted on the third day of the landings. Model was forced to concede and set his sights on an attack in the Wyler-Zyfflich area the following day using existing troops reinforced by *Kampfgruppen Becker* and *Hermann* from the parachute corps.

Meanwhile, *Frundsberg* troops began arriving in Nijmegen via the Pannerden ferry. The crossing of the division, which began on the night of D-Day, was slow and laborious. The Germans were relentlessly attacked by Allied aircraft, their sole defense at the crossing provided by a detachment from *Flak Abteilung* 10. The ferry was not capable of carrying large or heavy vehicles so the Germans resorted to anything they could find. Sixteen *Panzer* IV tanks had to wait for *Wehrmacht* engineers to build a forty-ton raft to transport them. None, it seems, were able to get across in time for the Nijmegen battles. The Germans were, however, able to get across four lethal *Jagdpanzer* IV tank destroyers, which were of comparable weight.

The first German troops to arrive in Nijmegen (by truck and bicycle) were a company of engineers under SS-Lieutenant Baumgaertel, who began to prepare the bridges for demolition in anticipation of an express order from Model's HQ, as well as defenses of the southern approaches to the bridges. At about midday, SS-Captain Karl-Heinz Euling arrived with his *Kampfgruppe* of about a hundred men; it is said via Elst and not by the usual route along the Waal from Pannerden.

Euling had disengaged his group, platoon by platoon, from Arnhem, the night before. At Lent, he met with SS-Captain Leo Hermann Reinhold, the overall commander of the *Frundsberg* troops defending Nijmegen and whose own battalion had already arrived via Pannerden. Reinhold would establish the defense of the northern bank of the Waal from his command post in Lent, while Euling's *Kampfgruppe*, with Baumgaertel's engineers, would take command of Colonel Henke's forces on the south side. The four tank destroyers moved across the 2,000 feet of the road bridge but Allied fire was so strong that Euling had to get his men across in rubber boats, not the last time he would cross the Waal in such a way

By midnight on D-Day north of the Lower Rhine at Arnhem, the *Hohenstaufen* had formed a rough but complete blocking line around the British First Parachute Brigade, preventing any major move east and, at the same time, cutting off the paratroopers at the north end of the road bridge. In the north, *Kampfgruppe von Allworden*, with three understrength companies and Graebner's self-propelled guns, held a line forward of the Amsterdamscheweg. Adjoining them and facing west was Krafft's SS Training and Replacement Battalion of 300 men. Adjacent to Krafft was the *Kampfgruppe Gropp* with 87 men, ostensibly anti-aircraft troops, though this number had declined to seven by the end of the battle.

Toward the Lower Rhine, *Kampfgruppe Moeller* was dug in after successfully holding off the Third Parachute Battalion the evening before. Spindler's artillerymen covered the rest of the line down to the river. A second blocking line had formed closer to the bridge. This consisted of *Kampfgruppe Harder*, with three companies of infantry. It was likely Harder's troops that Major Lewis' company ran into when they tried to break through to the road bridge. Three Panther tanks from the original *Hohenstaufen Panzer* Regiment 9 were lost on either D-Day or D+1.

To the east of Frost's force on the road bridge were units of *Frundsberg*. At dawn, the Germans estimated that there were about 120 British paratroopers on the bridge, a gross underestimate which may help to account for Graebner's apparent rashness when he advanced over the bridge from the south at about 0900 hours. In place on the east side was the *Frundsberg* reconnaissance battalion, now *Kampfgruppe Brinkmann*. Also in place was the Third Company of the *Frundsberg*

Panzer-Grenadier Regiment 21, fighting in the *Hohenstaufen* sector to the west of the bridge, by the market place and the St. Eusibius Church; that is, close to the bridge ramp.

The *Wehrmacht* Training and Replacement Battalion, *Bocholt,* comprised of convalescents not quite yet fit for action, arrived before dawn; the battalion had been supplied to Bittrich by *Wehrkreis* VI. Its commander, the one-legged Major Hans-Peter Knaust, a first-class soldier, had the task of relieving the last company of Euling's battalion so that it could disengage and take the route to Nijmegen via Pannerden. To the west, von Tettau, with the equivalent of about five battalions of uneven quality, was assembling his troops for his dawn attack, along a line roughly five miles in length. He was ordered by Model to attack the Arnhem landing zones from the west and the north.

Ranged against the Germans were the 1st Airborne Red Devils, so called because of their maroon berets, which were to become the emblem of paratroop forces worldwide. To the west was stationed a battalion of the Border Regiment, guarding the western edge of DZ-X, where First Parachute Brigade had dropped the day before and which was to be the LZ for the glider lift on D+1. One company occupied an isolated position a mile and a half to the southwest of the main position, in the Renkum brickworks overlooking the river.

To the northwest, on Ginkel Heath, were a battalion of the The King's Own Scottish Borderers (KOSB). These troops were to protect DZ-Y, where Fourth Parachute Brigade was to drop in the afternoon. Facing north, the line was thinly held by two companies of the South Staffordshire Regiment (South Staffs) since Dobie's battalion of First Parachute Brigade had moved to reinforce that of Frost at the road bridge. In the center were divisional troops and the Divisional HQ. Facing east were the two battalions of First Parachute Brigade. At the bridge, Frost's battalion held an area stretching about 300 yards each side of the river and about 700 yards to the north, terminating at about the point where the embankment and bridge ramp begin.

By the morning of D+1, the paralysis in command, caused by the disappearance of Roy Urquhart, had become acute. Lt. Colonel Charles Mackenzie, the 1st Airborne Chief of Staff, advised Brigadier Hicks of the Airlanding Brigade early in the morning that, in the absence of both Urquhart and Lathbury, he should take command of the division. Hicks agreed, realizing that the situation was ominous. The perimeter was under pressure from the north and west, while the two battalions of

First Parachute Brigade in the east had made little progress toward Frost at the bridge. Because of the weather, the arrival of the second lift was uncertain and Hicks could spare few troops to push east while protecting the drop and landing zones. Hicks at 1030 hours ordered the two companies of the South Staffs under Lt. Col. Derek McCardie, around 420 men, to proceed to the eastern face of the perimeter where they linked up with Dobie's battalion after dark. To replace them on the northern face of the perimeter, Hicks sent a reconnaissance squadron from the divisional area along with a contingent of glider pilots, the former a mark of how short of infantry he was.

As soon as Hackett landed in the second lift, Mackenzie told him that Hicks was now in command of the 11th Parachute Battalion which was to drive toward the bridge. Hackett was angry at both of these prescriptions and demanded that another battalion be transferred to the command of the Fourth Parachute Brigade. He later got control of the KOSB. Hackett was told to report to Hicks' HQ as soon as practicable. He spent the next few hours trying to extricate 10th Parachute Battalion from the northern reaches of DZ-Y and move 156th Battalion toward Arnhem. The 10th Battalion had virtually destroyed the SS *Wach* Battalion in the combat on the DZ and was replaced by the *Sicherheit* (Security) Regiment Knocke. The 156th began its move at 1700 hours, the same time that Hicks was pulling back the Borderers, hard pressed in von Tettau's attack, east toward Arnhem and a more constricted perimeter. The far positions in Renkum had been lost.

Hackett reached Hicks' HQ shortly after 2300 hours on D+1, complaining of a "grossly untidy situation" and the confirmation of orders which he regarded as vague. That the situation was untidy was undoubtedly true but whether it was of Hicks' making is doubtful. He had certainly issued orders to the battalions of First Parachute Brigade in the absence of a Brigade HQ and attempted coordination. He was receiving reports, despite an almost total lack of radio communication.

There were in fact two issues, not one, in which commentators have generally sided with Hackett. One was the question of command, in which Hackett was enraged that one of his battalions had been taken from him unilaterally by a junior commander, whose grip on the battle seemed to him to be loose and tenuous. But there was another issue, formally quite distinct, and that was tactics. Hackett wanted to "stick to the original plan" of taking his brigade to the northern face of the bridgehead. Hicks tried to persuade Hackett that what was now needed was not a continuation of the original dual purpose plan but a sin-gle-minded thrust east toward the bridge. The British could hold the bridge without a bridgehead but there could be no bridgehead without a bridge. Hackett did not agree and wished to advance north before he moved east, in accordance with the battle plan. Understandably, Hicks did not try to force this on Hackett, but the fact remains that it was Hicks, not Hackett, who had the better grasp of the realities on the ground.

The issue did not end there. When Urquhart finally returned from his expedition to First Parachute Brigade and resumed command at 0725 hours on D+2, he ordered the 11th Parachute Battalion to move north in support of the rest of Fourth Parachute Brigade. Though the message was not received for two hours, Hackett got his battalion back to support the ill-conceived continuation of his northern advance.

During the night of D-Day, the two battalions of First Parachute Brigade were assembling for a second phase of the advance on the northern end of the road bridge. Lieutenant Colonel Fitch of 3rd Battalion conferred with Brigadier Lathbury and General Urquhart, and received clearance to abandon the middle route to the bridge and to make for the southern route taken by Frost the afternoon before.

Starting at 0430 hours as planned, the battalion moved east and by the end of the day, one platoon had fought its way to within a mile or so of the bridge. But Spindler's *Kampfgruppen* made Fitch's progress slow and costly. At 1600 hours, Urquhart and Lathbury left to rejoin the former's HQ and Fitch, no doubt relieved to be left to command his bat-talion as he saw fit, launched another attack. This was soon abandoned in the face of heavy German fire, leaving Fitch with little choice but to terminate the advance for the day. His troops dug in west of the St. Elizabeth Hospital, in the built-up area of Arnhem. The battalion had lost fifteen killed and about fifty wounded during D+1; by the end of the day it was at little more than company strength.

Lieutenant Colonel Dobie of 1st Battalion had decided to take the middle route to the bridge, assuming that 3rd Battalion had already taken the crossing. Dobie too started before dawn and advanced unop-posed until his lead troops ran into the Germans along the rail embank-ment, losing seven killed. He decided to side-step to the south, effec-tively along Frost's original route, but when the battalion moved east from the Oosterbeek Laag underpass, they came under fire from the same troops who had opposed Fitch's battalion an hour or so before.

The German line was already stiffening when Dobie made contact with a company of 3rd Battalion.

In the afternoon, the Germans set up light flak emplacements in some industrial buildings on the south bank of the Lower Rhine, a treat in store for First Parachute Brigade on the following day. Dobie attacked down the river road but was stalled near the bulk of 3rd Battalion at about the same time the latter was halted. The battalion also dug in to the west of St. Elizabeth Hospital, after losing twenty-five dead, reducing it to about the same strength as Fitch's battalion. There was now no chance of First Parachute Brigade advancing to the bridge without reinforcements.

As of D+1 the British made no progress to restore the link to the bridge. Frost for his part had been unable to push over to the south side of the Lower Rhine. On the contrary, he was attacked from that direction and was increasingly hard pressed. Yet it was arguably Frost's stand at the bridge until the afternoon of D+3 that prevented the proper reinforcement of the *Frundsberg* south of the Waal thus enabling the British to establish what became the Nijmegen bridgehead.

The Germans made three attacks against Frost's battalion on D+1, taking a building north of the school from Mackay's positions and other buildings close to the river on the east side, losing one tank and several half-tracks from Brinkmann's *Kampfgruppe*. Heinz Harmel, the commander of *Frundsberg*, had come back from Berlin in the early hours of D+1. He found the armored car company of the *Frundsberg* Reconnaissance Battalion covering the disengagement of the last company of Euling's battalion. Since the prime responsibility of *Frundsberg* was at Nijmegen, Harmel moved his advance HQ to Pannerden, where some of his troops had already crossed the canal.

There followed one of the most famous episodes of the whole operation: SS-Captain Graebner's reconnaissance detachment's reopening of the route north. With a force consisting of five eight-wheeled Puma armored cars, nine half-tracks and eight truck transports (the troops protected by bags and drums of sand), the German column moved out at 0930 hours, 20mm cannon and machine guns blasting away. The British held their fire, some at first thinking Graebner's force was British. The leading armored cars negotiated the debris on the bridge, passing through Frost's positions and into friendly lines. There had seemed to be so little fire that Graebner was perhaps tempted to have his half-tracks and trucks follow up immediately. In any event, he did not wait for a reconnaissance report from his armored cars. As the half-tracks appeared over the arc of the bridge, they were met with a storm of fire from mortars, machine guns, PIATs, small arms and anti-tank guns.

Two, perhaps three, half-tracks were knocked out by Mackay's engineers, according to Stainforth. The convoy of half-tracks was now stopped between the bridge footings and the ramp on the north side of the river, the troopers mowed down as they jumped from their halted vehicles, burning fuel now spreading over the road. Those that could sought refuge in the superstructure at the sides of the ramp. At least two more half-tracks were destroyed.

Then the half-tracks made their second foray. The driver of the first was wounded, reversed into a second and blocked the way of a third. The first two, locked together, swerved to a halt and all three were destroyed. In the pile up of vehicles, some were said to have driven off the ramp, falling onto the street below. The infantry again sought cover, a few jumping into the river in an attempt to save themselves. For nearly two more hours the battle raged, with a great expenditure of ammunition by the British, their 3-inch mortars and machine guns directed against the trucked-in infantry that followed the half-tracks. As the second rush stalled, there arose the battle cry "Whoa, Mohammed!" from the elated paratroopers, a cry, it is said, in imitation of Arabs in Tunisia in 1942. "Thereafter it echoed from house to house whenever a garrison had beaten off the enemy's assault—a cry of victory and grim defiance." According to Mackay, the cry was also used for identification: "It was one which the Germans, with all their cleverness, could not imitate."

Those panzer grenadiers who could crawled back along the side of the bridge to the friendly south bank. Altogether twelve vehicles were lost. Of these, the eight half-tracks depicted on Mackay's diagram tally with the eight recorded in Hibbert's diary. But there was still enough German firepower to cause much grief to the First Parachute Brigade from the south bank on the following day, including the five armored cars that succeeded in moving over the bridge, plus perhaps fifteen vehicles in Elst, the self-propelled guns in Nijmegen and along the Amsterdamscheweg, and the *Hohenstaufen* Reconnaissance Battalion. Graebner was killed in the first foray. His staff car was recovered but his body was never found; his grave at IJsselstein is empty. British stretcher bearers collected the German wounded from the bridge. The dead, estimated at about seventy, were left for two days. As the battle died down, the British intercepted a clear signal from XXX Corps, giving rise to further yet false optimism.

While the battle was raging, the Germans were reinforcing their positions with two infantry howitzers, two *Panzer* IVs and six *Panzer* IIIs, obsolete tanks of the *Panzer Ersatz* Regiment Bielefeld, used for driver training. These were given to Knaust, whose battalion was upgraded to *Kampfgruppe*. In the afternoon, Brinkmann launched a further armored attack which succeeded in driving part of Major Lewis's company and the Brigade HQ defense platoon out of the buildings to the north of the ones lost in the morning.

For most of the night, until the early morning of D+1, the engineers holed up in the Van Limburg Stirium School were under siege. They fought heroically and with a flair for the creative, firing unmanned Bren machine guns by remote control. Soon after dark on D+1, the Germans set fire to the school and the office building to the north of it with a flame thrower. The fires spread to the two wrecked German half-tracks at the foot of the building which the engineers blew up while fighting the fire in the attic of the school. It took three exhausting hours under enemy fire for the engineers to put out the conflagration, using Dutch ARP equipment and their own parachute smocks to beat out the flames.

After this episode, the south wing of the school was badly damaged by a *Panzerfaust* round. At 0300 hours on D+2, the Germans, apparently thinking that resistance had ceased, left their positions. The engineers waited for the right moment, then blazed away, killing at least twenty and leaving a few in the open, horribly wounded. The engineers, most of them completely exhausted, again raised the cry of "Whoa, Mohammed!" By now, four had been killed, twenty-one badly wounded, and most of the others injured in some way. Ammunition was low; food and water virtually non-existent. For the wounded, there were only morphine capsules and field dressings. Benzedrine to keep hungry, debilitated men awake, caused as much aggravation among the men as it did alertness. This was the tenor of battle experienced by Frost's troops: confused fighting and attacks from all sides; rest and sleep almost impossible.

By dusk, after the repulse of Graebner's force and the subsequent attacks, Frost's battalion was in crisis. Nineteen had been killed during the day and a hundred, perhaps a hundred and fifty, wounded. The plight of the wounded was piteous, since no medical units had yet arrived at the bridge. Food, water, ammunition and medical supplies were all in short supply; the paratroopers had to make dangerous forays to recover water and obtain arms and ammunition from the dead of both sides. The whole area of the bridge, particularly on the west side, was in flames, including two churches, St. Eusibius and St. Walburgis. By now, the Germans were using ground attack aircraft in support of their troops at the bridge.

Frost, in Lathbury's absence, took command of First Parachute Brigade on the evening of D+1, leaving his deputy, Major David Wallis, to command his battalion. When Wallis was killed, mistaken by his own men for a German, the command of the battalion passed to Major Digby Tatham-Warter, the commander of A Company.

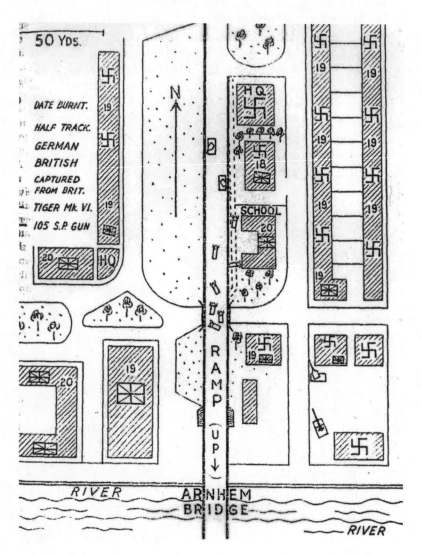

A sketch by Captain Eric Mackay depicting the action northeast
of the Arnhem road bridge.

6

BLACK TUESDAY

On D+2, XII Corps reported "some progress" out of its Lommel bridge-head, though the advance toward Kasterlee and Turnhout was counter-attacked by the formations that had defended Gheel and Aart so fierce-ly in the earlier operations on the Meuse-Escaut Canal. There was no advance north but the British got a message to the 101st Airborne that they could handle the opposition in the Wintelre area and that no patrols from the east were needed. This was an indication that XII Corps could begin the task of protecting the southern end of the Corridor.

At Lille St. Hubert to the east, the VIII Corps crossing of the Meuse-Escaut Canal began at midnight on D+1. Like the crossing point of XII Corps at Lommel, the banks at Lille St. Hubert were heavily wooded. In the darkness, troops of two infantry battalions crossed rapidly with little opposition, aided by a five-ton ferry. Once across, however, the woods on the north side favored the defense; the early reports empha-sized that the bridgehead was a small one. A third battalion was over the canal by morning, followed by the balance of the infantry division. The engineers began constructing a nine-ton bridge over the 160 foot width of the canal, all the while under small arms fire. The bridge was completed by 0830. Later, artillery and mortar fire delayed work on a forty-ton bridge, completed in the evening.

Early in the day, the armored division requested the use of the XXX Corps crossing at Neerpelt since the nine-ton bridge at Lille St. Hubert could not support tanks. By the following morning, VIII Corps units were in Achel, Budel and Hamont while contacting 50th Division in the Corridor and threatening Maarheeze above Weert. The corps was ordered to advance in three directions: the armor north toward Helmond, the infantry toward Weert on the Zuid-Willemsvaart Canal to the east, and the Belgian brigade southeast to the Meuse.

Within the Corridor, the build-up continued. The Americans received more paratroopers, a supply drop and their glider-borne artillery, badly missed at Best. Even so, Taylor did not get all he expected: only 79 of 136 jeeps, 40 of 68 75mm guns, and none of the twelve 105-mm guns allotted to his division. His main concern was the western sector bounded by the Wilhelmina Canal and the Eindhoven-Boxtel road, since the strength of the German opposition posed a threat to Hell's Highway. Accordingly, he organized a forceful offensive, ably supported by British tanks, against the Germans west of Best and the Eindhoven-Boxtel road. This was entirely successful, with a total of 1,100 prisoners and at least 600 enemy killed. At the roar and squealing of the tanks, many of the Germans bolted and were cut down en masse as they fled. The Americans surmised that the German troops were from "march battalions," not the hardened troops of the 59th Division.

The Americans then repulsed a reconnaissance in force directed on the rebuilt Son bridge from the southeast by the 107th *Panzer* Brigade, Taylor himself driving a jeep to the area, towing an anti-tank gun. They established a perimeter with a narrow minefield on both sides of the canal, which was the scene of a violent defensive battle the following day, in which Taylor was again well supported by ten British tanks.

St. Oedenrode was also threatened from the direction of Schijndel. When the battalion of the 502nd PIR came under heavy fire, Lieutenant Colonel Cassidy asked the commander of a disabled British tank to assist. The tank had dropped out of the Irish Guards' advance as it could not move any faster than five miles per hour. Sgt James M. "Paddy" McCrory responded willingly, supplementing his depleted crew with two Americans, one of whom would soon be killed while firing a borrowed Sten machine gun from atop McCory's Sherman. His crew destroyed a battery of three 20mm guns in quick succession, followed by an "88" and an ammunition truck.

This severely dampened the German advance, and Cassidy's battalion was able to move forward several hundred yards, reinforced by a further troop of three tanks from Son. There Cassidy called a halt, in accordance with Taylor's general instructions not to push too far out, for fear of thinning out the defense of Hell's Highway. McCrory's response at the end of the action was "When in doubt, lash out," which was adopted by some as the unofficial motto of 1st Battalion. Cassidy found time to write to Vandaleur the next day, commending McCrory and offering him a place in the battalion.

On D+1, Lt. General Matthew Ridgeway of the U.S. Airborne Corps flew to Antwerp with Brereton to join his troops at Eindhoven. That night they were caught in a German air raid of over a hundred medium bombers. After the devastating raid, Ridgeway became separated from Brereton and in the morning drove north only to be halted by a British tank officer, who told him he could go no further because of heavy small arms fire. He waited forty minutes, then proceeded on foot without being fired on. Ridgeway arrived first at Taylor's command post in Son, then sent for his jeep and met up with Gavin near Grave. According to Gavin, the meeting actually took place on D+3, at Gavin's HQ. Like Brereton commenting on the advance from Valkenswaard, Ridgeway "found the sluggish actions of the ground armies in that campaign inexcusable." Both Brereton and Ridgeway knew from Taylor the plans for the Airborne's contact with the Guards Armoured, which neither party had been able to achieve.

Gavin met with Browning soon after the arrival at Grave of the advance elements of the Guards Armoured at 0830 hours on D+2. Browning's first thought was to use the British tanks to force the Waal crossings. After the second lift had arrived on D+1 by 1430 hours, Browning had asked Gavin to prepare a plan for the capture of the two bridges. Gavin prepared such a plan, using a battalion of the 504th PIR, with the 508th attacking from the flanks. Browning then changed his mind, reaffirming the need to protect the Groesbeek Heights. This was one reason there were no attacks on the Nijmegen bridges on D+1.

The Allied plans for the bridges were restored and developed at the meeting on the morning of D+2. After the repulse of the German attacks on the Groesbeek Heights on D+1, Gavin felt able to move his reserve, a battalion of the 505th PIR, under Lt. Colonel Ben Vandervoort from Groesbeek to the Nijmegen bridges. Gavin had a mind to keep Vandervoort out of the 82nd's operations for fear that his valiant subordinate would not be able to sustain his luck in what the 82nd called "refugees from the law of averages." In return for this battalion, Gavin got as his reserve a Battle Group of the Coldstream Guards, mixed infantry and tanks, the latter welcome in view of the armor still thought to be hidden in the *Reichswald*.

Pressure against the two regiments on the Groesbeek Heights continued with some heavy fighting in the area of Devil's Hill near Berg-en-Dal. By the end of the day, the 508th PIR had secured Beek, Devil's Hill and Wyler along the Kleve-Nijmegen highway. German pressure at these points was reduced owing to Feldt's decision to postpone the offensive until D+3. The lift on D+2, disrupted by the weather, was disappointing. Only 221 of 385 gliders reached the LZ, and the 258 gliders carrying Gavin's Glider Infantry Regiment did not take off at all. A mere 40 of 265 tons of food and ammunition in the subsequent supply drop were recovered.

In the late afternoon, Gavin met again with Browning, Adair, commander of the Guards Armoured, and Horrocks near his new command post in Malden. The meeting took place in a roadside café close to the Grenadiers' Group HQ in the monastery at Marienboom. Gavin was still in great pain from his jump injury. Nearby, the 82nd Airborne's artillery was hammering away at the Germans on the north bank of the Waal. Also present were Norman Gwatkin of the Fifth Guards Brigade, Lt. Colonel Reuben Tucker of the 504th PIR and Colonel George Chatterton, the commander of the Glider Pilot Regiment, who had flown in with Browning's Corps HQ on D-Day. Others present were said to have included Lt. Colonel Edward Goulburn, Major A.H.M. Gregory-Hood and Captain the Duke of Rutland Charles John Robert Manners from the Grenadiers.

At the meeting Browning told Gavin that the Nijmegen bridge must be taken today or tomorrow. When the decision was made to put the Americans across the Waal in boats is not known, but it was likely at a time before dusk when it became clear that the day's assaults on the road and rail bridges had failed. These afternoon attacks on D+2 began at 1530 hours, before the start of the meeting of "the brass." They were in the form of three attacks by the Americans, with British infantry, tanks, artillery and air attacks, one toward the rail bridge, one in the center and one toward the road bridge.

By this time, the Germans were prepared. The *Frundsberg* had amassed a large number of artillery pieces on the north bank, well supplied with ammunition. The records are silent on the progress of the artillery from Arnhem via Pannerden so the number available is not easily estimated. In a famous interview which Harmel gave in 1987, the eighty-four year old said that his artillery commander, SS-Lieutenant Colonel Sonnenstahl had a total of seventy-two guns available, some of which had been commandeered from an abandoned train in Arras during the retreat from Normandy. To this we would have to add the twenty-nine 88mm guns that Allied intelligence estimated for the defense of Nijmegen and more 20mm antiaircraft guns. What is certain is that the artillery was exceptionally well organized, with forward observers on the south side and a pre-arranged fire plan whereby targets could be identified rapidly through named and numbered squares. When radio contact was lost, the observers continued to direct fire by Verey pistol. The dispositions of the SS artillery on the north bank are less certain, but it is likely that they stretched from Lent through the area of a large fort or tower called the Hof van Holland, to Oosterhout in the west.

By the afternoon, too, *Frundsberg* formations on the south side of the Waal were well dug in. There were essentially two defensive positions; the more heavily defended position was adjacent to the road bridge. The approaches to the bridge begin at a traffic circle, the Keizer Lodewijkplein, along what was then the Arnhemseweg, now the General James Gavinweg, the superstructure of the *Waalbrug* beginning about five hundred yards to the north. The Hunner Park stretches both east and west of the Arnhemseweg. Looking north, the more extensive west side of the park is dominated by a lookout point, the Belvedere, and further to the west, by the Valkhof, the ruin of a palace of Charlemagne. The medieval chapel still stands. The rail bridge is visible from the Valkhof, which dominates the road bridge and both of its approaches, north and south.

Euling fortified the edges of the park with a defensive zone on both sides of the Arnhemseweg, siting his own HQ in the huis Janssen, a hundred yards or so to the northwest on a street jutting into the park and set up an observation post in the Belvedere. In the Valkhof, on the summit were stationed Baumgaertel's engineer company and an artillery observation post under SS-Captain Krueger.

SS troops continued to arrive throughout D+2, as well as troops from an *Ersatz* (Replacement) Regiment. After the Allied attack on D+2, Gavin's G-2 Intelligence estimated that there were 500 first class SS troops defending the road bridge alone, an exaggeration which is a tribute to Euling's defenses. It was also estimated that there was an 88mm gun at the traffic circle, five lighter guns in Hunner Park, and mortars and other artillery north of the Waal. Some of the guns there could fire straight at the bridge; others were stationed in Lent, directed by Krueger at the Valkhof. Euling's four *Jadgpanzer* IVs were sited around the southern end of Hunner Park.

The defenses of the rail bridge, a mile or so from the *Waalbrug*, were less strong, with no SS troops known to have supported Henke's *Kampfgruppe*. The Allies approached the rail bridge from the southwest at the Keizer Karelplein traffic circle. After two blocks, there is an oval-shaped park, the Kronenburger, on the east side of the approach road, the Kronenburgsingel. The Germans had an unknown number of 88mm anti-tank guns guarding the approaches to the rail bridge and at least one 20mm cannon. Since the Allies were stopped in their tracks, it is likely that the artillery north of the Waal was the most decisive factor on D+2.

In the assault on the road bridge, Euling's *Kampfgruppe* defended its positions with valor and professional skill, hitting the Allies with crossfire in the maze of streets around the Hunner Park and luring the tanks into positions subjected to clear fields of fire. Even when Vandervoort took personal command, leading from the front, the attack died down in the face of German counterattacks and a truce in which the Germans collected their wounded. Euling's perimeter had shrunk from 500 to 300 yards from the water's edge, at the southern end of Hunner Park, but his positions had survived the attack. The Germans also held the river line in the central sector and at the rail bridge. By the evening of D+2, the whole waterfront on the south bank of the Waal was ablaze from the fires of hundreds of houses which the Germans had torched to help illuminate the attackers.

At Arnhem in the late morning of D+2, Knaust attacked A Company positions from the east with three tanks from the Bielefeld Training Regiment, causing the loss of positions at the northeast of the ramp; these were regained with the loss of one of the German tanks to a PIAT. Thereafter the Germans changed tactics, using their tanks as artillery to support the infantry, instead of risking themselves to British anti-tank fire.

More German fire support arrived in the evening with the first two of fifteen Tiger tanks from Heavy *Panzer* Brigade 506 in support of Brinkmann's *Kampfgruppe*. They moved down past Mackay's positions in the school, pasting it with fire as they went, then turned their 88mm guns onto the buildings on the east side, forcing the evacuation of a line already compressed during the day. As the rest of the Tigers arrived they were assigned to *Kampfgruppe Knaust*. Yet the night of D+2 passed, Frost wrote, "fairly peacefully."

What befell the remainder of the two parachute brigades at Arnhem was nothing short of disaster. The first reinforcements to arrive for the renewed onslaught on the bridge were the South Staffs. The battalion made contact with First Parachute Battalion at 1700 hours on D+1, having covered six miles in seven hours, coming under fire on the middle route before shifting south to the Oosterbeek Laag underpass. The 11th Parachute Battalion deployed around midnight, having been delayed for two hours at Hicks' HQ en route. Dobie assumed command of this force and briefed Lt. Colonel McCardie of the South Staffs and Lt. Colonel George Lea of 11th Battalion about an attack at 0400 hours on D+2. Dobie did not know that Fitch with his depleted 3rd Battalion was preparing to attack, also along the lower route to the bridge, at the same time. Fitch moved off first. The British were also unaware that the Germans had moved back before dawn to a good defensive position on high ground.

The terrain did not favor an offensive for the First Parachute Brigade. The frontage was barely four hundred yards from the east-west railway in the north to the river in the south. The ground rose gently to the east. Astride the railway with its cutting and sidings were placed Gropp's SS anti-aircraft group, with Moeller's group south of the railway facing west. By now, Spindler's *Sperrverband* (blocking line) had been reinforced by a further *Kampfgruppe* from SS Panzergrenadier Regiments Nineteen and Twenty, overlooking the axes of advance. Harder's group still manned a second line behind Spindler's first *Sperrverband*. South of the river, surrounding a brickworks and other industrial buildings, were the mobile troops of Graebner's reconnaissance battalion, armed with 20mm and 37mm cannon mounted on half-tracks and more armored cars. All told, the brigade had six combat groups, most of not more than company strength, supported by self-propelled guns, mortars and light flak, the last mainly from positions south of the river.

Running along the river, split off from the Utrechtseweg by the St. Elizabeth Hospital, was another road, the Onderlangs. The brigade aimed to advance along both axes. On the southern route, 3rd Battalion, operating independently of Dobie's command, advanced east in the darkness and ran into Spindler's blocking line and retreated. In doing so, it made contact with Dobie's battalion. Fitch, with little more than fifty men left, also joined Dobie's advance along the Onderlangs.

The first onslaught by the two battalions was so ferocious that

Moeller's veterans thought the day was lost. But at first light, the British battalions came under heavy fire from three sides. Dobie's battalion was soon down from 140 men to 39, most of whom were wounded. The battalion was surrounded, with a barrage of fire from the north, self-propelled guns supporting Spindler in the center, and the guns of the *Hohenstaufen* reconnaissance battalion across the river. They surrendered soon after 0730 hours. For 3rd Battalion, on the flank of the First, the outcome was nearly as bad. They were forced back in the direction of the Rhine Pavilion and their leader, Lieutenant Colonel Fitch, was killed by a mortar round.

The *Wehrmacht Sturmgeschutz* Brigade 280, with about ten assault guns, were arriving from the north and assembling near the railway station around the Utrechtseweg, the route of the northern prong of the brigade's advance. The South Staffs advanced along this route with the 11th Parachute Battalion behind and in support. They moved past St. Elizabeth Hospital, brightly illuminated, beyond the Museum, until stopped by heavy fire from the assault gun brigade.

The fighting was as ferocious as that on the southern route and, again, Moeller thought that his position was in danger of dissolution. But the South Staffs were overwhelmed by the sheer volume of fire, including Gropp's group in the north, firing over the rail yards from the upper floors of buildings. The South Staffs held their own until they ran out of PIAT ammunition. The Germans then counterattacked with assault guns backed by infantry and most of the British troops were taken prisoner, including McCardie. Even among the carnage, each side ceased firing to allow the other to attend to the wounded. Major Robert McCain took command of a company of about forty men that had been held back, together with the survivors of the advance, and attempted to regroup around midday.

The 11th Parachute Battalion was forming up to support the South Staffs when the order not to proceed was given. At some time before 1100 hours, the battalion next got an order to occupy high ground at the Heijenoord Diependal, to the northwest, in support of Fourth Parachute Brigade, north of the east-west railway. Lieutenant Colonel Lea ordered McCain of the South Staffs to occupy Den Brink, a shallow rise on his left flank.

The Germans, however, saw the 11th forming up at around 1430 hours and hit them hard with mortar fire, mauling the battalion so badly that, in Roy Urquhart's telling, it "disintegrated" and now numbered barely 150 men. McCain too was driven off Den Brink, one of several engagements for which he was awarded the Victoria Cross, the only one in the operation that was not awarded posthumously. The ragged groups of survivors retreated to Oosterbeek; those that remained were captured or killed when the Germans, with their self-propelled guns, cleared the area surrounding St. Elizabeth's Hospital.

The eastern side of 1st Airborne's perimeter began to form before the retreat of the brigade when on the morning of D+2, some panic-stricken stragglers retreated through the artillery park. The bulk of the survivors, about 400 men and some anti-tank guns were later organized as Lonsdale Force, under the second-in-command of 11th Parachute Battalion, Major Dickie Lonsdale. Of the remainder of the brigade, 120 had been killed and as many as 1,700 taken prisoner or sheltered by the Dutch. McCardie, Dobie and Lea had all been taken prisoner, and Fitch was dead, leaving the remnants without their battalion commanders. Like Eberwein against the Tenth Parachute Battalion in the northwest, Spindler lost an opportunity to move into Oosterbeek, and two assault guns were lost to a British anti-tank gun when they tried to infiltrate into the lightly defended area south of the Utrechtseweg.

If the 11th Battalion could not save the day for the First Parachute Brigade, it is equally true that the order to move northwest caused its destruction. The aim of the order was to support Fourth Parachute Brigade either as a pivot when it moved east or as a flank guard when it moved north, but the maneuver was dubious. Since German troops were occupying the area to the north of the railway in strength all the way west to the Dreijenseweg, it is unlikely that the battalion could have done more than form a bridgehead over the east-west railway, with Fourth Parachute Brigade still a mile away to the west.

While First Parachute Brigade was being destroyed, something similar befell the Fourth. The 156th Parachute Battalion had spent the night in the woods north of the Ede-Arnhem railway, having run into the outposts of Spindler's defense line along the Dreijenseweg. It was this line that the battalion was to attack at dawn on D+2. The Tenth Parachute Battalion was to protect the left flank of the 156th from positions along the Ede-Arnhem Road (Amsterdamseweg), a few hundred yards east of the Dreijenseweg.

By this time, Spindler's forces were formidable. In addition to Sepp Krafft's newly formed *Kampfgruppe, Kampfgruppe Bruhn (Wehrmacht)* was arriving by truck from *Wehrkreis VI*, with an eventual strength of eight infantry companies, some *Luftwaffe*, commanded by the one-legged Hans Bruhn. Numerous flak guns had also arrived behind the Dreijenseweg, in time to blunt the attacks of 156th Parachute Battalion. By the end of D+2, all that remained of the 156th was Major Geoffrey Powell's C Company and some supporting troops.

Major John Pott of A Company, did manage to cross the Dreijenseweg with six men but the position could not be held. Wounded, Pott was left until rescued the next night by two brave civilians. Tenth Battalion was not assigned any part in 156th's attack but, prompted perhaps by the flow of wounded, Lt. Colonel Smyth moved the Tenth toward the east at 1000 hours, then was obliged to retreat back to the rail crossings in the early afternoon. Another company under Captain Lionel Queripel crossed the Dreijenseweg before retiring. Queripel, badly wounded, covered the retreat back to the rail crossings, earning him a posthumous Victoria Cross, one of five awarded in Operation *Market*.

Tenth Battalion's attack stalled at the same time as that of the 156th. Urquhart arrived at Hackett's HQ in the early afternoon, harassed by strafing fire from three German fighter planes. Hackett wanted to withdraw his brigade south of the railway embankment, re-cross it further east, and join up with his 11th Battalion, supposedly advancing on the Heijenoord Diependal rise. Urquhart concurred, though the agreement does not seem to have been firm. He also ordered Hicks' Airlanding Brigade to take the Oosterbeek Hoog station to enable Hackett to pass his troops and transport under the rail embankment. This was no easy thing to do in view of the shortage of troops. The only way that Hackett's guns and vehicles could cross under the rail embankment was at Wolfheze station farther west, now abandoned by the British and threatened by Eberwein's *Kampfgruppe*. Eberwein took a hundred prisoners south of the embankment on the afternoon of D+2 and the bag would have been even greater had von Tettau appreciated the disorder of the British retreat.

In Urquhart's own version, he was sceptical about Fourth Parachute Brigade's northern advance from the time he arrived back at his HQ on the morning of D+2, although this is difficult to square with his order to 11th Battalion to strike north instead of east. He discussed a plan with Hackett to withdraw over the railway in order to take the old middle route into Arnhem but told him not to move until he, Urquhart, had ascertained the whole divisional picture. He then set off back to his HQ.

Half an hour later, Hackett heard that the battalion of the Border Regiment was under pressure at the southern end of the western perimeter. He feared that if the Wolfheze crossing was denied him, his vehicles and guns would be caught north of the embankment and his troops all forced to move over it on foot. So he ordered the Tenth Battalion to disengage immediately and reoccupy the abandoned Wolfheze underpass and prepare for the withdrawal of the entire brigade. It was then that they clashed with the Polish glider landing in the area of the retreat. In the confusion, the Poles and British fired on each other until order was restored.

The Poles lost more men as prisoners than they did to the British friendly fire. They also lost most of their jeeps, supplies and three of their eight anti-tank guns. Sosabowski's jeep from his HQ contingent was captured, along with a suitcase bearing his name. Based on this evidence, the Germans announced that he was dead when he was of course still in England.

During the retreat, some of the battalion vehicles became bogged down in a culvert close to Wolfheze, blocking the tunnel. Urquhart ordered all of Fourth Parachute Brigade to withdraw and take a more southerly route into Arnhem. The hastiness of the retreat under fire struck some who took part as perilous and unprofessional. The Tenth Battalion emerged south of the railway with about 250 men, roughly half its normal strength, and the 156th was not much better off. Their ordeal on D+2 was not yet over.

The loss of the better part of two brigades in a single day was not uncommon for the Germans on the Russian Front, but for the British it was an appalling loss—a "Black Tuesday" only two weeks after "Mad Tuesday" had seen a disorganized German rabble in chaotic retreat. Much comment about the performance of 1st Airborne on D+3 has concerned the numbers of troops involved on each side, with the observation that, overall, the division was not outnumbered. While this is true, more significant is the fact that the paratroopers were never intended to attack such a well entrenched opponent with a profusion of mortars and cannon, supported by self-propelled guns. When attacking in the dark, they were often successful, causing the Germans so much consternation that they failed to realize just how disadvantaged the Red Devils were. But with the *Hohenstaufen* veterans having formed a strong defense line, it was very unlikely that the British could have achieved any further objectives beyond those reached in the first few hours of the operation.

Despite the valiant efforts of all concerned, from Urquhart on down, there was, with hindsight, little chance of relieving Frost at the bridge. When the British were forced into the defensive at the bridge and in static positions around the Oosterbeek perimeter, they fought sturdily in the great tradition of the British infantry: the thin red line.

7

SUCCESS CLASHES WITH FAILURE

Gavin's idea of an assault crossing of the Waal was provided for in the planning of *Garden*, except that it was to be the responsibility of the British 43rd Division, not the American 82nd Airborne. But on the morning of D+3, the 43rd was still at Hechtel, behind the ground forces' start line. The assault boats for the Waal crossing were almost certainly attached to the Guards Armoured from the engineers' pool at Bourg St. Leopold. Horrocks' staff decided they could provide about twenty-eight folded canvas boats and thought they could have them ready by daylight on D+3.

When Gavin returned to his command post from his meeting with the British, he thought he could be ready by 0800 hours and that the 504th PIR would have the south bank of the Waal cleared of Germans by that time. He would have preferred to wait for a night assault but thought that the British in Arnhem would need relief immediately. Gavin planned to launch the boats from a concealed position in the Maas-Waal Canal out onto the Waal. Before the assault over the river and the move east into Nijmegen, Vandervoort's battalion, with the Grenadier Guards, would resume the advance over the Nijmegen bridges.

Then two things went wrong. The boats did not arrive, to Gavin's disgust. Further, it took Lt. Colonel Tucker until midday to clear the Germans from the south bank of the river. During the morning the crossing was twice postponed. Gavin himself was not present at the crossing of the Waal. He received a radio message that Beek and Mook had been overrun in what was Feldt's D+3 attack and made the difficult decision to leave Tucker's regiment to cross the Waal while he restored the defenses at Mook to remove the threat to the Maas-Waal Canal crossing at Molenhoek.

Feldt's plan was to capture Mook, then the Moelenhoek bridge, after which his men would join up with the troops moving from Beek, then move up the Maas-Waal Canal to Nijmegen. The German attack began at 1100 hours with a barrage from 88mm shells and rockets. Though buttressed by ten 75mm howitzers, the thinly-spread 505th PIR was forced back, and by mid-afternoon the Germans were on the edge of Mook.

Gavin arrived just in time to witness the second of two British tanks hit and disabled by German fire, and immediately had his driver send word back to his reserve, the Coldstream Guards detachment, to move straight away to Mook. Meanwhile Gavin, along with a lieutenant and a sergeant, held off the Germans until the tanks arrived, even capturing a German paratrooper.

Unbeknownst to Gavin, Major Long of the Guards had already put two platoons of infantry on the road, to be joined in the afternoon by six tanks. Still, Gavin credited his own troops with driving the Germans back before the British tanks arrived. In other accounts, the action was largely British and indeed Mook was retaken at the cost of twenty British killed who are buried at Mook. When the Germans withdrew, the threat to the Moelenhoek Bridge was removed.

After the regimental commander had assured Gavin that the position was secure, he moved to Berg-en-Dal, learning at the same time that Tucker's troops had started to cross the Waal. In the Groesbeek-Wyler-Beek area, Feld had two battle groups, which along with the group in the south were scheduled to attack at 0630 hours but, as has been seen, the Mook offensive did not actually begin until 1100 hours. The Americans, having had a relatively quiet time in these sectors on D+2, were not expecting a three-pronged attack in such strength.

Major Greschick's group advanced about a kilometer but ran into the Americans outside Groesbeek. Hand-to-hand fighting ensued; the Germans at 1600 hours reported a little progress but no actual further advance was made for the rest of the day. Major Becker's group drove two platoons out of Wyler but the Americans held the high ground and, with fire support from the Coldstream Guards' tanks, the Germans could proceed no further.

Becker then attacked Beek and had a parachute battalion in the village by the early evening. Two platoons of the 508th PIR retreated up the hill, at the summit of which stood the Berg-en-Dal hotel. The fighting was bitter with the Germans gaining the upper hand with their mobile 20mm cannon. When Gavin arrived, crawling over the summit of the hill to avoid enemy fire, he found the troops weary and shaken but in good spirits. With the assistance of the Coldstream Guards' tanks, they had succeeded in knocking out a half-track, which blocked further German progress up the hill. Lieutenant Colonel Mendez' tactics were typical of the American airborne forces, shifting platoons back and forth according to local threats while at the same time giving an impression of greater strength than the state of his troops warranted.

Of course Mendez could not do this indefinitely, and Gavin hoped that the Germans would do as they usually did: cease the attacks at nightfall. Gavin was still without his glider infantry regiment and could not promise more infantry, only artillery support. At dawn on D+4, the 508th recaptured Beek and, in a move that has not been generally acknowledged, reached the bank of the Waal at Erlekom by D+6. The 82nd now had a front extending from the Maas to the Waal, with no open flanks. Gavin said later that if Becker's group had sidestepped a shade to the right, they could have walked to the edge of Nijmegen almost unopposed. Quite so, but German tactics were to move first to Mook and Moelenhoek, which mirrored the initial priorities of the 82nd Airborne itself.

Scherbening reported to Feldt in Kleve that Wyler and Riethorst near Mook had been taken but heavy fighting was still going on at Mook and Groesbeek. But by then it was clear that the attacks of the three *Kampfgruppen* had failed and the news coming in from Nijmegen was so discomforting that Feldt took over personal command of the sector, at what time is not recorded.

At the waterfront on the Waal, the Allies had assembled a formidable force of a hundred British guns, two squadrons of tanks, some of the 82nd's divisional artillery, the 504th PIR's mortars and all the smoke that the attacking force could lay its hands on. On the other side, the Germans had troops at the water's edge and a defense line along a dyke road somewhat less than half a mile beyond flat fields. Their firepower came from two sources: 20mm guns and machine guns positioned near the rail bridge and in the tower known as the Hof van Holland and the guns of SS-Lt. Colonel Sonnenstahl's regiment in the sector from the rail bridge, through the Hof van Holland area to Oosterhout. These guns were, however, fully engaged in supporting Euling and Henke across the river and the most that could be spared was a battery under SS-Captain Schwappacher. The 250 rounds allocated to Battery 19 were enough to cause heavy casualties among the 504th troops crossing the river. When the Americans landed on the north shore, Schwappacher pressed into the infantry all the artillery men he could spare to defend the dyke road, while other formations at platoon strength were summoned from as far away as Valburg, six kilometers to the northwest.

On the American side, H-Hour, scheduled for 1330 hours, had to be postponed because the assault boats had not arrived, first to 1400, then to 1500 hours. The boats finally arrived at around 1430 hours, close to the time that the artillery barrage was about to begin. The Americans did not quite know what to expect but they could hardly have been reassured. Twenty-six boats were disgorged from three Bedford trucks which had been so far behind the advance that they had been caught up in the air raid on Eindhoven. The boats were nineteen feet in length, of plywood construction with collapsible canvas sides, and a draught of thirty inches. Some had fewer than the eight paddles per boat. They carried thirteen men plus equipment and were crewed by three engineers to allow them to return to the south shore.

The boats were overloaded on the first crossing. Few of the troops had ever used a paddle before and even fewer had any training on assault boats at all. They had to cross a river about three hundred yards wide, with a strong current of eight to ten miles per hour. According to plan, the first across would be 3rd Battalion commanded by Major Julian Cook, then 1st Battalion under Lt. Colonel William Harrison, who had taken the Molenhoek bridge on D-Day. After that, the assault force would split into two, a larger force aiming for Oosterhout and another east toward the two bridges, bypassing the Hof van Holland.

The softening of German defenses began with an air attack by eight Typhoons at 1430 hours followed by tank, mortar and artillery fire beginning fifteen minutes later. The artillery first began with high explosive (HE) shells, then white phosphorus for smoke, then back to HE. The smoke was not highly effective, at first shielding some of the paratroopers from the German gunners, only to be soon dispersed by a changeable wind. For the some 260 men attempting to cross the river there was no time to familiarize themselves with the assault craft, nor an opportunity to launch from concealed positions. Those without a paddle used their rifle butts. Even the launching was difficult, some having to haul their boats across in shallow water to launch further out.

Crossing was invariably erratic, some boats zigzagging, others turning around and around before they hit the shore. As they crossed, the Germans opened up with artillery and machine gun fire. Only half the boats reached the north shore and those who observed the crossing were both moved and astonished by the sight of the brave crews going back through the fire to pick up more passengers. "I never saw such a gallant action," commented Browning. Major Brian Urquhart, who had doubted whether XXX Corps would ever reach Nijmegen, could not have imagined that the untrained Americans could reach the north bank of the Waal in an assault crossing under fire.

Cook's men killed about fifty Germans near the water's edge, then they ran across the open fields to the dyke road, enraged at the slaughter of their comrades on the river. Though the German artillery and machine gun fire continued, the defenders of the dyke road kept their heads down and were overwhelmed by the fury of the American assault. Many of the Germans, some of them young teenagers, others old men, tried to surrender but were bayoneted or gunned down without hesitation at short range.

The eleven boats that returned from the first run made a total of six trips across the river. Two rafts were employed to carry the regiment's anti-tank guns across. The rafts were courtesy of Lt. Colonel C.P. Jones, the Guards' chief engineer, an energetic and popular officer who had supervised the rebuilding of the bridge at Son. A platoon of the 3rd Battalion took the Hof van Holland off the march, silencing its guns. The Third's Sergeant Leroy Richmond swam the moat and beckoned his platoon across the causeway to capture the fort. The battalion had companies at the rail and road bridges before being reinforced by 1st Battalion.

Meanwhile, British preparations for the assaults south of the Waal had begun at 0830 hours. The plan was to attack toward the road bridge from the west via the heights as well as from the southern end of Hunner Park. It took five hours to secure the western start line, including the police station and a convent north of it, which overlooked the river bank. Other Grenadier companies, including one earmarked for the road bridge, were to attack from the south, with the Americans on the extreme right between the park and the access canals to the east of the bridge.

The assault on the road and rail bridges by Vandervoort's battalion and the Guards began at 1620 hours. At the rail bridge, the Americans who had crossed the Waal were held up at the north end by a large number of machine guns and anti-aircraft artillery. At the advance from the southern end, however, the defenses suddenly cracked and the Germans came streaming north over the bridge. A total of 267 were killed by the assault troops on the north bank and many more were captured. Captain Karl W. Kappel of Company H radioed Cook, urging him to get tanks across and capture the highway bridge. Colonel Tucker arrived on the scene and ordered his troops on to the other bridge. The Grenadiers and Americans finally took the southern end of the rail bridge at 0900 hours on D+4.

In its water-borne assault, the 3rd Battalion, 504th PIR, had suffered twenty-eight killed, one missing and sevety-eight wounded, a far greater number than either 1st Battalion or Vandervoort's from the 505th. Gavin wrote that the action of the regiment was "brilliant and spectacular" in the most dramatic day of all for the division.

South of the road bridge, the Grenadiers climbed up an embankment in a surprise attack on Valkhof from the western side. Two platoons of the King's Company got through the barbed wire before the Germans knew what had hit them. Bitter hand-to-hand fighting ensued in which the company commander, the Hon. V.P. Gibbs was killed. From the German accounts, SS-Captain Krueger's artillery post was overwhelmed at about 2030 hours, much later than the other strongpoints on the heights. Though an attempt was made by the British to move to the bridge, they were obliged to halt because of friendly fire coming from the south and from the Americans to the southeast. The fighting in the area was again very heavy, a platoon of eleven men taking the Belevedere along with thirty prisoners. The Second (Armoured) Battalion was now in a position to go for the bridge, with covering fire from two points on the heights and others close to the western start line.

Euling's troops, defending the southern approaches, at first put up a strong resistance, but facing the combined might of Goulburn's tanks and Vandervoort's paratroopers, the Germans broke and retreated, some up to the Valkhof, some to the southern end of the bridge, yet others further east along the river. The four *Jagdpanzer* were lost in the park. The first attack on the bridge through Hunner Park by a troop of four tanks at about 1830 was stalled by anti-tank fire and one tank was lost. Then the troop led by Sergeant Peter Robinson, advanced again at 1900 hours. The episode was watched, with bated breath, by Horrocks, who expected the bridge to be blown at any moment.

Before they reached the bridge, Robinson's tank was damaged by artillery fire and its radio knocked out. He ordered Sergeant Billingham behind him to switch tanks. By this time, Sergeant Pacey in the third tank assumed the lead across the bridge; the Grenadiers' history states that two of the four tanks were hit by anti-tank fire. The tanks engaged a sandbagged "88" at the north end and what was thought to be a *Jagdpanzer* in the distance. Vandervoort witnessed the engagement, which he described as "pretty spectacular." One tank exchanged four rounds with the German gun, all the time spitting tracer fire at the German troops above them positioned in the bridge's superstructure. Then Robinson's gunner, Guardsman Leslie Johnson, knocked out the 88 while still not yet halfway across the bridge. The four tanks then ground across the bridge, firing their machine guns at the Germans on the bridge girders.

At the north end, Pacey moved off the road to protect the three tanks advancing behind him. Robinson recalled that the smoke and the noise were terrible; he tried to direct the driver and the gunner while on the radio to HQ. As they neared the north end, Robinson yelled orders to his gunner, who destroyed a second 88 and a *Jagdpanzer,* then turned his machine gun on the Germans who were evacuating their positions. His record equalled that of Paddy McCrory's gunner with the 101st Airborne.

In the slaughter, Robinson felt the tank bump over the bodies on the road—or so it seemed, since human corpses offer little resistance to thirty-two tons of tank. Robinson caught sight of some figures in a ditch by the side of the bridge approaches, who turned out to be Americans. They greeted the British with great warmth, as well they might. Behind the tanks came Lieutenant Tony Jones and a party of engineers, who removed demolition charges and cut all the wires they could find, taking prisoners, said to be seventy in number, along the way. The rest of the tank squadron, led by Captain Lord Carrington, followed and established a defensive perimeter with the Americans.

Then, to the disquiet of several of the Guardsmen, the British halted.

As at Valkenswaard exactly three days before, no patrols or reconnaissance units were sent ahead, nor were any orders received to move forward. One reason given for the halt was that the Guards were preoccupied with establishing and extending the Nijmegen bridgehead while fighting was still taking place on the south bank of the Waal. At dusk, an hour after crossing the road bridge, two companies of infantry from the Irish Guards crossed the bridge, along with two troops of engineers, four seventeen-pounder anti-tank guns and more Sherman tanks.

At least three tanks from the initial assault had proceeded further, commanded by Sgts. Robinson, Pacey and Knight. The crew of the third of these baled out upon being hit but Knight returned to the tank to find it in working order and picked up a volunteer crew of American paratroopers. Robinson's tank destroyed an assault gun en route to Lent where, in the dark, they pushed forward to be halted by two German anti-tank guns. The two leading tanks then withdrew behind the railway line which intersected the road just north of Lent. In the Grenadier Guards' History, a total of four tanks spent the night in isolation at the rail crossing, described as a bridge, and it was there that they linked up with the American paratroopers.

Beyond the actions of Robinson's tank troop, the failure of the British to make an advance of any sort during the night of D+3 stands in need of explanation. The answer has much to do with the attitude and outlook of the British leadership, Horrocks in particular. The 43rd Division, with its five thousand vehicles, did not begin to move from the Hechtel area, south of the Neerpelt bridgehead, until 0900 hours on D+3 and the attached Eighth Armoured Brigade, not until 1600 hours. The 130th Brigade arrived at the Grave bridge at 2300 hours when Brigadier Ben Walton decided to halt for the night. The Welsh Guards Group was at this time defending the Grave bridge, a task later delegated to a single company of Polish paratroopers. No one urged these units on or to be prepared to move forward from the Nijmegen bridgehead at first light. The excuse that the rule was "night movement only" is hardly valid, since there was an exception in the orders for tactical necessity.

During all of D+3, the forces striking north to 1st Airborne still believed that the Arnhem road bridge was held. This accounts for the American urgency in getting to Arnhem. Gavin had wanted the relief forces to cross the Waal during the night of D+2, while Tucker was so appalled by the British sluggishness on the morning of D+4 that he contemplated striking north with his regiment without orders. Only his duty to Gavin deterred him. That 1st Airborne in Oosterbeek was in deep trouble became clear during D+3.

Second Army radioed 1st Airborne at midnight that the Guards Armoured would go all out for the Arnhem bridges at dawn. The

Guards intercepted the message and interjected that the enemy was still strong north of the Waal and not to expect an advance before 1200 hours on D+4. Adair's claim that he waited till dawn to check out the terrain north of Nijmegen and that its unsuitability for tanks delayed the advance is not borne out by the historical record. At 0300 hours on D+4, Brigadier Walton was ordered to protect the Grave and Neerbosch (Honinghutie) bridges, which he did with two companies, and to advance to help the Guards clear Nijmegen.

By early afternoon, the Fifth Dorsets were on the north bank of the Waal. Major General Thomas told Brigadier Hubert Essame of the 214th Brigade that the plight of 1st Airborne was "vague but desperate." He was told to advance around the Guards west flank "in the direction of Arnhem." Accordingly, he routed his brigade over the Nijmegen rail bridge on the west side. The Welsh Guards Group moved in time to take part in the Irish Guards' advance along the main axis Nijmegen-Elst-Arnhem. Essame got the order to take Oosterhout "with only two hours of daylight left." In addition, the Seventh Somersets were delayed, having mistakenly taken the route over the road bridge while some elements of the brigade were still south of the Waal. The 4th/7th Dragoon Guards tanks from Eighth Armoured Brigade were, however, north of the Waal on the afternoon of D+4.

According to the *History of the 43rd Wessex Division*, no attack on Oosterhout was possible until dawn of D+5. Surprisingly, 130th Brigade was not ordered to reinforce the Guards on the Nijmegen-Elst-Arnhem road. The Dutch brigade took over responsibility for the Grave Bridge and the 130th stayed in Nijmegen, ostensibly to secure the city and clear out any remaining German troops. It was then to be relieved by the Sixty-ninth Brigade of 50th Division that was following the 129th brigade of 43rd Division. This brigade was ordered to advance on the right (east), up the main axis north of Nijmegen, but since it was the last brigade in the 43rd's column, it was strung back to Eindhoven and did not even arrive at Grave until dawn on D+6.

Horrocks was at great pains to argue that, far from attacking on the late afternoon of D+4, Essame did well to assemble his brigade overnight to advance at dawn on D+5. He did not mention that 214th Brigade had been ordered to take Oosterhout at 1630 hours on D+4. The reason for this order was that the Guards' advance, which allegedly began at midday on D+4 but actually at 1330 hours, was halted by strong opposition two miles from the start line and Horrocks needed an alternative route north. Horrocks' motive, no doubt influenced by his co-author, Essame, was to defend the 43rd from charges that it was slow and "sticky."

These charges, first made by author Chester Wilmot, were indeed baseless; but both critics and apologists miss the point. As with the Guards Armoured, the trouble was not that they were slow once they had started but that they were painfully slow in getting off the mark. The units concerned, at whatever level, may not have been directly responsible for the late start; but somewhere up the chain of command either no orders were given or the orders were given too late—or there was no sense of urgency conveyed to the leaders on the spot.

When Gavin met with his regimental commander on the north side of the road bridge at dawn on D+4, he found Reuben Tucker absolutely enraged. His regiment had fought hard and performed heroically to relieve 1st Airborne only to find the British doing little more than drinking tea. Tucker was told that the Guards could not advance until the infantry had come up. Gavin blamed Browning for the failure to advance, but the ground operation was not his responsibility. The Americans considered that if Ridgeway had been in charge of the paratroopers and Patton the ground troops, there would have been no hesitation in moving north. Just as deplorable was the fact that nothing was done to prepare for an advance at first light. At least six more hours of daylight elapsed before the Guards moved forward, even then without their armored cars to lead the advance. It would not be exaggerating much to say that the paratroopers counted in hours while the ground troops counted in days. The leading troops of 43rd Division did not arrive on the north bank of the Waal until after the Guards had resumed their advance, even though the 130th Brigade had arrived at Grave early on the night before.

The "lost opportunity" school, however, can sometimes get it wrong. Between 1900 hours and midnight on D+3, there was, Robert Kershaw says, at most "a few security pickets" to block the approach from Nijmegen to the southern approaches of the Arnhem road bridge. The British might possibly have been able to push an armored battle group into Arnhem. But the balance of Graebner's reconnaissance battalion at Elst and on the south bank of the Lower Rhine were stronger than what Kershaw makes out. Further, tanks and vehicles had been passing freely over the Arnhem bridge since the afternoon. "All fighting had ceased in the area of the bridge," the official accounts contend.

It is one thing to argue the sluggishness of the Guards, which is correct considering that the Guards believed the Arnhem road bridge was still held. It is another thing altogether to argue that an armored group could have advanced into Arnhem, since the state of the Germans north of Nijmegen was not known and the Arnhem road bridge had in fact been lost. How far Sgts. Robinson, Pacey and Knight could have pushed on toward Arnhem if they had not been stopped north of Lent is a matter of speculation. Harmel's idea that "four Panzers" could have swung the battle north of Nijmegen is not convincing. Even a whole squadron of tanks could not have held the Arnhem bridge without infantry support. The fault of the Guards was that, apart from Robinson's troop, no attempts were made to move north between the evening of D+3 and the early afternoon of D+4.

South of the road bridge, resistance continued into the evening of D+3, after the Guards had established their position on the north bank. Euling rallied the last of his *Kampfgruppe* at his command post, still in the Robert Janssen house. His men disabled a tank outside the house, the last of the nine that the British lost in the day's action. This attracted enemy fire, and by 2230 the house was in flames. With the British now well established on the north bank of the Waal and along the approaches to the bridge, there was no alternative but to retreat.

Not realizing that there might be survivors, the British allowed Euling's sixty men to retreat around the Valkhof and along the river bank. In the night, they passed through the Guards' infantry who had been stood down, sometimes by stealth, sometimes braving enemy fire, over the access canals on the south bank of the Waal. The group crossed the Waal in small boats much further up the river in the vicinity of Haalderen. For his lustrous exploits, as great as those of Frost at Arnhem, Euling was awarded the Knight's Cross and survived the war. His engineer commander, SS-Lieutenant Baumgaertel, who was also decorated, was killed at Stettin early in 1945.

When the attack on the bridges began, Harmel moved rapidly from Pannerden to Lent, where he observed the first British tanks crossing the road bridge. He attempted to blow the bridge after the first few tanks had crossed but this was abortive. Since Lieutenant Jones had removed the demolition charges only after Sergeant Robinson's troop had crossed, the wires must have already been destroyed either by artillery fire or by the Dutch Resistance. Some of the Dutch claimed that the wires for the demolition charges were destroyed on D+1 by a twenty-two year old student, Jan van Hoof, who worked in intelligence for the Resistance. Van Hoof was killed on D+2 while escorting the British to the rail bridge to destroy the demolition charges. Exactly what van Hoof achieved is uncertain; that he was a hero of the Dutch Resistance, there is no doubt.

The fact that Harmel was defying Model's orders is of no consequence since Model was not one to insist on the letter of his law and he had in any case complete confidence in Harmel. Orders to hold or destroy the Nijmegen bridge were received the next day. By then, Harmel had moved back to Bemmel, the new HQ of *Kampfgruppe Reinholt*. His worst fears had come true. Despite his initial order not to destroy the Nijmegen bridge, he never believed in holding a line south of the Waal and would have preferred to destroy the bridges and establish a strong defense line on the north bank. For XXX Corps, the German failure to destroy the Nijmegen bridge was a stroke of good fortune.

From Bemmel, Harmel organized the defense of the Island, to prevent the British from reaching the Lower Rhine. His main resources came from the Pannerden Canal crossing. Some units were already on the west bank of the canal when they were called upon to move, not to Nijmegen, but to a defense line centring on Elst. While the Guards dallied, Harmel had, by the afternoon of D+4, established a rough defense line stretching from Oosterhout, through a line south of Elst and Bemmel, and so back down to the Waal around Reithorst. In Oosterhout were SS-Lieutenant Schwappacher's artillery battery and the *Frundsberg* artillery HQ.

As units arrived from Pannerden, they were placed in line. The most powerful was the squadron of sixteen *Panzer* IV tanks, attached to SS *Panzer* Grenadier Regiment 21, with the strength of a reinforced battalion. A weak battalion of reservists organized as *Kampfgruppe Hartung* also moved from Pannerden. Artillery reinforcements were stationed at Flieren, east of Bemmel and anti-aircraft guns at Pannerden could also be called down from Reinhold's HQ at Bemmel. Over the Arnhem bridge came the *Kampfgruppe Knaust*, which had eight tanks under command, a mixture of *Panzer* IIIs and IVs and assault guns. Since four tanks, said to be Tigers, were destroyed by the British on the route from Oosterhout to Driel, it is likely that these were under Knaust's command. By 1600 hours, Knaust's *Kampfgruppe* was in Elst and had established contact with the forces in Oosterhout. Hartung's reservists were stationed between Elst and Bemmel where the *Panzer* IVs were concentrated and the line, held by SS *Panzer* Grenadier Regiment 21, continued down to the Waal.

The 82nd Airborne had every reason to be proud of its achievement, but the men were rather embittered by the fact that the press played down their role or ignored them altogether. This they put down to the British military authorities wishing to present Arnhem as a victory of British arms. Subsequently, most British books passed lightly over the Americans' achievements; it is the great merit of Ryan's *A Bridge Too Far* that it rescued the 82nd at Nijmegen from oblivion. The performance of the Guards in the battles for the Nijmegen crossings has also not received the recognition it deserves, again because British historians have focussed nearly all of their attention on 1st Airborne at Arnhem. Author William F. Buckingham's claim that the Guards fought poorly is not the same as the contention that they were slow off the mark and it cannot be substantiated.

Two allegations of atrocity were made against the 82nd Airborne, including the killing of the artillery coordinator, SS-Captain Kreuger, at the Valkhof. Both are highly dubious, mainly because there were very few (if any) American troops located where the atrocities were to have taken place.

In contrast to Nijmegen, the situation at Arnhem on D+3 worsened to the point of failure. The German attacks on Frost's battalion at the bridge began again in the morning, this time with the goal of destroying the bridge. Twice the British, led by Lt. Jack Grayburn, had to scour the columns of the bridge ramp for detonators and charges planted by German sappers, which earned Grayburn a posthumous VC. Urquhart spoke to Freddie Gough of the Reconnaissance Squadron on the civilian phone around 0800 hours, telling him he could expect no relief from 1st Airborne, only from XXX Corps. In the early afternoon, Frost was wounded in both legs and Major Gough took command of the defense forces at the bridge.

Two German tanks, said to be a Tiger and a Porsche Ferdinand tank destroyer, both armed with 88mm guns, blasted Mackay's engineer positions in the school at 1500 hours. There were now fourteen men on their feet and twenty five badly wounded. Of the fourteen, eight were then hit. In Mackay's account, the last cry of "Whoa M'hammed" at 1400 hours was met by silence from the other positions at the bridge.

After an abortive breakout in which one man was killed, Mackay himself led five men in the second attempt, when they surprised a party of about fifty German infantry accompanying two *Panzer* III tanks. The engineers opened up, each with a magazine from their Bren guns, and killed many at the cost to themselves of one killed and one wounded.

Mackay then continued with the breakout, only to be captured and taken to a camp at Emmerich. From there he escaped with Lt. Dennis Simpson ("Stiffy") from First Parachute Squadron and two corporals. By then, Mackay was wounded in three places, a serious septic wound to the foot, a slight head wound and a bayonet wound in the pelvis, incurred when he was captured. He had been without sleep for ninety hours. The party went down the Rhine in a commandeered boat and arrived at Nijmegen early on D+5. In Stainforth's version, the escape party of four consisted of Paul Mason, Tony Miles and two NCOs. According to Stainforth, it was Mason, not Mackay, who received the bayonet wound "in his seat."

German infantry assaults, along with artillery and tank fire continued all day. In the afternoon of D+3, the radio link in Major Hibbert's Brigade HQ was destroyed, with the result that nothing further was known about the defense of the bridge; the relieving troops from XXX Corps could only assume that the north end of the bridge was still held. In the evening, a truce was arranged to evacuate the British, German and civilian wounded, around 280 altogether, including Frost. The Germans used the truce to reconnoitre the British positions and advance their own, but by then organized resistance had ceased. Small parties of the defenders attempted to break out. Almost all were captured. Members of the Dutch Resistance and some of the many Dutch civilians who had sheltered the British wounded were shot out of hand. Traffic started to flow over the bridge in both directions, opening the direct route for the defense of Nijmegen.

After the truce had ended, there were two groups left. The first of these was centerd around the Brigade HQ and consisted of about 120 men. These attempted to break out toward the Oosterbeek perimeter in parties of ten; it is likely that all were captured, including Major Tony Hibbert. The 2nd Battalion party, led by Tatham-Warter, decided to hold out, but were either killed or captured that night. Tatham-Warter had led many of the engagements at the bridge with courage, skill and eccentric good humour. Thirty-seven of the eighty-one who died at the bridge were killed in the final day of fighting. Of the 188 Dutch civilians who died in the Battle of Arnhem-Oosterbeek, an unknown number were killed in the fighting around the bridge.

Though there was still shooting on D+4, the battle really ended when the bridge became passable on the afternoon of D+3 and Knaust's armored *Kampfgruppe* prepared to move south to Nijmegen. Some of the Germans who received the captured paratroopers were impressed not only by the fight they had put up but by the proud and defiant bearing of their prisoners, almost all of whom were exhausted, bloody, filthy and wounded in some way. As the prisoners were assembled for the move north, they were congratulated and applauded by the *Waffen-SS*.

The tentative plan for Fourth Parachute Brigade to switch from its northern offensive to the reinforcement of Frost at the bridge came to nothing in the retreat on D+2. Hackett and the remainder of his brigade spent that night just south of Wolfheze, the beating they had taken not yet over. By morning, the troopers were wet, cold, tired, very thirsty and hungry, as well as low on ammunition. For many, this predicament was to last for the next week. Hackett had wanted to withdraw to the divisional positions during the night but was persuaded to collect his forces, including some still north of the rail line, and move at dawn.

They moved off at dawn on D+3, but by then, the enemy were between their positions and Oosterbeek. After a charge with fixed bayonets, between sixty and seventy men of 10th Battalion reached the divisional perimeter. Among them was the wounded Lieutenant Colonel Smyth. Hackett's HQ and the 156th Battalion were pinned down and, led by the brigadier, charged their way out of a besieged hollow at 1630 hours. The group reached the positions of the Borders where, in Powell's account, a young captain, seeing the "gang of haggard, filthy ragamuffins" advised they be "removed" before, it was said, they destroyed the morale of the Borders.

Hackett reported to Urquhart with about seventy men, barely fifty of them from 156th Battalion, at 1850 hours, minus Lt. Col. Sir Richard Des Voeux. The badly wounded commander of the battalion, revered by his fellow officers, ordered his troops to continue the withdrawal and was killed shortly afterward.

Elsewhere on D+3, the day went well. Attacks on the Screaming Eagles at the Son perimeter, which extended both north and south of the Wilhelmina Canal on the eastern side, were all fought off with the aid of British tanks from the 15/19 Hussars. The only airborne mission of the day was the drop of Battery B of Taylor's parachute artillery battalion. All this time, Major von Maltzahn of the 107th *Panzer* Brigade at Son was out of contact with Poppe's infantry in Best. In any case, LXXXVIII Corps was not at this time in any position to offer significant help from the west. The 107th's tank workshops had already left for the Eastern Front before the brigade was diverted west, so disabled tanks could not be serviced, far less recovered. This was the reason that Maltzahn broke off his attacks on D+3, convinced that only a coordinated offensive could break the Americans.

At the very time when, by Taylor's admission, the Screaming Eagles were feeling the absence of VIII and XII Corps most acutely, they won a spectacular victory, comparable to the engagement in the Sonsche Forest the day before. The 501st PIR in Veghel advanced along the north side of the Zuid-Willemsvaart Canal, inflicting 500 casualties on the Germans, and established a bridgehead south over the canal in the area of Dinther-Heeswijk. This was to form one arm of a pincer movement against the Germans the following day.

Yet XII Corps on Taylor's left flank was also making unexpected progress. After hard fighting, Ritchie's forces had reached a line just below Rethie-Postel-Bladel-Wintelre. In doing so, they made more progress on the flank of XXX Corps than had been planned for the main Turnhout-Tilburg/'s-Hertogenbosch axis. As a result of his continuing commitments further west at Herenthals, Dempsey was concerned that the forces in the Eindhoven area were getting "very stretched." Yet he was so optimistic that he observed on D+3 that he would probably pass the 101st Airborne from XXX to XII Corps "shortly," just as he had passed 50th Division in the Corridor to VIII Corps.

For VIII Corps progress was quite slow. The tanks passed through the infantry at Hamont-Achtel and at Budel clashed violently with the SS *Kampfgruppe Richter* which was withdrawing from the Corridor toward Weert. The armor pushed on to occupy Leende by darkness. Patrols moved further north toward Heeze. Meanwhile, the Belgian brigade, deployed south of VIII Corps' starting-point, were assembling at Bree, Muizenduik and Elikom. The aim was to cross the Zuid-Willemsvaart Canal to their east and head for the Meuse. All the while, VIII Corps was reporting German patrols moving south across the canals. At the same time, Belgian civilians welcomed the liberators. The lone soldier killed at Hamont was given a full civilian funeral with a profusion of flowers and several hundred mourners at his grave.

The Predicament of 1st Airborne Division on D+3

When the withdrawals of the First and Fourth Parachute Brigades took place on D+2 and D+3, Urquhart's first concern was to prevent the destruction of his entire division. This led to the fortification of the divisional area, forming a Rhine bridgehead, not in Arnhem but near the original landing zones. Bittrich, for his part, moved from the containment of 1st Airborne Division to its elimination, and took von Tettau's division under command. However, his prime concern was still to prevent the relief of the British north of the Rhine. He had moved his advance HQ to that of Harmel, three miles west of Pannerden, on the Island. In support of Harmel at Nijmegen, he gave orders in the evening of D+3 for *Kampfgruppe Knaust* to move south, at about the same time as Harmel moved his command post back from Lent to Elst.

In the west at Oosterbeek, the British line, almost a mile and a half long, was held by the battalion of the Border Regiment, still largely intact. They were reinforced by parachute engineers and glider pilots on the northern sector of the west-facing line. On the short northern face, with a frontage of about a third of a mile, the KOSB with about 270 men arrived late on D+3, reinforced by the Independent Parachute Company, the pathfinders, and by more engineers.

The northern part of the eastern face of the perimeter, along the Stationsweg, was held by the Reconnaissance Squadron, then further south by the 156th Parachute Battalion and, down to the junction with the Utrechtseweg, by two squadrons of glider pilots. Major Geoffrey Powell, now leading the sixty survivors of the 156th Battalion, took over command of the Reconnaissance Squadron, which was severely depleted after an ill-advised patrol toward the Amsterdamseweg the day before.

Seven jeeps with thirty men from C Troop ran into German positions; only seven men and two vehicles returned, reducing the squadron essentially to dismounted infantry. South of the Utrechtseweg, the 10th Parachute Battalion was linked by a squadron of glider pilots to Lonsdale Force. The 11th Battalion was pulled into reserve. The Polish glider troops were scattered with their five anti-tank guns, some reinforcing the glider pilots in the east, others the Borders in the west.

All told, there were perhaps 3,600 men in the perimeter, about a third of the division prior to the operation. Of these, 1,200 were glider or parachute infantry with over 900 glider pilots and roughly 1,500 from the support services and administrative staff. The given figure of

2,500 Dutch civilians inside the perimeter sounds inflated; in any event, they suffered as much as the British troops.

Attacks around the perimeter were beaten off with lost positions reoccupied or recaptured. In the South Staffs sector, Lance-Sergeant John Baskeyfield, leading a crew of a six-pounder, destroyed at least three German armored vehicles. Severely wounded and with all of his gun crew killed or disabled, he manned another six-pounder unaided until he was killed, earning a posthumous Victoria Cross.

Communications

Up to D+3, communications from and within First Airborne had been virtually non-existent. Urquhart's divisional signals comprised the *Phantom* radio net (GHQ Signal Liaison Regiment Detachment), the *Jedburgh* radio net of the Dutch Resistance, and radio links for artillery and air support (U.S. Air Support Signals Teams). Urquhart made no contact with the Airborne Corps Main HQ until early on D+3, either through divisional signals or *Phantom*. On D+4, Urquhart raised the Sixty-fourth Medium Regiment, RA, using the powerful HP19 sets, which also provided a relay to XXX Corps. *Jedburgh* did not arrive intact and the air link never did function, which was the main cause of the failure of fighter-bomber support.

Division HQ established contact with Frost at the bridge through the artillery link on D+1. Within the division, communications were otherwise as poor as the links to other headquarters. The 1st and 3rd Battalions made contact with Frost at the bridge on the night of D-Day but throughout the operations of the First Parachute Brigade, D-Day to D+2, there was otherwise no radio contact between the battalions. The result was that the two battalions heading for the bridge were unaware of each other's presence, leading to attacks in sectors where a previous advance had been frustrated. Nor was there radio contact with the divisional HQ. Radio communications between the division and Fourth Parachute Brigade, as well as between the battalions advancing on the road bridge, were also poor to non-existent. Within the battalions, the SCR-56 walkie-talkies in Fourth Parachute Brigade worked intermittently in the daytime but not at night; in First Parachute Brigade, they seemed not to have worked at all.

The breakdown in communications between divisional HQ and the bridge on D+3, meant that neither Urquhart nor Horrocks knew whether or not the north end of the bridge was still held. Poor communications were not, however, the decisive factor in the failure of the two parachute brigades to reach the Arnhem bridge or bridgehead; the real reason was that the Germans were too well-armed and too well entrenched. However, the failure of the supply run on D+2 can, it is true, be put down essentially to Urquhart's inability to contact the War Office in London as well as other HQ on *Phantom* and through divisional signals.

A salient feature of D+3 was a great improvement in communications. Contact with the Arnhem bridge on an alternative frequency, the B wave, using the type 76 radio sets, was established at 1000 hours. Before that the artillery link was used. However, communication between division and 2nd Battalion broke down almost completely soon afterward. Frost did get a message to XXX Corps at about 1000 hours on D+2, stating his position and receiving a reply that the Nijmegen bridge would be attacked at 1200, with no time of relief estimated.

There were several poor contacts between 1st Airborne and Corps Advance, Main and Rear HQ prior to D+3, though none resulted in significant information being exchanged. The first definite contact from 1st Division with Airborne Corps Signals was at 0300 hours on D+3, when Urquhart advised Browning's HQ of the change in DZ for the Polish paratroopers and of a new drop zone for the day's supply run. Both messages got through to the airfields in England.

The Poles' drop was again cancelled owing to the weather while the supply planes were directed on to a zone two hundred yards west of Urquhart's HQ at the Hartenstein Hotel. At a final supply tally of 135 tons recovered out of 386 tons dropped, the run was more successful than in the past, even though thirty-three of the 164 Stirlings dropped their supplies on the old LZ-Z, two miles outside the perimeter. The total delivered would have been higher but for the smoke obscuring the DZ and the likelihood that the Germans had laid down decoy identification smoke and panels.

The Driel-Heveadorp Ferry

From 0800 hours on D+3, Urquhart was able to send via radio a series of situation reports to Airborne Corps HQ. One message was received by Browning at 0950 hours, stating that 1st Airborne required "immediate relief." Again, Urquhart signalled at 1505 saying that the situation was serious for First Parachute Brigade at the bridge, that he was forming a perimeter, and that "relief essential both areas earliest possible." He also reported that the ferry crossing was held. By the evening, it was known by all commands that Frost's paratroopers were isolated at the bridge and could not be resupplied. It was also known that the resupply zones for the division were almost entirely in enemy hands, that the fighting was intense, and that the predicament of 1st Airborne was not good.

At 0900 hours on D+4, Horrocks got a message from Urquhart's HQ via the Sixty-fourth Medium Artillery Regiment that the north end of the road bridge was still being held, and reiterated that the Driel-Heaveadorp ferry was in British hands. Neither was correct. The previous message on D+3 had said that it was a Class 24 ferry capable of carrying six tanks per load, a great exaggeration. At 2045 on D+3, Airborne Corps Rear HQ in England sent a message to Exfor Main, Eisenhower's HQ, stating that the British retained control of the ferry. For this reason, Sosabowski's brigade prepared to aim for the ferry crossing rather than attempt to fight their way along the south bank of the river to the road bridge.

In the small hours of D+4, Lt. Leo Heaps, with two companions, was sent to take supplies to the bridge, the second such task for the Canadian. Heaps decided to try the ferry crossing. The late Leo Heaps left two accounts of his experience. In his second, *The Grey Goose of Arnhem* (1978) he said that he found the abandoned ferry on the north bank, its cable winch gear disabled and thus inoperable and reported this to Colonel Mackenzie. This report to Mackenzie is not mentioned in Heaps' first account, *Escape from Arnhem* (1945).

In the 1st Airborne War Diary, the failure of Heaps' supply mission was recorded at 0340 hours on D+4 but the loss of the ferry is not mentioned. However, in his first book, on the night of D+6, Heaps claimed the ferry was sunk, having seen the prow of the boat protruding from the water. He was not the only party to have mistaken the piles of the destroyed landing for a sunken boat. In fact, the ferryman, Pieter Hensen, had cast it adrift and it ended up on the north bank, downriver and beyond the landing points of the relief forces. According to Cornelius Ryan's sources, a patrol went down to the ferry site and found it abandoned, with no sign of the ferry for several hundred yards along the river. Perhaps this occurred after Heaps' expedition. Either way, Urquhart knew by morning that there was no ferry.

In a *Phantom* message sent at 0515 hours on D+4, Urquhart reported that troops north of the ferry had been withdrawn, an understatement of what his patrols had reported during the night. This message was, however, not logged until 1415, the time that the Poles took off from their bases in England. In his memoirs, Urquhart strongly implies that he knew the ferry had been lost before about 1715 hours on D+4, the time of the Polish parachute drop. Inexplicably, Urquhart did not report the loss of the ferry on D+4 but later, in two *Phantom* messages at 0830 and at 0931 on D+5. The Poles had known of the loss of the ferry on the evening before. At 1900 hours on D+5, Airborne Corps Rear reported the ferry's loss to Eisenhower's HQ and the British War Office. This news had come from Urquhart and via both Sosabowski and Colonel Mackenzie on the radio of the troop of the Household Cavalry in Driel, on the south bank of the Lower Rhine.

Among those who had been informed of the plight of First Airborne was Maj. Gen. Edmund Hakewill Smith, the commander of the 52nd (Air-Portable) Division. Due to fly in on D+5 at Deelen, he was unable to do so because there had been no advance from the Arnhem bridgehead and so, of course, the American engineer battalion was not able to prepare a landing strip for the gliders and troop carriers. Nor had the Polish paratroopers landed as planned, and whether Hakewill Smith was aware of the change in their DZ is not known. His staff prepared a plan to land a small brigade group on the south bank of the Lower Rhine, to assist 1st Airborne "if required." Just where is not clear since the Poles had been diverted west and away from the southern approaches to the road bridge. Browning replied: "Thanks for your message but offer not, repeat, not required as situation better than you think. We want lifts as planned including Poles. Second Army definitely require your party and intend to fly you in to Deelen airfield as soon as situation allows."

The reference to the Poles may be due to the fact that their 1st Battalion had still not arrived. Quite apart from the implied optimism about the prospects of the XXX Corps advance from Nijmegen, the message reveals something alas typical of the planning of the operation—utter rigidity, a failure to consider alternatives, and a reluctance to consider changing the plan as circumstances developed or when things went wrong. But Browning may not have been entirely to blame. The reference in his message to Second Army suggests that he had raised the matter at the Army level, as was proper.

A message from Second Army to the Airborne Corps late on D+8 directed that no elements of 52nd Division were to be flown in for the time being; when this message was confirmed at 21AG, the latter HQ stipulated that no movement of the 52nd was to take place without the permission of the Army Group. Perhaps by then, Montgomery was afraid of reinforcing defeat. Since Second Army's message also included notice of an airfield being prepared for emergency supplies and for RAF Eighty-three Group, it is possible that a fly-in of the 52nd had been contemplated for the Nijmegen airfields or possibly the grass airfield at Grave.

8

POLONIA RESTITUTA

The terrain north and west of Nijmegen was not suitable for an armored advance. North to Elst, stretches of the road were on top of a dyke, with deep ditches at the sides. Anti-tank guns concealed in woods adjacent to the road would make Adair's armor a sitting target. If the road were blocked, it was sometimes possible to move along the embankments, partly for concealment and partly to bypass the obstacle. Along these stretches, maneuvering was impossible, something well known to the Dutch military establishment. Such conditions pertained also among some stretches of the western route to the Rhine through Oosterhout, though here the main problem was small and muddy roads, again with ditches at the sides, from which stuck vehicles could not be easily extricated. The heavier the vehicle, such as the DUKW amphibians, the worse the going, something which afflicted the Germans' heavy tanks as much as it did the British. Added to this, the weather worsened from D+4 on, making the going even tougher.

As armored vehicles crossed south over the Arnhem road bridge on the afternoon of D+3, the continuing German priority was to block the northward progress of the British ground forces. When the Poles landed on the south bank of the Rhine around 1700 hours on D+4, Harzer feared that they would head for the Arnhem road bridge. The Germans took the Polish parachute drop so seriously that Harzer was made responsible for opposing the Poles south of the Rhine as well as 1st Airborne north of it.

For SS-Colonel Lippert on the western face of 1st Airborne's perimeter, the concern was that the Poles would reinforce the British by crossing the Rhine on the Driel-Heaveadorp ferry, which he had not yet captured (but unknown to him had already been destroyed). There was a grand mix of false expectations: Lippert had correctly divined the purpose of the Poles' mission, but neither he nor Sosabowski before the drop was aware that the ferry was gone. Harzer anticipated a Polish advance along the south bank of the Rhine to the road bridge, but this was never Sosabowski's intention, even after he ascertained that the ferry was lost.

Harzer was ordered to set up a *Sperrverband,* or blocking line, running from Elst up to the Rhine. In addition to the troops at his disposal, *Kampfgruppen Knaust* and *Brinkmann* were in Elst, under the command of *Frundsberg.* Bittrich detached Brinkmann and put his *Kampfgruppe* under the command of *Hohenstaufen* (Harzer) to lead an attack on the Poles. Harzer then got a regimental HQ from Model and the blocking line became *Sperrverband Gerhard,* with its HQ at Elden. Knaust was given responsibility for the sector from Ressen in an arc southwest to Oosterhout and the Rhine. The Germans then had a line to hold XXX Corps advancing north and northwest and a blocking line to prevent the Poles from moving toward the Arnhem road bridge.

For Horrocks on the morning of D+4, the aim was still the Rhine at the Arnhem road bridge, the north end of which, as far as he knew, was still held by 1st Airborne. This was true both of the direct route north through Elst and of the flanking move through Oosterhout, where the troops were ordered to move "in the direction of Arnhem." A move west toward Driel from Elst was only to take place if the route north were blocked; apparently, Horrocks, like Harzer, thought that the Poles were still to aim for the southern end of the road bridge rather than to cross by the Driel-Heveadorp ferry. Even the next day, when the 5th Battalion, the Duke of Cornwall's Light Infantry (Fifth DCLI) arrived in Driel, the first thought of its commander, Lt. Colonel George Taylor, was to head east to the road bridge rather than attempt to cross the river in boats. Only on the morning of D+6 did Urquhart learn from the *Phantom* net that 43rd Division would cross the Rhine west of Arnhem and not adjacent to the city as previously intended.

The Irish Guards advance north from Nijmegen began at 1330 hours on D+4, along the elevated road, but they lacked effective artillery support and the VHF communications with the cabrank of Typhoons failed. By mid-afternoon, both the main attack at Ressen and a flanking move just east came to nothing. An attack by the Welsh Guards Group along the Oosterhout dyke road was, by darkness, similarly stalled.

The Polish paratroop lift finally took place on D+4. According to the German sources, the paratroop drop was preceded by RAF Spitfire attacks on positions and gun emplacements west of Driel and at Flieren. The 114 C-47 aircraft carried 1,568 paratroopers. Owing to a radio message interpreted as a recall and perhaps also because of the weather, forty-one aircraft returned either to their bases or to the nearest airfield they could find. Sosabowski's force was now severely depleted with 1st Battalion almost entirely absent. When aircraft carrying what was left of the Polish Brigade arrived over the DZ they encountered heavy flak, the German gunners having been alerted by a listening post at Dunkirk. They were also set upon by twenty-five Messerschmitt fighters. Altogether, 1,003 men landed at about 1700 hours, of which fewer than 200 were from 3rd Battalion, which was also without its commander, Captain W. Sobocinski. Of Sosabowski's units, only 2nd Battalion under Major W. Ploszewski was nearly intact.

The area of the Poles' new drop zone was not the *polder* of the previous DZ. The terrain was one of fields and orchards and the heavy clay of the area supported a brick-making industry. The orchards were not just in outlying fields but extended into the center of the villages and small towns, as in the case of Driel itself. The estate of the prominent Balthussen family, who were to play a vital part in the battles ahead, was located on the southern outskirts of Driel. These roads too were generally poor, narrow and muddy. Toward the river's edge, at the north of Driel, the town was protected by two dykes, behind which the Poles could take cover. But beyond the dykes, to the river's edge, there was an open area of *polder* and tidal land, a thoroughly exposed position which made crossings in both directions extremely hazardous. The quagmire along the river's front made the launching and landing of boats difficult and that of amphibious vehicles impossible. No troops, Polish, British or Canadian, stayed on the bank any longer than was necessary.

On landing, Sosabowski's two battalions made straight for the river, one through the eastern edge of the town, directly toward the ferry crossing. En route, Cora Balthussen, a Red Cross nurse, approached Sosabowski. She told him that the ferry had been destroyed and that the site was covered by machine gun and artillery fire. From that point on, Cora Balthussen became a pillar of strength for the Poles, even holding a council of war with them at the family farmhouse. She informed them that German guns were positioned on both sides of Urquhart's perimeter, subjecting the river to a lethal crossfire. A patrol confirmed what

Cora had said and Sosabowski set up a command post among the orchards in the center of the town and began work on a new plan.

Soon after, "a near-naked man" staggered in. Captain L. Zwolanski, Sosabowski's liaison officer to Urquhart had swum the Lower Rhine. Zwolanski told the general that the ferry had been lost on the night of D+3 and that Urquhart would provide rafts to get the Poles across. A British engineer, Lt. David Storrs, then arrived in a dinghy and confirmed Zwolanski's messages. The engineer returned to the north bank with Zwolanski and Lt. Colonel R. Stevens, Sosabowski's liaison officer, who presented Urquhart with Thursday's copy of the London *Times*. He then swam back. Zwolanski carried a message from Sosabowski that his troops would cross the same night with Sosabowski, "Stary," in the lead.

The British engineers prepared makeshift rafts that night, made out of jeep trailers minus the wheels, but they sank like stones. This was just as well. Sosabowski observed that the Germans subjected the river and the south bank to covering fire all night. His two battalions were withdrawn to Driel before dawn.

When the Poles arrived, Cora Balthussen organized a first aid station for the wounded in an empty school that had a number of beds in it. She had three Red Cross volunteers to help. She then remained at the hospital, day and night, until D+8, caring for the wounded, whose stoicism and whose stories of tragic lives amazed her. She related to George Cholewczynski, "I have never been under the impression of such courage. You did not hear one sound of screaming and crying. These were people from hundreds of miles away waiting for a doctor to operate or amputate. A people so very earthy, so honest and with a sincerity that has always impressed us."

After four sleepless nights, covered in the blood of the wounded as well as her own, having been hit by shrapnel in the head, shoulder and thigh, Cora cycled home under shellfire and fell asleep on the floor of her home, which was crowded with refugees. When she returned to Driel the next day, most of the British and Poles had gone.

For the Germans, events further down did not deter them from planning to sever the Corridor from both sides. There, the day caused less consternation than the failure of an early attempt to attack the Nijmegen bridgehead, which was impractical, and the subsequent landing of the Poles. In the area of the 82nd, Gavin withdrew Tucker's regiment to the south of the Waal, where his positions were still under threat from the forces of *Wehrkreis VI*.

Yet further down the Corridor, General Taylor was in radio contact with VIII and XII Corps and took heart at the prospect of the two corps taking over responsibility for the southern end of Hell's Highway. With XII Corps troops exerting pressure on the Germans, he felt the position of the 101st Airborne secure enough to move the bulk of the 506th PIR north out of Eindhoven. Taylor planned to push one battalion north to occupy Uden at the limit of his operational area, beginning the next day. He also planned an offensive to trap the Germans northwest of St. Oedenrode in a pincer movement, one arm of which was the 502nd PIR in the south, along with the Hussars' armor and Paddy McCrory's tank. The other arm was from the 501st PIR in the Dinther-Heeswijk bridgehead over the Aa River that it had acquired to the north in the successful operation the previous day.

Both arms of the offensive were packed with drama. The Germans retreated across the Zuid-Willemsvaart Canal and lifted the drawbridge. An American squad rowed across to the south bank, dropped the bridge and were joined by the balance of the platoon from the north bank. In such episodes, the Americans routinely took several hundred prisoners. On the southern arm, Paddy McCrory again came to the rescue, destroying an 88mm gun, machine gun position and an armored car, before bagging a young pig with his pistol. "Tonight we eat," he said. An anti-tank gun and shortage of ammunition forced McCrory to withdraw. He was recommended for the Silver Star.

On Taylor's left flank, the progress of XII Corps was slow and hard. Corps troops reached the Wilhelmina Canal at Oirschot, closer to XXX Corps than had been planned, and were over the waterway by the evening. But German resistance was strong; other patrols over the canal had to be withdrawn and the enemy resisted for two more days south of the canal at Middelbeers. There a famous incident took place. During the heavy fighting an SS trooper came forward under a white flag and asked for a doctor to assist in a difficult childbirth at the house they were defending. "All fighting ceased and recommenced when the child was born." Elsewhere south of the canal, the troops took Wintelre, Westelbeers and Bladel.

That same day, Dempsey met with O'Connor at his HQ, now near Helmond. He recorded that VIII Corps was holding an extended front with three divisions, the third being the 50th in the Corridor. The infantry were ordered on to the Zuid-Willemsvaard Canal at Weert, which they approached in the evening, to the sound of the Germans blowing the canal bridges. The armor was to establish itself in the area of Helmond-Asten-Deurne-Bakel and to cut the roads between Helmond and the XXX Corps axis. The operations began at first light the next day.

The Crossing Point of XII Corps over the Meuse-Escaut Canal
at Lommel on the afternoon of D-Day. The crossing was
virtually unopposed.

The Crossing Point of VIII Corps over the Meuse-Escaut Canal at
Lille St. Hubert, late in the night of D+1. The wooded banks of the canal
made it easy for the attackers to form up but, once across, they met resistance from defenders concealed by the woods on the south bank (right).

The Dommel River bridge in St. Oedenrode, looking south,
captured by the 101st Airborne on D-Day.

The bridge over the Wilhelmina Canal at Best.
The firefight by Lt. Wierzbowski's valiant band took place downstream
on the left bank, before the bridge was destroyed by the Germans, then
later replaced by British engineers.

US paratroopers of the 82nd Airborne Division unload a wrecked glider after landing some way to the south of Arnhem. (Imperial War Museum).

The monument to Pfc. Joe Mann, Congressional Medal of Honor, near the Wilhelmina Canal bridge.

The Maas-Waal Canal, looking south from the Malden bridge with the Heumen bridge in the far distance. The bridges at Malden and Hatert were destroyed by the Germans on D-Day before troops from the 82nd Airborne approached.

The Pannerden-Doorenberg Ferry, looking from the east side toward the Island. The first troops from the 10th SS Panzer Division crossed the Pannerden Canal on the night of D-Day, bound for Nijmegen.

A Lloyd carrier of the anti-tank platoon of 3rd Battalion, Irish Guards, explodes during XXX Corps' advance up the Eindhoven road at the start of Operation Market Garden. (Imperial War Museum)

The grave of Major-General Friedrich Kussin at IJsselstein. Kussin, the Town Commandant of Arnhem, was killed by troops of 1st Parachute Brigade at Oosterbeek on D-Day.

The Polenplein monument to the Polish Paratroopers in Driel, on the south bank of the Lower Rhine.

Driel Church. The plaque at the left was installed by the 5th Battalion, DCLI Old Comrades, commemorating their dash to Driel for the relief of the 1st Airborne.

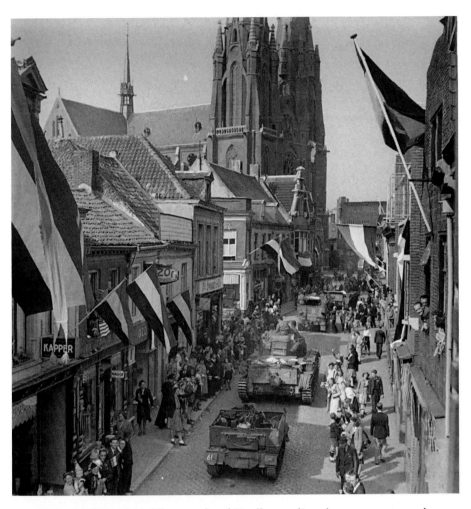

18 September 1944: The people of Eindhoven line the streets to watch armored vehicles of British XXX Corps pass through. The 101st (US) Airborne Division had captured the town on the previous day. (Imperial War Museum)

The house on Stationsweg in Ede where Brigadier Hackett, as an evader, was briefly sheltered by Theodoor Boeree and his family. A retired artillery colonel and member of the Resistance, Boeree was one of the first critics of the Battle of Arnhem, fair to both the British and the Germans.

The remains of the sophisticated Luftwaffe night fighter control center at Deelen air base, destroyed by British bombers on the night of D-13.

Kasteel Doorweerth on the Rhine, west of Arnhem.
The castle was the headquarters of SS-Colonel Lippert, who was enraged when he discovered that a report from his superiors that his HQ had been occupied by the British was false.

Anthony Deane-Drummond, second-in-command of 1st Airborne Signals, takes the 60th Anniversary salute, September 16, 2004.

Major John Pott, who advanced further than anyone in 4th Parachute Brigade on D+2. The wounded Pott was rescued by two brave Dutch civilians that night.

Jasper Booty, Staff Captain, 4th Parachute Brigade. Known for his wit and bravery, Booty, formerly of the Royal Sussex Regiment, was the co-author, with Brigadier Hackett, of the brigade's after-action report.

A 6-pounder anti-tank gun of the 1st Border Regiment, 1st Airborne Division at Arnhem, 20 September 1944. The gun was at this moment successfully engaging a German tank. (Imperial War Museum)

Lance-Bombardier John Mills (center). Mills was the No. 2 gunlayer of a 17-pounder anti-tank gun, which destroyed a German tank outside the Hartenstein Hotel, Urquhart's HQ. The gun still stands outside the hotel, now the Airborne Forces Museum.

Tony Hibbert, Brigade Major, 1st Parachute Brigade,
the most senior officer of Brigade Headquarters at the Arhhem road
bridge during the siege.

Chelsea Pensioner Sgt. Arthur Parker, No. 1 (Army) Commando.
Parker was one of a four-man signals team dropped with the 101st
Airborne on D-Day, an event not recorded in the reports and histories.
Since the Corps Signals detachment did not arrive, the 101st was initially
plagued by communications failures, but the British commandos
did not, evidently, have any success either.

Major Michael Tucker (1907–1981), commander of the 23rd Field Company, Royal Canadian Engineers, won the DSO for his role in evacuating the remnants of 1st Airborne Division across the Lower Rhine from Oosterbeek on September 25, 1944.

Russell Kennedy MC, now over 90, formerly Reconnaissance Officer, 23rd Field Company, Royal Canadian Engineers.

Diorama of 23rd Company Engineers at the Arnhem evacuation in the Canadian Airborne Forces Museum, Petawawa, Ontario, Canada.

Russell Kennedy in 1945. As a lieutenant in the 23rd Field Company, RCE, he won a Military Cross and was officially credited with organizing the evacuation of nearly 2,400 paratroopers, making his last run across the Rhine in a stormboat in full daylight under German fire. Without the efforts of the 23rd Company RCE the evacuation would have failed.

Operation Market Garden, 17–25 September 1944. Four men of the 1st Paratroop Battalion, 1st Airborne Division, take cover in a shell hole outside Arnhem. (Imperial War Museum)

9

STAGNATION

On D+5, Horrocks was still aiming for the road bridge at Arnhem but he switched the axis of advance from Arnhem to Driel. The direct route to Arnhem was blocked; the Poles were in Driel and the ferry was reported held. Messages from Urquhart on the *Phantom* net to the effect that the ferry was lost were logged at 1207 and 1630 hours. Urquhart was sent a message earlier in the morning, giving him permission to withdraw to, or even cross, the river by the ferry if necessary and that 43rd Division was taking all risks to effect relief on D+5. The 129th Brigade was indeed to advance north, directly toward the road bridge. The Germans were known to have prepared defensive positions in Elst and though it was possible that the brigade would make progress, the main aim of that thrust was to take pressure off the main attack by 214th Brigade in the Oosterhout sector.

In the evening of D+4, the Second Household Cavalry Regiment, which had led the Guards' advance from Neerpelt, Valkenswaard and Son, was given orders to cover the advance from Oosterhout. C Squadron, under the command of Captain the Hon. Richard Wrottesley, was assigned the job. On the morning of D+5, he led one troop through the fog along the river bank south of Oosterhout, routed through Valburg, swept around through Heteren and linked up with the Poles from the west.

Taking advantage of the fog while it lasted, the squadron commander directed a second troop under Lieutenant Young to Driel, by the same route. A third troop under Lieutenant Hopkinson lost a scout car and driver to a German tank and did not arrive at Driel. From this, Wrottesley concluded that the route behind him was closed and so declined to take 1st Airborne Colonels Mackenzie and Myers to Nijmegen. (They had crossed the river to Driel around midday.) The two troops of the Household Cavalry were to perform many useful, even crucial, duties during the day, helping the Poles resist German attacks and providing a radio link with the advancing ground troops.

The attack on D+5 by 214th Brigade initially took the same route to Oosterhout along the exposed dyke road as the Welsh Guards on the afternoon before. The Brigade had cleared Oosterhout by 1700 hours, preparatory to the advance toward Driel of the DCLI. The leading formations of the DCLI, supported by Eighth Armoured Brigade tanks, arrived in Driel within half an hour. A plaque of Cornish slate on the Driel Church commemorates the drive. Horrocks himself had briefed the west countrymen's commander, Lt. Colonel Taylor, on the urgency of making contact with the 1st Airborne Division and delivering two DUKW amphibians loaded with ammunition and medical supplies. Taylor was surprised that there were only two DUKWs.

By the time that Taylor conferred with Sosabowski, Mackenzie and Myers, he had his whole battalion present, less B Company. Another battalion of the 214th Brigade, the First Worcesters, moving in DUKWs, established a defense line in Valburg and was not ordered on to Driel. The Forty-third Reconnaissance Regiment was stationed on the Waal at Slijk Ewijk, known to the British as "Slicky-Wick," while the Seventh Somersets of Essame's brigade were regrouping in Oosterhout.

The attacks of the brigade up the Nijmegen-Elst road were intended to take the pressure off the flanks, but the timing was all wrong. The brigade had first to wait for Essame's brigade to complete its crossing of the Waal and it was not until 1130 hours that the advance of the battalion of the Wiltshire Regiment began. Its aim was to capture Elst. This attack was stalled for reasons similar to that of the Irish Guards the day before.

At 0600 hours on D+5, Sosabowski's signalers made contact with his units in Oosterbeek. All day, the Germans shelled and mortared Driel from the north bank and from the southeast. They also fired on the drop zones, where the brigade's supplies were being collected. At the same time, Sosabowski sent out patrols in the direction of Elst, Elden and Hateren. The Polish commander moved about the brigade's positions on a lady's bicycle, which the troops found hilarious but which boosted morale, already high, since *Stary* was known to be lucky. He was with a company at the western edge of the positions at around 0830 hours when he saw armored vehicles approaching. This was the troop of the HCR, with two scout cars and two armored cars, under Captain Wrottesley. Through Wrottesley's radio, Sosabowski was able to give a detailed account of his positions directly to XXX Corps HQ.

Soon after midday, Sosabowski got a radio report that the troops collecting supplies had been driven off the DZ and that a German attack, supported by tanks, was expected in that sector. He made his own reconnaissance and sent his PIAT teams forward. At least six half-tracks from *Kampfgruppe Brinkmann*, followed by panzer grenadiers advancing through the orchards, moved onto the Honingsveldstraat, moving west along the southern edge of the town. The Poles and the PIAT teams retreated, some leaving their anti-tank weapons behind.

On getting the news that the Germans had broken through, Sosabowski enlisted the support of the Household Cavalry. These troops were reluctant to assist since their radios were so valuable, but Sosabowski persuaded them with the observation that, if they did not help, there would be no positions left on which to report. He escorted one of Young's armored cars to the southwest, on his bicycle. The armored car opened up on the half-tracks with its two-pounder, then loosed off a whole belt of machine gun bullets. The Germans, startled by the armor and what they thought were regular infantry, withdrew. A second attack by half-tracks was also halted. A third, with a half-track and a tank, was stopped by the Poles using a PIAT as if it were a mortar, at maximum range, in all a remarkable success against veteran troops.

Sosabowski, knowing that he was needed to coordinate the battle, rode back through Driel to his HQ. He found the town under shellfire, with the steeple of the Catholic Church a particular target. After a late lunch and an attempt at sleep, he was awakened at about 1500 hours by Lieutenant Colonel Mackenzie, Urquhart's Chief of Staff, and Lieutenant Colonel Myers, the commander of the engineers, who had rowed across the river in a rubber dinghy and were very lucky to have arrived unscathed. They said that they were on their way to inform Horrocks of the critical situation facing 1st Airborne in Oosterbeek. Wrottesley was shocked that they talked to HQ on his radio in the clear, and also by the dire situation of 1st Airborne.

Despite the daring and fortitude of these officers, there was something very odd about their venture. Horrocks had been in radio contact with Urquhart for more than two days and, if he did not know of the gravity of the predicament of 1st Airborne, this was because Urquhart's messages were a blend of optimism and vagueness about his prospects. Yet when Mackenzie urged Sosabowski to get as many men across the river as possible—he needed no urging—he said that "even five or ten might make a difference." Again, this was odd because lightly armed men could not provide relief for 1st Airborne; as soon as their food and ammunition ran out they would become a liability, not an asset. What was needed were thousands of men and heavy equipment—in other words a bridge.

The two officers stayed in Driel. Myers directed the Polish crossing that night with six two-person rubber dinghies and a bigger RAF dinghy. These could be pulled back and forth in a line across the water with a hawser. If unopposed, a maximum of two hundred paratroopers could be got across, in batches of about fifteen.

At dusk, Sosabowski got a report that a column of vehicles was arriving from the southwest. This was the DCLI. Lt-Colonel George Taylor told Sosabowski that his brigade would be in Valburg, five miles to the south, sometime before the early morning. The Pole was pleased but wondered why they had not followed behind the Household Cavalry. Perhaps he wondered out loud in that manner which had raised eyebrows, if not hackles, in the briefings for *Comet* and *Market Garden*.

The night's crossing, supervised by Myers, was by 3rd Battalion, scheduled for 2100 hours at a point opposite the Oosterbeek Church; that is, well to the east of the ferry site and toward the western edge of Urquhart's perimeter. Taylor's battalion had brought along two DUKWs, each loaded with 2.2 tons of supplies. These belonged to the 536th General Transport Company, equipped with sixty-six such vehicles attached to 130th Brigade. As Sosabowski's Chief Engineer had predicted, these became inextricably bogged down on the south bank.

The crossing started quietly but the current was swift and the hawser, made of signal cable, kept breaking or running foul of rocks on the north bank. The Poles were reduced to paddling, depositing individual soldiers one at a time. Lt. David Storrs, the engineer who had crossed the river the previous night, was said to have rowed a two-man dinghy twenty-three times across the river. The Germans put up parachute flares and Sosabowski stopped the operation at 0400 hours on D+6, after fifty-two Poles had got across. There were fatal casualties both on the south bank and on the perilous route to Divisional HQ, including Captain Ignacy Gazurek, the acting commander of 3rd

Battalion. The Poles were assigned a sector occupied by the Independent Parachute Company in the northeast along the Stationsweg.

Further down the XXX Corps axis, the 101st Airborne came under a coordinated attack on Hell's Highway from both east and west. Student had put the attacks on from the west under the local command of Major Jungwirth, a highly experienced and accomplished paratroop officer. Jungwirth was to enjoy a notable success, severing the Corridor from the west on D+7–9. Under Jungwirth's command was *Kampfgruppe Huber*, with a mixed group of veteran troops from the 59th Division, paratroop infantry battalions, artillery, seven anti-tank guns and four assault guns from *Kampfgruppe Chill*. Added to this, thus far on paper, was Parachute Regiment 6, another sub-standard battalion having been added to von der Heydte's command. The regiment disengaged from the British at Best and made its way north. Completely exhausted, Heytdte's men marched night and day via the Tilburg-Boxtel road, perhaps sixty miles in all, arriving too late for the attacks on D+5.

On the east side, Model had created a new Corps HQ, the LXXXVI, led by Lt. General Hans von Obstfelder, to relieve Student of the responsibility for the eastern side of the Corridor. Under command were *Division Erdmann*, the 716th Division and *Kampfgruppe Walther*. Colonel Walther's *Kampfgruppe* now consisted of the 107th *Panzer* Brigade, the *Waffen-SS* units from II SS *Panzer* Corps, an impressive amount of artillery, and SS-Captain Roestel's tank group, likely still of squadron size, even with new assault guns and crews picked up in Gemert. The reason that the formations on the eastern side were so far north was that they had been pushed up the Corridor by VIII Corps troops, bringing them even higher than the German forces on the western side. The *Kampfgruppe* was ordered to capture Veghel and cut the Corridor there, and make contact with the formations attacking from the west. The plan was to advance on both sides of the road from Erp, where the bridge over the Aa had been secured.

At 1430 hours, the 501st PIR called off the northern arm of the pincer movement on getting word that German tanks had attacked Veghel from the east and cut Hell's Highway. British tanks supporting the regiment were ordered to block the German advance while the Americans conducted a fighting retreat, taking with them 250 prisoners, and dug in for the northwestern defense of Veghel. The regiment as a whole suffered a grievous blow when a shell landed on the HQ, wounding

Colonel Michaelis, killing his orderly and seriously wounding twelve other officers. Lt. Colonel Cassidy assumed command of the regiment until Lt. Colonel Chappuis took over. By the late afternoon, meanwhile, the 502nd's move north was also called off and the regiment pulled back to St. Oedenrode with 125 prisoners.

The German attacks began at 0900 hours when an advance party of the 1st Battalion, 506th PIR arrived in Uden from the Eindhoven area at 1100 hours. The party was cut off until 1700 hours the next day when the 107th *Panzer* Brigade tanks went north around the Americans and cut the Veghel-Uden road. The 2nd Battalion of the 501st halted the German advance on the Erp road outside Veghel but Brigadier General Anthony McAuliffe, the Deputy Division commander, was in a tight spot. Fortunately, the balance of 1st Battalion arrived in Veghel en route to Uden.

By this time, Taylor's glider infantry regiment had joined the troops north of Veghel. McAuliffe and Sink moved the bulk of them south, no doubt because of the German attacks from the west, which began at 1400 hours. The Germans, because of poor communications, were barely aware of what was happening on the eastern side, and advanced on the road bridge over the canal. They brought the bridge under fire, driving off the crews of a column of British 3.7 inch anti-aircraft guns. McAuliffe ordered the crews back to the guns and drove the Germans away with the fire of these powerful weapons, the British equivalent of the German 88, even though the gunners were not trained in such a role.

This at least is the American version. In the British accounts, two Field Regiments of Artillery took part and, in conjunction with tanks and the American paratroopers, were heavily engaged for two days. A group of Sherman tanks from the Royal Tank Regiment, coming up from the south, added to the defenders' strength, as did the 3rd Battalion of the 506th PIR, which McAuliffe and Sink held in reserve.

The Germans withdrew to cut the Corridor to the south. But the balance of the glider infantry, with artillery, were moving up from the south and pushed the Germans off the road, arriving at the bridge at 1600 hours and taking seventy prisoners. The Germans were also caught from behind by the paratroopers from the southern arm of Taylor's aborted pincer movement, in the vicinity of Schijndel, which closed in to form the western defense of Veghel. In doing so they cut off the rear elements of Huber's *Kampfgruppe*, some killed when the Americans released hydrochloric acid from a factory into the ditches in which Germans were taking cover. Student himself was reported as taking part in these engagements. Elements of the Green Howards from British 50th Division were also engaged in the defense of Veghel, in accordance with the task of the 50th to protect the Corridor. Attacks on the town from the west and the north continued into the night, with constant shelling by the Germans.

For VIII Corps, D+5 was a great success and a turning point in their operations. One armored brigade got between Helmond and XXX Corps, closing within half a mile of the town. British tanks and armored cars destroyed three German tanks and three other vehicles thought to be assembling for the attack further north. Advancing northeast on the Deurne road, the tankers took 300 prisoners. They occupied Maarheeze, between Weert and Leende early in the day, while the Belgians took Bocholt, still on the west side of the Zuid-Willemsvaart Canal. The Germans evacuated Weert, which was occupied by first light, the occasion of much celebration by the Belgian civilians. After a forty-ton bridge was built to replace those blown by the Germans, armored patrols penetrated deep into the Belgian sector, where Oppiter, Maaseik, Kinrooi, even Dilsen were found to be clear of the enemy. Dempsey put the 101st Airborne under VIII Corps command at 1830 hours to reopen Hell's Highway, in conjunction with 50th Division troops in the vicinity of Veghel. At the same time, he announced the joint responsibility of the two flanking corps for the main axis.

By now, Dempsey was gravely concerned with the XXX Corps axis. His XII Corps on the left flank was tied down at Best, unable to disrupt the German attacks on Hell's Highway to the north. Dempsey saw Ritchie at his HQ "and told him to place one brigade group of 15th Division at Son and not to be moved without orders from me." The corps made slow but steady progress in the Best area and had a nine-ton bridge constructed over the Wilhelmina Canal by 0900 hours. Further east, a battalion of the KOSB pushed over the canal in the area held so valiantly by Wierzbowski's platoon of the 101st. They outflanked Best to the northeast and by 0800 had a forty-ton bridge over the canal, close to the demolished road bridge. There, the advance stalled, with little prospect of spoiling the German operations against the Corridor.

First Airborne Division
landing zones, September 1944

British landing zone
Polish landing zone

10

THE POLES' SECOND CROSSING OF THE RHINE

The American task on D+6 was to clear Hell's Highway between Veghel and Uden, for which tanks from the Guards Armoured were promised from the north, Horrocks being obliged to break the rule of "no turnabout." The Guards received the orders to move at 1430 hours on D+5. A group from the Grenadiers was to move on Veghel and another from the Coldstreamers to advance on Voekel, off the main axis to the southeast. By the time the groups arrived at their rendezvous, the Guards had lost a tank to a *Panzerfaust*; it was nearly dark and, there being no pressure from the Americans to advance until the next day, the British called a halt. By this time, VIII Corps had forty-ton bridges over the Zuid-Willemsvaart Canal at Beek and Helmond, which threatened the rear of *Kampfgruppe Walther*. Two reconnaissance regiments, one an advance party of the 52nd (Air-Portable) Division, moved east out of the Corridor and made contact with armored cars of the Inns of Court Regiment, VIII Corps.

On D+3, Dempsey had planned to put the 101st under the command of XII Corps, but this did not happen until D+6, with the dire threats to the western side of the Corridor. The VIII Corps liaison officer remained with the 101st. So stalled was the XII Corps flanking advance that the 7th Armoured Desert Rats linked with the Grenadier Guards Group of XXX Corps, southwest of Heesch, only on D+12. As Montgomery later remarked, the moves of the flanking corps had been "depressingly slow," an observation less pertinent in the case of VIII than XII Corps. The British made substantial gains on the western side of the Corridor, but only after *Market Garden* had officially concluded. In one respect, events moved in favor of XII Corps. On D+6, Dempsey recorded that the enemy had withdrawn to a line at Antwerp-Turnhout-Reusel, with Kasterlee, Retie, Postel and Arendonck reported clear. This enabled the Desert Rats to move to the Eindhoven area.

The day began with German attacks close to Veghel from the west by Parachute Regiment 6, which continued until 1400 hours. There were no other supporting troops, *Kampfgruppe Huber* having been virtually wiped out in the previous day's fighting. Nor did von der Heydte have any knowledge of the plans or the dispositions on German forces to the east of the Corridor, again ruling out a coordinated attack. His whole regiment, arriving piecemeal from Boxtel, was halted by the 501st PIR and a squadron of British tanks, west of Eerde. General Reinhard, at a meeting with Chill and Poppe at the 59th Division's HQ, reluctantly concluded that the advance had failed, though Fifteenth Army directed that it should continue, as per Model's orders. Von der Heydte dug in where his regiment stood.

Before the German halt at 1400 hours, McAuliffe was able to move two battalions of the 506th PIR up the road to Uden, where they met surprisingly little resistance. Maltzahn had probably withdrawn because of the threat to his rear from VIII Corps. Indeed, Taylor's aim was to destroy all the German forces east of Hell's Highway. He sent jeeps from his Divisional Reconnaissance Platoon through enemy-held territory west of the road to the Guards coming down from the north, with the aim of a double envelopment of the 107th *Panzer* Brigade; the Guards making a wide sweep from the northeast and the two battalions of parachute infantry from the southeast.

The Guards were in two groups. The Grenadiers Group consisted of a troop of tanks from the armored battalion, mortar platoons from the Grenadiers and the Northumberland Fusiliers (Second Army troops) and an artillery battery from the Leicestershire Yeomanry. The Grenadiers moved south and made contact with the Americans, and with Royal Tank Regiment armor, at 1500 hours. The task of the Coldstreamers group was to make a wide sweep to the southeast, link up with the Americans and catch the Germans in a bag east of the Corridor. But the Guards delayed for several hours until midday, and initially refused to move off the road, even though they came under the orders of the 101st Airborne.

Possibly, the Coldstreamers did not regard their task as anything greater than reopening the Corridor at the main road. Their actions, though belated, were successful. They advanced on the Volkel airfield and took the town after a sharp fight at 1330 hours with the loss of one tank. They then moved to Erp and to Boekel in a truly wide sweep and occupied the latter the next day. Troops from 50th Division took over Volkel on D+8. Taylor's sweep was thus accomplished, though the bag was not nearly as full as had been expected. Hell's Highway was not again threatened from the east, and from the west, Jungwirth gathered his strength for an attack the next day, sending out reconnaissance patrols to probe weak points in the defenses of the Corridor.

The final lift on D+6 dampened the Germans' resolve. By impersonating a British officer over the civilian phone lines, Colonel Walther had found out that VIII Corps was about to assault Deurne, and moved his HQ back to Venray before the Guards arrived, to withdraw and defend a line west of the Meuse. Walther had lost a fifth of his infantry and a quarter of his tanks, all of which came from the 107th *Panzer* Brigade since, it seems, the SS *Kampfgruppen* of Richter and Dr. Segler had not been deployed; nor for that matter had Roestel's assault guns.

During D+6, the last of Taylor's artillery finally arrived, including the 105mm guns of the glider field artillery battalion. The sea tail of the 101st Airborne, having landed on Omaha Beach early on D+3, arrived on the nights of D+5 and D+6, taking advantage of Horrocks' order of "day movement only" in the Corridor. The full sea tail comprised 1,077 officers and men and over 400 vehicles. The 101st Airborne was at last at full complement. Model considered the landings on D+6 as part of a push to keep his troops away from the Corridor. Though he was on the verge of a complete victory over the British at Arnhem, he thought that he had achieved little, and requested reinforcements that he knew he would not get.

By the morning of D+6, Horrocks had decided to relieve 1st Airborne via a Rhine crossing at Driel and not Arnhem. Second Army sent a message to Urquhart at 0830 hours, stating that 43rd Division would now cross to the west of Arnhem. Urquhart responded, observing that the first task of the DCLI would be to take the Westerbouwing Heights to "help the crossing of armor." "Relief" for Urquhart clearly meant the reinforcement of the 1st Airborne bridgehead, contrary to the tone of the previous messages he had sent to XXX Corps via Mackenzie and Myers on the previous day.

While Horrocks had now clearly set his sights on the Driel crossing, the relief of 1st Airborne in that direction was still not his singular aim for he also ordered 214th Brigade to attack east in the direction of Elst.

The relief moves by 130th Brigade on Driel and the preparations to attack Elst got entangled with each other in a sector that was still under German fire. The First Worcesters in Valburg and the Seventh Somersets behind them around Oosterhout were attempting to move toward Elst while 130th Brigade in their unwieldy DUKWs were passing through their assembly area, delaying the movements of both brigades.

By the evening, the three battalions of 130th Brigade had closed to the Lower Rhine: the Fifth Dorsets were in Driel, the Seventh Hampshires near Heteren on the river bank to the northwest, and the Fourth Dorsets in reserve. There were very few assault boats and those belonged to the Dorsets. Brigadier Walton in Valburg promised Sosabowski both boats and engineers for the night's crossing. These were, supposedly, following behind 130th Brigade, although Urquhart was told on the *Phantom* net in the early afternoon that the *head* of 130th Brigade had the boats which were to be used to supply his divisio. Just how retarded were the relief effots will soon be seen.

On Saturday morning, D+6, Mackenzie and Myers were driven by Wrottesley's troop in a hazardous trip to Browning's HQ in Nijmegen. Mackenzie pointed out to Browning the perilous state of 1st Airborne, upon which Browning gave ambivalent signals about the possibility of relief. Mackenzie returned to Driel and was in one of the first boats to cross that night. Despite his own deep reservations, he gave Browning's more positive gloss on the prospects of relief to Urquhart. Myers too returned by tank in time to supervise the night's crossing.

In the morning, Sosabowski heard that 214th Brigade had been held up in the area of Valburg and was trying to approach Driel by an alternative route. At 0900 hour, a liaison officer arrived from the British Airborne Corps. He forecast the arrival of 130th Brigade during the day and said that the Poles were to attempt another crossing that night. Sosabowski thought this curious since, unlike the Poles, 43rd Division had been briefed, trained and equipped for assault crossings. The officer also brought news of Sosabowski's 1st Battalion, which was to be dropped onto the grass airfield at Grave along with the 82nd Airborne's glider infantry regiment. Sosabowski said he would need more boats, food and ammunition, which the officer promised him. He further pointed out that there were no plans for supplying food and ammunition to 1st Airborne, a matter which the officer "agreed to look into."

Sosabowski had sent out a patrol in one of the DCLI jeeps to 130th Brigade in Valburg. There Brigadier Walton promised eighteen 24-man motorized stormboats, manned by Canadian sappers, to arrive at 2030 hours, with artillery support. At 1430 hours on D+8, at least some of the 43rd Division assault boats were still south of the Corridor cut at Koevering. The Canadians, however, were just south of Nijmegen and north of the cut, under the command of the 204th Field Company RE. The reason they were not sent to Driel with their boats was, in Major Tucker's words, that the British engineers had "no confidence in them and it looks as if we and our boats have just come along for the ride." The next day, their commander asked rhetorically, "Why won't they let us play?" Sosabowski later learnt that he would have to supply his own engineers to paddle a different batch of boats, which came from the Fourth Dorsets, in the brigade reserve. In his draft report of 28 September, Sosabowski stated that he did get the help of sixteen engineers from the north bank, that is, from 1st Airborne Division, at 0400 hours, not long before the operation was called off. If possible, Sosabowski intended his whole brigade to cross.

His boats arrived late, after midnight, and without any supplies for 1st Airborne. The boats were reputed to be those that survived the 82nd Airborne's crossing of the Waal on D+3. They had a capacity of twelve men, not the expected twenty-four, so the Polish engineers would have to make twice as many trips in a craft with which they were in any case unfamiliar. The crossing was lit up by the light of a burning factory on the north bank and raked by machine gun fire. In addition, the whole area from the *polder* to the dyke was covered by artillery fire. Sosabowski, directing the operation from behind the higher dyke, was blown off his feet by an exploding shell.

The crossing, bloody and chaotic, was witnessed by Myers, who found no fault with the performance of the untrained Poles. Inexplicably, no trained engineers were provided with the Dorsets' boats. Even more perplexing is the fact that a platoon of British engineers from the 204th Field Company RE was in the vicinity, among other things to give assistance to the Poles. Lieutenant Kennedy, of the Canadian Twenty-third Company, was attached to the 204th for forty-eight hours but had no contact with the Poles. Most critics would find it unthinkable that senior British officers would have recklessly jeopardized a relief effort and sent their allies to a watery death.

In all, 153 Poles got across, ninety-five from 3rd Battalion, forty-four from the complement of the anti-tank battery, and fourteen from Brigade HQ. As in the previous crossing, there were several casualties, as well as one group that surrendered en route to the positions on the Stationsweg. The Poles were dismayed at the debilitated state of the British, but impressed by their determination. The British, for their part, found the Poles "brave and dedicated." Both parties got it right.

11

DITHERING AND DECEIT

On D+7, Model reorganized his command. All German troops west of the Corridor came again under Fifteenth Army, Chill moving his HQ to Schijndel the next day. Student's First Parachute Army was given command of all troops east of the Corridor, including Meindl's II Parachute Corps, the Corps Feldt and von Obstfelder's LXXXVI Corps, with *Kampfgruppe Walther*, so that *Wehrkreis VI* had no further authority over operations in the Netherlands. Student, who had been visiting his troops in Gemert by crossing the severed Corridor, also got the II SS *Panzer* Corps, including the Division von Tettau, taken from Model's direct command. But there was no immediate possibility of attacking from the east, where the initiative had passed to the Allied VIII Corps.

From the west, the Germans were to have more success than the strength of the available forces indicated. There, the Germans threw together a number of ad hoc units, including the remnants of *Kampfgruppe Huber*, the Battalion Jungwirth, some surviving elements under the command of 59th Division, and some self-propelled guns from Tank-Destroyer Battalion 559. The main aim was still to retake the rail and road bridges over the Zuid-Willemsvaart Canal, but reconnaissance by Battalion Jungwirth the previous day had revealed gaps in the defenses of Hell's Highway further south. The attack by von der Heydte's parachute regiment began at 1000 hours against the battalion of the 502nd PIR defending Eerde.

At midday, the Americans counterattacked the Germans in the sand dunes outside Eerde in which there was an incident comparable to that when the 82nd crossed the Waal in assault boats. One platoon, led by Lt. Harry Mosier charged over open ground facing five machine guns, a mortar and the German infantry, well dug in. The entire platoon was seized with a bloodlust, a "brute battle-rage" that can lead equally to heroism or to atrocity. In the more mundane parlance of the British rank and file, the Americans "got their wild up." The Germans were overwhelmed, suffering fifteen killed, seven prisoners and about fifty who retreated through the dunes.

On the west side, the Americans also beat off the Germans, whose artillery plastered Hell's Highway throughout the afternoon and into the night. However, two assault guns did reach the highway, where they halted the British supply columns, shot up several trucks and destroyed three tanks sent down from Veghel.

In the late afternoon, Battalion Jungwirth began its advance and by nightfall it had reached Hell's Highway. On the morning of D+8, Jungwirth, who had been joined by some companies of von der Heydte's regiment, reported about fifty vehicles destroyed, including three tanks, forty prisoners taken and two British tanks captured, their crews unaware of Jungwirth's presence. Two companies of the paratroopers from St. Oedenrode and the guns of the glider field artillery were not able to dislodge the Germans, who not only cut the highway but severed the main signals cable connecting the division's rear in St. Oedenrode with the formations around Veghel and Eerde.

At about 1000 hours on D+7, after only an hour's sleep, Sosabowski was awakened to be told that Horrocks had arrived in an armored car. With Myers, they met in the tower of the Driel church. According to author George Cholewczynski, based on the testimony of Sosabowski's liaison officer and interpreter, Lt. J.H. Dyrda, Sosabowski said that 1st Airborne needed supplies and support from heavy weapons, otherwise they would have to conduct an orderly withdrawal across the Rhine. To this Horrocks replied that a battalion of the 43rd Division would cross that night, with supplies for 1st Airborne, and the Polish brigade would cross at the points used on the previous two nights. He then drove off, smiling and waving to the troops with Sosabowski in tow, to attend a meeting at 43rd Division HQ at Valburg.

This meeting was very different in tone. Major General Thomas, who was among the officers present, greeted Sosabowski "in a cool, almost cold, manner." Horrocks stated he had been ordered by Dempsey to open a "strong bridgehead" on the north bank of the Rhine, and there would be two crossings under the command of

Thomas of the 43rd, who then took up the briefing. The first crossing would be by the Fourth Dorsets, with supplies for 1st Airborne, then Sosabowski's 1st Battalion, now arriving from Grave, under the command of Brigadier Walton of the 130th. These units would cross just to the west of the ferry landings. The remainder of the Polish Brigade, essentially 2nd Battalion, would then cross at the same points as the previous two nights.

Sosabowski heard all this with mounting anger, not least because he was being reduced to a mere battalion commander under the direction of a brigadier, his junior. A violent argument over tactics ensued between Sosabowski and Thomas, Sosabowski claiming that the forces employed were too small and that they were to land where the German opposition would be the strongest. He urged that the whole of 43rd Division should cross the Lower Rhine at a point well to the west of the planned operation. After this Horrocks concluded the meeting, stating angrily that his orders would stand. To Sosabowski and his interpreter, it seemed that the British, with their slight and perfunctory orders, were overcome by a supine indifference to the outcome of the battle.

Outside the tent, Thomas was giving orders for the Polish brigade to Lt. Colonel Stevens, Sosabowski's British liaison officer. When Sosabowski walked over to them, Thomas ignored him, continued to give orders to Stevens, then walked away without any word or gesture to the Pole. Browning, present at the Valburg meeting, had invited Sosabowski to lunch in Nijmegen, then to his caravan. At the meeting, Browning indicated that his main concern was to keep the Corridor open from Eindhoven to Nijmegen. Sosabowski, anxious for a strong and early crossing, asked Browning what the chances were of successfully assaulting the Lower Rhine. As Sosabowski later recalled:

> Browning's reply positively amazed me:
> "The river crossing may not succeed as there is no adequate equipment."
> Thunderstruck, I asked: "Why in heaven's name not?"
> "Because it is impossible to get the equipment up to the river."
> "But ambulances are getting through regularly to Driel; they have evacuated some of my wounded and, if they can do it, so can the bridging lorries."
> Browning repeated what he had said, adding that the

Germans had cut the road and nobody knew when it would be clear again. He hoped it would be soon. I felt it was incredible and, speaking my mind freely, I told him so.

"Every hour, every minute that 1st Airborne Division is left on the other bank means more killed and wounded. We are so near to them—we must make a final effort."

I fear that my forthrightness hurt Browning's feelings, for he quickly ended our conversation.

Within Second Army, Sosabowski was rapidly becoming a small minority of those still believing in the reinforcement of 1st Airborne, but the bigger, official picture was still one of optimism. That day, there were yet plans afoot to fly engineer and defense units into Deelen on D+9 and the 52nd (Air-Portable) on D+10. Brereton was equally optimistic, citing Browning's decline of the 52nd as an encouraging sign.

In the event, only the Dorsets under Lt. Colonel Gerald Tilly crossed the river that night, beginning at 0100 hours, three hours late. Six DUKWs loaded with supplies were supposed to take part in the crossing, but only half arrived. The other three were launched from the Driel ferry site and landed west of the Heveadorp ramp. This was either because the Heveadorp terminal was under fire or because it was feared that the DUKWs would become ensnared with the putatively sunken ferry boat or with its cables.

On the north bank, the DUKWs bogged down in the mud and only half the supplies were salvaged and none reached the perimeter. Myers, who rode in the last of the DUKWs, moved east along the north bank and delivered messages to Urquhart, two of which from Browning were out of date and one from Major General Thomas. He also reported on "the obvious failure of Fourth Dorsets to help us in any way." Major Grafton, second in command of the Dorsets, also got through with a similar message.

Of the assault boats, each had a crew of two or three sappers and held ten soldiers with food and ammunition for four days. How many boats were used and how many crossings they made is not recorded, although twenty had been promised. Colonel Powell claimed that nine had arrived by lorry, plus, according to Cornelius Ryan, three that had survived the Polish crossing the night before. Since a battalion's complement was thirty boats, there were not enough to transport all the men in a single wave. A heavy artillery barrage covered the crossing, as well as machine gun fire from neighbouring units, the Fifth Dorsets and the Seventh Hampshires. Burning buildings in Heavedorp illuminated the river, which was swept by machine gun and mortar fire. At least one boat sank; others were swept downstream. The result was that those who arrived on the north bank did so in scattered groups. Brigadier Walton called off the operation at 0215, in view of the intensifying German fire.

The north bank was not initially strongly held, contrary to what Sosabowski had predicted, but the German reaction was swift. At 0515 hours on D+8, von Tettau informed the II SS *Panzer* Corps that the enemy had crossed the Rhine under an artillery barrage. By 0610, the Germans knew that only a battalion had crossed. The Dorsets had disembarked in the sector of a naval battalion, the *Schiffsturmabteilung* 10. One battalion of Security Regiment 26 counterattacked from Renkum. A battalion of another formation, the Security Regiment *Knocke*, was also sent in, taking two *Luftwaffe* field companies under command.

By the time the operation was called off, 315 of 350 Dorsets who had launched had got across. But by the morning about 200 had surrendered, including Lt. Colonel Tilly, and thirteen had been killed. Most of the rest reached the 1st Airborne lines or hid out on the river bank. For the second time in the campaign of 1944, the Fourth Dorsets had been nearly destroyed. The Dorsets who got into the perimeter were spread among the companies of the Borders to stiffen the western side of the defenses. Of particular value was the artillery support from 43rd Division, called in through two radio channels, one fom the Dorsets and the other from artillery observers who had accompanied them.

Both Urquhart and Sosabowski thought that 43rd Division had moved too slowly to the relief of 1st Airborne. More generally, commentators since the war have asserted that the British manpower crisis and the troops' unwillingness to take risks in a war that was thought to be virtually over, led to "stickiness" on the part of XXX Corps.

In *Corps Commander*, Horrocks went out of his way to refute the charge of stickiness on the part of 214th Brigade. Since Hubert Essame was a co-author of the book, though not nominally responsible for those passages, the cynical might suppose that Horrocks was engaged in special pleading. On the more general charge, Horrocks was surely correct: there is no evidence that any of XXX Corps' troops fought badly in Operation *Garden*. Where 43rd Division was found wanting was in the sluggishness of its movements, right from the time that it moved from Hechtel on D+3 to the time that 130th Brigade arrived at Driel. This was a failure of command from Horrocks on down, not a comment on the fighting qualities of the troops.

When the Fifth DCLI made its dash to Driel on D+5, there was no attempt to follow up with the First Worcesters. From then on, faulty tactics were responsible for the delays. Instead of advancing on Driel with two brigades, Thomas switched the Driel movement from 214th Brigade to the 130th and had the former attack east toward Elst, when the move to the Arnhem road bridge had been abandoned. The movements of the two brigades became entangled with each other, with the result that the 130th did not arrive at Driel in its entirety until twenty-four hours after the DCLI, which then moved east to join its parent brigade.

CONTROVERSIES

By the morning of D+6, Horrocks had decided to cross the Rhine in the vicinity of Driel rather than by the Arnhem road bridge. This gives rise to two important questions:

> 1. What preparations did XXX Corps make, by way of assault crossings and a bridge, to relieve First Airborne in Oosterbeek?
> 2. When was the decision made to move from the reinforcement of 1st Airborne to its evacuation?

There were never enough assault boats to get a single battalion with supplies across the Rhine, never mind a whole brigade and certainly not a division. The idea of getting an entire division across with only assault boats is absurd. For that a forty-ton bridge was needed and over this, the higher commands were quite clear. Sosabowski, when he met with Browning, assumed that a column of "bridging lorries" would be brought up to the Rhine. Browning's evasive and "amazing" reply was to the effect that it was impossible to bring up the bridging columns, with the implication that this was due to German threats to the Corridor in the rear.

Sosabowski was not the only one who thought that a bridge was needed to get a division across. Urquhart, when he was confined to the

Oosterbeek perimeter, continued to believe that a bridgehead could be maintained north of the Rhine. In his view, in the earlier days "it might even have been possible to put a floating bridge across the river and thus enable us to extend the perimeter with a view to a further advance when the force had been sufficiently built up." His troops evidently thought so too, since a Class 40 bridge is mentioned in the dialogue of the film *Theirs is the Glory,* made in 1945. Second Army clearly envisaged the need for a bridge in order to maintain the bridgehead. In the evening of D+6, before the meetings at Driel, Valburg and Nijmegen, Second Army signalled to 1st Airborne that there would be assault crossings by 130th Brigade during the night and, as noted in Dempsey's diary, "RE will then build a Class 40 bridge." The idea that 130th Brigade would be in any position to cross was quite unrealistic, but it does show that Dempsey considered that a bridge capable of carrying tanks was necessary for the maintenance of the Rhine bridgehead.

So where were the bridging columns? In the Guards Armoured Division Operational Order No. 12 of 15 September, the division was notified that a bridge column of 450 vehicles was to be given a "new priority" in the move north to Grave. This included enough equipment to provide close support rafts and, initially, a Class 9 bridge over the Lower Rhine. Two Class 40 bridges were to follow, one on pontoons and the other on barges. In fact the whole column of 483 vehicles was in Nijmegen by D+4 "to be ready for the Arnhem crossings, there then being little hope of securing the road bridge." Lt. Kennedy saw the dead at the water's edge from the American assault on the previous day.

Among the engineer units were the 260th and 553rd Field Companies RE, the Twentieth and Twenty-third Field Companies, RCE and, possibly, the 204th Field Company, RE. They had travelled "with such priority that even their own commander and his reconnaissance parties had to make way for them." In other words, the bridging equipment was available, *north of the cut of the Corridor.* The question of a bridge was still a sore point after the war, one which, on the whole, commentators preferred to avoid.

Brigadier Essame said that it would have been impossible to bring bridging lorries to the crossing point and that, even if a bridge were built, it would have come under German fire from the north bank. This, of course, assumes that the crossing had to be at that site, contrary to what Sosabowski had urged, and that plans had been made for bringing the bridging equipment forward. In fact the Canadian troops, trained in crossing large rivers, were ordered to marshal their bridging train "for a move to the river bank" only at about noon of 24 September, D+7, but were stood down before the lorries were mobilized. The Twenty-third Field Company RCE was alerted for a night assault crossing before it was cancelled. "Plans were changing." They certainly were.

Horrocks later said that he issued orders to Thomas and Sosabowski on D+7. First, 130th Brigade, with at least one battalion, would cross the Rhine that night, followed by the Poles, "with as many stores as possible." This all depended on the number of assault boats he could muster. Second, Thomas was to conduct a reconnaissance to the west since, if things went well, he would "side-slip the 43rd Division, cross the Neder Rijn further west, and carry out a left hook against the German forces attacking the western perimeter of the airborne troops." This is remarkably like the plan that Sosabowski had proposed and which had been angrily rejected by Horrocks on D+7! On the face of it, Horrocks seemed to some to have been serious about the maintenance of the Rhine bridgehead. But as there were not even enough assault boats for the small crossing that night, never mind rafts and bridging equipment, Horrocks' orders on D+7 seem unrealistic to the point of self-deception, fantasy or outright fraud.

In view of Sosabowski's words on what Browning had told him in their private meeting that day, the more extreme and damning diagnoses of Horrocks' reasoning are the most plausible. It is difficult to avoid the conclusion that the statement that there were tentative plans to have the 43rd cross the river was anything other than disingenuous. Historians have rightly commented on the ill-preparedness of a division that was assigned, trained and equipped for a Rhine crossing. A much greater point is that the maintenance of the bridgehead required a bridge, which was hardly even considered in the efforts to relieve 1st Airborne. The four bridging companies south of Nijmegen remained there from D+4 to D+8; they were never brought forward for relief or reinforcement, only for the evacuation of 1st Airborne on D+8.

After issuing his order on D+7, Horrocks moved south to meet Dempsey in St. Oedenrode. The commanders agreed that unless 43rd Division's left hook could be carried out quickly and with a considerable chance of success, 1st Airborne would have to be withdrawn. Since neither condition had the slightest chance of being met, it has to be concluded that the decision to evacuate 1st Airborne was in fact made on

D+7, as was definitively stated in the coded message that Myers carried across the river that night from Thomas to Urquhart. A decision would be given to XXX Corps at 1200 hours on the following day.

Dempsey met with Montgomery at the HQ of 50th Division at 1100 hours on D+8. Montgomery agreed to withdraw 1st Airborne that night and a message to this effect went to XXX Corps at 1215 hours. Urquhart had pondered Thomas' letter and, at 0800 agreed to a withdrawal. He got on the radio to Thomas at 0808 and told him "Operation *Berlin* must be tonight." A message on *Phantom* soon afterward suggested a possible collapse if contact was not made "early September 25." A further message of 1550, more in line with the radio contact at 0808, confirmed the crossing that night. When the order to withdraw went out from Second Army, it was stated that the reason was an inability to build a bridge across the Rhine. Horrocks contended that it was he and Browning who had decided to order the withdrawal, on the morning of D+8. Urquhart claimed that Dempsey met with Browning at his HQ at Nijmegen on D+7. It was clearly Dempsey who ordered the withdrawal of 1st Airborne, endorsed by Montgomery.

Thomas had jumped the gun, no doubt with Horrocks' knowledge; the evacuation was thus a foregone conclusion on D+7. Essame's idea that the bridgehead over the Rhine was evacuated because it had "no military value" is ridiculous, serving only as a feeble excuse for the failure to build a bridge. Horrocks and Thomas never had any intention of building a bridge over the Lower Rhine, invoking all kinds of excuses, including the severance of the Corridor behind them. In *Corps Commander*, Horrocks claimed that he should have attempted a left hook with 43rd Division much earlier, in order to relieve 1st Airborne. In so far as major elements of the 43rd were still attempting the direct route north while the left hook was in progress, this is a reasonable contention. Otherwise, what Horrocks regretted was what Sosabowski had advocated all along, though he had received only insults and humiliation for something that Horrocks later claimed was the right strategy.

Sosabowski received written orders for his Rhine crossing at 1700 hours. Shortly afterward, he was joined by Major Tonn's 1st Battalion which had been dropped near Grave on the day before. Sosabowski's two battalions were ready to cross by 2100 hours when Lt. Colonel Stevens arrived at HQ with a message from Major General Thomas, saying that the operation had been delayed because of the non-arrival of the assault boats. When Sosabowski asked him when the boats would arrive, Stevens said they did not know and that they may never get them at all. With a deep breath, Stevens then asked whether Sosabowski would give up the boats he held so that the Fourth Dorsets could use them for the main crossing. Since he figured that the Dorsets' crossing was more important, Sosabowski sadly but willingly agreed and ordered his Chief Engineer, Captain P.P. Budziszewski, to take the boats to the Dorsets' crossing point.

Officially, all of the Fourth Dorsets were to cross the Rhine. However, Brigadier Walton made it clear that the aim of the operation was not to broaden the perimeter of 1st Airborne but to hold the banks for its evacuation. The Dorsets' crossing was not to be the precursor of a major crossing the next night. Walton clearly did not believe even in this altered task since he also directed Lt. Colonel Tilly not to take his whole battalion across and intimated, remarkably, that he need not lead it. Tilly realized then that his battalion was being sacrificed, "chucked away."

Both Browning and Montgomery claimed afterward that the Dorsets had performed a vital service in covering the evacuation. Browning wrote to the CO of the Fourth Dorsets: "I want to thank you and your [battalion] personally for the magnificent show you put up in enabling the survivors of the First Airborne Division to withdraw over the river." The Dorsets were in no position to do any such thing, as Myers recorded. Further, the engineers carrying out the withdrawal on the following night made no distinction between the main body of 1st Airborne and a covering force that had to be evacuated last of all; the operation to bring back the "covering force" ended earlier than the main operation. In all this, Sosabowski alone had a militarily sound conception of what it would take to reinforce 1st Airborne and he alone persevered with the idea until his brigade was withdrawn. From the meetings with Horrocks on D+7 onward, he had been subjected to an elaborate and deceitful charade.

Sosabowski was led to believe that the crossing of the Dorsets and his own brigade was the prelude to a major reinforcement the following night. He was then not told that the task of the Dorsets was to provide a flank guard for the evacuation of 1st Airborne, nor that XXX Corps officers did not even believe in this official change of plan. Why then did Brigadier Walton direct *any* troops to cross? The most obvious explanation is that Second Army expected a crossing that night as the precursor of a major assault, and the 43rd had to go through the motions.

Since XXX Corps and 43rd Division had no confidence in the usefulness of any crossing, there had to be a way of preventing the Poles from mounting their own relief operation. Sosabowski was convinced that the operation still had a military purpose and was mollified by the excuse, itself fraudulent, that no assault boats were available. The only difference was that the Dorsets were "chucked away" while the Poles were held back. Who suffered the most from this British disingenuousness and mendacity is for the reader to decide.

12

THE LAST HOPE FADES

The signal cable from the 101st Airborne headquarters in St. Oedenrode to the troops to the north was restored, then severed again, but not before plans had been made to reopen Hell's Highway.

The aim was to advance both from Veghel and from the area south of the Germans on Hell's Highway. The Americans' greatest asset was that they were able to move along minor roads east of the highway, no longer threatened by *Kampfgruppe Walther*, and though the Corridor had been severed the XXX Corps route to Nijmegen was still open. This enabled the Allies to box the Germans in from three sides. The two forces linked up at 1940 hours but the Germans still held a small section of the highway, stalling all traffic. All the while, the Germans made small-scale attacks on the paratroopers and glider infantry around Eerde and in Veghel.

Yet unknown to the Americans, the German position was precarious. *Battalion Jungwirth* was isolated, with no possibility of reinforcement or of linking with troops on the west side. Reinhard at LXXXVIII Corps received permission from Fifteenth Army to withdraw, von Zangen insisting that the original aim of the mission, the two canal bridges, remain in force. Much of the withdrawal had taken place before daylight and the highway was soon cleared of German troops.

The Germans had been hit heavily, almost as badly as Battalion Huber. In his memoir, Robert Bowen wrote, "We [3rd Battalion, 327th GIR] approached the woods cautiously because the enemy could still have been there. They were, but all of them were dead. Great gaps had been blasted in the trees by artillery fire, and bodies of Germans were sprawled as if tossed by a giant hand. We saw a heavy mortar position that had taken a direct hit, the mortar and crew blown to pieces. Dead horses, still in their traces, wagons and destroyed equipment also greeted us." The Germans had, however, mined the road and it took American engineers until 1400 hours on D+9 to clear it and get the traffic rolling again.

The Germans continued with patrols, probing attacks and artillery salvos after D+9, but there were no more threats to the Corridor. On 2 October, the 101st Airborne moved up to the Island, to the "surprise and disappointment" of most of the troops, believing as they did that *Market* would be an operation of only short duration. Among the division's achievements were the taking of 3,511 prisoners and the laying of 4,800 miles of signal cable. Their casualties up to D+8 stood at 2,110.

If we can ever speak of the business of killing as dazzling, then the 101st Airborne's defense of Hell's Highway was a dazzling performance. British guns and tanks, principally from the 44th RTR, played a vital part in some engagements, especially in the absence of Taylor's airborne artillery. The 44th RTR was down to thirty tanks until relieved by the Desert Rats on September 30. These armored troops performed in ways contrary to the usual American criticisms of the British tank arm. Intelligence gathered by the Dutch Resistance was also of great value, as was that provided by glider troops downed west of the Corridor.

The Germans in contrast suffered from two disadvantages. The first was that poor communications ruled out coordinated attacks from east and west. The second disadvantage was the overall poor quality of the troops at their disposal, which resulted in mass surrenders, especially on the western side. The repeated observation from LXXXVIII Corps that they were perilously short of artillery ammunition does not seem to have been correct, as German artillery continued firing, even after local defeats. Robert Bowen wrote: "We rushed into town [Veghel] among screaming shell bursts which rocked the ground under us. . . . The artillery fire was deafening, as bad or wose than in Normandy. Several houses in the town were aflame and a great pall of smoke was gathering above. The shells were falling fast and close, no more than 100 yards away. Startled, we huddled against the buildings, waiting for a shell to drop in our midst. It was one of the most terrifying moments of my life. . . . We waited nearly an hour as the shells tore the town apart."

The Germans' greatest success was keeping the XII Corps formations away from the Corridor, inflicting numerous casualties on the

British and preventing them from protecting the flank of XXX Corps further north. The cutting of the Corridor for the better part of five days disrupted British supply lines since the minor road to the east was not big enough for supply columns. On D+9, while the Corridor was still cut, a convoy of 1,500 vehicles was routed through the VIII Corps sector, moving from Eindhoven to Helmond and over the forty-ton bridge at Beek, through Gamert and Boekel to Uden. The disruption was otherwise too late to compromise *Market Garden.*

The retention of the 82nd Airborne for operations both south of the Waal and on the Island did not come as much of a surprise as it did to the Screaming Eagles. Several days after D+3, Browning told Gavin that the 82nd was to take part in an offensive to the north. When Gavin said he could not agree to such a thing without clearance from Ridgeway, Browning "seemed to understand." Dempsey met with Gavin and made his famous utterance, "I am proud to meet the Commanding General of the finest division in the world today." When this meeting took place is not recorded, but Dempsey was at the HQ of the 101st Airborne at 1200 hours on D+6. He met with Montgomery at 1600. The day before, Montgomery was at the HQ of his old division, the 3rd, at Hamont, his excuse for not being at Eisenhower's meeting with his top commanders at Versailles.

Gavin recorded that his meeting with Montgomery took place on the day after his conversation with Browning. There is no record of any discussion of the future role of the 82nd Airborne. According to the Guards histories, Montgomery was driven around the severed Corridor with an escort of six Bren Carriers and that the hazards of the route north were not apparent to the Commander-in-Chief. The subsequent performance of the 82nd Airborne impressed Dempsey no end. "This is a very fine division" he wrote in his diary, one of the few reflections that Dempsey permitted himself.

THE LAST DAYS OF 1ST AIRBORNE IN THE
OOSTERBEEK KESSEL

hen Roy Urquhart got command of the 1st Airborne, he replaced the highly capable Eric Down, leading to speculation that Browning got rid of a commander who might challenge his own reputation. Sosabowski thought that Urquhart's failing was that he treated airborne troops like infantry. Once on the ground, he never got a firm grip on the battle until the offensives of his two parachute brigades were over. But when the Oosterbeek perimeter was formed, he came into his own. He was constantly on the move, giving advice and encouragement, seemingly fearless and oblivious to enemy fire. Brereton recorded that fourteen men were said to have fallen beside him. He also took on the work of his men, as if he were a common soldier.

On one occasion in the dark, a trooper gave instructions to an unknown hulk of a man working beside him, only to find that this was his divisional commander. He called his men "son." Whenever he found them not fighting as they should, he did not ask them for name, rank and unit but told them to get back in line and get on with the job. As an airborne divisional commander, he was quite out of the league of Taylor and Gavin. Yet as a battlefield leader, he was their equal. His first move on D+4 was to reorganize his command, making Hicks responsible for the western face of the perimeter, and Hackett the eastern face. Hackett recorded that on D+6 he had about five hundred troops under command, which included roughly forty from his 10th Battalion, sixty from the 156th and seventy from the 11th. He was organizing the addition of about two hundred Poles when he was badly wounded by a mortar round in the stomach and thigh.

The main German reorganization also occurred on D+4 when Harzer was made responsible for all the forces attacking Oosterbeek, including the Division von Tettau, which was transferred to II SS *Panzer* Corps from Christiansen's Netherlands Command. Harzer also communicated directly with Army Group B, which made for more efficient supply and reinforcement, for instance the company of assault pioneers with flamethrowers that was flown in to Deelen, perhaps on the night of D+3.

On the morning of D+4 the Germans, having reoccupied the north end of the road bridge, resolved to destroy the Oosterbeek *Kessel*. The attacks were to begin at 0800 hours. Each group was given an assault pioneer section with flamethrowers and three assault guns from Assault Gun Brigade 280. On the previous day, Artillery Regiment 191 arrived from Army Group B and was transported to the front in what remained of the II SS *Panzer* Corps vehicles. On D+4, SS Mortar Group Nickmann, with two groups of six *Nebelwerfer* were put under a unified artillery command as ARKO (Artillery Command) 191. The previous day, Army Group B had ordered the civilian evacuation of Arnhem, except for the emergency services, the sick and the wounded. Many simply moved to Velp, a move "silently tolerated by Harzer." That "the partial evacuation of Arnhem" had been ordered by the Germans was known to the British through *Ultra* on D+7.

For Urquhart, D+4 began badly, when B Company of the Borders was driven off the Westerbouwing Heights. The Germans, however, lost three of four captured French Char B tanks and suffered numerous casualties, so much so that the commander of the Worrowski Battalion, Colonel Schramm, was dismissed three days later, at the insistence of *Luftwaffe* Colonel Fullriede.

The Borders appreciated the seriousness of the loss of the Heights since they mounted two further counterattacks by fresh companies, but neither was successful. B Company, down to the strength of a single platoon, was pulled back to a defense line, half a mile back from the restaurant on the Heights and became known as "Breeseforce" after Major Charles Breese, the acting second-in-command of the Borders. Not only had the Heights been lost but the base of the perimeter on the river bank narrowed to less than 700 yards. It was not feasible to mount a counterattack with such a small and exhausted body of troops; but Breese's defensive positions were not seriously attacked during the following four days.

In the recriminations that followed the loss of 1st Airborne, Urquhart was blamed for losing the Westerbouwing Heights. The most extreme criticism came from Lt. Colonel Theodoor Boeree, the retired Dutch artillery officer and one of the earliest commentators on the Arnhem battles. Boeree observed that Urquhart should have abandoned the relief of Frost at the road bridge earlier than D+3 and established a bridgehead with the Westerbouwing Heights at its center. The 43rd Division apologists implied that the loss of the Westerbouwing Heights caused the failure of the relief efforts, since the crossing areas were covered by fire from the Heights and the arriving troops would have been confined to the exposed north bank. This of course assumes that crossings would be made in this area. The truth was more prosaic; the Borders were driven off the Heights by a strong enemy attack and were not strong enough to retake them.

Throughout D+4, there was heavy fighting all around the perimeter, in which the main German success was in Hackett's eastern sector. In vicious house-to-house fighting, the Tenth Battalion was reduced to a handful of men and no officers left unwounded. Lt. Colonel Smyth was wounded for the second time and died a month later, in spite of the best efforts of the Germans who captured him. The enemy, however, was able to advance only about two hundred yards, one assault gun being abandoned by an untrained crew. Hackett withdrew the remnants of Tenth Battalion into reserve on the night of D+5, putting the Independent Parachute Company, still near to its full complement of 186 men, in their place.

A second round of German attacks in the afternoon made some gains on the British perimeter. This was one of the engagements for which Major Robert Cain was awarded his Victoria Cross. The last German assault was at 1630 hours, against the KOSB in the narrow northern neck of the perimeter. The Germans were driven back by a bayonet charge led by Lt. Colonel Payton-Reid, but the price was heavy, with the Borderers down to 150 men from the 270 with which they had started on the morning of D+3. Urquhart ordered a small withdrawal to shorten the line.

The British defense on D+4 was aided by much greater artillery support than before. At 0945 hours, the First Airborne Light Regiment made radio contact with the Sixty-fourth Medium Artillery Regiment of XXX Corps, about eleven miles away. The first requests for artillery support were made at 1035 hours. The Sixty-fourth was a Territorial Army unit with one 5.5-inch and two 4.5-inch batteries. They were joined shortly by a battery of four 155mm guns from the Fifty-second Heavy Regiment. Urquhart called their performance "one of the most exciting and remarkable artillery shoots I have experienced," as some of the targets were a mere hundred yards from the British lines.

A total of 160 shoots were carried out during the siege, which includes those from the 43rd Division's artillery. One shoot was brought down inside the perimeter on D+8 along one of the planned evacuation routes, which had been infiltrated by Germans. Lt. Colonel Loder-Symonds directed the guns from atop a high building beyond the target, the artillery being about 15,000 yards away. There were several cases of friendly fire on D+4, one of which killed three Polish anti-tank gunners; the last of the five Polish guns was put out of action on D+8.

Over the four days following D+4 there was a marked decrease in the power of German attacks, along with an apparent change in tactics, the assault guns standing off rather than providing close support. German artillery strength had increased to 110 guns, not including the *Nebelwerfer* companies and the 20mm light flak. On D+5, German attacks were led by *Kampfgruppe Bruhn*, north of the Airborne perimeter, *Wehrmacht* Battalion 'Junghahn' and Krafft's battalion, all without significant success. The Dutch SS battalion performed badly, suffering heavy losses. Lippert dismissed Helle in disgrace and ordered his battalion disbanded, the survivors coming under Eberwein's command.

Despite heavy mortar, artillery and *Nebelwerfer* fire, the British held the Germans off with almost complete success. When Eisenhower wrote to Urquhart after the battle, saying that for nine days they checked "the furious assault of the Nazis . . . pressed from every side, without relief, reinforcement or respite," this was absolutely correct. Even a hardened soldier such as SS-Captain Moeller was perplexed and depressed at the ferociousness of the fighting and the refusal of the British to give in.

Bittrich reiterated orders to reduce the bridgehead on D+6, again without significant success, athough 145 prisoners were taken amid signs that the British were being worn down. On D+7, the Germans mobilized fifteen Tiger IIs ("King Tigers") from the 506th Heavy *Panzer* Battalion, the formation that had arrived on D+3. These were deployed in support of infantry and assault pioneer detachments. The British destroyed at least one King Tiger, setting it on fire. The Tigers proved useful as artillery but were never used to spearhead an attack and their success in Oosterbeek was limited. Like Fullriede, Harzer pulled the inexperienced troops out of the line and relied on veterans as the core of the assault teams.

The British had in fact countered the German armor at Oosterbeek with considerable success. By D+7, all eight tanks of *Panzer* Company 224 were destroyed; *Panzer* Brigade 280 lost three of its four self-propelled guns; the Hermann Goering Training Regiment lost two Panthers; and three of eight PzKpwf IIIs of the Bielefeld Training Battalion were lost. Frost claimed a further six tanks at the bridge and a Tiger damaged, with the usual proviso that tanks were often identified as Tigers when in fact they were other marks, usually the long-gunned *Panzer* IV. Perhaps 50 percent of German tank strength had been lost, the majority at the western face of the perimeter. Tettau deplored the lack of co-ordinated tank-infantry attacks and put the remaining tanks into platoons instead of operating singly. They were assigned only to the experienced battalions of Schultz and Eberwein. Harzer adopted similar tactics with the Tigers on D+8.

By D+8 von Tettau had relieved Lippert of his command. Lippert complained that he was not properly supplied by Tettau and had to rely on Rauter's SS commissariat. Tettau contended that Lippert's HQ in

Kasteel Doorwerth on the Rhine just west of Heveadorp was in British hands. When Lippert went back to investigate, he found this to be completely false. Enraged, Lippert returned to von Tettau's HQ and vented his spleen at the *Wehrmacht* general. Tettau in turn worked himself into a rage and dismissed Lippert, as the latter had done with Helle, the commander of the Dutch SS battalion. Lippert returned to *Hohenstaufen* where, on December 27, he was mentioned in dispatches for his part in the reduction of the Oosterbeek bridgehead.

By all accounts, both Lippert and von Tettau were good soldiers. The best explanation for the animosity is a personality clash between the old-fashioned von Tettau and the outspoken Lippert, possibly also the tension between the Army and the *Waffen-SS* over command and supply. Fullriede's comment that von Tettau's HQ resembled an old gentlemen's club, proves nothing about von Tettau's ability. There was still a Division von Tettau fighting east of the Maas in October. The last reference to Tettau is in March 1945, when his formation at the northern end of the Eastern Front took troops from the 33nd SS (French) Division under command.

By the time of Lippert's dismissal, von Tettau had moved the troops from the rear areas, where they were guarding against future paratroop drops, into the battle front. Fullriede, however, had taken 1,600 of his *Luftwaffe* recruits out of the front line and sent them back to Germany, for fear of another massacre like that of the Worrowski Battalion on the Westerbouwing Heights. He was able to do this by appealing around the Army and *Waffen-SS* chain of command to *Oberkommando der Luftwaffe*.

Conditions inside the British perimeter were grim. Sleep was impossible because of the constant artillery bombardment, especially at night. Urquhart's HQ at the Hartenstein was under constant daytime sniper fire. Once there, visitors from the perimeter had difficulty finding the HQ of the specialized services, which were in other bulidings or in holes in the ground. Louis Hagen found a supply of PIAT ammunition under a bush, unsupervised and overlooked by its custodians, the RASC.

The troops were invariably short of water and food, often relying on the meager supplies of the Dutch householders who offered their guests as much help and support as they could, resulting in friendships for life. Rifle and Bren ammunition was rarely in short supply but there were, often enough, dangerous deficits in 9mm rounds for Sten submachine guns as well as munitions for the specialized weaponry such as mortars and the all-important PIAT and six-pounder anti-tank guns.

For the wounded this meant no ticket home. Leo Heaps recorded: "Sitting in the garden, Kettley discovered a lost, dazed lieutenant from the glider-borne troops. One arm hung limply at his side. The stump was bandaged, but the muscle and bone were exposed. Sickened by the sight, Kettley could not move for a few seconds. When he recovered, he helped the wounded officer to the regimental aid post near the Oosterbeek church, where the casualties were laid out in the garden. A stack of bodies about three feet high was piled one on top of the other like cordwood, and while the horrified Kettley watched, one of the bodies on top of the pile moved to scratch his nose. When Kettley reported this to the medical orderly the body was pulled out of the stack and brought inside the first aid post. Many years later this ghoulish incident became Kettley's recurring nightmare." Throughout the divisional area, there was an overpowering stench of unwashed bodies, excreta and putrid wounds.

Inside the perimeter there were about 1,200 wounded British, Polish, German and Dutch distributed among five Regimental Aid Posts (RAPs) and two Main Dressing Stations. One of the former was in the house of Kate ter Horst, the "Angel of Arnhem," who became a legend throughout most of the division. Not only were the medical services overwhelmed by the casualties, but the facilities were under near constant shellfire. Colonel Graeme Warrack, the senior medical officer approached Urquhart to arrange for a truce for the wounded to be evacuated. Urquhart agreed, provided it was made clear to the Germans that there were no implications of British military weakness. Warrack led a team of emissaries, which included the senior Dutch officer with the division, Lt. Commander Arnoldus Wolters (purporting to be a Canadian named Johnson) and a Dutch civilian doctor, van Maanen. They proceeded to the Schoonoord Hotel, a British RAP then behind the German line. There they met the senior medical officer of the *Hohenstaufen*, Dr. Egon Skalka, who claimed that he too had the idea of a "battlefield clearing." He agreed in principle to a truce but said they would have to get permission from Harzer, and he had Warrack and Wolters driven to Harzer's HQ in Skalka's captured jeep.

Skalka was an enigmatic figure. Warrack found him effeminate and anxious to ingratiate himself with the British, but genuine in his willingness to cooperate. Skalka took the two emissaries to Harzer's HQ by a tortuous route without blindfolds. Skalka claimed that he did so to confuse the British; Wolters thought that Skalka wanted to illustrate German strength by taking them along a path of devastation and carnage. When they reached the HQ, Harzer was angry at Skalka for not blindfolding the pair but said that he would agreed to the truce. Wolters, however, noted that Harzer balked at the proposal and that the acting chief of staff, SS-Captain Schwartz, said the matter should be referred to Bittrich.

While they waited they were offered brandy, which they at first declined, yet took the drink when also given sandwiches, which the Germans found amusing. Then Bittrich strode in. "Everyone snapped to attention and there was much 'Heil Hitlering,'" Warrack wrote. Bittrich said that he deeply regretted this war between "our two nations." He listened to Warrack and consented to the plan, and had his staff give the British a bottle of brandy "for your general." En route back, they were permitted to visit the St. Elizabeth's Hospital and the Allied wounded there. They were also allowed to take morphine and medical supplies from the hospital, and briefly exchanged information with the British surgeon, Lipmann Kessel. The Dutchman Wolters was pleased to get out of the German lines, especially after Schwartz said to him, "You don't speak English like a Britisher."

The truce was to last for two hours starting at 1500. At that time, the firing slackened, then stopped. There were outbursts of firing and the Poles in particular had to be convinced that the truce was in a good cause. Some 250 wounded were taken out of the perimeter in relays of jeeps and other vehicles from both sides. About 200 walking wounded also got out. At 1700, the fighting resumed "as though it had never stopped."

The worst cases were taken directly to Apeldoorn, lesser ones to St. Elizabeth's Hospital. The medical evacuation continued the next evening, just before the 1st Airborne withdrawal. About 500 were left in the RAPs, part of the 2,000 caualties who remained north of the Rhine. At the St. Elizabeth's Hospital, Peter Stainforth saw the walking wounded come in: "I have never been so proud. They came in and the rest of us were horror-stricken. Every man had a week's growth of beard. Their battle dress was torn and stained; and filthy, blood-soaked bandages poked out from all of them. The most compelling thing was their eyes—red-rimmed, deep-sunk, peering out from drawn, mud-caked faces made haggard by lack of sleep, and yet they walked in undefeated. They looked fierce enough to have taken over the place there and then."

There was universal agreement on the British side that the Germans thoroughly respected the medical conventions both during the truce and generally. The respect was mutual. Both north and south of the Rhine, a pause after each engagement to collect the wounded became almost a ritual, each side making little distinction between their own and the enemy.

The German infantry and artillery attacks began again in strength on D+8, the renewed resolve to eliminate the British north of the Rhine possibly prompted by the Dorsets' crossing the night before. There had been about eighty deaths a day inside the perimeter; this day it rose to 120, thirty-two of them glider pilots. The weather worsened in the morning; cold rain continued intermittently during the day and throughout the evacuation, increasing the misery. The worst attack was on Lonsdale Force by *Kampfgruppen Harder* and *von Allworden*, which overran an artillery battery and threatened to cut the eastern escape route, if not the entire access to the river.

Until the end, Urquhart was plagued by shortage of supplies of all sorts: food, water, medical supplies and ammunition, especially 9mm and PIAT rounds. But there were also shortages of things needed to keep a modern army going, such as rifle oil, spare batteries and crystals for the radio sets. The supply drops on D+4 and D+6 were failures. The situation was not helped when mortar fire destroyed the division's main reserve of ammunition on D+4, and much of Borders' the following day.

13

THE NIGHT OF THE CANADIANS

By D+9, XII Corps in the vicinity of Best was, in the words of a divisional history, "bogging down into something like positional warfare." Still, troops of the 15th Division outflanked Best to the northeast, providing some protection for the XXX Corps axis in that area. They also linked up with the 101st Airborne in St. Oedenrode, and one company of the KOSB was guarding the forty-ton bridge at Son.

At Nijmegen, the surface of the road bridge was damaged in an air attack on D+8, which forced Horrocks to cross the river in a DUKW. The central span of the rail bridge was destroyed by enterprising German frogmen on the night of D+9. They used equipment and techniques from the Italians, who were recognized as experts in this form of warfare. The road bridge was spared since the frogmen had been unable to affix the unwieldy charges properly to a central bridge column. There were possibly twelve frogmen, of whom ten were captured by the Dutch Resistance and handed over to the British. After the sabotage attempt the road bridge was floodlit and a DUKW made night patrols to guard against more German swimmers. German night bombers did not attempt to take advantage of the illuminated target, though it came under shellfire and the Americans on the Island observed fighter-bomber attacks on the bridge at dawn and dusk.

The advance of VIII Corps on the right flank proceeded apace. Helmond was occupied by D+8 as was Nederwetten, above Neunen, where Sink's regiment from the 101st had sent out armored patrols. By then too, the Belgian Brigade, a rather small but highly mobile unit, had reached the Meuse (Maas) at Euen, gaining access over a forty-ton bridge on the Zuid-Willemsvaart Canal at Bree. British armor broke the opposition at Deurne beyond Helmond, drove through Bakel and Gamert as ordered, reached St. Anthonis, and sent patrols down the Meuse. On each day, 11th Armoured lost a small but steady stream of tanks. Five German half-tracks at St. Anthonis, retreating east, killed two British battalion commanders before all five were destroyed.

While on the Meuse, VIII Corps troops linked with reconnaissance patrols sent out by XXX Corps from the Corridor. On D+9, Inns of Court Regiment armored cars occupied Boxmeer on the Meuse which was now clear between Offelt and Vortum, though the rail bridge south of Offelt was blown. Overloon to the south was strongly held by the 107th *Panzer* Brigade—this became the northern anchor of the German salient west of the Meuse and the scene of some terrible battles, the "Second Caen," as it became known, in October. On 29 September, D+12, the U.S. 7th Armored Division of XIX Corps took the Belgian brigade under command. Patrols from VIII Corps crossed the Meuse and linked up with the 82nd Airborne, the same day that XII Corps troops met the Grenadiers from XXX Corps on the eastern flank.

At his HQ in Oosterbeek, Major General Urquhart called a conference at 1030 hours on D+8, in which the evacuation plan was drawn up. Those present were his Chief of Staff, Charles Mackenzie, his chief engineer, Eddie Myers, his artillery commander, Loder-Symonds, and Lt. Colonel Iain Murray, the commander of the glider pilot wing, who replaced the wounded Hackett. All were embittered at the decision to withdraw, since they had expected imminent relief. For reasons of security and the morale of the rank and file, they were ordered to keep the evacuation a secret, and it was not until the early evening that the majority of the men were told of the plan. The troops would withdraw progressively from the northern end of the perimeter, leaving active pickets to simulate a continuing defense. The medical staff were to stay with the wounded and the military police would guard the German prisoners until the last moment.

The MPs withdrew at 0130 hours, when they were sure that there were no British troops to the north of their positions at the Hartenstein. A signals deception plan would operate overnight; the final message from 1st Airborne was received by 130th Brigade at 0330 hours on D+9. The last lone signaller, James Cockrill, made it back to Driel, having been pulled onto a boat by a burly Canadian engineer.

The artillery plan took six hours to construct, transmit in code and have verified by 43 Division. It called for solid shelling for three hours to keep the Germans in their positions, then "spasmodic concentrations" for the next five. Shells would fall on the evacuated positions, but only after the final pickets had left for the river. The crossings would also be supported by machine gun fire from the infantry battalions on the south bank. The evacuation would start at 2200 hours through marshy meadows along two white-taped routes prepared by the engineers in the afternoon. The Germans were deceived, thinking that the activity on the river was another reinforcement move. For some, the deception lasted into D+9, when German formations still thought the perimeter to be properly defended.

On the south side, there were available two companies of British engineers, each with sixteen assault boats and two companies of Canadian engineers in stormboats, powered by what to the British were huge, 50hp Evinrude engines. The engineers came under the command of Lt. Colonel W.C.A. Henniker, the Chief Engineer of 43rd Division (formerly of 1st Airborne).

Yet 43rd Division planners made a bad mistake, possibly influenced by the charade that the Dorsets' crossing had been the prelude to a major reinforcement of 1st Airborne. They assumed that the Dorsets had established and held an extended frontage to the west and that there would be a major evacuation in the west as well as in the east, north of the Oosterbeek Church. Officially, the Dorsets would "cover the left flank of the 1st Airborne withdrawal," but any pretence that they would be the last out was abandoned through the plan to evacuate both groups almost simultaneously. How such a misconception should have taken hold is entirely unclear; if Urquhart had known of this plan, he would surely have demurred. His *Phantom* message of 1550 on D+8 suggests that he thought that there would be only one crossing, albeit on a wide frontage designated by a four-figure map reference.

That 43rd Division really had convinced itself that a major evacuation would take place in the western sector is clear from the disposition of their resources: half the evacuation force—one British company and the other Canadian—was directed on the western crossing, with major artillery support. The Canadian company, however, had far fewer stormboats than their other company at the main crossing to the east, and in the end, forty-six Dorsets were brought back, all in British assault boats. This figure includes a section of Dorsets who crossed in an assault boat which they found abandoned on the north bank. If the figure of forty-six was a component of the total of seventy-five Dorsets brought over, then very few Dorsets had broken through to the perimeter, to be evacuated with 1st Airborne.

Perhaps three hundred men were left on the north bank after the evacuation, and in view of the misguided evacuation plan, the figure could have been far worse. The largest of those parties left in the perimeter was D Company of the Borders in the central part of the western face of the perimeter. They were out of radio contact, and a message sent by a runner failed to meet them. Of the three brigadiers, Hicks alone crossed that night, and of the battalion commanders, only Payton-Reid of the KOSB.

The units assigned the western crossing point, nearly a mile away from the eastern crossing were the 553rd Field Company, Royal Engineers, and the Twentieth Field Company, Royal Canadian Engineers under Major A.W. Jones, normally equipped with assault rafts. The Canadians were allotted six of the twenty stormboats and six of a party of twelve fitters and carpenters from the Tenth Field Park Company, RCE. On the main eastern crossing route were the 260th Field Company, RE and Twenty-third Company, RCE, under Major Michael L. Tucker of Montreal, with fourteen stormboats and six more tradesmen from the Field Park Company. The Twenty-third got the lion's share of equipment because, wrote Tucker, "It [was] thought that the main body of airborne survivors are opposite our site."

The Canadian motorized stormboats were made entirely of plywood, with a crew of three and carried fifteen passengers. The stormboats weighed 500 pounds, but when wet and fully equipped, they could weigh half as much again. They were thus extremely difficult to manhandle in the driving rain and pitch-black darkness, across the morass and over two dykes to the south bank.

Tucker had ordered a daytime reconnaissance of the route through Valburg to Driel, then along the river bank. This was carried out by Lieutenants Russell Kennedy and Bob Tate, both now living in retirement in Canada. The final orders for the two Canadian companies were given at 1800 hours, the stormboats to be ready for operation by 2130 hours at the two crossing sites. The Canadians left Valburg in three jeeps, one scout car and twenty lorries. Their orders were for the Twenty-third to kick off at 2140 hours, the Twentieth in the west two hours later.

The evacuation began at 2130 hours or soon after, preceeded by an artillery barrage. This barrage caused much destruction among the

Germans and Dutch civilians alike. At the north of the perimeter, Major Geoffrey Powell, acting commander of 156th Parachute Battalion, pulled out the remnants of his unit at 2015 hours, shortly after the men had been told of the plan. This procedure continued down both sides of the perimeter. The Fourth Parachute Brigade HQ party, for instance, left for the evacuation at 2100 hours. The evacuation concluded with the withdrawal of Breeseforce in the west and Lonsdale Force in the east. At around 0200 hours, the last ammunition dump was blown up, the artillery firing off their last shells before the guns were disabled. Urquhart's HQ took its place in the evacuation sequence and crossed under fire from the Westerbouwing Heights just after midnight.

For the move to the Rhine, the paratroopers blackened their faces and masked the noise of their boots and equipment with strips of cloth. Heavy, driving rain continued throughout the night. Some failed to find the northern nodal points of the evacuation route, getting lost in the dark and sometimes blundering into the German lines. Once on the taped routes, they held onto the lines to the river bank or onto the tails of the smocks of the men in front of them, since few wore belts. The walking wounded were helped along and into the boats. There were reports of troopers calling at the ter Horst house to assist any wounded who felt capable of walking to the boats. This was contrary to Urquhart's order that the wounded were to be left behind.

The routes came under mortar and shellfire; some parties were ambushed by German patrols that infiltrated through the perimeter, which had never been secure at night. Those wounded on the route had to be abandoned, one of the many grim aspects of life in the Oosterbeek *Kessel*.

Louis Hagen wrote: "Then as my eyes got used to the open darkness of the meadow—searching for the origin of subdued screams I began to distinguish the shapes of bodies dragging themselves towards the path. Feverish pleading eyes looked up towards me, arms clutched around my legs, it seemed that all the wounded were frenzied by the fear of being left behind. . . . Then someone with an authoritative voice came up from the river and ordered me to leave the wounded where they were as they could not be got over the river just now and a doctor would be left behind to look after them. Exhausted and dazed by my impotence and the ghastliness of the scene, I continued towards the river. All along the path were mortar pits and the bodies of dead and wounded soldiers."

Once at the river bank, men lay in the mud, waiting their turn. Some fell asleep in the rain. The evacuation was on the whole efficient and orderly. When fights broke out over places on the boats, the glider pilots and engineers restored order. On one final trip, Lieutenant Kennedy drew his pistol while standing in his boat, thought better of it, then his boat sank from under him in four feet of water. Many were obliged or elected to swim across, though some of these exhausted troops drowned. The world soon got to know of the evacuation from the emotionally charged dispatches of the Canadian journalist, Stanley Maxted, featured in *Theirs is the Glory.*

At the western crossing, it was agreed that the Royal Engineers would begin ferrying operations. This was ostensibly because the noise from the Canadian stormboats' engines would give away the Allied positions. Since there was a constant din of supporting fire, the real reason was probably a deep British distrust of the motorized boats. In the event, none of the six Canadian boats was launched. Toward the end of the night, the Canadians attempted to send four of the stormboats the 1,500 yards to the eastern site. One boat was sunk by mortar fire and a second, under machine gun fire, was abandoned when the engine failed. "No other stormboats were launched," the 20th Company recorded, the reason being that German machine-gunners had pinpointed the Canadian positions.

Tucker launched the first boat of the eastern crossing at 2130 hours but this sank, having been holed by rocks as it was dragged from shore. Under fire from artillery, mortars and machine guns, the second and fourth boats were also sunk. Number two was lost with its crew of three and its commander, Lt. Russ Martin, after a direct hit by a mortar shell. Number four capsized when its passengers instinctively threw themselves to one side as a mortar round descended on the other. Only five of the complement on the boat returned to the south bank. Boats that did get across returned, initially, overloaded with wounded men, who were cared for under the supervision of the Catholic padre, Captain Jean Mongeon. The engineers' first aid post treated about sixty stretcher cases and 100 walking wounded before they were transported by lorry to Driel. The medical facilities of the engineers were overwhelmed by the casualties.

By 0330 hours, all of Tucker's fourteen boats were in operation, less those sunk or disabled. A crossing took three or four minutes, but there were delays in loading and the Canadians were plagued by electrical failures due to the rain, which often enough disabled the boats in mid-river, under fire from the Westerbouwing Heights. This was the experience of Major General Urquhart, who was relieved when his Canadian crew managed to restart the boat to the tune of ripe curses. The Evinrude engines sometimes failed to restart when their propellers became stuck in the mud on the shores. The Field Park Company, "working like fiends," serviced or changed ten engines. Boats that were damaged when arriving on the south bank had to be abandoned.

By 0400, as the first dull light appeared through the darkness and rain, only two boats were still in service. A third came back into operation when Lt. Kennedy managed to get the engine of an abandoned stormboat started. In his penultimate crossing, Kennedy set out in this boat towing an assault boat from the British engineer company and another stormboat whose engine had failed. He returned with thirty-six passengers and others clinging to the boat. Kennedy's final crossing was in a stormboat, towing another. When on the north bank, the motor of Kennedy's boat initially refused to restart and the second boat cast off, the passengers paddling to the shore. Of the twenty-five men aboard, most succumbed to machine gun fire and only four made it to the south bank. In the last two crossings, Kennedy was said to have deposited a load of German life jackets on the north bank. This apocryphal act, which did not take place, is often recorded but the real achievements of the Canadians are usually noted briefly in passing, if at all.

The Twenty-third Company Report credits the organization of the evacuation to Kennedy as well as his bringing over 125 men. Tucker, who had directed operations on the beach under machine gun fire, was ordered to cease the crossings at 0545 hours. On the north bank, Kennedy finally got his stormboat restarted. His last run concluded at 0720 hours in daylight; Kennedy, with a dead paratrooper beside him, was the last off the stormboat. The western crossing had ceased at 0330 hours. At least 2,398 men got across, which included 160 Poles and seventy-five Dorsets. Tucker calculated that his stormboats had carried across all but about a hundred in 150 crossings. The Canadians were warmly praised by Lt. Colonel Henniker for the operation. Five were decorated, including a Military Cross for Lt. Kennedy and a DSO for Tucker. Six men from the Twenty-third Company were killed and five were wounded.

At the western crossing, the British assault boats were slower, with smaller capacity, fighting a fast current on a diagonal passage. The two-

man crews became four, then six or eight, decreasing the number of passengers, but the two companies suffered no casualties. Ninety-five Red
Devils were killed on the north bank or while crossing. The carnage
would have been much worse but for the fact that the machine guns on
the Heights were forced to fire downward, rather than traversing across
the river. Krafft reported a total of 615 captured on the north bank and
in Oosterbeek, a total which likely included such of the walking wounded and the 300 or so which the 1st Airborne estimated to have been left
on the north bank. Without the Canadians, the evacuation would have
failed. Essame, characteristically, got the number of stormboats wrong
and gave the Canadians no credit for their part in the evacuation.

The German assault on the evacuated British positions began at
dawn on D+9 with three coordinated attacks aimed at the Hartenstein,
led by Eberwein, Oelkers and Bruhn. By midday, Eberwein and Oelkers
were in the heart of the perimeter and had made contact with a battalion of the Hermann Goering Regiment that had advanced east through
what had been the Breeseforce positions. Despite "spirited opposition"
from rearguards, the operation was over by 1400 hours. The Germans
too were utterly exhausted; some simply collapsed into sleep as soon as
it was clear that the British had gone. The *Wehrmacht* troops were given
ten days' leave; the *Waffen-SS* were left to supervise the forced evacuation of the civilian population, then to continue the campaign on the
Island. Dutch homes were systematically looted and the contents sent to
the devastated Ruhr. The Dutch had no kind words for the conduct of
the *Waffen-SS* in the aftermath of the siege.

At the British collection points on the south bank, the men were
marched into Driel or, arriving in strange places, simply walked into the
town. Some collapsed exhausted by the roadside; others scrounged civilian clothes to replace wet uniforms. After tea, cigarettes, rum and hot
food, the survivors were taken by truck, jeep and ambulance to
Nijmegen; some chose to walk in the absence of transport. By the early
morning, Cora Balthussen reported that almost no 1st Airborne troops
were left in Driel.

In Nijmegen there were instances of recrimination aimed at the
Guards for their failure to reach the Airborne. Tensions between the
paratroopers and the ground forces continued after the war, though the
rank and file of the latter were the least to blame for the failure of the
relief effort. One of the more unfortunate consequences of this is that,
contrary to the depictions in *Theirs Is the Glory*, the airborne did not

always give the Canadians the recognition they so thoroughly deserved. When truckloads of British survivors passed through the area of the 101st Airborne, they were roundly cheered. The fifteen days that the Screaming Eagles later spent in a *Kessel* of their own, during the Battle of the Bulge, were every bit as hellish as what the Red Devils endured at Arnhem.

14

ASSESSMENT

"They have first raised a dust and then complain they cannot see."
—Bishop Berkeley

Strategically, the most important achievements of *Market Garden* were the Nijmegen bridgehead and the gains that VIII Corps had made when it closed to the banks of the Meuse down to Sambeek. Neither delivered the apparent promise. In heavy fighting on the Island, the British and the 101st Airborne beat off counterattacks and crossings of the Lower Rhine, until the Germans flooded large areas south of Arnhem and near Driel. When the British and Canadians took Arnhem in April 1945, they crossed the IJssel from the east rather than the Rhine from the south. The Germans thwarted Montgomery's plan for a "threatening bridge-head" on the Island.

The Allies had planned an offensive southeast from the positions west of the Meuse even while *Market Garden* was still in progress. What stymied them in this case was the Meuse Salient, sometimes known as the Battle of the Peel Marshes, which sucked in divisions, British and American, at terrible cost until it was reduced early in December. The British-Canadian offensive along the Rhine and through the *Reichswald* began only in February 1945.

After *Market Garden,* the idea of twin thrusts over the Rhine in Montgomery's M525 order persisted. Hodges was planning his U.S. First Army offensive toward Bonn and Cologne on September 22, the day of Eisenhower's meeting with his senior commanders at Versailles and the day that all offensive operations of his army were shut down. Held up initially by the German defense of Aachen, and stiffening resistance along the Westwall, the American push over the Rhine was never more than a theoretical plan.

As a result of the Versailles meeting, the twin thrusts across the Rhine to threaten the Ruhr, one British and the other American, remained the SHAEF official policy on paper until the Battle of the Bulge began in mid-December. Montgomery later claimed that SHAEF had altered its military policy in his favor, on the grounds that Eisenhower now fully supported a proposition like that of M525. This led to the myth of the lost opportunity, on the grounds that *Market Garden* had not been given nearly enough priority.

The objectives were reduced to something more modest: instead of two bridgeheads as a prelude to the Ruhr offensive, the new plan for operations would *conclude* with two bridgeheads, likely one in the Bonn-Cologne sector and the other at Wesel-Krefeld, the small part of the *Ruhrindustriegebiet* west of the Rhine. By 22 September the euphoria of the Allied advance had evaporated. The strategic promise of *Market Garden*, which few other than Montgomery had believed in, came to nothing. Late in March 1945, the British crossed the Rhine at Rees, close to Dempsey's preferred site at Wesel.

The Players

After the war, Harzer said that the German achievement in *Market Garden* was the more remarkable because the battle was won using troops untrained in the role in which they were employed. Some were also badly equipped. Equally true is that, by rapid reaction and improvisation the Germans built up an opposition along the Corridor and at Ressen sufficient to derail the Allied plans and timetable. While Harzer paid tribute to the British, he did say that their stand at Arnhem was something that the Germans on the Russian front routinely had to do.

Some of the troops pitched against Second Army and the paratroopers had never even fired a rifle. Their leaders on the battlefield were as strange to them as were the enemy. Thus the degree of control the officers achieved over their green troops was remarkable. The *Wehrmacht* by 1944 had long begun to wither; but it was far from dead. Generally, a unit that was comprised of veterans or which had a core of veterans in its ranks fought as well during *Market Garden* as the *Wehrmacht* did in Normandy.

When this did not happen, such as the engagements on the western face of Hell's Highway, there were massacres and mass surrenders.

There were also episodes in which control broke down in the absence of a pre-existing command set-up. In some engagements, particularly with the *Wehrkreis VI* component, the Germans fought for a couple of hours, then faded away, a pattern that became comfortingly familiar to the Allies only in April 1945. Equally important were poor communications which led to uncoordinated attacks along the Corridor.

The failure of *Market Garden* can be put down to several mistakes, both in the planning and in the conduct of the operation. Yet when all these are accounted for, the fact remains that the Germans outfought the British. The two key points at which the Germans prevailed were the defense of the Nijmegen road bridge on D-Day and D+2, with a delaying action on D+3, and the defense of Ressen on the Island, from D+4 onward. Both engagements were carried out directly or under the command of II SS *Panzer* Corps. It was these two episodes, rather than the onslaught against the First and Fourth Parachute Brigades on D-Day to D+3, that proved decisive. Without the *Waffen-SS,* it is likely that the British would have reached the north bank of the Rhine at Arnhem.

The view that II SS *Panzer* Corps fought well was not universally shared. Private James Sims, who fought at the Arnhem road bridge, thought their performance patchy. Glider pilot Sergeant Louis Hagen, who interrogated prisoners, considered their morale poor, and their offensives hesitant and half-hearted.

As for the British, the central contention of this book is not that British troops were sluggish in their fighting and campaigning, but that they were invariably too slow in starting a new phase of the operation. The usual explanation for this is that Horrocks failed to instil a sense of urgency among the three divisions of XXX Corps. It is quite true that he never led from the head of an advance, nor did he use the radio or other means of communication to urge his units on. All through the night of D+3 for instance, it was abundantly clear that the Guards would advance from Nijmegen only at midday on D+4; in fact they started at 1330 hours. It is not that Horrocks failed to impart a sense of urgency; he never even tried.

When we see a constant pattern of delay, of the Guards at Valkenswaard and Nijmegen, and the 43rd Division at Grave, Nijmegen, Oosterhout, Valkenburg and Driel, some deeper explanation is needed than a failure of urgency. The explanation is that the leaders of the ground troops simply failed to understand the nature of *Market Garden*: the timetable for establishing the Arnhem bridgehead and the sequence of events needed to achieve it. Neither in outlook nor in training were the British ground troops cut out for an operation such as *Market Garden*. This was never factored in to the planning of the operation. Doubts about the feasibility of *Market Garden* should not have been confined to the possible strength of the opposition but of the ability of XXX Corps to move according to the timetable required. The attitude of a Patton and his Third Army toward the circumstances would have been very different.

There is a small example in the 5th Guards Brigade War Diary, a beautiful hand-written document which gives the impression, quite false, of having been written in the study after dinner. In it there is a telling phrase: "As usual the situation eased up in the evening." At the very time in which the advance needed to be pursued with the utmost vigor, the tanks and armored cars were harboured for the night.

And so it was with the infantry. Urquhart was clearly disgusted at the failure of General Thomas and the 43rd Wessex to close up to the Lower Rhine and relieve his division in the Oosterbeek bridgehead. But infantry training put no premium on such urgency so it was not likely to happen. The demand for more effort concealed deep-seated flaws in the whole system, not one particular division or its commander. Further, the demand for more effort fails to put the emphasis where it surely should lie.

There have been many plausible designations of the point at which the Arnhem operation failed: the loss of the Son bridge and the failure of the Guards to advance out of Valkenswaard; the inability of the 82nd to take the Nijmegen Bridge on D-Day; the inability of Frost's battalion to prevent the German armor from moving south across the Arnhem Bridge on D+3; the failure of XXX Corps to advance from the north end of the Nijmegen bridge that same evening. But the point of failure is best located where XXX Corps failed to advance north to the Arnhem road bridge beyond the German positions at Ressen, and turned west instead. Without immediate plans to build a bridge and cross the Rhine in force, the move was really an admission of failure. The British leadership was far from incompetent; the truth is that the British Army was incapable of carrying out the Arnhem operation.

The Battle

In the Arnhem battle, there were really two operations in one, and not simply *Market* for the paratroop drop and *Garden* for XXX Corps.

In its grand conception and strategic aim, there was one operation to advance three Corps of the British Second Army over the Rhine to the IJsselmeer with bridgeheads over the IJssel River to the east. The paratroop operation was merely to ensure the success of the advance at key points: Son, Grave, the Maas-Waal Canal, Nijmegen and Arnhem. This strategic operation was a total failure, as de Guingand acknowledged. It was far too ambitious to succeed.

The second operation was an advance by XXX Corps to secure a bridgehead over the Lower Rhine, assisted by the paratroopers in a more ambitious version of *Comet*, as one arm of the dual thrust to the Rhine planned on 6 September. To have secured a bridgehead over the Rhine would have been a momentous success. This operation too was a failure, though it liberated a large area of the Netherlands and secured the Nijmegen bridgehead. So the question then becomes: were the strength of the enemy and the training and outlook of the British ground forces such as to warrant such a major tactical operation? There is no clear answer since the operation nearly succeeded, but the assessment of the ground forces suggests that the verdict should have been negative.

We cannot ascribe all of the failures of the Arnhem operation to the confounding of two distinct but overlapping operations; but many of them can. On paper, XXX Corps should have had no trouble on the flanks, but because neither XII nor VIII Corps kept pace with XXX Corps, the latter was constantly harried from both sides. The XXX Corps was still on its own when it crossed the Nijmegen bridge and had to fight the battle for the Oosterbeek bridgehead solely with its own resources. The cutting of the Corridor and the diversion of resources to deal with the German threat on both sides was not decisive or crucial. But it does serve to illustrate the strategic failure of the Arnhem operation in the inability to bring all of Second Army up to the Rhine as a unified force. To sum it all up: the tactical operation for a Rhine bridgehead began too late to exploit the German retreat, while the strategic operation to secure the IJsselmeer was premature and too ambitious to succeed.

After the operation was concluded, both Eisenhower and Montgomery expressed confidence that the attempt had been worthwhile. And so they would and should have, because Eisenhower had endorsed, authorized and supported Monty's offensive, which was neither modified nor compromised from its original conception. Alan Brooke and the British official military historian, L.F. Ellis, later expressed the opinion that the operation should never have taken place, the former casting doubt on Montgomery's military judgment in this unique case, the latter putting the onus on both Montgomery and Eisenhower. It is thus instructive to see what Montgomery himself said about the operation.

Montgomery's first contention in his *Memoirs* was that the operation was not properly supported in terms of "administrative resources," "additional resources" and "full logistic support." Montgomery in 1958 regarded the Arnhem operation as "the spearhead of a major Allied movement on the northern flank designed to isolate, and finally to occupy, the Ruhr." It "should, and could, have been the decisive blow of the campaign in the West." According to Montgomery, SHAEF did not regard the operation as such and failed to give it the supplies and support that it needed.

This apologia is a travesty of the facts. Throughout September, Montgomery had been most anxious to open the Channel ports to Allied supply, principally Le Havre, Boulogne and Calais. This he regarded as essential to his strategic plans. But he undertook *Market Garden* without these ports and with a supply line extending from his rear maintenance area around Bayeux directly to the divisions of Second Army. The inadequacy of this arrangement led him to ask for more supplies. When he got them, he rescinded the delay in the launch of *Market Garden* and to Crerar he wrote that he had won a "great victory" at SHAEF.

There was indeed a delay in gasoline deliveries and in getting the additional supply transport that Bedell Smith had promised, though this was not crucial for operations and the supply arrangements persisted long after the *circa* October 1 sunset that Eisenhower had laid down. Montgomery never requested more transport for his divisions on the Seine. Montgomery got all the logistical support he requested, with only minor delays.

Montgomery also said that the ground forces were inadequate for the job; but he made no such contention at the time, at best merely grumbling that Eisenhower had not curtailed operations by the U.S. Third Army, which was irrelevant to the question of what he himself considered adequate. The truth was that the operation was too ambitious. In launching it with a tenuous supply line, no reserve build-up of supplies, a shortage of ground transport, and both VIII and XII Corps unready at the start, Montgomery's professionalism had deserted him. (These logistical issues are fully discussed in Appendix 2.)

Montgomery conceded that he had underestimated the enemy. In this he was not alone, yet there is some indication that he knowingly did so. The principal reason that *Comet* was cancelled was that opposition along Second Army's front had stiffened, making relief of the paratroopers by the ground forces uncertain. There was really no reason then to think that the Germans would crumble along the frontage of three Corps in a matter of hours. With no plan for the eventuality of a major stall and no hands-on direction of the battle in the event that the plan, such as it was, were thwarted, is it any wonder that Gavin asked in his memoirs why the battle was so badly planned?

Second, Montgomery said that he should have ordered a whole Parachute Brigade to drop "quite close" to the bridge so that it could have been captured in a matter of minutes. This is quite correct, though the story is more complex. In the case of 1st Airborne, the question was not only the distance from the road bridge but the fact that, because of the need to guard the DZ/LZ as a base of operations, only half of the forces available on D-Day could make for the road bridge. In the case of the 82nd Airborne, there was a comparable flaw in the battle plan, with the additional fact that the Nijmegen road bridge was only the third on the list of priorities. There was also the need to land on both sides of the key crossings of Son, Grave, the Maas-Waal Canal, Nijmegen and Arnhem: the Five Bridges. The need was all the more acute because the operation was in daylight; even *coup de main* parties could not rely on surprise.

Chester Wilmot blamed the Americans for overturning "Montgomery's plan" to drop on both sides of the Son bridge, when this benefit of the original seven-point plan was incidental. Equally, it was Dempsey as much as Maxwell Taylor who endorsed the plan to drop paratroopers two miles from the Son bridge and not on the south bank.

With regard to the Grave crossing, Gavin decided to drop a company south of the bridge only at the last minute. That he was able to do so without objection from First Allied Airborne Army is a credit to American organization, which had a flexibility that their British counterparts lacked. With the Maas-Waal crossings, it was a matter of luck and good soldiering that the Heumen bridge over the Maas-Waal Canal was captured before it was blown, since there were no troops in the vicinity on either side of the bridge and the other three bridges over the canal were not a top priority on D-Day.

Third, Montgomery blamed the weather, saying that it was an uncertain factor that had to be accepted. The weather did indeed prevent effective air support, though the inadequacy was mainly due to poor and clumsy communications. Montgomery said that the weather could have been offset by additional resources and more aircraft. But at Arnhem, all air transport was fully engaged in airborne operations and supply. To have pulled in more aircraft would have meant converting medium and heavy bombers to a transport role, which could never have been done in the time available, even if it were well-advised.

The salient factor with the weather was the delay in bringing in reinforcements. These delays accounted for five hours lost at 1st Airborne's second lift on D+1, the postponement of the Polish paratroop drop for two days, the delay of Polish 1st Battalion for a further two days, and the delay of the 82nd's glider infantry and the 101st's artillery for four days. Robert Kershaw is surely correct when he says that the Germans, through rapid improvisation, easily won the battle of the build-up.

Yet there is a real question of how important these delays actually were. Most of the things that went wrong did so on the first day of the battle: the hiatus at Valkenswaard, the destruction of the Son bridge, the failure of the 101st Airborne and the Guards Armoured to meet in Eindhoven; the frustration of the 82nd Airborne's limited attempts to capture the Nijmegen bridge, and the inability of 1st Airborne to secure the south end of the Arnhem road bridge. These failings are not related to the battle of the build-up. With regard to *Garden*, it has been argued that the key points of the battle were the failure to advance over the Nijmegen bridges until D+3 and the halt the Germans imposed on the British on the Nijmegen-Elst-Arnhem road. In none of these cases was the lack of airborne troops a cause of failure. The one serious contention about a lack of airborne troops was the refusal of 1AAA to agree to a second lift on D-Day. (In Appendix 3, it is argued that this was not the reason that the initial assaults on the Arnhem and Nijmegen bridges failed.)

Fourth, Montgomery attributes the lack of full success to the fact that the II SS *Panzer* Corps was refitting in the area. "We knew it was there . . . we were wrong in supposing that it could not fight effectively." Here, Montgomery was at the very least being economical with the truth. The brigadiers, plus Freddie Gough, were told only of Second Army intelligence that two depleted SS *Panzer* divisions were in the area. This information was not passed on to the battalion commanders.

No one in 1st Airborne knew of the *Ultra* information, not even in ways that disguised its source, nor of Brian Urquhart's photo-reconnaissance findings. Browning knew of the latter but, it must be assumed, not the former, since *Ultra* information went down only to Army level commands.

Montgomery knew about the *Ultra* information. When Bedell Smith and Kenneth Strong, Eisenhower's Intelligence chief, met with Montgomery on September 16, they talked of transport and Montgomery's supply situation. But equally important were the *Ultra* decrypts revealing the presence of the two SS tank divisions and some indication of their strength. Bedell Smith made some proposals, which Montgomery "waved airily aside." In refusing to modify the plan in any way, Montgomery's professionalism had again deserted him. Nothing was to be allowed to qualify the grand design.

Could the operation, in so far as it meant a bridgehead over the Rhine, have succeeded? The answer is yes, because it nearly did. To have undertaken the operation with a prospect of success would have entailed a single-minded push toward the Arnhem Bridge, with the ground troops knowing that they had one urgent task and one only. When Eisenhower is faulted for not "reining in" Montgomery, this criticism is properly applied to the bigger plan, not to the limited aim of securing the Arnhem Bridge.

Instead of an advance by Second Army, the Arnhem Corridor should have been kept clear of anything that was not needed for the immediate relief of the three groups of paratroopers. Extra troops from Second Army should have been available to expand and defend the Corridor from the inside. Among the equipment needed for immediate relief were bridging columns. The evidence shows that 43rd Division planned carefully for the eventuality of a major bridge being lost and the bridging columns did get the priority that they were accorded by the Transport Office. But when the question arose of having to cross the Rhine in force in the area of Heaveadorp-Driel on D+5, the 43rd was ill-prepared. The four bridging columns were not alerted until D+7 and the plans to move to the Rhine were immediately cancelled.

When we have examined all the merits and defects of Allied strategy, the final result comes down to one thing. Buoyed and blinded by the success of the Allied advances of August 1944, the Allies launched an operation which assumed a German response of a sort that only materialized in April 1945, during and after the Battle of the Ruhr Pocket.

Among the few who disputed this false appreciation of the enemy were
Brian Urquhart, John Hackett, Stanislaw Sosabowski and Oscar Koch.
This being so, the Germans outfought the British and the battle was lost.
Lest anyone think that the Arnhem operation was a unique blunder, let
them look first at engagements which were a far bigger waste: Patton's
needless hammering away at the Metz fortresses or Hodges' throwing
division after division into the Battle of the Huertgen Forest, like some
mythical donkey of the Great War.

A MAGNIFICENT DISASTER

Christopher Hibbert, writing long before *A Bridge Too Far* had made
Market Garden famous, describes the Battle of Arnhem-Oosterbeek as
being "one of the great epic tragedies which ennoble the history of the
British Army," and as having "a special quality, a flavour almost of mys-
tique. . . . It is, for many reasons, unique." Major G.G. Norton
described the battle as a "magnificent disaster," Peter Harclerode as a
"glorious defeat." Foreigners have often observed that the British have
a curious way of celebrating defeat, in the Second World War most obvi-
ously the Dunkirk evacuation of 1940 and Arnhem in1944. This is a
mischaracterization. What is being celebrated is not defeat but the combatants and their battles. The celebrations have historical connections in
sagas, oral traditions and epic poetry; the combatants are not soldiers
but warriors.

The language used, of epic battles, of glory, but above all, of magnificence, are expressions of the warrior culture, many of whose values
were absorbed into the ethic of the professional soldier many centuries
ago. This language is essentially class-based, since it is to be found far
more frequently among officers than among the rank and file. Yet survival of the warrior culture can be detected more widely, since the rank
and file notoriously respected a worthy enemy who fought fiercely and
skilfully and was expected to accord decency in victory. This is the real
import of the warm regard of "Old Jerry" in the First World War and
"Old Rommel" in the Second.

What is less clear is how far the British saw themselves as warriors
as opposed to professional soldiers. The paradigm case is that of Lt.
Colonel John Frost, who assumed that not only did he enjoy fighting
and combat but that his men did too. He thought it wrong to hate the
enemy. When among civilians during the war he praised the prowess

and the chivalry of the Germans, for which he was "almost ostracised."

Frost was a tall, big-boned, taciturn man, in Urquhart's words "with an anxious moon face and permanent worry lines across his forehead," hardly the model of a modern hero. How far his attitudes were shared by his fellow officers is not known, since there are few writings comparable to Frost's *A Drop Too Many*. The most likely conclusion is that there were warrior vestiges in the culture of the British Army, reflected in the language of magnificence, glory and epic tragedy. But the vestiges were just that: remnants of an earlier time, not the essence of modern military society. To discern the ethos of the battle in the language used is not to characterize it falsely but to accord pre-eminence to only one of its many facets. A disaster Arnhem certainly was; its magnificence was a view seen from an oblique angle and described in language from a distant past.

The German troops of *Hohenstaufen* and *Frundsberg* certainly had a respect and admiration for the British, perhaps even affection. Here, the import of their attitudes is harder to discern. Himmler saw the SS as a warrior caste, comparable to the Teutonic knights who would dwell in fortified manors of the conquered east. There they would hold sway over a depleted Slav population of serfs. Whether many of the *Waffen-SS* troops held such views is doubtful, except perhaps among the original premiere SS regiments of pre-war days. The *Waffen-SS* armored divisions, of which the Ninth and Tenth were two of seven, were an elite, yet marred in almost every case by atrocities committed against the soldiers they fought and civilians unfortunate enough to have crossed their path. The Ninth and Tenth divisions were exceptional, in that the Nazi ethos was minimal, irrespective of the number of Nazis in their ranks. They were among the SS divisions that Himmler considered insufficiently Nazi and too akin to the *Wehrmacht*. They committed very few criminal acts; the original mustering in 1943 was marked by protests against having to join a Nazi organization. Bittrich, aware of the impact of this on morale, allowed both Catholic and Protestant Chaplains into *Hohenstaufen*. The senior officers of the Corps, led by Bittrich, regarded themselves simply as professional soldiers for whom, self-deceptively no doubt, the Nazi military structure was of no consequence.

Against the British they performed and conducted themselves as such, to the surprise of some of the enemy, who thought they would be shot when captured. There may well have been warrior vestiges in the II SS *Panzer* Corps, but the dominant impression is one of professional soldiery little different from the elite of the *Wehrmacht*. The airborne would have had no objection at all to inviting their old enemy to the Arnhem observances; there seems to have been some social contact, for example, between Frost and Harmel after the war. That there were no such invitations was out of respect and deference to the Dutch, whose memory of the SS after the battle is of a band of boorish louts who pillaged and defiled what was left of their households and killed those who had aided the British with arms or merely with succor.

EPILOGUE

"I had been thrown not long before into yet another
thunderous demonstration of man's inhumanity to man, its
impact all the greater for the speed with which the airborne operation
had developed. I had seen dreadful destruction, great kindness, cruel
pain, and high fortitude—a catastrophic mixture of opposites,
all of man's contriving, not forced upon him but his own
work, in a universe surely intended for some better end.
What had gone wrong?"
— General Sir John Hackett, 1978

On 1 October, the *Hohenstaufen* was withdrawn to Siegen in Germany, a move that had been planned three weeks before. On the 10th, Sylvester Stadler resumed his command of the division and Harzer was appointed commandant of the Divisional Officers' Course at Hirschberg. *Hohenstaufen* received replacements from the *Luftwaffe*, the *Kriegsmarine* and *Volksdeutscher* from Hungary and Yugoslavia. As in the original mustering in 1943, unpromising draftees soon met the high standards of *Hohenstaufen*. The division was restored almost to the strength it had on 28 June, when it arrived in Normandy. As late as April 1945, both *Hohenstaufen* and *Frundsberg* were reinforced and re-equipped for new operations at a level approaching normal establishment.

On 9 December, in sixty-two trains, *Hohenstaufen* moved to the German Eiffel to take part in the Battle of the Bulge. Early in March 1945, the II SS *Panzer* Corps, with the *Frundsberg* detached, was moved to Hungary for *Unternehmen Frühlingserwachen* (Operation Spring

Awakening), the recapture of Budapest and the Hungarian oilfields. Stadler surrendered to the Americans on 8 May, 1945. After its last battle, the *Hohenstaufen* was down to two battalions, fifteen Panther tanks and eight *Panzer* IVs.

Frundsberg remained on the Island until 18 November, when it was withdrawn from II SS *Panzer* Corps. The division was directed to Alsace to face the U.S. Ninth Army at the West Wall, sixty miles to the south. In January 1945, it might have been returned to the II SS *Panzer* Corps but for another crisis on the Eastern Front. The *Frundsberg* was directed to Stettin on February 10 and fought on the east bank of the Oder until 19 March. Eight days later it was ordered to the *Frankfurt am Oder* sector, then to an assembly area seven miles from Goerlitz. At the end of March, while in Berlin for medical treatment, Harmel briefed Hitler on the state of his division and learned on 16 April that the Russians had begun their last great push from the Oder-Neisse bridgeheads. He rushed back to his division to lead a counterattack on the Russians around Spremberg.

By the 19th, *Frundsberg* was split into three parts. Ordered by Field-Marshal Shoerener to close a gap between Cottbus and Spremberg or die trying, Harmel ignored the order and attempted a break-out northwest to the units covering the sector south of Berlin. On the 28th Harmel was recalled to Schoerner's HQ, relieved of his command, then sent to lead, in Michael Reynolds' words, "a hotchpotch of units in the Klagenfurt sector of southern Austria." He surrendered to the British on 8 May. SS-Lt. Colonel Franz Roestel, who had led the armored squadron on the eastern side of the Arnhem Corridor, became the final commander of *Frundsberg*. In the last days the division broke up, its members killed or captured by the Czechs and Russians. One formation, however, Brinkmann's Tenth SS Reconnaissance Battalion, crossed the Elbe and surrendered to the U.S. 102nd Infantry Division.

From the initial work of Lt. Colonel Theodoor Boeree and Christopher Hibbert to Cornelius Ryan, the chief written and oral source of the German perspective on Operation *Market* was Walther Harzer. He became a consulting engineer in Stuttgart and died in 1982. Heinz Harmel, *der alte Frundsberg*, became a salesman in Duisberg and died in 2000 at the age of 94. Willi Bittrich surrendered his corps HQ to the Americans at Linz on 8 May, 1945 and was handed over to the French. He was accused of ordering the hanging of twelve resistance fighters by SS military police in August 1944. This act, a war crime, did not have on it the mark of the other *Waffen-SS* armored divisions, with their atrocities and reprisals; rather it reflected the brutality of the German occupation forces.

At a hearing in 1953 before a military court in Bordeaux, Bittrich claimed that he did not know of the event until after it had happened, and the charges were dismissed. The real reason for his exoneration was that he had already spent far more time in jail than most convicted war criminals. He returned to Germany in 1954 and provided a wealth of information to scholars, both German and foreign. Hackett and others spoke in his defense as a fair and honorable enemy. Bittrich died in 1979, an outstanding corps commander of the Second World War.

Bittrich's colleague in the Netherlands, *Luftwaffe* General Friedrich Christiansen, was sentenced twelve years for three cases of criminal reprisals against civilians, in one of which the *Luftwaffe* Colonel Fullriede was involved. Christiansen, "a former tug-boat skipper," was known to his German associates and to the Dutch as a mild man; to the latter, he was certainly not the object of retribution or revenge. Arthur Seyss-Inquhart, *Reichskommissar* for the Netherlands, was hanged at Nuremberg in 1946. He said of his fellow Austrian, the Higher SS and Police Chief Hanns Albin Rauter, that he was "a big child with a child's cruelty." Rauter, who had offered help and advice to Model, von Tettau and Lippert, was shot by the Dutch in 1949.

Those German officers who did their best to mitigate the worst effects of the occupation were treated with leniency, including Colonel Fullriede. Among them was the Town Commandant of Apeldoorn, Major Eckbrecht Freiherr von Oldershausen, who was declared a "non-enemy" by the Dutch after the war. Though some, such as Graeme Warrack, did not trust him, Olderhausen was in fact a German patriot and a traitor to National Socialism.

The British found it easy to liaise with the Dutch Resistance in the complex of four hospitals in Apeldoorn to which the wounded Red Devils were transported. The lax security was likely due to von Oldershausen, who turned a very blind eye to the activities of the Resistance at the hospitals, even giving them sheafs of blank transit passes. Oldershausen was imprisoned by Rauter and then released by General Johannes Blaskowitz on 5 May 1945. Blaskowitz was to some extent a kindred spirit; he had incurred Hitler's lasting enmity for protesting the treatment of Polish civilians in 1940. Oldershausen ended up as an interpreter for Blaskowitz when he conducted the surrender negotiations with the Canadian General Foulkes and Prince Bernhard at Wageningen.

As for the Americans, the 82nd Airborne was ordered to pull out of the line and assemble near Paris on 11 November (D+55), a withdrawal that was completed two days later. On 25 November (D+71), the 101st Airborne began their withdrawal and also completed it in two days. They were transported across the Waal in the stormboats of the Twenty-third Field Company, RCE, in numbers estimated at 6,500 by Major Tucker. The withdrawal took place in the nick of time, since they were to act as ground troops by the middle of December in the Battle of the Bulge.

The casualties of the 82nd Airborne from D-Day to D+8 were 215 killed, 790 wounded and 427 missing. For the 101st Airborne the figures were 315 killed, 1,248 wounded and 547 missing. The battles on the Island and, for the 82nd in the *Reichswald*-Groesbeek sector south of the Rhine, were a catalogue of hard fighting, constant shelling, perpetual exhaustion, waterlogged trenches, rain and squalor.

The Americans' two brilliant divisional commanders went on to distinguished careers. Maxwell Taylor became Chairman of the Joint Chiefs of Staff, then Ambassador to South Vietnam in the opening stages of that war. James Gavin also stayed in the Army, then became a civilian consultant and was twice Ambassador to France. He died, much mourned, at the age of eighty-two in 1990. His friends said of him that he had such strength of character and diversity of talent that he should have been President of the U.S.

After the war the Americans, like the other combatants, suffered the delayed after-effects of their wartime experiences. This aspect of the audit of war is in constant flux, because of changing perspectives on warfare and the emergence of new evidence, sometimes centuries after the event. The general pattern is well-known: guilt at survival, remorse at killing, reclusiveness, sleeplessness, nightmares and memories of maimed and dismembered bodies, alcoholism, unhealed wounds, the inability to hold a job or keep a marriage together. At least the veterans enjoyed mutual support among their own kind and the recognition that they had acquitted themselves well, in a just war. The next generation of veterans, those of the Vietnam War, had no such consolation; for many, that war was an unmitigated personal and social tragedy.

For the British, it seems plausible that there were parallel phenomena; but among the reasons put forward for the annual observances at

Arnhem, the notion of veterans coming to terms with a harrowing experience has not yet been advanced. Even the strongest were not exempt: after the war, Roy Urquhart assaulted his wife in bed, believing in his sleep that he was still at Arnhem.

The 1st Airborne Division was not immediately disbanded as expected, but Hackett lost his beloved Fourth Parachute Brigade, barely a hundred members of which had been evacuated across the Rhine. Parts of the division were sent to Norway to oversee the German surrender in May 1945 and disbandment came in August. Four hundred troops were released to Arnhem in the summer for the making of the movie, *Theirs Is the Glory.*

When Sosabowski met Urquhart in Nijmegen after the battle, he found him "in a low state, both physically and mentally." On the 28th, Urquhart had lunch with Dempsey then went overnight to Montgomery's Tactical HQ, where he was received with evident gratitude and sympathy. The next day, Major General Williams sent his own aircraft to Brussels, from which Urquhart was flown to RAF Cranwell, to be met by Brereton and Major General Crawford, the IAAA Director for Air. Though Urquhart, like Montgomery, put a brave face on *Market Garden*, he was deeply dejected by the event. He seems to have been "tainted by defeat," since he remained a Major-General until he retired in 1955. He died in 1988. Montgomery, too, according to one account, was dejected, since he became withdrawn, "usually a sign of anger." How Browning reacted is not known; he soon after became Mountbatten's Chief of Staff at South East Asia Command, retired in 1949 and died in 1953. According to Brian Urquhart, he was as dejected as the others.

Of the corps commanders, General Sir Brian Horrocks remained GOC of XXX Corps till the end of the war, then commander of the British Army of the Rhine, formerly 21AG. His less than adequate command performance in *Market Garden* did not detract from his service record in World War II. Lt. General Sir Richard O'Connor became GOC East India early in November 1944. A possible reason for his transfer and promotion was that he refused to write an adverse combat report on Major General Lindsay McDonald Silvester of the U.S. 7th Armored Division when it came under VIII Corps command in the early stages of the Battle of Overloon. Though Silvester's dismissal by Bradley was upheld by a court of inquiry after the war, there is no reason to doubt that O'Connor's position was principled and correct.

Lt. General Sir Neil Ritchie, still clouded by his poor performance as commander of Eighth Army in the Western Desert, retired from the Army in 1951 and took up residence in Toronto, where he died in 1984. General Sir Miles Dempsey finally retired in 1953. He lived the life of an obscure country gentleman and died in 1969, having served his country if not with distinction, then at least a thoroughgoing competence.

On the air side, 474 air crew, passengers and glider pilots were killed in the British part of *Market,* a figure which includes 79 RASC dispatchers. The Glider Pilot Regiment needed about 500 replacements after *Market Garden,* since it suffered 615 casualties in the battle, of whom 147 were killed. In the event, Colonel Chatterton used the old-boy network to recruit 1,500 replacements, not from the Army but from Bomber Command, much to the disgust of most of those drafted.

Of the 7,000 from 1st Airborne taken prisoner, more than 130 escaped over the Lower Rhine to the British lines. Hundreds more evaded capture. The greatest concentration of evaders was in and around the small town of Ede, in which were garrisoned many hundreds of German troops. Most evaders had arrived with the help of the Dutch Resistance after escaping from Oosterbeek, from German captivity en route to prison camps, and a few from the four large hospitals in Apeldoorn.

The first exodus in the Renkum area was well organized by the Dutch Resistance and British officers, the leading light of whom was Tatham-Warter. The party of 128 that crossed the Rhine in assault boats crewed by Robert Sink's parachute infantry on the night of October 22 (*Pegasus I*) included Brigadier Lathbury, CO of First Parachute Brigade, Tatham-Warter of 2nd Battalion, Deane-Drummond, second-in-command of 1st Airborne Signals, and Tony Hibbert, Brigade Major of First Parachute Brigade. The escape was supervised by Lt. Colonel David Dobie of First Parachute Battalion and Lt. Leo Heaps, who had crossed earlier at Maurik independently of each other. A subsequent crossing (*Pegasus II)* in the stormboats of the 23rd Company, RCE on the night of 19 November, was much less successful. Lieutenant Kennedy brought across one paratrooper and two Dutch civilians; two subsequent crossings by the 23rd brought over four more.

The wounded Brigadier Hackett had been spirited out of the St. Elizabeth's Hospital on October 4. He was hidden and nursed in Ede by the de Nooy sisters, three older spinsters, and members of their family, with extreme care, kindness and selfless bravery. Still weak, he was escorted out of Ede on 30 January, 1945. He and Colonel Warrack, the chief medical officer, crossed at the western confluence of the Waal and the Maas on February 5, the surgeon Captain Lipmann Kessel the following night, and yet another doctor, Captain T.F. Redman, a few nights later. So it was that the last of the three brigadiers of First Airborne returned to England.

By 2004, most of Torenstraat in Ede had vanished in favor of a large commercial development in the center of the town. No. 5, where the de Nooy sisters had cared for Brigadier Hackett for nearly four months, was demolished much earlier. The house on Stationsweg, damaged by Allied bombing, where Hackett was sheltered briefly by Lt. Colonel Boeree and his family, still stands. Hackett's memoir, *I Was a Stranger*, is a classic of the Second World War.

Appendix I

Chronology of Events

September 1: Dieppe captured.

September 2: Airborne Operation *Comet* first planned.

September 3: Field-Marshal Montgomery orders an all-out effort to "bounce the Rhine."

Brussels liberated by the Guards Armoured Division.

Deelen airfield and nightfighter control center bombed.

September 4: General Eisenhower issues a general order to the Allied Expeditionary Force.

Montgomery given control of First Allied Airborne Army.

Antwerp captured by the 11th Armoured Division and the Belgian Resistance.

September 5: *Mad Tuesday*: the German retreat reaches its height and begins to slow down.

German evacuation of Fifteenth Army elements from the south bank of the Scheldt to Walcheren and South Beveland begins, through the ports of Breskens and Terneuzen.

Field-Marshal Gerd von Rundstedt reappointed Commander-in-Chief West.

Field-Marshal Walther Model retains command of Army Group B.

Colonel-General Kurt Student ordered to the line of the Albert Canal as Commander, First Parachute Army.

September 6: British Second Army plans for a ground advance articulated.

	Leading elements of the retreating II SS *Panzer* Corps arrive in the Arnhem area.
	Operation *Comet* repeatedly postponed.
September 7:	Gheel crossing of the Albert Canal.
	Beeringen crossing of the Albert Canal.
September 9:	Ostend occupied.
September 10 (D-7):	*Market Garden* definitively planned; first planning meeting held the same day.
September 12 (D-5):	De Groot Barrier crossing on the Meuse-Escaut Canal, the Neerpelt bridgehead for *Market Garden*, established.
	XII Corps takes over responsibility for the Gheel sector on the Albert Canal.
September 13 (D-4):	Aart crossing of the Meuse-Escaut Canal by XII Corps troops.
	Le Havre assaulted and captured.
September 15 (D-2):	Port of Marseilles opened.
	Model's HQ, Army Group B, opens in Oosterbeek.
	VIII Corps Advance HQ opens near Beeringen.
September 16 (D-1):	Eisenhower authorizes *Market Garden*.
	Heinz Harmel, commander, 10th Waffen-SS Division *Frundsberg*, leaves for Berlin.
	Plans for the ground advance explained at a XXX Corps commanders' meeting.
September 17 (D-Day):	*Market Garden* opens with massive bombing raids on Arnhem and points south, the airborne landings and the XXX Corps advance.
	The 9th *Waffen-SS* Division *Hohenstaufen* Reconnaissance Battalion moves south over the Arnhem Bridge to Nijmegen.
	First Allied Airborne Army units capture the Grave and Molenhoek bridges, the demolished Son bridge, and the north end of the Arnhem road bridge.
	Plans are abandoned to use the Aart bridgehead over the Meuse-Escaut Canal as the XII Corps starting point for *Market Garden*.
	Dutch national rail strike begins.

September 18 (D+1):   Brest falls to U.S. Ninth Army.

Lommel bridgehead over the Meuse-Escaut Canal established as the XII Corps starting point for *Market Garden*.

The 82nd Airborne captures the Honinghutie bridges.

The 101st Airborne occupies Eindhoven; German air raid on the city, the same night.

Most of British 3rd Division established in its VIII Corps sector.

The leading elements of the 10th *Waffen-SS* Division *Frundsberg* arrive in Nijmegen.

September 19(D+2):   VIII Corps establishes a bridgehead over the Meuse-Escaut Canal at Lille St. Hubert as its starting point for *Market Garden*.

The Guards Armoured Division reaches Grave and Nijmegen.

September 20 (D+3):   82nd Airborne's assault crossing of the Waal.

Nijmegen road bridge captured by the Guards Armoured Division and elements of the 82nd Airborne.

German vehicles cross south over the Arnhem bridge, through the positions of the Second Parachute Battalion.

Terneuzen, Dutch port used to evacuate German Fifteenth Army from the Breskens Pocket, captured by First Polish Armored Division.

September 21 (D+4):   German evacuation of the Breskens Pocket completed, leaving 64th Division in place.

First Polish Independent Parachute Brigade drops south of the Lower Rhine around Driel.

British First Airborne establishes a perimeter opposite the Poles at Oosterbeek.

September 22 (D+5):   Boulogne captured by Canadian First Army.

All offensive operations of U.S. First Army shut down.

Eisenhower meets with his senior commanders at Versailles.

Leading elements of Second Household Cavalry Regiment, then the 5th DCLI, join the Poles in Driel.

First crossing of the Rhine into the Oosterbeek perimeter by the Poles.

Arnhem Corridor cut from the east between Veghel and Uden by 107th *Panzer* Brigade.

Weert captured by British Third Division troops, in the VIII Corps sector.

XII Corps operations stalled in the area of Best.

September 23 (D+6): Second crossing of the Rhine by the Poles.

Arnhem Corridor route restored by the 101st Airborne and Coldstream Guards tanks.

130th Brigade of 43rd Division arrives at the Polish positions in Driel.

The remaining elements of the Polish Parachute Brigade dropped near Grave.

September 24 (D+7): Valburg meeting: XXX Corps, 43rd Division and Polish Parachute Brigade.

Crossing of the Rhine by the Fourth Dorsets.

Germans cut the Arnhem Corridor south of Veghel from the west; an alternative route north remains open.

September 25 (D+8): First Airborne Division evacuated from Oosterbeek by 23rd Field Company, Royal Canadian Engineers.

Patrols of First Belgian Brigade, under VIII Corps, reach the Meuse.

Helmond occupied by VIII Corps troops.

September 26 (D+9): *Market Garden* officially concludes.

Boxmeer on the Meuse occupied by VIII Corps troops.

Alternative supply route to Uden in the Corridor opened through the VIII Corps sector.

Arnhem Corridor route restored.

First crossing to the south bank of the Rhine by troops of the Division von Tettau.

September 27 (D+10): German frogmen destroy the Nijmegen rail bridge.

September 29 (D+12): The Grenadier Guards of XXX Corps and the 7th Armoured of XII Corps meet near Heech.

The British 3rd Division of VIII Corps and the 82nd Airborne meet on the Maas.

Peel Marshes (Meuse Salient) Campaign opens west of the Meuse with offensives by First Belgian Brigade Group and U.S. 7th Armored Division, both under U.S. XIX Corps.

October 1(D+14): 10th Waffen-SS Division *Frundsberg* attacks British positions on the Island from the east.

Second crossing to the south bank of the Rhine by elements of the Division von Tettau.

October 7: Arnhem road bridge rendered unusable by the RAF.

Appendix II

The Supply Situation of 21st Army Group on the Eve of Market Garden

". . . the Commanders, with full knowledge of the risks involved, undertook the operation without allowing time for planning and provision. Under normal circumstances, it would be an act of administrative folly to allow an operation to begin without the proper supplies in the Army Roadhead and Corps FMCs."
—XXX Corps response to the Second Army draft report, 3 November, 1944

The SHAEF planners had envisaged the Allies gradually closing up to the German frontier by May 1945. The supply system would be built up progressively as the front line advanced. In September, the Allies were eight months ahead of schedule and the advance had been so rapid that logistical planning was now void of meaning. The American armies were up to 400 miles from their supply bases at Cherbourg and the Normandy beaches. The aim had been to use the Brittany ports as supply bases and to develop Quiberon Bay as a supply reception point. But by early September, none of the Brittany ports had been captured and the American armies continued to be supplied from Normandy. For Eisenhower, supply was thus a constant concern, so much so that he acknowledged that even tactical advances would have to be halted for want of supply. Something had to change before strategic advances could be contemplated. During the first week in September, SHAEF abandoned the idea of using the Brittany ports and Quiberon Bay as supply bases. Brest, which fell on 18 September, was to be used only as a collection point for American troops, as it had been during the Great War.

217

In place of the Brittany ports, the Allies would use Marseilles in the south and open Antwerp in the north. Antwerp, with its cranes, gantries, sluices and dock facilities, had been captured intact on 4 September, but since the Germans dominated the Scheldt Estuary, there was no telling when the great port would be reopened. The electrical power supply for the Antwerp docks at Merxem was still in German hands. So the American planners earmarked Le Havre as an American supply port. Le Havre was the westernmost of the Channel ports and, after Marseilles, the second port of France, with a capacity of 20,000 tons per day. The port and city were captured on 12 September. The cranes and gantries were wrecked as badly as at Cherbourg and the port was not opened till 9 October. In the event, the supply situation continued to be unsatisfactory until Antwerp was opened on 28 November.

The situation of 21AG was somewhat less acute, partly because the distances involved were shorter and partly because of the prospect of capturing and opening the Channel ports. The British envisaged capturing these ports progressively as the front line advanced over a period of months; but again events outstripped the planning. Dieppe fell without a fight on 1 September. The first freighter unloaded its cargo on 8 September and the port was soon unloading a thousand tons a day, 3,000 in mid-month, rising to 6,000 by the beginning of October. Perhaps deceived by the ease by which Dieppe had been captured, then opened, Montgomery began to make plans to supply his two armies for his northern offensive, which crystallized in *Market Garden*. On 5 September, Calais and Boulogne were invested, Dunkirk soon afterward. Ostend was entered unopposed on 9 September, though it was not opened for shipping until 26 September, when it received petrol and stores. Montgomery had no objection to the Americans earmarking Le Havre for their own use, since it was almost as far from the front line as his Rear Maintenance Area in the vicinity of the Normandy city of Bayeux. By 18 September, PLUTO, the cross-Channel gasoline pipeline had been extended on land only as far as Rouen.

By his own admission, Montgomery still needed a Channel port. On 6 September, de Guingand, Montgomery's Chief of Staff, warned that the Channel ports would be strongly defended by the Germans and that he needed such a port for the development of his offensive plans. Dempsey, the commander of British Second Army, estimated that without a good port in working order, only one corps of three divisions, together with airborne forces, could be maintained for offensive operations. On the evening of 6 September, Montgomery signalled to Crerar, commander of the Canadian First Army: "Immediate opening of some port north of Dieppe essential for the development of my plan and I want Boulogne badly," and he asked him what the chances were of capturing it soon.

Crerar invested Boulogne that same night but the port did not fall until 22 September and was so badly damaged that it was not opened until 12 October. Calais fell on 1 October, again so thoroughly wrecked that it could not be opened until November. As it transpired, Montgomery made no attempt to capture Dunkirk, which was besieged by the First Czech Armored Brigade and held out to the end of the War. From Dunkirk, the Germans reported on the air movements over the southern route to the Arnhem Corridor.

Thus, early in September, Montgomery's supply problems were similar to the Americans'. Though the British Mulberry Harbour had been damaged in transit and was working well below capacity, the problem was not with the Normandy beaches. At their peak, the beaches were delivering up to 17,000 tons per day, but they were 300 miles from the 21AG front lines. Montgomery's difficulties were twofold. He needed ground transport and at least one major port closer to the fighting troops. On 9 September, he had only Dieppe and Ostend, the former delivering around a thousand tons per day and the latter not yet opened. On that date, he calculated he could get to Berlin with Dieppe, Boulogne, Dunkirk and Calais, together with 3,000 tons of supplies through Le Havre. With "one good Channel Port," 1,000 tons per day airlift and more trucks, he could get over the Rhine and reach the Muenster Triangle: Rheine-Osnabruck-Muenster. On the 7th and the 9th, however, Montgomery told Eisenhower that *even with a Pas de Calais port working*, he could not get over the Rhine without additional administrative resources. Specifically, he wanted assurance that the current 750 tons of daily air supply would be brought up to 1,000 tons and that, when and only when he had the Pas de Calais port working, he would then require about 2,500 additional three-ton lorries.

For the time being, Antwerp took second priority to the Channel ports of Boulogne, Calais and Dunkirk. On 13 September, Montgomery signaled to Crerar that he was to capture Boulogne, Dunkirk and Calais *and* "tackle the Antwerp business," saying, in an uncharacteristically vague statement, that "the latter is probably more important." This was a tacit acknowledgement that the opening of the Channel ports would be too late for *Market Garden*. Montgomery's directive for his two armies of 14 September ordered Crerar to direct all his energies to the opening of Antwerp, even though he was still to capture Calais and Boulogne. Crerar freed his 2nd Infantry Division to take part in the Scheldt operations, which had begun on 12 September, against the Breskens Pocket, covering an isolated province of the Netherlands which had the south bank of the Scheldt as its northern boundary. Only on 19 September, after the start of *Market Garden,* did British I Corps of Canadian First Army take over the Antwerp sector from British XII Corps, Second Army being greatly in need of troops to support XXX Corps' left flank.

If the capture of a working port to supply *Market Garden* was a failed project, the transport problem was difficult to resolve, at best. The first problem was the quality of the transport. The main lorry used by the British was the Ford or Bedford three-tonner, with a light chassis, unsuitable for the rough conditions in which it operated, and an underpowered, unreliable engine. In the parlance of the day, they were "not man enough for the job." To cap it all, 1,400 such vehicles, and their replacement engines, were found to be defective, the equivalent of twenty-one 200-ton truck companies, and the capacity of a working port. These lorries were not replaced by the start of *Market Garden;* they comprised one reason why Montgomery had to ask for American supply trucks.

To resolve the problem of transport, Montgomery grounded VIII Corps and used most of its transport to maintain XII and XXX Corps. Within XXX Corps, the Guards Armoured Division used the transport of the Sixth Guards Armoured Brigade, which was not part of *Market Garden.* In Crerar's Army, 51st Division was halted and its transport used for moving other units and supplies. Since supply at the beaches was more than adequate, Montgomery cut imports from 16,000 to 7,000 tons per day and diverted the extra transport from the beaches-Bayeux run to Bayeux-Army Roadhead near Brussels. Transport was centralized under an organization called Tranco; tank transporters were pressed into service with crude side panels welded to the flatbeds.

This was not enough. Montgomery's calculations had been based on the working of a Channel port. Without such a port, the supply situation was even more acute. Montgomery told Eisenhower that without more logistical help, he would be unable to start *Market Garden* until 23 September. Eisenhower's chief of staff visited Montgomery on 12

September and promised him 500 tons a day by air and a further 500 tons delivered to the front by American trucks diverted from moving three newly-arrived American divisions, the 26th, the 29th and the l04th. The hasty arrangements for this "Red Lion Route" were greatly successful. The Red Lion ran 300 miles from Bayeaux to Brussels. It was understandable that the Red Lion Route should have started late, on 16 September; but it delivered 650 tons per day instead of the 500 promised. Nearly half of the total of 18,000 tons went to the two American airborne divisions in *Market Garden*, again nearly half the tonnage being Petrol, Oil and Lubricants (POL).

Well satisfied, Montgomery wrote to Crerar that "we have had a great victory with SHAEF" and moved *Market Garden*'s D-Day forward from the 23rd to the 17th of September. The arrangements were to last until about 1 October and though Eisenhower did not respond to Montgomery's request to continue the road supply arrangements until 7 October, the arrangements continued until 12 October. The plans of both Montgomery and Dempsey had, however, been predicated on the capture of a Channel port and the subsequent issue of thousands more lorries. Colonel Stacey said that Montgomery's calculations "turned out to be unsound." A more pertinent judgment would be that, in pursuing a legitimate military ambition, Montgomery's professionalism deserted him to the point of irresponsibility. He simply did not have enough resources to take a whole army and four airborne formations to the Ijsselmeer to the north and over the IJssel to the east. Further, two out of the three corps of Second Army were by no means fully deployed on 17 September, nor did they have bridgeheads over the Meuse-Escaut Canal. This, in the event, was more important than the question of supply, but the two considerations are related. Montgomery's decision to move the operation forward did not compromise the airborne; it did, however, have consequences for the ground troops in *Garden*. On 17 September, XII Corps was still responsible for the Antwerp sector, and in VIII Corps, 3rd Division had not even arrived in its entirety at its start-line, let alone deployed. The reason for the delay was the shortage of transport.

It is not clear that anyone could have dissuaded Montgomery from mounting the Arnhem operation with resources he *knew* to be inadequate; both Brigadier Belchem, Montgomery's G-3 Operations, and Brigadier Williams, his G-2 Intelligence, tried to dissuade Montgomery from launching *Market Garden* at the scheduled time. Freddie de

Guingand was off sick in England during the planning of *Market Garden,* arriving back on the afternoon of 17 September. From his sickbed, de Guingand phoned to warn Montgomery that German resistance and the need for Channel ports made the northern thrust doubtful, even if Arnhem were reached. Montgomery's later statement that the operation was 90% successful on the grounds that XXX Corps had advanced nine tenths of the way to the Arnhem bridge, or that he had resources enough to get over the Rhine is deeply ambivalent, to say the least, because he neatly conflated the aim of reaching the Ijsselmeer with getting a foothold over the Rhine.

In the event, there were only local supply difficulties such as artillery ammunition for XXX Corps in the Nijmegen bridgehead and a similar initial shortage in VIII Corps. The slow movement of VIII and XII Corps in *Market Garden* was caused not by supply deficiencies but by the strength of enemy opposition. Montgomery reported that 400–500 tons per day of supplies were delivered by air, in spite of the use of troop carriers for the Arnhem operation, from 17–20 September. Airlifts of gasoline to Liege, which comprised a commitment in addition to the 1,000 tons a day by air and road, began with a fleet of seventy Halifax bombers, from units other than those engaged in *Market Garden;* they lifted a total of 325,000 gallons between 25 September and 2 October. This was a result of a complaint by Montgomery on 20 September that air deliveries of supplies, particularly gasoline, were behind schedule. Montgomery also complained that there was a shortfall of 12,000 tons of rail deliveries. In view of the state of the rail system on that date, it is not clear whether anyone was to blame for a situation that was remedied only in the first half of October.

There have been many criticisms of Eisenhower and SHAEF that *Market Garden* was not properly supplied, thus was doomed to failure. This is a fallacy. First, the main reason for inadequate supply was that Montgomery's own plans to supply 21AG from the Channel ports were abortive, and the dearth of road transport in 21AG was in no way the fault of SHAEF. It is quite true that both air and ground supply were late in starting. When they did start, they more than fulfilled the extra supplies promised by SHAEF. No one in SHAEF promised more transport to alleviate the situation in which VIII Corps' and 51st Highland's lorries were diverted to other units, nor did Montgomery make such a request. What critics have done is to cite the extra supplies collared by Patton's Third Army and his wilful "misinterpretation" of orders as the reasons for the failure of supply and in turn the operation itself. In view of what Montgomery requested and what he actually got, it is both false and beside the point to argue that Second Army got too little because Third Army got too much.

Montgomery had only a week to plan the operation, and it was launched without any reserve of supplies at all. When he said that *Market Garden* was less than a full success because it was not properly supplied, he implied that SHAEF was at fault, remaining silent on the failure of his own supply measures. Just how alarming his supply situation ought to have been can be gleaned from the American predicament in October and November. In a situation in which not even daily supply quotas were being met, U.S. Communications Zone estimated that it would take about sixty days before a substantial reserve of supplies could be built up in the advanced bases. As for Montgomery's idea of a drive on Berlin, this was a sheer fantasy.

Appendix III

The Air Forces in Operation *Market Garden*

Until *Market Garden,* airborne operations had been tactical in nature, securing key objectives until the paratroopers were relieved by advancing ground forces which would bear the brunt of the fighting. In a strategic operation, the case was altered. In *Market Garden,* the relationship between the ground and airborne forces was reversed, so that rather than securing particular objectives like bridges, fortifications and airfields, as done previously, the airborne forces would hold relatively large areas of territory until relieved, hopefully quickly, by ground forces. Here, the basic assumption was that the ground forces would have to do little fighting and so move at high speed toward the airborne forces. There was no doctrine for such a venture; Gavin's attempt to articulate one, appearing with *Airborne Warfare,* was not published until after the war's end.

The idea of an airborne operation entirely in daylight was also new. One consequence was that it was deemed impossible to do two lifts entirely in daylight. Yet virtually all of the British commentators have contended that the single-lift decision was mistaken. Air Vice-Marshal Hollinghurst, who had been responsible for training the British glider pilots, was prepared to do two lifts, as he had been for *Comet,* confident that his aircrews were up to the job. But he had to rely on the U.S. IX Troop Carrier Command to drop the British paratroopers, so the decision over a single lift inevitably and squarely involved the American decision-makers. British historians have uncritically assumed that the arguments for a second lift entirely outweighed the considerations of Brereton and Williams. This is debatable, partly because the American arguments were well-founded and partly because the benefits of a double lift have been distorted. A premise of the airborne operation was that the major crossings had to be secured in a matter of hours, before a defense could be assembled and enemy demolition crews had carried out their work. Yet a second lift would arrive, at the earliest, eight hours after the first, due to flying time, maintenance, assembling the second flight and refueling. The turnaround time in *Comet* was in fact ten hours. Further time would also be taken up in assembling the troops on the ground, rendering the fresh troops too late for the first assault on the bridges. Urquhart, in his report of January 1945, stated that a delay of even four hours, due to the remoteness of the paratroopers from the Arnhem road bridge, was a severe disadvantage.

Losing Sight of the Tactical Objectives

The combination of the daylight operation and only one lift on D-Day meant that there could be no *coup de main* operations by night, as precursors to the main drop and landing. The daytime operation implied that any *coup de main* parties would have to be dropped or landed at the same time as the rest of the airborne. Alternatively, the DZ/LZ would have to be close to the key tactical objectives. There is very little discussion in the documentation and the accounts of the participants of *coup de main*, other than pointing out that *coup de main* parties were a positive feature of *Comet*. What seems to have happened is that in the hasty planning of *Market,* the need to take key tactical objectives in a matter of hours was overlooked.

How this came about differs in the case of each of the three airborne divisions. With regard to the 101st, Chester Wilmot blamed the Americans for overturning "Montgomery's plan" to drop on both sides of the Son bridge. It is indeed true that one of the benefits of the original seven-point plan was that troops would be dropped close to the Son bridge and that Taylor gave up this benefit when he got Dempsey to agree to a different assault plan. The Americans were dropped two miles from the bridge on the north side only; the Germans blew the bridge at the imminent assault and when the Americans were in sight of it.

In the original plan for the 82nd, none of the airborne were to be dropped or landed close to any of the seven bridges that were to be taken by the time that XXX Corps arrived: two over the Waal, up to four over the Maas-Waal Canal, and the Grave bridge over the Maas. The plan to capture the rail bridge at Mook was to block any German advance there. The wise decision to drop a company south of the Grave bridge was taken only thirty-six hours before the operation, at the request of the commander of the 504th PIR, Lt. Colonel Tucker. It was too much to hope that troops from the 504th could first take the Heumen bridge over the Maas-Waal Canal, then advance to the Grave bridge with any prospect of surprise. The success of the company assigned the Grave bridge was achieved by speed, stealth, surprise and good soldiering.

With 1st Airborne, Urquhart pushed for the landing of troops both close to, and on both sides of, the Arnhem road bridge. That this did not happen was undoubtedly a flaw in the assault plan. In the case of both the 82nd and the 1st Airborne, the plans violated the first principle of airborne assaults articulated by Gavin in *Airborne Warfare*: proximity to the objectives. But in both cases the flaws went deeper, into the very heart of the assault plans.

Hasty Planning and Staggering Tasks

Like Sosabowski in *Comet,* Gavin's chief of staff thought that the task of the 82nd called for two divisions, not one. It was difficult and risky to first secure the airhead, Gavin's essential task, then attempt to capture the Nijmegen road bridge as well as the Grave bridge and at least one bridge over the Maas-Waal Canal. Though the Nijmegen bridge was a tertiary objective, Gavin did try on D-Day to strike out for the bridge. But the troops did not move straight to it, they were not concentrated in a single force, and they had to be recalled on D+1 owing to threats to the airhead and the need to retake the LZ, parts of which were occupied by German troops.

The plan for the 82nd, and in particular the early capture of the Nijmegen bridge, could only succeed on the assumption of minimal German opposition. Even then, Gavin could not be sure that the airhead was reasonably secure until after several hours had elapsed. There could be no question of "racing for the bridge" in Cornelius Ryan's words, as if Gavin were in the position of First Parachute Brigade at Arnhem on the afternoon of D-Day. With anything more than minimal German opposition, it was extremely unlikely that the Nijmegen bridge would be captured intact. That it was taken on D+3 by the Guards Armoured and a battalion of the 82nd was due not only to the enterprise of the troops but by a major stroke of good fortune. Model had ordered the Nijmegen bridge not to be destroyed on the grounds that it was needed for a counterattack. The attempt by the Germans to blow the bridge in defiance of Model's orders failed as the Guards' tanks were crossing in the evening of D+3. The deep flaw in the plan was that the 82nd had to secure the Groesbeek Heights at all times, while taking several tactical objectives without which XXX Corps could not stick to its timetable of advance, if indeed it could advance at all.

There was a parallel flaw in the case of 1st Airborne at Arnhem. Though Urquhart's task would have been much easier by landing troops on both sides of the Arnhem bridge, there was still the problem of holding the DZ/LZ until after the second lift on D+1. This meant securing and holding a passage to the Arnhem road bridge for more than twenty-four hours. There was no reason to think that this could be done except on the assumption that there were minimal German troops who were either in place or within striking distance. Not only was this not correct, but the British at Army level and above knew from *Ultra* that both the II SS *Panzer* Corps and formidable *Waffen-SS* training units, including Krafft's battalion, were in the vicinity.

Only Hackett of the Fourth Parachute Brigade took the likelihood of a rapid and violent German response seriously; like Urquhart, he was ignorant of just what was in store for the division. Gavin, on the other hand, knew that he was faced with a "staggering task." Characteristically, he tried to rise to the challenge of a bad plan without complaint and, luck notwithstanding, achieved a remarkable success. In both cases, things would have had to have been very different for the plans to have had a reasonable chance of success: the 82nd could hardly hold the Groesbeek Heights and take the key bridges at the same time, and the 1st Airborne could not hold the road bridge while simultaneously holding open the route from the airhead. The presumption of minimal German opposition can be put another way: there was no margin of error for the operation, which was open to the assumption of maximum risk.

Construed as a strategic operation, *Market* was peculiar. We should have expected a large but compact landing in which the troops formed a perimeter, or "box" in the parlance of the Desert War, sent out patrols and waited for the ground forces to relieve them. Inside the box, there would be important tactical objectives necessary to facilitate the advance. Gavin, in *Airborne Warfare,* pursued such ideas, with a forty-five mile perimeter circumference for an airborne corps, bigger for an army. But the area of landings for *Market* was long and slender, with most of the tactical objectives outside, not within the landing areas. The result was that there was a tension between the wider aims of securing ground for the offensive and securing immediate objectives without which the ground forces could not advance. This tension is seen at its most acute when the urgent need to capture the bridge crossings took second place to the need for consolidation of the airhead.

As a strategic offensive, *Market* was not quite the "big one" that the senior American commanders had envisaged, certainly not six divisions committed in a single operation. Eisenhower acknowledged as much when he wrote in his order of 4 September that First Allied Airborne Army was to operate in the north up to and including the crossing of the Rhine and *then* be prepared to engage in large-scale operations for the advance into Germany. This explains Brereton's constant agitation for the return of the airborne divisions after the conclusion of the operation. Eisenhower made it clear in approving the operation that as soon as the airborne were relieved by the ground troops, they must be "instantly released" for future operations, e.g. for other crossings further up the Rhine.

As it transpired, the American components of First Allied Airborne Army in *Market Garden* were used as ground troops until the conclusion of the war. In so far as there never was a six-division airborne operation, there is a case for saying that the Allied Airborne Army was not unreservedly a good idea: the Army would either wait around indefinitely for the "big one," or it would be underused in smaller, traditional operations, or the troops would be used, contrary to doctrine, as light infantry. James Huston, the most judicious critic of *Market*, wrote "The results seemed to cool some of the sentiment for . . . long-range strategic envelopment and prolonged action from an independent airhead."

There was actually a positive retreat from long-range envelopment. In Operation *Varsity*, the Allied crossing of the Rhine in March 1945, more airborne troops were landed than on the first day of *Market Garden*. Yet so great was the fear of the airborne troops being cut off in a deep penetration that they were landed close to the river and the German "gun line." The result was an airborne casualty rate far higher than the river crossing and assault.

Air Supply

In the planning for *Market*, supply for 1st Airborne was to be handled by First British Airborne Corps, but this was to be in the form of "requests" to the Allied Expeditionary Air Force. For the rest, the airborne would have to use their own troop carriers. The U.S. XVIII Airborne Corps was given responsibility for supplying the two American airborne divisions, which were assigned 252 B-24 Liberator bombers. Additional support was requested in the form of five truck companies based in Brussels. The reason that the landing of the 52nd (Air Portable) Division was not scheduled until D+5, earliest D+4, was that the troop carriers were needed for supply, envisaged to last for up to ten days, the duration of the entire operation.

Supply for 1st Airborne was compromised in several ways. The Germans were alerted to incoming aircraft by their listening post in Dunkirk. They also knew from plans found on a captured British officer of the sites of the DZ/LZ and of the supply drop zones. This enabled them to site their light flak accordingly and to release yellow smoke to attract the transport aircraft. Finally, the breakdown of the British assault plan and the failure of communications meant that supplies were dropped according to the original plan and in the wrong place.

In the first supply run on D+1, thirty-three Stirlings dropped eighty-three tons of supplies on a dedicated DZ just to the north of Oosterbeek. Of these, only twelve tons were recovered. On D+2, Urquhart's radio message that DZ-V was in enemy hands did not get through. The Polish glider lift and the supply run took the southern route to Arnhem, on which their movement had been reported by the German garrison at Dunkirk. This time, the supply transports faced an even bigger contingent of both flak and the *Luftwaffe*. Only thirty-one of the 390 tons of supplies were recovered. On D+3, Urquhart successfully sent a message advising of the change of drop zone, with the result that 135 out of 386 tons were recovered, a relatively large proportion. On D+4, 117 aircraft carried supplies, of which twenty-nine were lost, a terrible attrition rate in which in minimal amount of supplies were recovered. On D+6, 123 aircraft dropped a total of 291 tons, of which Urquhart reported that only "a minute portion of the panniers came our way." Six aircraft were lost.

By the end of D+4, the supply flights to 1st Airborne were also in jeopardy; though the severe losses of that day may have been a factor, the circumstances remain murky. The report of 38 and 46 Groups, RAF, states that no supply missions were flown on 22 September (D+5) since no supply requirements had been received from HQ, Airborne Troops. Bad weather could, alternatively, have been cited as a factor, since the supplementary Polish paratroop drop had been postponed on that day.

The trouble is that there is a message from AEAF (Leigh-Mallory) in the file dated 22 September (D+5) stating categorically that no supply flights were to be flown that day, and no explanation was given. The message was received by 21AG the same day. There is no record in the 38/46 file of an order from Hollinghurst stating that no more supply missions were to be flown; but Urquhart claims that such an order was given on the grounds of heavy losses and a reluctance to carry out supply flights after D+4, the latest date that the ground troops were estimated to reach the Arnhem bridgehead.

In the light of subsequent events, the order was evidently issued. Exactly when is again not clear, but it was likely on Saturday the 23rd (D+6) for two reasons. On that day, 123 aircraft dropped 2,624 containers, with the result that "ground reports indicate that the drop into the very restricted area" without navigational aids such as Rebecca-Eureka, was "not sufficiently accurate." This was the last supply mission flown from England to 1st Airborne Division.

The second reason is that Urquhart's representative at First Allied Airborne Army, Lt. Colonel Bill Campbell, was well prepared to take action on that Sunday morning, D+7. He contacted Brereton's Chief of Operations, Brigadier General Ralph Stearley, a go-getting, "can-do" sort of character whom the best of the British admired immensely. Stearley got an immediate commitment from U.S. Eighth Army Air Force that they would drop food and small arms ammunition in fighter auxiliary fuel tanks right away, pending clearance from Second TAF. Fighter-bombers were loaded with food and ammunition, but no clearance came from Second TAF by the deadline of midday. When the clumsy communications network finally responded, it was too late. The 38/46 Group report talks of tentative plans to drop supplies from Mosquitoes and Typhoons on D+8 and D+9, but the British did not have the flexibility of organization to permit this to be arranged in time.

Meanwhile, another plan had been developing. Air Commodore Darvall has been a shadowy figure in *Market Garden,* usually rating little more than a mention as the officer commanding 46 Group, RAF. But he was evidently a forceful and influential character, especially as he went against the grain of his superiors' prescriptions. Since there was difficulty in obtaining information about the situation and the casualties at Arnhem, he flew over the area of operations and landed at Nijmegen on D+5, meeting with Broadhurst of 83 Group, RAF. His light aircraft had been forced down over the severed XXX Corps

Corridor; one previous flight had been shot down and another crash-landed.

The next day, 525 Squadron of 46 Group flew into Brussels under the local command of 83 Group. There, the squadron could get the latest information on the tactical situation: escorting flights would be easier; short flights would make for more sorties; and the content of supply containers could be changed more readily. The following day, twenty-one aircraft flew in a supply mission, no doubt the entire squadron. Four aircraft were damaged by flak and forty-one tons of supplies dropped, of which, evidently, none were recovered. On D+8, seven aircraft dropped food and medicine in the vicinity of Heaveadorp. The little information that is available suggests that none of the supplies were retrieved, and one aircraft was lost. The operations were a credit to the squadron and to Darvall in the general picture of the failure of supply.

However, lest it be thought that the failure of supply related only to the 1st Airborne, it is worth recalling that only 68% of the 82nd's supplies were recovered. For the 101st, the success rate varied between 64% and a low of under 30%. Less than 30% arrived on D+3, leading to shortages of gasoline and food, the latter to the extent that it affected battle performance. After the war, planners concluded that the most reliable way of bringing in supplies was to land them by glider. In fact, 33 gliders were used to supply the 101st, with a very high success rate. The U.S. Airborne were also able to utilize two transport companies dedicated to the British 52nd (Air Portable) Division, the sea tail of the 1st Airborne, and four transport companies of the U.S. Communications Zone.

Air Support and Ground Attack

Browning reported after the operation that of 95 requests for air support, only 49 were fulfilled by the RAF. All requests were from XXX Corps, from the Airborne Corps or from 1st Airborne. There are no recorded complaints about lack of air support for the 101st Airborne, and there are virtually no records of air support, either requests or action, from the 82nd. Browning alleged that the RAF was somehow at fault, through overcaution and conservatism. This explanation is in fact the least likely. Bad weather accounted for some of the rejections. With others, the RAF considered that the targets were insufficiently identifiable to warrant an air strike. Colored smoke to identify targets was only due to arrive with the 52nd Division on D+5 and, at least initially, it would have been available only in the division's immediate area of operations north of Arnhem, at the limit of the airborne's advance. It should also be added that while air support from Typhoons was good for morale, it was not greatly effective unless targets were precisely identified. The chances of this happening at Arnhem were remote, even if the aircraft had been on call, since the pilots had to rely solely on the identification of friendly forces and six-figure map references, hardly precision targeting.

The chief complaint about lack of air support came from 1st Airborne, but again this was not the fault of the RAF. The equipment of the U.S. Air Support Signals Team was improperly tuned, then destroyed by artillery fire. This meant that the division had to rely on the overloaded artillery link or on the *Phantom* net. This route was slow and tortuous: from division to the XXX Corps artillery, through XXX Corps, Second Army, 83 Group RAF, then to the airfields. With *Phantom,* the requests went directly to Second Army, but there were only four requests made on *Phantom.* One of these, on D+4, was possibly identical to a message sent via the artillery link at 1700 hours for air support at 1830, or not at all. Since the turnaround time from request to delivery under ideal communications was one hour, it is no wonder that air support failed. A dozen Spitfires flew over the drop zones on D+2, chasing away German fighters. Typhoons later sought out targets of opportunity near 1st Airborne, without any direction from the ground. Other requests from the Airborne Corps experienced a similar problem of clumsy communication routes, since there was no direct contact with 83 Group RAF, only through XXX Corps.

Appendix IV

The Humiliation of
General Sosabowski

The First Polish Independent Parachute Brigade was formally established in October 1941, the brainchild of Colonel Stanislaw Sosabowski. Its commander was a veteran of the Great War, the Polish-Soviet War of 1919–20 and of the Warsaw battles in September 1939. Sosabowski had no airborne experience but he had a small cadre of highly capable paratroop officers who instructed the British as well as the Poles. Admired by both Urquhart and Hackett, Sosabowski was nicknamed "Old Sosab" or just "Stary" ("Old"), which is in Polish a mark of great affection rather than deference to a superior. The English translation as "Pops" is a poor rendering. He was known to be difficult, even by his Polish peers and superiors. Sosabowski, in a Polish tradition, also considered it the duty of a commander to point out the flaws in the plans of his superiors. This was one reason why the British thought him uncooperative, from the planning of *Comet* and *Market Garden*, through the encounters with the arriving ground forces at Driel to the planning of the relief of 1st Airborne at the Lower Rhine.

The strongest allegation that Sosabowski was uncooperative is to be found in Hubert Essame's *The 43rd Division at War, 1944–1945* (1952). How much Essame's thoughts were shared by the higher commanders is not known, but Browning was well aware of the attitudes of 43rd Division officers when he recommended Sosabowski's dismissal. Essame's first contention was in regard to the Poles' crossing on the night of D+5. "It has to be recorded that General Sosabowski's attitude was the reverse of cooperative." Why, we may ask, did it have to be recorded? Since there was nothing to be uncooperative about and there were no British troops involved except for Lt. Colonel Myers, this can be discounted as a canard, perhaps reported to Essame by Lt. Colonel Taylor of the DCLI. Sosabowski was not at all impressed with the British efforts to get to Driel and said so in no uncertain terms. Myers had no complaints about the untrained Poles, who crewed the boats in no worse a fashion than their American comrades at the crossing of the Waal.

When Sosabowski met with Horrocks for the second time on D+7 in Valburg, Horrocks' attitude was very different from that at the earlier meeting. Certainly, Horrocks was under great pressure and maybe suffering from the unknown ailment that had afflicted him in August. But it is also possible that he had been influenced by Taylor, who came under Essame's brigade; Taylor recorded that his meetings with Sosabowski "did not go well." At the meeting, Sosabowski alone had a sound conception of military purpose and tactics. Essame again blamed Sosabowski for being uncooperative, but it was the Pole who had been deceived, insulted and humiliated.

Essame said that in the crossing on the night of D+6, the troops were ferried over by 204th Field Company RE and Fourth Dorsets' engineers in sixteen assault boats, of which neither contention is true, as Myers testified. Lt. Russell Kennedy of the Twenty-third Field Company RCE was attached to the 204th Field Company RE for about forty-eight hours on D+5; but there is no indication that the 204th played any part in the Poles' second crossing. Further, Essame alleged that the Poles' assault boats from their second crossing were left on the north bank where most were destroyed during the day, which had "unfortunate results" for the next night's crossing. This snotty insinuation is typical of Essame—trying to blame the Poles for the shortage of assault boats which they were supposed to use on the night of D+7. Essame did not even mention the plan to put the Poles' 1st Battalion across with the Fourth Dorsets, saying again that the Poles were uncooperative and that their crossing was suspended at about midnight. Again, not true: Lt. Colonel Stevens asked Sosabowski to give up his assault boats at about 2100 hours.

When the Poles along with the Red Devils crossed the Rhine at the evacuation, most ignored the order to move to Nijmegen and rejoined their brigade in Driel. Sosabowski marched his brigade, with its heavy equipment, the fourteen miles to Nijmegen where he received new orders from Browning. They were first sent to guard the grass airfield near

Grave, where Sosabowski's 1st Battalion had dropped on D+6. This was later extended to guarding the Nijmegen road bridge and the Maas-Waal Canal crossings as a response to the success of German frogmen in destroying the rail bridge on the night of D+10. By this time, a forty-ton bridge had been built over the Maas at Grave, a precaution against the destruction of the road bridge. Earlier, on D+9, the Polish brigade had been brought under the command of the 157th Brigade of the 52nd Division. The 157th Brigade HQ was part of the sea tail of the division; at Grave, the formation was of little more than battalion strength. Sosabowski protested this insult, by now familiar, of being subordinated to a brigadier, his junior. The decision was reversed, Sosabowski recording that Browning appeared deliberately to have slighted him. On 7 October, the Polish brigade was taken out of the line, arriving in England by air and sea on or before 12 October. They were followed out of Nijmegen the next day by Browning's HQ on the Groesbeek Heights.

In his report to the Polish President on October 16, Sosabowski said, in an understatement, that the lack of appreciation of his brigade had led to insufficient numbers of gliders allotted to him for Operation *Market*. He requested the expansion of the brigade to divisional size. With training in Scotland, replacements, re-equipment and the recruitment of specialists, the unit should be ready for action in the spring of 1945. He asserted that the brigade had received little recognition for its help to 1st Airborne and to XXX Corps. Sosabowski did not request the restoration of the independence of the brigade, only that its "independent character" should be recognized. Yet, in subsequent events, he said that the question of command was being decided by the Polish authorities.

The circumstances of Sosabowski's dismissal from command of the brigade are obscure. The group that most needed a scapegoat for the failure to relieve the Red Devils were the officers of 43rd Division. Their mendacious hostility to Sosabowski is a matter of public record. However, if they needed an alibi they were covering themselves against future recrimination, since at the time there were far more important things to do than assigning blame for disaster. An alternative explanation, put forward by William F. Buckingham, is that Browning too was looking for a scapegoat.

Early in October, with the Polish Brigade still in Nijmegen, Sosabowski wrote to Browning, congratulating him on receiving the Order *Polonia Restituta* from the Polish Government. Browning wrote him a curious reply, in which he asserted that "my relationship with you and your Brigade has not been of the happiest during these last few weeks." Sosabowski was mystified and replied, offering "my apologies if at any time my opinion was expressed in such a way or with words you did not like." He saw the matter as a personal one; there is no reason to doubt his sincerity when he said that he had always considered it an honor and a pleasure to serve under Browning's command. Even after his dismissal he continued to regard the matter as a personal one, of "differences that grew out of all proportion."

Whatever Browning's motives, or the pressures on him, it was he who betrayed Sosabowski, writing to the Deputy CIGS on 20 November that Sosabowski had been uncooperative throughout the period of training, planning, the operation and the aftermath at Nijmegen. He alleged that Sosabowski had been "argumentative and loath to play his full part in the operation." Browning said that Horrocks and Thomas would bear out these criticisms of Sosabowski's attitude. He recommended that Sosabowski be employed elsewhere. He gave Sosabowski full credit for raising the brigade and said, condescendingly, that Sosabowski was a "knowledgeable and efficient soldier and up to the average of his rank." He recommended that his replacement be Lt. Colonel S. Jachnik, the Deputy Commander, or, on Stevens' recommendation, Major Tonn.

It is, however, hard to see Browning's move as a way of defending his reputation. Browning seems to have played little part in the decisions to reinforce or evacuate 1st Airborne. The more likely explanation is that Sosabowski was seen by those in high authority as a thorn in their side and that Browning gave them spurious reasons for telling them what they wanted to hear. Montgomery, who had flatly refused any provisos in bringing the Poles under British command, wrote to Alan Brooke, the CIGS, on 17 October that the Poles had "fought very badly here, and the men showed no keenness to fight if it meant risking their own lives. I do not want this Bde [Brigade] here again, and possibly you may like to send them to join other Poles in Italy." Someone had clearly been feeding Montgomery's prejudices with a gross distortion of the facts. And prejudices they were. The only compliment that Montgomery ever paid the 1st Polish Armored Division, which had fought so valiantly in the Falaise Gap and throughout the Normandy campaign, was that it needed a kick in the pants. Sosabowski was relieved of command on December 9, 1944.

On the other hand, Sosabowski continued to believe that he had come under British command only for *Market Garden*. When, in October, he was told that he was to come under the command of the 1st Airborne, he replied to Urquhart on 4 November, saying he would be delighted to see him but, "regarding the matter of command, I was awaiting instructions from the Polish HQ." He saw the question of command as evidence that his brigade "was fast losing its independence and was well on the way to being integrated into the First Division." It was on 4 November also that Sosabowski got a short telegram from Browning, confirming that the brigade would continue to come under command of 1st Airborne Division. The most likely explanation for Sosabowski's dismissal was his obsessive refusal to accept that the independence of his brigade had gone for good. In doing this, uncomfortable facts, distortions and outright lies were used to justify an action that was in no way related to Sosabowski's performance as a commander. His dismissal was a political move, not military or personal.

At the same time, Sosabowski continued to enjoy the respect and friendship of the British paratroop commanders. He warmly acknowledged the help and support he had received from Browning and Eric Down, as well as General Crawford who, as Deputy CIGS, went out of his way to get Sosabowski's son Stanislaw out of Russian-occupied Poland. As a soldier, the younger Sosabowski had been blinded in the Warsaw Uprising of September. General Sir Richard Gale, who succeeded Browning as commander of the British Airborne Corps, wrote the preface for Sosabowski's memoirs, *Freely I Served*. In this work, Sosabowski was assisted by two anonymous British officers, one of whom was almost certainly General Sir John Hackett. The other officer was quite possibly Gale himself, since he says nothing in his preface about the content of the memoir.

It was altogether in Hackett's character that he should recognize Sosabowski for what he was: an individual of fanatical loyalty and determination, outstanding in his bravery and organizational talent, truly among the very best that the Allies produced. To be brought down by lesser men on spurious grounds over a genuine but peripheral flaw is the stuff of tragedy. When, on Christmas Eve, members of his old brigade refused to enter the mess at Wansford and Peterborough in protest at his dismissal, Sosabowski persuaded them to end their demonstration and relaxed with them over a meal. *Stary*, a modern Belisarius, was never forgotten by those who came close to him.

After the war, Sosabowski established two small businesses, which failed in turn. He became a store man at a factory in 1949 until he was laid off at the age of seventy-five in 1966. It is said that Polish veterans who worked in the factory kept his identity secret; it is more likely his workmates respected his privacy. He and his brigade were honored in Driel and the surrounding towns. They were also honored in Poland long before the fall of the Communist regime. He died on 25 September, 1967, believing that the loyalty of his troops were what made his life worth living. Among his last written words were: "Hard and desolate was my entire life. In the midst of all these miseries there were also bright times. These I had witnessed with my own eyes, that through my efforts, and through the efforts of those who believed and followed, that they did not go for nothing."

Appendix V

Brian Urquhart's Recollections of Intelligence at Arnhem

At the time of the Arnhem operation, Corps Intelligence was under canvas at Moor Park. The G-2 Intelligence comprised about ten officers and men. There were no formalities, parades or general orders because of the exceedingly heavy workload. Since the commands under the Corps were scattered, I spent much of my time in a jeep, particularly back and forth from Ascot, the HQ of the Allied Airborne Army. As there was less than a week to plan *Market Garden,* there was of necessity much improvisation.

The reason for this goes back to the circumstances of the time. After the victories of August, the fall of Brussels, then of Antwerp (but not the approaches to it), there was a feeling that the Germans were finished. One last push and it would be over. The light-hearted way in which Lt. Gen. Frederick Browning, the commander of the airborne operation, referred to "the party" and the carpet of airborne troops leading into the Fatherland, indicated the opinion that it would be a walkover. This attitude I did not share. I did not think that the German Army would give up at the borders of the *Reich*.

There was perhaps another and deeper reason why my attitudes were not taken seriously. In my view, junior officers were given responsibilities out of all proportion to their age, experience and seniority. They did not have the standing to make a mark that their rank and position would suggest. There were in any case few who shared my misgivings. Brigadier John Hackett, the commander of Fourth Parachute Brigade in 1st Airborne Division, was uneasy in private but never broadcast the fact; he thought the operation unprofessional and badly planned. The planning meetings at Ascot were top heavy with

241

much brass, though senior staff officers from XXX Corps were not in evidence.

My first reaction to *Market Garden* was that it was unbelievably risky, a plan for which there were grossly insufficient resources. I could not understand why Eisenhower and his headquarters allowed it to take place. As an operation to get across the Rhine, it was in the wrong place, requiring the capture of three major bridges, not one. Strategically, the operation made no sense. It would have been far better to have supported Patton's drive, which was proceeding against light opposition and which had a much better chance of getting across the Rhine. My own explanation, which I arrived at only much later, was that the operation was to feed Montgomery's ego and secure his reputation by a dashing manoeuvre to end the war.

Tactically, the planning was very poor. I studied the route of XXX Corps' advance to the Grave Bridge and concluded that it could never relieve the airborne in time. I thought at best that the troops would reach Nijmegen but not get across the road bridge. At the time that the Arnhem operation was authorized, XXX Corps was stuck on the Albert Canal, with no prospect of an easy breakthrough. Then there were the controversies about the role of the British 1st Airborne: the fact that troops were to land eight miles from the Arnhem Bridge, in a single lift on the first day, with no paratroopers on the south bank of the Rhine.

During the planning of previous operations, I had established a working relationship with the Spitfire Reconnaissance Squadron at RAF Benson in Oxfordshire. Through this contact, I was able to obtain air photos of the Arnhem drop zones. When I saw German armor on the photos and took them to Browning, the commander of the Airborne Corps, I did not know quite what to expect. I thought that 1st Airborne was too light on anti-tank weapons, and that troops should land on the south side of and near the bridge. I considered it possible to change both of these factors. I knew that the operation would not be postponed and that changing the plans with only two days to go would be exceedingly difficult. What distressed me was that the intelligence was dismissed as irrelevant without considering possible options—this from Browning, a commander who was much more open to argument than most of his peers.

At the time, I put the response down to Browning's ambition to get into action, and to command airborne troops in a major operation before the war's end. Later, I realized that I had done Browning a great injustice. Browning was certainly keen to get into action; but he had received firm orders for an operation about which he may well have had reservations. Nonetheless, the idea of landing the Corps HQ in the 82nd's bridgehead was ill-conceived; the HQ was unwieldy, took up thirty-seven gliders and was not much use in a situation in which the airborne units could not be manoeuvred, once they had landed.

In retrospect, I am surprised that Browning put up with me as long as he did. Browning was a very loyal and decent man. I was indeed exhausted, as were most of the staff (five operations had been planned since D-Day, June 6th, and several others reviewed); but this was hardly the reason for being sent on sick leave. Colonel Austin Eagger, the Corps Chief Medical Officer, had qualms about the move too. Long after the war, I heard from Brian Courtney, the Australian doctor who had treated me for my serious parachuting injury in 1942, that Eagger deeply regreted never having told Browning that I thought the operation "madness." Instead, he was ordered by Browning to send me on sick leave. I was as much mortified by the fact that I would miss the operation as I was convinced that it was heading for certain failure. When I was recalled to Nijmegen, it was under constant shelling. Even worse was the fact that on a clear day I could see the V2 rockets taking off from the Dutch coast for Antwerp or London.

I regard the assault crossing of the Waal at Nijmegen by U.S. troops as an extraordinary and completely unpredictable piece of soldiering. Nobody believed they could do it, nor that they would capture the bridge intact. I had a very high opinion of Gavin and Taylor, the American divisional commanders; they lived in a different world from the British. However, the British Parachute Regiment officers, especially in the original battalions, were soldiers in a similar mould to the Americans, very different from the normally hidebound British Army generally.

I was so appalled by *Market Garden* that I hardly spoke about it for forty years. I was so totally shocked by what had happened that I did not want to think about it. I concede that I may have been overly antagonistic to *Market Garden* because, if the operation had succeeded, it would have been regarded as a great *coup*, even if it was in the wrong place. On the other hand, the odds against it succeeding were overwhelming. When I left the Airborne, I got a friendly letter from Browning in which he suggested that neither of us say anything about our differences. I don't believe Browning wished to cover anything up.

Browning's motive, I believe, was that too many good men and close friends had been killed at Arnhem; a public controversy, which implied that the operation should never have taken place, would serve no good purpose. Though Browning continued to defend the effort and the achievements of the operation, I believe he was deeply damaged by the tragedy of the 1st Airborne. His only operational command in World War II had ended in costly failure.

I put the responsibility for the operation squarely on the shoulders of Montgomery, who launched it, then refused to listen to anyone who wished to modify a bad plan. Finally, he made the incredible statement that the operation was ninety percent successful.

When I left the Airborne, I took with me no documents or photos, which would in any case have been a breach of security. Browning's private letter did not survive the war. Nor did the photos of the Arnhem drop zones. The official history is even sceptical as to whether the reconnaissance actually took place. However, in 2004, Tony Hibbert, the Brigade Major of First Parachute Brigade, recalled seeing them in my office at Moor Park, after he returned from Arnhem. At the time, when I was still scheduled to fly in with Browning's HQ, I told a friend I thought the plan is so bad that I'll have to write a letter and put it in a safe, because I don't want to be the person who failed to tell them what was going to happen. The story that I wrote such a letter and addressed it to Churchill is not correct. I have to stress that as I took no documents with me, I may be inaccurate on some dates and times.

—Edited transcript of an interview with Brian Urquhart given in
New York City, 15 May 2003

Appendix VI

Glossary of Terms and Acronyms

1AAA: First Allied Airborne Army

AEF: Allied Expeditionary Force (western Europe)

AEAF: Allied Expeditionary Air Force

21AG: Twenty-first Army Group (Montgomery)

Alarmheiten: German "alarm companies" (rapid response)

ARP: Air Raid Precautions

Battalion: Constituent unit of a brigade (British) or regiment (American and German), typically three in number; a British infantry battalion comprised 700-900 troops

Battery: A number of artillery pieces, often three or four

Bazooka: Nickname for the American infantry anti-tank weapon

Brigade: British infantry divisions were usually comprised of three brigades, each of about 5,000 troops

Brigade Group: Brigade with additional units attached

GIGS: Chief of the Imperial General Staff

Company: A British infantry company comprised around 130 troops divided into platoons

Corps (*Korps*): A tactical HQ, taking a number of divisions under command (typically 3)

Division: A British infantry division comprised up to 17,000 troops, divided into brigades and divisional troops

DCLI: Duke of Cornwall's Light Infantry

DSO: Distinguished Service Order (American and British)

DUKW: Wheeled amphibious vehicle with a capacity of 2.2 tons

DZ: Drop Zone

Flak: Anti-aircraft artillery

GFA:	Glider Field Artillery (American)
GIR:	Glider Infantry Regiment (American)
GOC:	General Officer Commanding
GSO:	General Staff Officer, often abbreviated to G- , e.g. G-2, Intelligence
HCR:	Household Cavalry Regiment
Jagdpanzer:	German tank destroyer
Kampfgruppe:	Battle Group, a unit reduced in size or formed ad hoc from other units
Kessel:	Cauldron
KOSB:	King's Own Scottish Borderers
Kriegsmarine:	German Navy
Luftwaffe:	German Air Force
LST:	Landing Ship Tanks
LZ:	Landing Zone
MC:	Military Cross, usually awarded to British officers
MM:	Military Medal, usually awarded to British other ranks
Nebelwerfer:	German multi-barrelled rocket launcher.
Oberbefehlshafer:	Commander-in-Chief
OC:	Officer Commanding
Oberkommando der Wehrmacht (OKW):	Supreme Command of the Armed Forces
Panzer:	Tank (German)
Panzerfaust:	German infantry anti-tank weapon
PFA:	Parachute Field Artillery (American)
PIAT:	Projector Infantry Anti-Tank; British infantry anti-tank weapon.
PIR:	Parachute Infantry Regiment (American)
Platoon:	Three sections (squads) of up to twelve troops
PLUTO:	Pipeline Under the Ocean
POL:	Petrol, Oil and Lubricants
POW:	Prisoner(s) of War
RA:	Royal Artillery
RAF:	Royal Air Force
RASC:	Royal Army Service Corps
RCAF:	Royal Canadian Air Force
RCE:	Royal Canadian Engineers
RE:	Royal Engineers
Reichsarbeitsdienst:	German Labor Service, later para-military in nature

Reichsbahn: German national railways
REME: Royal Electrical and Mechanical Engineers
RTR: Royal Tank Regiment
Ruhrindustriegebiet: Ruhr industrial region
Sappers: Engineers
SHAEF: Supreme Headquarters Allied Expeditionary Force
Squadron: In the British Army, a unit of tanks, engineers or reconnaissance formations; in armored units, a squadron comprised up to eighteen armored vehicles, divided into troops, usually of three vehicles
Sturmgeschutz: Armored, tracked assault gun
VC: Victoria Cross, the highest British military decoration
Waffen-SS: The military arm of the Nazi state
Wehrmacht: German Armed Forces, strictly speaking, ground forces
Wehrkreis: German Military District

NOTES ON THE TEXT

Chapter 1: The Prospects for the Western Allies
The sources for this chapter are the works listed in the Bibliography by Ambrose, Belchem, Bennett D.(1), Bennett R., Blair, Bowen, Brereton, Burgett, Deane-Drummond, de Guingand, D'Este (3), Ehrman, Eisenhower (2) and (3), Gavin, Goerlitz, Hamilton, Horrocks (1), Huston, Liddell-Hart (1) and (2), MacDonald, Montgomery (1) and (2), Ridgeway, Rapport & Northwood, Ryan, Sims, Urquhart B, Urquhart R. and Webster; interview with Brian Urquhart, May 15, 2003. The SHAEF strategic planning of May 1944 is covered in Pogue, MacDonald and Weigley.

Throughout, an essential source is the *Twenty First Army Group Report on Operation Market-Garden, 17–26 September 1944* (124 pages), PRO AIR 37/1249. The 21AG internal memo of September 17, 1944 is in 21AGpOp/20765/G(Plans); PRO AIR 37/1249.

Chapter 2: Two Weeks of Allied Preparation
For Operation *Comet,* the sources are *Warning Order from U.S. IX Troop Carrier Command on September Sixth,* PRO WO 205/850; and First Airborne Division Operational Instruction No. 8, *Confirmatory Notes on Divisional Commander's Verbal Orders for Operation Fifteen,* PRO WO 171/393. Other primary sources for this chapter are *First Airborne Division Intelligence Summary, September 7th,* PRO WO 171/393; the Dempsey Diary, PRO WO 285/10-15; *Orders for Arnhem* in Horrocks (2), 99; Montgomery's M525 Order, reproduced in *Memoirs,* 258–64; the endorsement of M525 in the *Eisenhower Papers,* 2152; Horrocks' doubts about an early breakout in a letter to Ritchie, quoted in Martin H.G., 146; *Operation Market, First Airborne Division,*

Operational Instruction No. 9, 12 September 1944, reprinted in Urquhart R., as Appendix II; and 101st *Airborne Report,* PRO AIR 16/1026. Divisional and unit histories consulted are Third Division (Scarfe), 15th Division (Martin H.G.), 43rd Division (Essame), the 50th Division (Clay), the 52nd Division (Blake), 7th Armoured, 11th Armoured, the Guards Armored (Briant, Rosse & Hill and Verney), the 44th RTR (C.G. Hopkins) and the Fife and Forfar Yeomanry (R.J.B. Sellar).

The primary sources for VIII and XII Corps are the Dempsey Diary, PRO WO 285/10; *VIII Corps War Diary,* September 1944, PRO WO 171/287; *VIII Corps Operational Instruction No. 10, 17 September 1944,* which delineates the tasks of XII Corps (sic), PRO WO 171/287; *VIII Corps 'G' Branch, Battle Log of September 1944,* PRO WO 171/287; *War Diary, Eighth Armored Brigade,* PRO WO 171/613; *XII Corps War Diary,* which includes operational instructions and Intelligence Summaries, PRO WO 171/310. The background to the Battle of the Meuse Salient is covered in Altes & Veld.

Other sources used in this chapter are the works in the Bibliography by Baynes, Blair, Brereton, Bradley (1) and (2), Buckingham, Burgett, Cholewczynski, Delaforce, Eisenhower (2), Ellis, Frost, Gavin, Golden, Hamilton, Hibbert, Horne, Horrocks (1) and (2), Huston, MacDonald, Middlebrook (1), Montgomery (1) and (2), Piekalkiewicz, Rapport & Northwood, Ryan, Tedder, Urquhart R., Weigley, Wilmot and the Deelen Airbase Museum exhibits.

Chapter 3: The Other Side of the Hill

For the German retreat of August-September 1944, an essential source is still Schulman, also Stacey. The argument that the Allies made a great mistake in failing to advance from Antwerp to Woensdrecht is summed up, most recently in Beale, *The Great Mistake;* see also Horrocks (1), 203–6, 232; Liddell Hart (1), 591; Thompson R.W., *Montgomery,* 204; Schulman, 231–2; Ryan, 60; Horne, 279; MacDonald,123; Kershaw, 23–4. A lone dissenting voice is to be found in Copp (2), 39.

For the *Waffen-SS* generally, the sources are Hausser, Hoehne, Keegan, Reitlinger and Stein. For the quality, leaders, composition, deployment, actions and movements of the II SS *Panzer* Corps, the sources are Bauer, Harzer, Kershaw and Tieke. These sources are used throughout.

Trevor-Roper ed. contains the Directives for the defence of the West Wall; other sources are Farrar-Hockley, *Student* and Seaton (1). German anticipation of the Allied attack is to be found in Heiber and Glantz ed., in Warlimont and in the *Ultra* decrypt of September 16 in PRO DEFE 3/225.

The account of British Intelligence on German dispositions and intentions rests on Bennett R., Ellis, Hinsley Vol. III, Part II, which includes an Appendix on Intelligence during *Market Garden,* Lamb, Lewin, Ryan, Saunders *The Red Beret,* Smith, Strong, Urquhart B., Urquhart R., and an interview with Brian Urquhart, May 15 2003. The documentary sources are *First Airborne Division Intelligence Summary No. 2, September 7* PRO WO 171/393, the *XII Corps War Diary* PRO WO 171/310, *First Airborne War Diary* PRO WO 171/393; *Forty-third Division, Intelligence Summary No 49, 30 September 1944* in PRO WO 171/480; *Second Army Intelligence Summary, 29 September,* PRO WO 285/4.

The English translation of Krafft's War Diary is in AFM File 48, in PRO AIR 20/2333 and as Appendix II to Chatterton. Other sources used in this chapter are the works in the Bibliography by Graham & Bidwell, Mitcham and Wilmot. Persuasive evidence that there could have been no easy advance from Antwerp to Woensdrecht, *contra* Thompson's *Montgomery,* is to be found in Ellis, Moulton and in the History of the 11th Armoured Division (Taurus Pursuant).

Chapter 4: An American Triumph
Chapter 5: Airborne Hiatus
Chapter 6: Black Tuesday
Chapter 7: Success Clashes with Failure

The sources for the Guards Armored Division are the histories by Briant, Verney and Rosse & Hill; for the history of the Irish Guards (Fitzgerald); The Coldstream Guards (Howard and Sparrow), The Grenadier Guards 1939–1945; the histories of the Grenadiers by Martin F., and Nicolson & Forbes; the history of the Second Household Cavalry Regiment (Orde), the Royal Engineers' History (Packenham-Walsh), the Royal Canadian Engineers' History (Kerry & McDill) and the memoirs by Adair and Vandaleur. British Intelligence on the German response is in PRO DEFE 3/226, September 18 0525 hours. British underestimate of German strength is acknowledged in the 21AG Report, PRO 37/1249, Section II, especially para.12. Instructions for the Guards to pause before Eindhoven is in *The Guards Armored Division Operational Order No. 12, September 15,* PRO AIR 33/1249. Orders for 5th Armored Brigade are in *5th Armored Brigade Operational Order No. 1, 16 September,* PRO WO 171/605.

The indispensable authority on American airborne military organization and tactics is Huston. The main documentary source consulted is *Reports of First Allied Airborne Army and 82nd and* 101st *Airborne Divisions on Operation Market,* PRO AIR 16/1026.

The main source for the 101st Airborne is still Rapport & Northwood; there are also superb memoirs by Bowen, Burgett and Webster; as well as the accounts by Ambrose, Saunders T. (1), and those in Blair, MacDonald and Ridgeway.

The story of the 82nd Airborne rests heavily on Gavin as well as Blair, Ryan, Saunders T.(2), and MacDonald, who cites Gavin's Letter to Army Historians, July 25, 1945. Gavin's accounts of tactics over the capture of the Nijmegen road bridge are in Gavin (1), Gavin (2), and in Ryan, where there is testimony from Gavin, Lindquist and Warren. There are many experiences of the participants recounted anecdotally in the history of the 505th PIR (Nordyke). Also consulted were the histories of the 504th PIR (Mandle and Whittier), the 508th PIR (Lord) and the 82nd Airborne (Dawson), which is little more than a picture book.

For the battles in Nijmegen, the Guards' histories, cited above, were used extensively; also Maass, *Nijmegen 1944* (in Dutch) and *War Diary, Second (Armored) Battalion, Irish Guards,* PRO WO 171/1256.

There are a large number of works, including participant accounts, on the 1st Airborne and the Battle of Arnhem-Oosterbeek, including those by Bauer (based on information supplied by Lt. Col. Theodoor Boeree), Baynes, Buckingham, Cholewczynski, Dekkers & Vroemen, Fairley, Farrar-Hockley, Frost, Hagen, Harclerode, Harvey, Heaps (1) and (2), Hibbert, the article by Mackay (1945), Mackenzie, Middlebrook (2), the article by Myers (1988), Powell (1) and (2), Sims, Stainforth, Steer, Thompson J., Urquhart R., and the accounts in Lamb, MacDonald, Ryan, Weigley and Wilmot. In addition to the documentary sources cited above, there are *First Parachute Brigade, Outline of Events, Operation Market,* PRO WO 171/592; and *4th Parachute Brigade War Diary,* reconstructed after the battle, PRO WO 171/594 and the Lathbury Diary in the AFM, File 53. The reference book, *Who Was Who During the Battle of Arnhem* (van Roekel) is a list of officers who fought at Arnhem.

For communications in *Market Garden,* see *Report on Operations 'Market' and 'Garden,' Part III Signals Report,* PI, Archive pages 81–120; Bauer, 127, 232–3; Belchem 135; Bennett D. (3); de Jong (2), 381ff; Deane-Drummond, 196, 200–210; Golden 139–69; Lathbury Diary; Hills, 257; Middlebrook (2), 136, 142; Nalder 434; Powell (2), 42, 61, 67, 87, 96; and the 21AG message log in PRO AIR 37/1249. Especially useful is the Appendix to Warner, 1st Airborne Div. *Phantom* message log.

Chapter 8: *Polonia Restituta*
Chapter 9: Stagnation
Chapter 10: The Poles' Second Crossing of the Rhine
Chapter 11: Dithering and Deceit
Chapter 12: The Last Hope Fades

The sources for the First Polish Independent Parachute Brigade and the attempts to relieve 1st Airborne Division are Sosabowski's memoirs, Buckingham, Cholewczynski, Essame, Horrocks (1) and (2), Middlebrook (2), Ryan, Saunders T. (3) and the article by Myers. The chief documentary sources are Sosabowski's draft report, *Krotkie Wstephe Resume,* September 28th, PI AV, 20/31/56, especially para 7d (the original is sadly damaged); *War Diary, 130th Brigade,* PRO WO 171/660; *130th Brigade, Operational Directive No. 1, September 25th,* PRO WO 171/660; *4th Dorsets War Diary,* PRO WO 171/1286; also in the same file, Browning to CO, 4th Dorsets, in *Military Observer's Report,* 2 October, 1944, *The Dorsets Saved the Airborne.* Conditions in the Poles' field hospital in Driel are derived from Cholewcznyski and a conversation with Lt. Leonard Mackiewicz, September 16, 2004. Sosaboski's nickname *Stary* is explained in Appendix 4.

For medical activities in Oosterbeek, see ter Horst, *passim;* Warrack, 47–50; Middlebrook (2), 383; Lipmann Kessel, 21–3 and Ryan, 550–59, the best account of the medical truce.

Dutch contributions to the Battle of Arnhem-Oosterbeek were in the form of military personnel who landed with 1st Airborne, the Resistance and civilians. See *Appendix C of Operational Instructions to Airborne Troops, September 13, 1944, Resistance in Holland,* PI AV.20/31/5; The Dutch Resistance Movement and the Arnhem Operations, n.d., AFM File 53; L.de Jong, *Het Koninkrijk,* Deel 10a; L.de Jong, *De Bezitting;* van der Krap Ch. 24; Maass, 179–81; Heaps (2), especially115, 161–92, 178–9; Internet article by Stewart W. Bentley, *The Dutch Resistance During Operation Market Garden;* references in Bauer, Hackett, ter Horst, Ryan, Urquhart R., and Warrack.

Chapter 13: The Night of the Canadians

The chief primary sources for the Evacuation of 1st Airborne Division from Arnhem-Oosterbeek are M.L. Tucker, *The 23rd Story;* R. Kennedy, *Whispers and Shadows;* Russell Kennedy's notes to this author on Operation *Berlin,* "*Kennedy Notes*"; *Evacuation Report of the 20th Field Company, RCE, September 29th, 1944,* NA, file T 18399; *Evacuation Report of the 23rd Field Company, RCE,* NA file T 18578; *Market*

Garden Report, *Engineers, Re Aspects of Operation Garden, Appendix D to Part 1, Para 5,* PRO AIR 37/1249.

Other sources listed in the Bibliography are *The Pegasus and the Wyvern* (Anonymous, 1946); Bauer, Bennett D.(2), Essame, Hagen, Heaps (2), Kerry & McDill, Middlebrook (2), Packenham-Walsh, Powell (2), Ryan, Sosabowski, and Urquhart R.

Chapter 14: Assessment
The main references from which the assessment is constructed, are Bennett D. (1), Blair, Brooke, Eisenhower (2), Harzer, Hibbert, de Guingand, Kershaw, Montgomery (1) and (2), Urquhart R., and Weigley.

Epilogue
The main sources for the Epilogue, listed in the Bibliography, are Reynolds for the fate of the II SS *Panzer* Corps, Ambrose, Bauer, Belchem, Chatterton, D'Este (1), Bowen, Dekkers & Vroemen, Hackett, Heaps (2), Kennedy, Lamb, Lipmann Kessel, Maass, Middlebrook (2), Tucker M.L., Warrack, and conversation with Tony Hibbert, September 16, 2004.

Appendix 2: The Supply Situation of 21st Army Group on the Eve of *Market Garden*
The chief documentary sources for this Appendix are *XXX Corps Response to the Second Army Draft Report, 3 November 1944,* AFM File 55A; Montgomery, *Normandy to the Baltic; British Airborne Report,* January 1945, PRO AIR 37/1214; *21AG Operation Market-Garden, 17–26 September 1944; Aspects of Operation Garden, Appendix D to Part I; Part III* and 21AGGpOp/20765/G(Plans), PRO AIR 37/1249.

Other sources, listed in the Bibliography, are Belchem, de Guingand, Eisenhower (2) and (3), Golden, Lamb, Liddell-Hart (1), Middlebrook (1), Montgomery (1) and (2), Ruppenthal, Vol. 1, Ruppenthal in *Command Decisions,* Stacey, and van Crefeld. Graham & Bidwell are inaccurate and misleading on supply, because of a silly anti-Americanism.

Appendix 3: The Air Forces in *Market Garden*
The chief documentary sources for this Appendix are *38 and 46 Groups RAF—Report on the British Airborne Effort in Operation 'Market',* PRO AIR 37/418; *21AG Messages, Operation Market-Garden, 17–26 September, 1944,* PRO AIR 37/1249; and Browning's Report, quoted by Wilmot, in PRO AIR 37/1214.

Other sources are Brereton, Cholewczynski (for the final supply run by 525 Squadron), Copp (1) (on fighter-bomber turnaround times), Eisenhower (2), Gavin, Golden, Horrocks (2), Johnson, Rapport & Northwood, Urquhart R., Warner (*Phantom* messages 7, 13, 14, 24, 34, and 36), Wilmot, and (especially) Huston.

Appendix 4: The Humiliation of General Sosabowski

The documentary sources for this Appendix are *War Diary, First Airborne Corps Main*, PRO WO 171/366; Sosabowski's Report to the Polish President, *Pan Prezydent Rzecpospolitie Polskiej*, PI, A.V. 2031/56; Browning's letter to the Deputy CIGS is reproduced in the Appendix to Cholewczynski.

Other sources, listed in the Bibliography, are Blake (52nd Division History), Brereton, Buckingham, Cholewczynski, Eisenhower (2), Essame, Lamb (quoting Montgomery), Middlebrook (2), Morgan (on the likes of Stearley), Powell (1), Saunders T. (3) (for the DCLI's relations with the Poles), Sosabowski, Urquhart R., Warner and Wilmot.

BIBLIOGRAPHY

GENERAL NOTE

The only work to come close to a complete, balanced and comprehensive account of *Market Garden* is Cornelius Ryan's *A Bridge Too Far* (1974). Prior to Ryan, there were a number of more general books which had chapters on *Market Garden* and various memoirs, of which the most notable were those of Major General Roy Urquhart, *Arnhem* (1958) and Major General Stanislaw Sosabowski, *Freely I Served* (1960). Apart from these, works available in English were largely confined to accounts of the Battle of Arnhem-Oosterbeek, principally Christopher Hibbert's *Arnhem* (1962), Anthony Farrar-Hockley's *Airborne Carpet, Operation Market Garden* (1970), and Cornelis Bauer's *The Battle of Arnhem* (1966), based on information supplied by the retired Dutch Artillery officer and Resistance member, Lt. Col. Theodoor A. Boeree. Bauer's work is particularly valuable because it is based on reports, correspondence and interviews with the German participants, such as Rauter, Harzer, Lippert and Bittrich. Though none of the three works are annotated and all have inevitably dated, they remain useful works. Both Urquhart's memoirs and Hibbert's work soon became known to German scholars.

Cornelius Ryan's main achievement was to bring out the major role played by the two American divisions (the 82nd and 101st Airborne). He also had much more to say than previous writers about *Garden,* the ground advance of British XXX Corps, and his use of Dutch oral sources is very extensive. His chief claim to fame was in the form of a *genre* which he virtually invented: the construction of a battle from the experiences of the surviving participants, a huge number of whom were interviewed in the course of writing the book.

257

At a distance of a generation, *A Bridge Too Far* remains a considerable achievement, but it is less comprehensive than it appears to be. The book is extremely weak on the strategic background and objectives of *Market Garden*. It fails to convey the fact that *Market Garden* was an operation by all of Second Army, not just of XXX Corps: the operations of VIII and XII Corps are not even mentioned! Next, the narrative is in fact very patchy: the progress of XXX Corps to the Island, between the Waal and the Rhine, fades away soon after the breakout from the Neerpelt bridgehead; the 101st Airborne virtually disappears after the D-Day landings; and the battle in Oosterbeek between the second lift on D+1 and the evacuation on D+8 is skimpy in places. For some events, Ryan provides the most detailed description of the action; in others he over-dramatizes apocryphal events.

Many of these flaws can be traced to a common source: a reliance on interviews with the surviving participants at the expense of the written primary sources. There is a comprehensive bibliography in *A Bridge Too Far*, but few works seem to have been consulted. One result is that Ryan did not compare the oral contributions of the participants with what they previously wrote. Brian Horrocks, Roy Urquhart, Walther Harzer, George Chatterton, Peter Stainforth, Stanislaw Sosabowski, Eric Mackay, Joe Vandaleur, Graeme Warrack and Kate ter Horst all fall into this category.

The best composite picture of the Battle of Arnhem-Oosterbeek can be constructed from a combination of Ryan's book and Martin Middlebrook's *Arnhem 1944: The Airborne Battle, 17–26 September* (1994). Middlebrook based his account on written primary sources at the Airborne Forces Museum but on few other sources; there are a smaller number of participant accounts and interviews than in Ryan. Middlebrook also ignores Ryan completely, even where Ryan provides a better account, such as the circumstances of the crossing of the Lower Rhine by the 4th Dorsets on D+7, the part played by the Dutch in the battle, and the medical truce on the eve of the evacuation.

After Ryan, the next milestone in *Market Garden* historiography was the publication in 1990 of Robert Kershaw's *It Never Snows in September: The German View of Market Garden*. Before Kershaw, the only author to make significant use of the German sources was the official American historian, Charles B. MacDonald, in *The Siegfried Line Campaign* (1963). This book contains what is still the best short account of *Market Garden*. After Ryan, there was a flood of books, mainly British, about *Market Garden*, some more balanced than those published before Ryan's work. Despite a great deal of repetition, most have something useful to say. None of them, however, are comprehensive and very few written primary sources are cited.

More generally, almost nothing has been written about the operations of VIII and XII Corps. Few have consulted the unit histories written in the immediate post-war period and even fewer have put these two corps into the context of Second Army operations in September 1944.

GENERAL BIBLIOGRAPHY

Documents in the British National Archives are identified as **PRO** (Public Record Office).

Documents in the Polish Institute and Sikorski Museum are identified as **PI**.

Documents in the Airborne Forces Museum at Aldershot are identified as **AFM**.

Documents in the Canadian National Archives are identified as **NA**.

Unit histories consulted include that of the Royal Corps of Signals, the Royal Army Service Corps, the Royal Engineers, the Royal Canadian Engineers, the 23rd Field Company RCE, the British 3rd Division, the 15th (Scottish) Division, the 7th Armoured Division, the 11th Armoured Division, the 43rd (Wessex) Division, the 50th (Northumbrian) Division, the 52nd (Lowland) Division, the Royal Tank Regiment, the 44th Battalion RTR, the Second Household Cavalry Regiment, the Guards Armoured Division, the Grenadier Guards, the Coldstream Guards, the Irish Guards, the Fife and Forfar Yeomanry, the Parachute Regiment, the 2nd Battalion, the Parachute Regiment, the 1st Airborne Division, the U.S. 82nd Airborne Division, 101st Airborne Division, the 504th, 505th and 508th Parachute Infantry Regiments and the II SS *Panzer* Corps.

Adair, Allan. *A Guards' General, The Memoirs of Major General Sir Allan Adair,* London: Hamish Hamilton, 1986.

Alanbrooke, Field Marshal Lord. *War Diaries 1939–1945*. Edited by A. Danchev and D. Todman. London: Phoenix Press, 2002.

Altes, A. Korthals, and N. K. C. A Veld. *The Forgotten Battle, Overloon and the Maas Salient, 1944–45*. New York: Sarpedon Publishers, 1995.

Ambrose, Stephen E. *Band of Brothers, E Company, 506th Regiment, 101st Airborne from Normandy to Hitler's Eagle's Nest*. 1992. Reprint. New York: Simon and Schuster, 2001.

Bauer, Cornelis. *The Battle of Arnhem, The Betrayal Myth Refuted.* 1963. Reprint. London: Hodder and Stoughton, 1966.

Baynes, John. *Urquhart of Arnhem: The Life of Major-General R.E. Urquhart.* London: Brasseys, 1993.

Beale, Peter. *The Great Mistake: The Battle for Antwerp and the Beveland Peninsula, September 1944.* Gloucestershir, UKe: Sutton, Stroud, 2004.

Belchem, David. *All in the Day's March.* London: Collins, 1978.

Bennett, D. "Airborne Communications in Operation Market Garden." *Canadian Military History* 16(1): (Winter 2007).

———. "A Bridge Too Far, The Canadian Role in the Evacuation of the British First Airborne Division from Arnhem-Oosterbeek, September 1944." *Canadian Military Journal* 6(4): (Winter 2006).

———. "British and American Paratroopers in Operation Market Garden." *The Airborne Quarterly* 18(3): (Fall 2005).

Bennett, Ralph. *Ultra in the West: The Normandy Campaign, 1944–5.* London: N.p., 1979.

Blair, Clay. *Ridgeway's Paratroopers, The American Airborne in World War II.* 1985. Reprint. Annapolis: Naval Institute Press, 2002.

Blake, George. *Mountain and Flood: The History of the Fifty-second (Lowland) Division 1939–1946.* Glasgow: Jackson, 1950.

Bowen, Robert M. *Fighting with the Screaming Eagles: With the 101st Airborne from Normandy to Bastogne.* London: Greenhill Books, 2001.

Bradley, Omar N. *A Soldier's Story.* 1951. Reprint. Toronto: Popular Library paperback, 1964.

———, and Clay Blair. *A General's Life: An Autobiography by General of the Army, Omar N Bradley.* New York: Simon and Schuster, 1983.

Brereton, Lewis H. *The Brereton Diaries: The War in the Air in the Pacific, the Middle East and Europe, 3 October 1941–8 May, 1945.* New York: William Morrow, 1946.

Briant, Keith. *Fighting with the Guards.* London: Evans, 1958.

Buckingham, William F. *Arnhem 1944: A Reappraisal.* U.K.: Tempus, 2002.

Burgett, Donald. *The Road to Arnhem, A Screaming Eagle in Holland.* New York: Dell, 2001.

By Air to Battle: The Official Account of the British First and Sixth Airborne Divisions, London: H.M.S.O., 1945.

Chatterton, George. *The Wings of Pegasus: The Story of the Glider Pilot Regiment.* 1962. Reprint. Nashville: The Battery Press, 1982.

Cholewczynski, George F. *Poles Apart: The Polish Airborne at the Battle of Arnhem*. New York: Sarpedon Publishers, 1993.

Clay, Ewart W. *The Path of the Fiftieth: The Story of the Fiftieth (Northumbrian) Division in the Second World War 1939–1945*. Aldershot: Gale and Polden, 1950.

Copp, Terry. *Fields of Fire: The Canadians in Normandy*. Toronto: University of Toronto, 2003.

———. *Cinderella Army: The Canadians in Northwest Europe 1944–1945*. Toronto: University of Toronto Press, 2006.

Crosswell, D. K. R. *Chief of Staff: The Military Career of General Walter Bedell Smith*. New York: Greenwood Press, 1991.

Dawson, W. Forrest. *Saga of the All American [Eighty-second Airborne]* 1946. Reprint. Nashville: Battery Press, n.d.

Deane-Drummond, Anthony. *Return Ticket*. London: Collins, 1953.

de Guingand, Francis. *Operation Victory*. London: Hodder and Stoughton, 1947.

de Jong, L. *De Bezitting*. Amsterdam: Amsterdam Em. Querido's Uitgeverij BV, 1966.

———. *Het Koninkrijk der Nederlanden in de Tweede Wereldoorlog, Deel 10a*. 1985. Reprint. N.p., 1995.

Dekkers, C. A. and P. L. J. Vroemen. *De Zwarte Herfst, Arnhem 1944*. Arnhem: Gijsbers and van Loon, 1989.

Delaforce, Patrick. *Churchill's Desert Rats, from Normandy to Berlin with the 7th Armoured Division*. 1994. Reprint. London: Chancellor, 1999.

D'Este, Carlo. *Decision in Normandy*. 1983. Reprint. New York: Harper paperback, 1994.

———. *Eisenhower, A Soldier's Life*. New York: Henry Holt, 2002.

———. *Patton*. New York: Harper Collins, 1995.

Ehrman, Jon. *Grand Strategy, vol. 5, August 1944–September 1944*. London: H.M.S.O., 1956.

Eisenhower, David. *Eisenhower at War 1943–1945*. New York: Random House, 1986.

Eisenhower, Dwight. *Crusade in Europe*. 1947. Reprint. New York: Avon, 1968.

———. *The Papers of Dwight David Eisenhower: The War Years, vol. 4*. Edited by Alfred D.Chandler. Baltimore: John Hopkins Press, 1970.

———. *Report by the Supreme Commander to the Combined Chiefs of Staff on the Operations in Europe of the Allied Expeditionary Force,*

6 June 1944 to 8 May 1945. Washington, D.C.: U.S. Government Printing Office, 1945.

Ellis, L.F. *Victory in the West, Vol. 2, The Defeat of Germany.* London: H. M. S. O., 1968.

Evacuation Report of the 20th Field Company, RCE. NA File T 18399.

Evacuation Report of the 23rd Field Company, RCE. NA File T 28578.

Essame, Hubert. *The Forty-third Wessex Division at War, 1944–1945.* London: William Clowes, 1952.

Farrar-Hockley, Anthony. *Airborne Carpet, Operation Market Garden.* London: Ballantine, 1970.

———. *Student.* London: Ballantine, 1979.

Fairley, John. *Remember Arnhem: The Story of the First Airborne Reconnaissance Squadron at Arnhem.* Aldershot: Beardsen, Pegasus Journal, 1978.

Fields, Stanley C., ed. *History of the 5th Field Company, Royal Canadian Engineers, 1941–1946.* Ottawa: N.p., n.d.

Fitzgerald, D. J. L. *History of the Irish Guards in the Second World War.* Aldershot: Gale and Polden, 1949.

Frost, John. *A Drop Too Many.* 1980. Reprint. London: Sphere, 1983.

Gavin, James. *Airborne Warfare.* Washington, D.C.: Infantry Journal Press, 1947.

———. *On to Berlin, Battles of an Airborne Commander 1943–1946.* New York: Viking paperback, 1979.

Goerlitz, Walter. *The History of The German General Staff 1657–1945.* New York: Praeger, 1959.

Golden, Lewis. *Echoes from Arnhem.* London: Kimber, 1984.

Graham, Dominick, and Bidwell, Shelford. *Coalitions, Politicians and Generals, Some Aspects of Command in Two World Wars.* London: Brasseys, 1993.

Greenfield, Kent Roberts, ed. *Command Decisions.* New York: Harcourt, Brace and Co., 1959.

The Grenadier Guards 1939–1945. Aldershot: Gale and Polden, 1946.

Hackett, John Winthrop. *I Was a Stranger.* Boston: Houghton Mifflin, 1978.

Hagen, Louis. *Arnhem Lift.* London: Hammond, 1945.

Hamilton, Nigel. *Monty: The Field Marshall 1944–1976.* 1983. Reprint. London: Sceptre paperback, 1987.

Harclerode, Peter. *Arnhem: A Tragedy of Errors.* London: Caxton, 1994.

Harzer, W. *Fallschirme ueber Arnheim,* in Hausser op cit., 131–136.

Harvey, A. D. *Arnhem.* London: Cassell, 2001.

Hastings, Max. *Armageddon: The Battle for Germany.* London: Macmillan, 2004.

―――. *Das Reich: The March of the Second SS Panzer Division through France, June 1944.* 1981. Reprint. London: Pan paperback, 1984.

―――. *D-Day and the Battle for Normandy.* 1984. Reprint. London: Pan paperback, 1985.

Hausser, Paul. *Waffen-SS im Einsatz.* Oldedorf: K. W. Schutz, 1953.

Heaps, Leo. *Escape from Arnhem: A Canadian Among the Lost Paratroopers.* Toronto: Macmillan, 1946.

―――. *The Grey Goose of Arnhem [The Evaders].* 1976. Reprint. Markham, Ontario: PaperJacks edition, 1977.

Heiber, Helmut, and David M. Glantz, eds. *Hitler's Generals: Military Conferences, 1942–1945.* New York: Enigma, 2002.

Hibbert, Christopher. *Arnhem.* 1962. Reprint. Moreton-in-Marsh: Windrush paperback, 1998.

Hills, R. J. T. *Phantom Was There.* London: E. Arnold, 1951.

Hinsley, F.H. *British Intelligence in the Second World War: Its Influence on Strategy and Operations, vol. 3, Part II.* London: H. M. S. O., 1988.

―――. *Hitler's Strategy.* Cambridge: Cambridge University Press, 1951.

History of the Eleventh Armoured Division (Taurus Pursuant). Aldershot: Gale and Polden, 1945.

History of the 44th RTR 1939–1945. UK: N.p., n.d.

History of the Second Battalion, The Parachute Regiment from its formation to the Battle of Arnhem. Aldershot: Gale and Polden, 1946.

History of the 7th Armoured Division, June 1943–July 1945. British Army of the Rhine, 1945.

Hoehne, Heinz. *The Order of the Death's Head: The Story of Hitler's SS.* 1969. Reprint. London: Pan paperback, 1972.

Horne, Alistair, and David Montgomery. *The Lonely Leader: Monty 1944–1945.* London: Pan Edition, 1995.

Horrocks, Brian. *A Full Life.* London: Leo Cooper, 1974.

―――, with Eversley Belfield and H. Essame. *Corps Commander.* Toronto: Griffin House, 1977.

Howard, M.E., and J. H. A. Sparrow. *The Coldstream Guards, 1920–1946.* Oxford: O. U. P., 1951.

Howard, Michael. *Strategic Deception in the Second World War.* 1990. Reprint. London: Norton, 1995.

Huston, James. *Out of the Blue: U.S. Airborne Operations in World War II.* Nashville: Battery Press, 1972.

Jackson, G.S. *Operations of VIII Corps*. London: Clements Press, 1948.

Johnson, 'Johnnie.' *Wing Leader*. Toronto: Clarke Irwin, 1956.

Kahn, David. *Hitler's Spies, German Military Intelligence in World War II*. 1978. Reprint. Cambridge, Mass.: De Capo Press paperback, 2000.

Keegan, John. *Waffen SS: the Asphalt Soldiers*. New York: Ballantine, 1970.

Kemp, Anthony. *The Unknown Battle: Metz, 1944*. New York: Stein and Day, 1980.

Kennedy, Russell. *Notes on Operations Berlin and Pegasus II*. N.p., 2005.

————. *Whispers and Shadows: Arnhem Fifty Years Later*. Kingston, Ontario: N. p., 1996.

Kershaw, Robert J. *It Never Snows in Septembe: The German View of Market-Garden and the Battle of Arnhem, September 1944*. London: Crowood Press, 1990.

Kerry, A. J. and W. A. McDill. *The Corps of Royal Canadian Engineers, Vol. 2, 1936–1946*. Ottawa: Military Engineers Association of Canada, 1966.

Krafft, Sepp. *Report of the SS Panzer Grenadier Depot and Reserve Battalion 16*. English translation in AFM File 48, in PRO AIR 20/2333 and in Chatterton, Appendix II.

Lamb, Richard. *Montgomery in Europe, 1943–45: Success or Failure?* New York: Franklin Watts, 1983.

Lewin, Ronald. *Ultra Goes to War*. London: Arrow Books Edition, 1980.

Liddell Hart, Basil. *History of the Second World War*. 1970. Reprint. London: Pan paperback, 1973.

————. *The Tanks: History of the Royal Tank Regiment, vol. 2 1939–1945*. London: Cassell, 1959.

Lipmann Kessel, Alexander William. *Surgeon at Arms*. 1958. Reprint. London: Leo Cooper, 1976.

Lord, William G. *History of the 508th Parachute Infantry*. Nashville: Battery Press, 1977.

Maass, Walter B. *The Netherlands at War: 1940–1945*. London: Abelard-Schuman, 1970.

MacDonald, Charles B. *The Siegfried Line Campaign*. Washington, D.C.: Office of the Chief of Military History, 1963.

Mackay, E. M. "The Battle of Arnhem Bridge." *Blackwoods Magazine* (October 1945) and reprinted in *The Royal Engineers Journal* (1954).

Mackenzie, C.B. *It Was Like This: A Short Factual Account of the Battle of Arnhem and Oosterbeek*. Oostebeek: Oosterbeek Airborne Museum, 1997.

Mandle, William D., and David H. Whittier. *The Devils in Baggy Pants: Combat Record of the 504th Parachute* Infantry *Regiment April 1943–July 1945*. 1945. Reprint. Nashville: Battery Press, 2004.

Martin, F. *History of the Grenadier Guards 1646–1949*. Aldershot: Gale and Polden, 1951.

Martin, H.G. *The History of the Fifteenth Scottish Division 1939-1945*. Edinburgh: William Blackwood and sons, 1948.

Middlebrook, Martin. *Arnhem 1944: The Airborne Battle*. 1994. Reprint. London: Penguin, 1995.

—————, and Chris Everitt. *The Bomber Command War Diaries: An Operational Reference Book 1939-1945*. 1985. Reprint. London: Penguin, 1990.

Mitcham, Samuel W. *Hitler's Legions: The German Army Order of Battle, World War II*. New York: Stein and Day, 1958.

Montgomery, Bernard. *Memoirs*. Cleveland: World Publishing, 1958.

—————. *Normandy to the Baltic*. 1947. Reprint. London: Grey Arrow paperback, 1961.

Morgan, Frederick. *Peace and War: A Soldier's Life*. London: Hodder and Stoughton, 1961.

Moulton, J. L. *Battle for Antwerp: The Liberation of the City and the Opening of the Scheldt, 1944*. New York: Hippocrene, 1978.

Myers, E. C. W. "At Arnhem: September 1944." *Royal Engineers Journal* (September 1988).

Nalder, R. F. H. *The Royal Corps of Signal: a history of its antecedents and development (circa 1800–1955)*. Aldershot: Royal Signals Institution, 1958.

Nicolson, Nigel, and Patrick Forbes. *The Grenadier Guards in the War of 1939–1945, Vol. 1*. Aldershot: Gale and Polden, 1949.

Nijmegen 1944. Nijmegen: N. p., 1994.

Norton, G. G. *The Red Devils: The Story of the British Airborne Forces*. London: Pan, 1971.

Nordyke, Phil. *Four Stars of Valor: The Combat History of the 505th Parachute Infantry Regiment in World War II*. St. Paul, Minn.: Zenith Press, 2006.

Packenham-Walsh, R. P. *History of the Corps of Royal Engineers, vol. 9, 1938–1948*. Chatham: Institution of Royal Engineers, 1958.

"The Pegasus and the Wyvern (The Evacuation of the First Airborne Division from Arnhem)." *Royal Engineers Journal* (March 1946).

Piekalkiewicz, Janusz. *Arnhem, 1944*. New York: Scribners, 1976.

Orde, Roden. *The Household Cavalry at War: Second Household Cavalry Regiment*. Aldershot: Gale and Polden, 1953.

Pogue, Forrest C. *The Supreme Command*. Washington, D. C.: Office of the Chief of Military History, 1954.

Powell, Geoffrey. *The Devil's Birthday: The Bridges to Arnhem, 1944*. London: Leo Cooper, 1984.

————. *Men at Arnhem*. Rev. ed. London: Leo Cooper, 1986.

Rapport, Leonard, and Arthur Northwood. *Rendezvous with Destiny: A History of the* 101st *Airborne Division*. Enl. Ed. Kentucky: Fort Campbell, 1962.

Reitlinger, Gerald. *The SS: Alibi of a Nation 1922–45*. New York: De Capo Press, 1957.

Ridgeway, Matthew B. *Soldier: The Memoirs of Matthew B. Ridgeway*. New York: Harper, 1956.

Reynolds, Michael. *Sons of the Reich, History of the II SS Panzer Corps in Normandy, Arnhem, the Ardennes and on the Eastern Front*. Haverton, PA: Casemate, 2002.

Rosse, L. M. H. P., and E. W. Hill. *The Story of the Guards Armoured Division*, London: G. Bles, 1956.

Ruppenthal, Roland G. *Logistical Support of the Armies, vol. 2: September 1944–May, 1945*. N.p., 1953.

Ryan, Cornelius. *A Bridge Too Far*. 1974. Reprint. New York: Popular Library Edition, n.d.

Saunders, Hilary St. George. *The Red Beret: The Story of the Parachute Regiment at War 1940–1945*. London: Michael Joseph, 1950.

————. *Royal Air Force, vol. 3, The Fight is Won*. London: H. M. S. O., 1954.

Saunders, Tim. *Hell's Highway*. Barnsley: Leo Cooper, 2001.

————. *The Island*. Barnsley: Leo Cooper, 2002.

————. *Nijmegen, Grave and Groesebeek*. Barnsley: Leo Cooper, 2001.

Scarfe, Norman. *Assault Division: A History of the Third Division from the Invasion of Normandy to the Surrender of Germany*. London: Collins, 1947.

Schulman, Milton. *Defeat in the West*. 1947. Reprint. London: Coronet, 1973.

Seaton, Albert. *The Fall of Fortress Europe: 1943–1945*. London: Batsford, 1981.

————. *The German Army*. London: Weidenfeld and Nicolson, 1982.

————. *The Russo-German War, 1941–45.* 1971. Reprint. Novato, Cal.: Presidio Press, 1993.

Sellar, R.J.B. *The Fife and Forfar Yeomanry, 1919–1956.* London: Blackwood, 1960.

Sims, James. *Arnhem Spearhead : A Private Soldier's Story.* London: Imperial War Museum, 1978.

Smith, Walter Bedell. *Eisenhower's Six Great Decisions: Europe 1944–45.* New York: Longmans, 1956.

Sosabowski, Stanislaw. *Freely I Served.* Nashville: The Battery Press, 1953.

Stacey, C. P. *The Victory Campaign, The Operations in North-West Europe (Official History of the Canadian Army in the Second World War, vol. 3).* Ottawa: The Queen's Printer, 1960.

Stainforth, Peter. *Wings of the Wind.* London: Falcon Press, 1952.

Stein, George H. *The Waffen SS 1939-45.* Ithaca, New York: N. p., 1966.

Steer, Frank. *Arnhem: The Bridge.* London: Leo Cooper, 2003.

————. *Arnhem, the Fight to Sustain, The Untold Story of the Airborne Logisticians.* London: Leo Cooper, 2000.

————. *Arnhem, the Landing Grounds and Oosterbeek,* London: Leo Cooper, 2002.

The Story of the Royal Army Service Corps. London: G. Bell and Sons, 1955.

Strong, Kenneth. *Intelligence at the Top: The Recollections of an Intelligence Officer.* London: Cassell, 1968.

Swiecicki, Marek. *With the Red Devils at Arnhem.* London: Max Love, 1945.

Tedder, Arthur William. *With Prejudice: The War Memoirs of Marshal of the Royal Air Force Lord Tedder.* London: Cassell, 1959.

ter Horst-Arriens, Kate. *Cloud over Arnhem, A Regimental Aid Post.* 1945. Reprint. N. p., 1959.

Thompson, Julian. *Operation Market: The Battle for Arnhem.* N. p., 1989.

Thompson, R.W. *The Eighty-Five Days: The Story of the Battle of the Scheldt.* London: Hutchinson, 1957.

————. *Montgomery: the Field-Marshal.* London: Allen and Unwin, 1969.

Tieke, Wilhelm. *In the Firestorm of the Last Years of the War: II SS Panzer Corps with the 9. and 10. SS-Divisions, Hohenstaufen and Frundsberg.* (1975) Winnipeg: J.J. Fedorowicz Publishing, 1999.

Trevor-Roper, H.R. *Hitler's War Directives 1939–1945.* 1964. Reprint.

London: Pan paperback, 1966.

Tucker, M.L. *The Twenty-Third Story (History of the 23rd Field Company, RCE)*. Montreal: N. p., 1947.

Urquhart, Brian. *A Life in Peace and War*. New York, Harper and Row, 1987.

Urquhart, R.E., with Wilfred Greatorix. *Arnhem*. London: Cassell, 1958.

van Creveld, Martin. *Supplying War, Logistics from Wallenstein to Patton*. Cambridge: Cambridge University Press, 1977.

van der Krap, Charles J.F. Duow. *Contra de swastika: De strijd van een onversetteljke Nederlandse marineofficier in bezet Europa, 1940–1945*. Amsterdam, N.p., 1981.

van Roekel, C. *Who Was Who During the Battle of Arnhem, The Order of Battle of Airborne Officers and Warrant Officers Who Fought at Arnhem in 1944*. N. p., 1996.

Vandaleur, J.O.E. *A Soldier's Story*. Aldershot: Gale and Polden, 1967.

Verney, G.L. *The Guards Armoured Division: A Short History*. London: Hutchinson, 1955.

Warlimont, Walter. *Inside Hitler's Headquarters*. Navato, Cal.: Presidio, 1964.

Warrack, Graeme. *Travel by Dark: After Arnhem*. London: Harvill Press, 1963.

Warner, Phillip. *Phantom*. London: Kimber, 1982.

Weigley, Russell F., *Eisenhower's Lieutenants, The Campaigns of France and Germany, 1944–45,* Indiana University Press, Bloomington, 1981

Wilmot, Chester, *The Struggle for Europe* (1952), Reprint Society/Collins, London, 1984.

MOVIES

There are two movies about Operation *Market Garden*, of which the first is *Theirs is the Glory*. This is a film about the Battle of Arnhem-Oosterbeek, produced in mid-1945 using members of First Airborne Division as actors and filmed in the ruins Arnhem and Oosterbeek. The production is interspersed with the small surviving footage of original war film from Arnhem. As such, the film is a superb, early and unique example of what is now called a docudrama. It is available in a special edition from the Airborne Forces Museum in Oosterbeek. Some of the acting, understandably enough, is wooden and slight; mostly it captures the spirit of the action and the demeanour of the troops. Some of the actors play themselves. Watch for Dickie Lonsdale, Tony Hibbert, John Frost, Dennis

Munford, Freddie Gough, Kate ter Horst and, above all, Stanley Maxted, the Canadian journalist whose despatches from Arnhem gripped the free world—and, in the film, still do.

A Bridge Too Far is a Hollywood-style blockbuster, based on Cornelius Ryan's book. Some of the scenes are lifted and adapted from *Theirs is the Glory*. Like the book, the movie covers the planning of the operation, the airborne landings, the advance of the Guards Armoured, the crossing of the Waal by the 82nd Airborne, the fighting at the Arnhem bridge and the evacuation of 1st Airborne. No movie can cover all the events in a nine-day battle; it has to be selective. For instance, Harmel and Harzer are collapsed into a single character, "General Ludwig." This is legitimate. But there are then distortions, to serve popular appetite. Brian Urquhart is given a fictitious name and is portrayed as a wimp, clumsy with projection equipment, entirely false. Bittrich is depicted as an arrogant young Nazi, when he was neither of these things.

Rundstedt's famous response to the question "What shall we do?" ("Make peace, you fools, what else can you do?") was the occasion of his dismissal in July, not following his reappointment as theatre commander in September. The meteorologists are played as disingenuous amateurs, in order to make Sosabowski more of a victim than he really was. Dirk Bogarde is miscast as Browning; his performance is languid and measured, when Browning was hawk-like and sharp.

Others are well cast, such as Sean Connery as Roy Urquhart and an outstanding performance by Edward Fox as Horrocks. The main fault of the movie is that there is no sense of the shape of the battle; it is not always clear what the players are up to and how they fit into the progress of the operation. Unless the viewer knows the battle, it is utterly inexplicable why SS troops should be approaching the Arnhem bridge from the south since they are not seen moving from north to south on D-Day. The Son bridge is shown as being destroyed by artillery fire, then restored by the Americans. It would have helped to have maps and diagrams shown, in order to plot the progress of XXX Corps, the declining fortunes of 1st Airborne, and the frustrations of the Poles. The net result is that all the drama is lost.

ACKNOWLEDGMENTS

This book would not have been possible without the help, advice and critical comments of Carlo D'Este, Brian Urquhart, Russell Kennedy, Anna Nitoslawska, Marikje Dollois, Ivor Green and Tom Goss. Special thanks are due to Henk Duinhoven, who generously shared with me his immense knowledge of the history and topography of the Battle of Arnhem-Oosterbeek. I also received valuable help from Barbara Derkow-Disselbeck, Nora Côté, Peter Stachura, George MacDonnell, Elsie Lafontaine and Nancy Stroud of the Canadian Department of National Defence Library and Dr. Andrzej Stuchitz of the Polish Institute and Sikorski Museum, London. Jean Bradburn tracked down rare articles and lent me Arnhem memorabilia belonging to her father-in-law, John Bradburn of the Second South Staffs. For interviews and conversations, I am grateful to Brian Urquhart, Tony Hibbert, Russell Kennedy, Ken Fleet, John Mills, Leonard Mackiewicz, Robert Taylor, Ted Lawson and Stan Fields.

Since relaxed conversation is as important to historical interpretation as reasoned inference from the written sources, I am grateful to my friends, Tom O'Brien, Mike Wright, Jack Bennett, a veteran of the U.S. 525th Engineer Company in the 1944–45 campaign, the late Dick Martin and the late Kurt Heine, formerly a signaller with the Fifth *Waffen-SS* Division *Wiking*. Ivor Green, formerly of the Royal Signals and REME, sent me critical comments on the passages dealing with communications at Arnhem and gave me a most valuable document: his wartime Specification Notes on the No.19HP wireless set.

Equally, I express my deep thanks to Russell Kennedy, formerly Reconnaissance Officer of the Twenty-third Field Company, RCE, for his critical comments on the passages in the book dealing with the Arnhem evacuation, for supplying me with his memoir *Whispers and Shadows, Arnhem Fifty Years Later* and for extensive notes on Operations *Berlin* and *Pegasus II*. My agent, Arnold Gosewich and my editor, Robert Buckland, guided me in turning a promising manuscript into a viable book, while David Farnsworth of Casemate Publishing saw the book into print without any needless complications whatever. Any errors and misconceptions in the text are, of course, the responsibility of the author alone.

The chief intellectual debt in regard to this book is to Colonel Albert Seaton. In *The Battle for Moscow, 1941–42* (1971), only one of Seaton's many accomplished works, we see a historian with all the grasp of a professional soldier constructing and reconstructing a battle from the few available Russian sources and a profusion of those German. On these constructions rest the attribution of reason and motive, then an evaluation of military purpose and conduct. Since Seaton wrote before the era of interviewing participants in the battle, he relied, among other sources, on divisional histories, partly for narrative information and partly to lend color to a terrible battle against the weather and the terrain as well as the enemy. By today's standards, Seaton's pioneering work is one of John Locke's underlaborer, essential basic history but old-fashioned. If the same accusation is levelled against this book, I can only plead that very many of the primary written sources have remained so far untouched and that *A Magnificent Disaster* should have been written a generation ago.

Tom Goss acted as navigator and historical consultant for a battlefield tour in September 2003, which included the Meuse-Escaut crossings, the German cemetery at IJsselstein, Nijmegen, Mook, the Groesbeek Heights, Wyler in Germany, Driel, Heveadorp, Oosterbeek and Arnhem. In blissful ignorance we passed the signs for the National Oorlogs-en Verzetzmuseum, wondering why the Dutch should make so much fuss about a clock museum. We realized our error and returned in haste to look at the splendid National War and Resistance Museum at Overloon, which contains some exceedingly rare exhibits, such as a restored 88mm flak gun, a towed Polsten light cannon and DUKW amphibians. If the 82nd Airborne had taken as much time to find a route off the Groesbeek Heights as we did in ascending them, they would never have reached Nijmegen! A further visit in September 2004 took in the 60th Anniversary of the Arnhem operation, Ede, the north bank of the Lower Rhine and the Deelen Airbase Museum.

Finally, I would like to thank Art-Tech Ltd in the UK for their expertise with the maps specially prepared for this work.

INDEX

A Bridge Too Far, xii, 127
Aachen, Germany, 44, 53, 191
Adair, Maj. Gen. Allan, 15, 106, 123, 137
"Airborne Warfare," 40
Albert Canal, 10, 21-24, 28, 45-46, 53-55, 212, 242
Allied Expeditionary Force, 5
Allied Joint Military Units, 44; *First Allied Airborne Army*, xv, 6, 8, 10-12, 21, 32, 35-36, 197-198, 212, 229, 241
Antwerp, Belgium, 5, 7-8, 10-12, 20, 22, 24, 28, 44-45, 219, 221, 241, 243
Apeldoorn, 23, 29, 42, 48, 178, 205, 208
Arnhem, vii, xii, 1, 6, 12, 14, 20-21, 23-26, 41-42, 50, 57-58, 64, 80, 82, 113, 192, 199; a disaster, 201-202; assessment, 194-195, 198; British casualties, 129; British defense of, 79, 154; British landings, 3-4; British troops need relief, 115; civilian evacuation, 172; D+2, 108; D+3, 122; D+5, 143; D-Day, 81; defense of, 123; disaster for parachute brigades, 109; flooded by the Germans, 191; German troops in Arnhem, 85; inside the British

perimeter, 176-179, 182; Montgomery's assessment, 196; night crossing the river, 163, 183-184; night evacuation, 182, 187-188; not a unique blunder, 200; Operation *Comet*, 19; presented as a victory of British arms, 127; where it failed, 194
Arnhem Bridge, xvi, 22, 38-39, 48, 52, 59, 84, 133, 212; air operations, 226-228, 233; D-Day, 79; Frost's main objective, 75; German attempts to cross, 73-74, 79; intel, 241; supply situation, 222, 231
Arnhem Corridor, see "the Corridor"

Balthussen, Cora, 139-140, 188
Baskeyfield, Sgt. John, 132
The Battle of Arnhem Bridge, 79
Baumgaertel, SS-Lt. (-), 93-94, 107, 125
Beek, 37, 91, 106, 115-117, 151, 171
Belgian Military Units, First Belgian Brigade Group, 15, 24, 181, 214-215
Belgian Resistance, 5, 45, 211
Best, 35-36, 61-63, 68, 130, 147, 149, 181, 214
Bestebreurtje, Capt. "Harry," 72, 92, 104

Bittrich, SS-Lt. Gen. Wilhelm, 47-56, 73, 81-82, 84, 95, 131, 138, 175, 178, 201, 205

Blaskowitz, Gen. Johannes, 206

Boeree, Lt. Col. Theodoor, 173, 209

Bowen, Robert, 169

Bradley, Gen. Omar, 4, 7, 11, 27-28, 208

Breese, Maj. Charles, 173

Brereton, Lt. Gen. Lewis, xv, 10, 34, 59, 172, 207, 225, 229, 231; a fundamental decision, 33; blamed for mistakes in planning, 33; flies to Antwerp, 105; gives Browning command of Market, 28; Hollinghurst, 39; initially favors British plan, 35; night crossing the river, 160; Ninth Air Force, 32; one of three blind mice, xvi; original plan came from Montgomery's HQ, 35; plans one drop on D-Day, 21

Breskens Pocket, 12, 22, 44

Brinkmann, SS-Major, 48, 100, 204

British Military Units, *1st Airborne Division,* xi, 3, 6, 10, 15, 22, 28, 30, 31, 33, 35, 37-42, 58-59, 81, 85, 95, 111, 122-124, 127, 131, 133-135, 137-138, 144-146, 153, 155, 158, 160- 166, 171, 173, 178, 182-184, 199, 207-209, 213-214, 227-233, 235, 237-239, 241-242, 244; D+3, 132; D-Day, 75, 197; drop zone, 74; night crossing the river, 159; night evacuation, 188-189; Operation *Comet,* 19; out of radio contact, 14; perilous state, 154; plan to capture Arnhem bridges, 29; plans immediately unravel, 75; route to target, 34; *First Airborne Corps,* 8, 58, 229; *First Airborne Light Regiment,* 174; *First Airlanding Brigade,* 38, 41, 80-81, 95, 112-113; *First Parachute Battalion,* 208; *First Parachute Brigade,* 38, 41, 49, 75, 77, 83-84,

94-99, 101, 109, 111, 131-133, 193, 208, 227, 244; *First parachute Squadron,* 128; *First Parachute Squadron of Engineers,* 78-79; *First Worcesters,* 144, 154, 162; *Second Army,* xiv, 3-4, 6, 10-13, 20-27, 45-46, 52, 58-60, 122, 135-136, 153, 160, 163, 165-166, 192, 195-199, 211, 217-218, 220-221, 223, 233; *Second Household Cavalry,* 68, 89, 90, 143, 214; *Second Parachute Battalion,* 213; *Second Tactical Air Force,* RAF, 33; *3rd Division,* 15, 24, 171, 213-215, 221; *4th Parachute Brigade,* 20, 38-39, 41, 75, 95-97, 110-112, 129, 131-132, 185, 193, 207, 228, 241; *Fourth Dorsets,* 154-155, 159-160, 166-167, 179, 183-184, 187, 214, 236; *Fifth Armoured brigade,* 69; *Fifth Dorsets,* 123, 154, 161; *Fifth Guards Armored Brigade,* 31, 106, 194; *6th Airborne Division,* 10, 40; *Sixth Guards Armored Brigade,* 220; *7th Armoured Division,* 24, 151-152, 215; *7th Dragoon Guards,* 123; *Seventh Hampshires,* 144, 154, 161; *Seventh Somersets,* 123; *Eighth Armoured Brigade,* 30-32, 122, 144; *Eighth Army,* 208; *9th Field Company Royal Engineers,* 80; *Tenth Parachute Battalion,* 96, 111-113, 129, 131, 172-174; *11th Armoured Division,* 5, 15-16, 24, 45, 182, 211; *11th Parachute Battalion,* 96-97, 109-112, 131, 172; *Fourteenth Field Squadron,* Royal Engineers, 90; *15th Infantry Division,* 23, 25, 91, 149, 181; *16th Parachute Field Ambulance,* 80; *21st Army Group,* xv, 4, 7, 12, 21, 30, 36, 44, 58-59, 66, 136, 207, 218-219, 222, 231; *21st Independent Parachute Company,* 38; *38 Group RAF Transport*

Command, 33, 230; *43rd Division*, 15, 29-31, 115, 122-124, 138, 143, 153-154, 158-159, 161, 164-167, 173-174, 182-183, 193-194, 199, 214, 235, 237; *43rd Reconnaissance Regiment*, 144; *Forty-fourth Battalion, Royal Tank Regiment*, 90; *46 Group RAF Transport Command*, 33, 230, 232; *50th Infantry Division*, 23, 29-30, 89-90, 103, 123, 130, 141, 149, 153, 165; *51st Infantry Division*, 220, 222; *52nd Division (Air-Portable)*, 10, 19, 22, 28, 33-35, 135-136, 151, 160, 174, 230, 232, 237; *53rd Infantry Division*, 23, 90; *Sixty-fourth Medium Artillery Regiment*, 32, 132, 134, 174; *Sixty-ninth Brigade*, 123; *83 Group, RAF*, 33, 66, 136, 231-233; *91st Anti-Tank Regiment*, 24; *129th Brigade*, 123, 143; *130th Brigade*, 122-124, 146, 154, 159, 162-164, 182, 214; *147th Field Regiment*, 32; *156th Parachute Battalion*, 96, 111-112, 129, 131, 172, 185; *157th Brigade*, 237; *204th Field Company Royal Engineers*, 155, 163, 236; *214th Brigade*, 123, 143-144, 153-154, 161-162; *231st Brigade*, 69; *260th Field Company Royal Engineers*, 163, 184; *525 Squadron, RAF*, 232; *536th General Transport Company*, 146; *553rd Field Company Royal Engineers*, 163, 184; *Bomber Command*, 33; *Coldstream Guards*, 31, 105, 116-117, 151-152, 214; *Duke of Cornwall's Light Infantry*, 138, 144, 146, 153-154, 162, 214, 236; *Fighter Command*, 33; *Glider Pilot Regiment*, 106, 208; *Grenadier Guards*, 31, 89, 106, 120-122, 151-152, 182, 188, 193, 215; *Guards Armoured Division*, 5, 15-16, 23, 29-31, 89, 93, 105-106, 115, 119, 122, 124-

127, 143, 151, 163, 171, 194, 198, 211, 213, 220, 227-228; *Household Cavalry*, 88, 135, 141, 144-146; *Inns of Court Regiment*, 151, 182; *Irish Guards*, 1-2, 23, 31, 67-69, 89, 104, 122-123, 138, 144; *King's Own Scottish Borderers*, 80, 95-96, 113, 129, 131, 149, 161, 173-174, 179, 181, 184; *Leicestershire Yeomanry*, 152; *Lonsdale Force*, 111, 179, 185; *Northumberland Fusiliers*, 152; *Royal Army Service Corps*, 78; *Royal Engineers*, 31; *Royal Tank Regiment*, 148, 152; *South Staffordshires Regiment*, 80, 95-96, 109-110, 132; *Welsh Guards*, 31, 89, 122-124, 138, 144; *I Airborne Corps*, 12, 29, 220; *VIII Corps*, 3, 15-16, 23-26, 30, 63, 89, 90, 103, 130, 141, 147, 149, 151-153, 157, 171, 181-182, 191, 195-196, 208, 213-215, 220-222; *XII Corps*, 2-3, 14, 23-25, 30, 46, 63, 90-91, 103, 130, 141, 149, 151, 170, 181, 195-196, 212-215, 220-222; *XXX Corps*, 3, 6, 10, 13, 23-27, 29-31, 35, 37-38, 41-42, 50, 54, 61, 63-65, 68-69, 75, 85, 89-90, 93, 100, 103, 119, 126-128, 130, 132-133, 135, 138, 141-142, 145, 147, 149, 151, 153, 161-162, 165-167, 169, 171, 174, 181-182, 193-195, 207, 212, 214-215, 217, 220, 222, 226, 228, 231-233, 237, 242

Brooke, Sir Alan, 5, 7, 195, 238
Browning, Lt. Gen. Frederick A.M. "Boy," 12, 21, 36, 42, 59, 241; air operations, 63, 232; argument over tactics, 159-160; assessment, 199, 242-244; bad communications, 85, 133; calls for seven drops, 35; changing his mind, 105; commandeered gliders for HQ, 39; compliments units crossing the Waal, 119; D+3, 133; D+4, 124; D+5, 135; D-

Day, 62; devious manipulator and a poor planner, 13; dismisses Sosabowski, 235-239; evasive and amazing reply to Sosabowski, 162; General Richard Gale, 40; given command of *Comet*, 20, 29; Horrocks' reasoning for night crossing, 164; ignores intel about German strength, 58; meets with Gavin, 106, 171; meets with Montgomery D+8, 166; night crossing the river, 154; Nijmegen bridges and the 82nd Airborne, 71; one of three blind mice, xvi; *Operational Instruction No. 1*, 41; orders capture of Nijmegen bridge, 106; orders withdrawl on D+8, 165; patronizing condescension toward Americans, 13; plans seven different zones for 101st, 40; post war, 207; quote "...a bridge to far....", 22; relieved Sosabowski of command, xvii; sketch and rigid planning, 13; takes command of "Market," 28

Bruhn, Hans, 112

Brussels, Belgium, 5, 21, 46

Buckingham, William F., 22, 127

Budziszewski, Capt. P.P., 166

Bulge, Battle of the, 192, 204, 206

Burd, Capt. W.S., 64

Burgett, Pfc. Donald, 3, 203

Cain, Maj. Robert, 174

Campbell, Lt. Col. Bill, 231

Canadian Military Units, *First Army*, 4-5, 12, 21, 213, 219-220; *2nd Division*, 220; *Tenth Field Park Company*, RCE, 184; *Twentieth Field Company RCE*, 163, 184, 186; *Twenty-third Field Company RCE*, 163-164, 184, 187, 206, 208-209, 214, 236

Carrington, Capt. Lord, 121

Cassidy, Lt. Col. Patrick, 64, 104-105, 148

Chatterton, Col. George, 106, 208

Chill, Lt. Gen. Kurt, 46, 54-55, 65-67, 152, 157

Cholewczynski, George, 140

Christiansen, "Luftwaffe" Gen. Friedrich, 44, 53, 56, 172, 205

Churchill, Winston, xiv, xvi, 5

Clark, Lt. Gen. Mark, xvi

Clifford, Alexander, xiv

"Club" Route, 26, 89

Cockrill, James, 182

Cole, Lt. Col. Robert G., 62, 87

Combined Chiefs of Staff, 5, 7, 11

Congressional Medal of Honor, *Cole, Lt. Col. Robert G.*, 87; *Mann, Pvt. Joe*, 88

Cook, Maj. Julian, 118, 119, 120

The "Corridor", xii, 29-30, 35, 46, 51, 54, 62-63, 65, 89- 90, 103-104, 130, 140-141, 147-149, 151-153, 155, 157-159, 163, 165, 169-171, 182, 192-193, 195, 199, 204, 214, 219, 232

Courtney, Brian, 243

Crawley, Maj. Douglas, 75

Crerar, Gen. Harry, 4, 13, 21, 196, 219-221

Crook, Bill, 80

De Guingand, Gen. Frederick, 9, 195, 218, 221

Deane-Drummond, Maj. Anthony, 3, 208

Deelan, 34, 39-40, 76, 135, 160, 172, 211

Dempsey, Lt. Gen. Miles, xiv, 4, 13, 24; air operations, 226; assessment, 197; bridges that won't hold tanks, 89; crosses Rhine River, 192; D+3, 130, 151; D+4, 130; D+5, 149; D+6, 151; D+8, 25; dispersal of efforts, 24; engineers, 30; heart never in the Arnhem operation, 28; "I am proud..." quote, 171; meeting with Taylor, 69; meets with

Horrocks on D+7, 164; meets with Montgomery D+8, 165; meets with O'Connor, 141; Montgomery proposes a large scale parachute drop, 21; more efficient than brilliant, 14; night crossing the river, 158, 163, no interest in Taylor's plan, 36; Operation *Comet*, 20; out of radio contact, 85; plans airborne drop, 22; post battle, 207; post war, 207-208; supply situation, 218, 221

Des Voeux, Lt. Col. Sir Richard, 129

Devers, Gen. Jacob L., xiii, 4

Dietrich, Sepp, 49

Dinther-Heeswijk bridgehead, 141

Dobie, Lt. Col. David, 75-77, 95-98, 109-111, 208

Doggart, LCpl. James, 2

Dommel River bridge, 29, 35, 64, 89-90

Dover, Maj. Victor, 75, 78

Down, Gen. Eric, 171, 239

Driel, 30, 126, 135, 138-140, 143-146, 153-155, 158, 160, 162-163, 182, 184, 186, 188, 191, 193, 199, 213-214, 235-236, 240

Driel-Heveadorp Ferry, 38, 56-57, 80, 133-134, 137-138

Dutch Resistance, 36, 58, 64, 125-126, 128, 132, 170, 181, 205, 208

Dyrda, Lt. J.H., 158

Eagger, Col. Austin, 243

Eberach, Gen. Hans, 49

Eindhoven, xii, 3, 20, 23, 25-26, 29, 35-36, 50, 64-69, 73, 85, 88-90, 118, 123, 130, 141, 148, 152, 159, 171, 198, 213

Eisenhower, Gen. Dwight D., xiii, 5-9, 11, 134-135, 211, 213; air operations, 229; assessment of the campaign,195-196, 199, 242; assurances to Montgomery, 28; authorized strategic offensive, 8; authorizes *Market Garden*, 212, 242; commands ground forces in Europe, 4; concerns about German armor, 19; D+6 meeting, 171; despised by Montgomery, 14; Montgomery proposes a large scale parachute drop, 21; Montgomery wants supply priority, 10, 27; need to open Antwerp, 12; note of caution, xiv; pitted against Montgomery, xv; planning for Market Garden, 26; pressure to use airborne units, xv; status on Antwerp, 12; supply situation, 217, 219-222; Urquhart's failing, 175; Versailles meeting, 191

Ellis, L.F., 195

Elst, 126-127, 131, 137-138, 143-144, 153-154

Essame, Brigadier Hubert, 123-124, 144, 161, 163, 165, 188, 235-236

Euling, SS-Capt. Karl-Heinz, 80, 93-95, 95, 98,107-108, 117, 120, 125

Feldt, Gen. Kurt, 54, 74, 93, 106, 115-117, 157

Fitch, Lt. Col. J.A.C., 75-76, 97, 109-111

Foulkes, Gen., 206

Frost, Lt. Col. John, xii, 48, 60, 73, 81; Arnhem defense, 79-81, 83, 85, 94-98, 100-101, 114, 125, 127-129, 133, 173, 175; arrives in Arnhem, 75-78; assessment of the battle, 200-201; bad communications, 132-133; D-Day, 75, 84; Driel-Heveadorp ferry, 38; hero of Arnhem bridge, 37; no re-supply available, 134; post war, 202

Fullriede, *Luftwaffe* Col., 55, 173, 175-176, 205

Gale, Gen. Sir Richard, 40, 239

Gavin, Brig. Gen. James, 1, 3, 6, 70, 140, 172; air operations, 225, 227-228; *Airborne Warfare* book, 40; assault crossing of the Waal, 115; assessment, 243; Browning orders offensive in the north, 171; capture of Nijmegen, 122; D+1, 92; D+2, 106; D+4, 124; disgust as boats did not arrive, 115; divisional responsibility, 72; Groesbeek Heights, 37; jump injury, 106; meets with Browning, 105-106; meets with Ridgeway, 105; memoirs, 197; Nijmegen, 92, 116-117, 120; Operation *Comet*, 20; post war, 206; satisfied with the progress, 71

Gazurek, Capt. Ignacy, 146,

German Military Units, *1st SS Panzer Division*, 47; *First Panzer Army*, 47; *First Parachute Army*, 44, 46, 51, 53-54, 157, 211; *First Parachute Brigade*, 56; *2nd Division*, 58; *Fifth Panzer Army*, 44, 46, 49; *6th Parachute Regiment*, 54, 65-66, 89; *Seventh Army*, 44, 46; *9th SS Panzer Division*, 1, 58; *9th SS Reconnaissance Battalion*, 48, 73-74; *9th Waffen SS Division Hohenstaufen*, 47-49, 52, 55, 60, 65, 82, 83-84, 94-95, 110, 113, 126, 201, 203-204, 212; *Ninth SS Reconnaissance Battalion*, 55; *10th SS Engineer Battalion*, 73; *10th SS Panzer Division*, 58, 73; *Tenth SS Reconnaissance Battalion*, 204; *10th Waffen SS Division Frundsberg*, 47-52, 60, 65, 80, 82- 84, 91, 94, 98, 106-107, 138, 201, 203-204, 212-213, 215; *Fifteenth Army*, 27, 44-46, 51, 53-54, 152, 157, 169, 211, 213; *24th Division*, 55; *33rd SS (French) Division*, 176; *59th Division*, 46, 51, 53-54, 61, 64, 87, 89, 104, 152, 157; *64th Division*, 213; *70th Division*, 45-46, 54; *84th Division*, 46; *85th Division*, 46, 54, 65-67; *107th Panzer Brigade*, 51, 53-54, 89, 104, 130, 147-148, 152-153, 182, 214; *116th Division*, 58; *191st Regiment of Artillery*, 84;

219th Coastal Division, 53; *245th Division*, 46, 54; *346th Division*, 44, 53; *406th Division*, 51, 54, 74; *506th Heavy Panzer Battalion*, 175; *711th Division*, 53; *712th Division*, 46; *716th Division*, 54, 147; *719th Coastal Division*, 46, 53; *Army Group B*, xiii, xiv, 43-44, 47, 49, 172, 211-212; *Army Group Center*, 43; *Artillery Regiment 184*, 55-57; *Artillery Regiment 191*, 172; *Assault Gun Brigade 280*, 172; *Battalion Bruhns*, 85; *Battalion Euling*, 49, 73, 80, 84, 93, 95, 98, 107; *Battalion Ewald*, 64; *Battalion Huber*, 169; *Battalion Junghahn*, 174; *Battalion Jungwirth*, 157-158, 169; *Battalion Knaust*, 85; *Battalion Richter*, 65; *Bielefeld Training Battalion*, 108, 175; *Division Erdmann*, 147; *Division Von Tettau*, 55, 157, 176; *Divisional Officer's Course*, 203; *Divisionsverband Walter*, 65-66; *Heavy Panzer Brigade 506*, 108; *Hermann Goering Training Regiment*, 175, 188; *Kampfgruppe Becker*, 93; *Kampfgruppe Brinkmann*, 82-84, 94, 98, 100, 108, 138, 145, 204; *Kampfgruppe Bruhn*, 111, 174; *Kampfgruppe Chill*, 53-54, 147; *Kampfgruppe Dr. Segler*, 153; *Kampfgruppe Eberwein*, 111-112, 175, 188; *Kampfgruppe Euling*, 108, 117, 120, 125; *Kampfgruppe Fuerstenberg*, 91; *Kampfgruppe Goebel*, 91; *Kampfgruppe Greschick*, 91, 116; *Kampfgruppe Gropp*, 94; *Kampfgruppe Harder*, 83, 94, 179; *Kampfgruppe Hartung*, 126; *Kampfgruppe Henke*, 54, 65, 91, 108, 117; *Kampfgruppe Hermann*, 93; *Kampfgruppe Hoffman*, 66; *Kampfgruppe Huber*, 147-148, 152, 157; *Kampfgruppe*

Knaust, 108, 126, 129, 131, 138; *Kampfgruppe Krafft,* 49, 111, 174; *Kampfgruppe Moeller,* 94; *Kampfgruppe Reinhold,* 73; *Kampfgruppe Reinholt,* 126; *Kampfgruppe Richter,* 130, 153; *Kampfgruppe Rink,* 88; *Kampfgruppe Spindler,* 82-83, 97; *Kampfgruppe Stargaard,* 91; *Kampfgruppe von Allworden,* 83, 94, 179; *Kampfgruppe Walther,* 54, 89, 147, 151, 157, 169; *Korps Feldt,* 54; *Kriegsmarine,* 55; *Luftwaffe Penal Battalion Six,* 65-66; *I Brigade Flakartillerie,* 85; *II Fallschirmjeager Korps,* 73; *II SS Panzer Corps,* 21, 43, 47, 51, 53, 56, 58, 65, 147, 157, 161, 172, 193, 198, 201, 204, 212, 228; *II Parachute Corps,* 93, 157; *LXXXVI Corps,* 147, 157, 169; *LXXXVIII Corps,* 53, 54, 67, 69, 130, 170; *Nacht Jagdgeschwader 1,* 40; *Netherlands Command,* 55; *Nijmegen Defense Force,* 54; *OB West,* xv; *Panzer Abteilung 503,* 85; *Panzer Brigade 280,* 175; *Panzergrenadier Regiment 21,* 48, 95; *Panzerjaegergruppe Roestel,* 65-66; *Parachute Regiment 6,* 152; *Parachute Training Division Erdmann,* 54, 66- 67; *Parachute Training Regiment von Hoffman,* 65; *Reserve Battalion 16,* 56; *Schiffsturmabteilung 10,* 161; *Security Regiment 26,* 161; *Security Regiment Knocke,* 161; *Sicherheit Regiment Knocke,* 96; *SS Lippert NCO Training School Arnheim,* 55; *SS Panzer Grenadier Depot,* 56; *SS Panzer Grenadier Regiment 21,* 84, 126-127; *SS Panzergrenadier Regiment 19,* 109; *SS Panzergrenadier Regiment 20,* 109; *SS Training and Replacement Battalion,* 94; *SS Wach Battalion 3,* 55, 96; *Tank-Destroyer Battalion 559,* 157; *Training and Replacement Regiment Hermann Goering,* 57; *Waffen-SS Kampfgruppe Eberwein,* 57; *Wehrkreis VI,* 53-55, 72-74, 95, 111, 141, 157, 193; *Wehrmacht Sturmgeschutz Brigade 280,* 110; *Worrowski Battalion,* 176

Gibbs, Hon. V.P., 120

Gough, Maj. Frederick, 75, 77-78, 80-81, 127, 198

Goulburn, Lt. Col. Edward, 106, 120

Graebner, SS-Captain Viktor-Eberhard, 1, 73-74, 82-83, 91, 94, 98-99, 109, 124

Grave Bridge, 19-20, 26, 29, 36-37, 69-70, 85, 90-91, 105, 122-124, 154, 159, 163, 165, 193, 195, 197, 212-214, 226-227, 237, 242

Grayburn, Lt. Jack, 78, 127

Greenwalt, Lt. Howard A., 71-72

Gregory-Hood, Maj. A.H.M., 106

Greschick, Maj. (-), 116

Groesbeek Heights, 29, 36-37, 39, 53, 71, 73-74, 91-92, 93, 105-106, 116-117, 206, 228, 237

Gwatkin, Brig. Norman, 31, 67, 106

Hackett, Gen. Sir John, 20, 22, 39, 58, 96-97, 112-113, 129, 172, 174, 182, 200, 205, 207, 209, 228, 235, 239, 241

Hagen, Sgt. Louis, 176, 185, 193

Harmel, SS-Maj. Gen. Heinz, 47-48, 50, 81, 98, 106, 109, 125-126, 131, 202, 204-205, 212

Harrison, Lt. Col. William, 70, 118

Harzer, SS-Lt. Col. Walther, 1, 47-48, 82, 84, 137-138, 172, 175, 177-178, 192, 203, 205

Hatert bridge, 37, 70-71

Hausser, Col. Gen. SS Paul, 47, 49

Heaps, Lt. Leo, 81, 134, 176, 208

"Heart" Route, 26, 89

Helle, SS-Capt. Paul Anton, 55-56,

175-176
Helmond, 25, 104, 142, 149, 151, 171, 181-182
Henke, Col. (-), 54, 73, 91, 94, 117
Henniker, Lt. W.C.A., 183, 187
Herclerode, Peter, 200
Heumen bridge, 37, 197, 227
Heydte, Lt. Col. Baron von der, 54, 65-67, 89, 147, 152, 157-158,
Hibbert, Maj. Anthony, 77-78, 80-81, 244,
Hibbert, Christopher, 84, 99, 128, 200, 204, 208
Hicks, Brigadier (-), 95-97, 109, 112, 172, 184
Higgins, Brig. Gen. (-), 68
Himmler, "Reichsfuehrer SS" Heinrich, 49, 201
Hitler, Adolf, xiv-xv, 43-44, 49, 51-52, 204, 206
Hodges, Gen. Courtney, 4, 21, 191, 200
Hoeppner, Col. Gen. Erich, 49
Hollinghurst, Air Vice-Marshal Leslie, 33, 39, 225, 231
Honinghutie rail bridge, 37, 71, 91, 92, 123, 213
Hoof, Jan van, 126
Hopkinson, Lt. (-), 143
Horrocks, Gen. Brian, 6, 13, 15, 17, 22, 26, 31, 90, 120, 144-145; argument over tactics, 159; assault crossing of the Waal, 115; bad communications, 132, 134; crosses the Waal River, 181; D+4, 134, 138; D+5, 143; D+6, 153, 162; D+7, 164, 166, 236; D-1 meeting, 30; failure of command, 193, 162; lack of advance on D+3, 122-124; launches D-Day attack, 66; meets Gavin, 106; meets with Sosabowski, 236; night crossing the river, 158; no evidence XXX Corps fought badly, 161; orders withdrawal on D+8, 165; out of radio contact, 85; plans

to replace 1st Airborne, 153; poor health, 14; post war, 207; Sosabowski, 238
Hunner Park, 107-108, 119-120
Huston, James, 229

IJmuiden, 12
IJssel, 9, 27, 29-30, 38, 84, 191, 195, 221
IJsselmeer, 4, 9, 27, 29, 41, 44, 51, 68, 195, 221-222
IJsselstein, 76, 99

Jachnik, Lt. Col. S., 238
Johnson, Leslie, 121
Jones, Maj. A.W., 184
Jones, Lt. Col. C.P., 119
Jones, Capt. Robert E., 61-62
Jones, Lt. Tony, 121, 125
Juettner, SS-Obergruppenfuehrer Hans, 50
Jukes, Pvt. Bill, 74

Kappel, Capt. Karl W., 120
Kennedy, Lt. Russell, 155, 163, 184, 186-187, 208, 236
Kershaw, Robert, 83, 124, 198
Kessel, Lipmann, 178, 209
Knaust, Maj. Hans-Peter, 95, 100, 108, 126, 129
Knights Cross, Graebner, Capt. Viktor-Eberhard, 1
Koch, Col. Oscar, 5, 200
Krafft, SS-Capt. Sepp, 56-57, 77, 82-84, 94, 111, 174, 188, 228
Krueger, SS-Capt., 107, 120, 127
Kussin, Maj. Gen. Friedrich, 56, 76, 84

Lamb, Richard, 59
Lathbury, Brigadier, 75-78, 80-81, 83, 95, 97, 101, 208
Lea, Lt. Col. George, 109-111
Lee, Cdr. Asher, 59
Leigh-Mallory, Trafford, 33
Lewin, Ronald, 59

Lewis, Maj. R.P. C. "Pongo," 76, 94, 100

Lindquist, Lt. Col. (-), 71-72

Lippert, SS-Col., 55-57, 137-138, 175-176, 205

Loder-Symonds, Lt. Col., 81, 174, 182

Lommel bridgehead, 2, 23, 90, 103, 213

London Daily Mail, xiv

Lonsdale, Maj. Dickie, 111

Maas-Waal Canal, 19, 25, 37, 70-71, 85, 91, 115-116, 195, 197, 209, 226-227, 237

Mackay, Capt. Eric, 79, 99, 108, 127-128

Mackenzie, Lt. Col. Charles, 59, 95-96, 98, 134-135, 144-146, 153-154, 182

Malden bridge, 37, 70

Maltzahn, Maj. Baron von, 54, 130, 152

Mann, Pfc. Joe E., 62, 87-88

Manners, Capt. Charles J. Robert, 106

Marshall, Gen. George C., 5

Martin, Lt. Russ, 186

Mason, Lt. Paul, 79, 128

Mattusch, SS-Capt. (-), 57

McAuliffe, Brig. Gen., 148, 152

McCain, Maj. Robert, 110-111

McCardie, Lt. Col. Derek, 96, 109-111

McCrory, Sgt. James M., 104-105, 121, 141

Meindl, Gen. Eugen, 73, 93, 157

Mendez, Lt. Col. Louis, 71-72, 117

Meuse-Escaut Canal, 1-3, 23-25, 29-30, 66, 90, 103, 212-213, 221

Michaelis, Lt. Col. John H., 62, 87, 148

Middlebrook, Martin, 40, 79-80

Miles, Tony, 128

Model, Field Marshal Walter, xv, 43-44, 47, 49-50, 54-55, 65, 84, 126, 138, 152, 205, 211-212, 228; Allied landings south of the Nijmegen bridges, 72-73; Arnhem best military moment, 53; D+1, 93; D+5, 147; D+6, 153; D+7, 157; headquarters at Oosterbeek, 59; orders bridges not to be blown, 52; orders Nijmegen bridge not to be destroyed, 227; orders to Von Tettau, 95; preparations, 51; rapid reaction, 52

Moeller, SS-Capt. Hans, 84, 110, 175

Molenhoek bridge, 37, 70, 91, 116, 118, 212

Mongeon, Capt. Jean, 186

Montgomery, Field Marshal Sir Bernard, xv, 4-5, 8, 15, 22, 29; a flair for publicity, 13; a man in a hurry, 9; advance to be rapid and violent, 31; air operations, 226; ambitions rescued from disaster by &&&naï..ve&&& and ignorant Americans, 17; ambitious aspirations, 11; American airborne units ace card, 17; assessment of the campaign, 195-199, 242, 244; brainchild is *Market Garden*, 13; bridges, 30; bridgeheads over the Ijssel, 9; complains about Eisenhower, 7; control of First Allied Airborne Army, 211; D+6, 171; despised Crerar, 13; did not care about transportation issues, 10; did not consult staff about Market Garden, 9; drive on Berlin was sheer fantasy, 223; Eisenhower, 192; excessive optimism, 6; explains decision about *Market Garden*, 25-26; failed to order additional transport, 10; feels betrayed, 11; felt Eisenhower was an amateur, 14; gives orders for *Market Garden*, 9; instructions to Crerar, 12; lack of concern about German armor, 59; meets with Dempsey, D+8, 165-166; methodical preparations hallmark of leadership, 16; movement "depressingly slow,"

151; no sense of diplomacy, 13; one of three blind mice, xvi; Operation *Comet*, 20; orders effort to cross the Rhine, 211; original plan came from Montgomery's HQ, 35; Patton, 14; planning for Market Garden, 26; post battle, 207; Prince Bernhardt's visit, 21; reinforcing defeat, 136; SHAEF, 192; Sosabowski, 238; supply situation, 218- 223; thwarted by the Germans, 191; wanted to be first in Berlin, 9; wants control over U.S. First Army, 27; wants supply priority, 27 wins promise of supplies, 10

Mosier, Lt. Harry, 157

Munford, Maj. Dennis, 78, 80

Murray, Lt. Col. Iain, 182

Myers, Col. Eddie, 144-146, 153-155, 158, 160, 165-166, 182, 235-236

Naumann, SS-Lt. Albert, 56

Neerpelt bridgehead, 2, 23, 29, 50-51, 65, 103, 122, 143, 212

Netherlands Armed Forces (German), 44

Netherlands Military Units; *Dutch Princess Irene Brigade*, 29; *Royal Netherlands Brigade Group*, 32; *Netherlands Command*, 53

Newport, George, 203

Nijmegen, the Netherlands, xii-xvii, 17, 21, 23, 25, 29-30, 42, 52, 65, 73, 82-83, 121, 129, 135, 137-138, 140, 144, 154-155, 159, 163-165, 169, 188, 195, 207, 212- 213, 231, 238, 243; assault on, 71, 92, 98; Browning orders capture of, 106; capture of, 120; D+1, 91-92, 100; D+9, 181; D-Day, 91; defense of, 193; extending the West Wall through, 44; failure to capture on D-Day, 46, 194; German defense of, 116-120; German reinforcements arrive, 93-99, 107; German reports

of landings, 57; inside the British perimeter, 181; Operation *Comet*, 19; river crossing, 119-120; supply situation, 222

Nijmegen bridges, 36-37, 68, 72, 74, 92, 115, 121-122, 128, 227, 237, 242; assessment, 198; battle around the, 100; capture of, 120, 125, 133; D+3, 131; D+4, 123; D-day, 85; German orders to destroy, 126; German reinforcements arrive, 106; important achievement, 191; no attack on D+1, 105; third on list of priorities, 197

Norton, Maj. G.G., 200,

Obstfelder, Lt. Gen. Hans von, 147, 157

O'Connor, Lt. Gen. Sir Richard, 15, 23-24, 141, 207-208

Oldershausen, Maj. Eckbrecht Freiherr von, 205-206

Oosterbeek, 52, 56-57, 59, 76, 78, 82-83, 97, 109, 111-112, 114, 117-118, 122, 128, 131, 145-146, 162-163, 171- 172, 175-177, 182-183, 185, 188, 194-195, 208, 212- 213, 214, 230

Oosterhout, 123, 126-127, 137-138, 143-144, 154, 193

Operation *Bagration*, 43

Operation *Comet*, 19-22, 26, 28, 43, 146, 195, 197, 211-212, 225-227, 235

Operation *Garden*, 2-3, 23, 115, 161

Operation *Linnet I*, 28-29

Operation *Linnet II*, 28-29

Operation *Market*, 2-3, 12, 19, 20, 50, 170, 204, 226, 228- 229, 237

Operation *Market Garden*, xi, xvi-xvii, 1, 12, 33, 49, 54, 91, 151, 171, 191-192, 194, 196, 200, 208, 213-214, 218, 220-223, 231, 235, 239, 241-242; air operations, 225; approved on Sept. 10, 27; assess-

ment of, 198, 207, 243; contained
the seeds of failure, xii; D+5 transportation issues, 10; D-day successes, 85; definitively planned, 212;
Dempsey's heart not in it, 28; failure
along the Corridor, 46; failure of,
193; flanking corps not given due,
25; German military units, 47;
Hitler's plans for Ardennes offensive, 51; Horrock's poor health, 14;
importance of the Mook rail bridge,
26; intent not to capture the Ruhr,
27; intent to capture V2 sites, 27;
Irish Guards did not understand
nature of, 68; Leigh-Mallory commands air forces, 33; limited strategic thinking, 53; military disaster,
xii; Operational directive M525, 27-
28; Origins of, 4-6, 8-10, 13, 21,
24; requires a lighting advance, 16;
scheduled completion on D+6, 29;
strategic airborne operation, 11;
VIII Corps territorial gains, 15
Operation *Varsity*, 229
Operational directive M525, 27-28

Paetsch, SS-Col. Otto, 82-83
Palmer, Lt. R.M.A., 68, 88
Pannerden Canal, 26, 73, 84, 94-95,
98, 125-126, 131
Parks, Brig. Gen. Floyd, 28, 36
Patton, Gen. George S., xiii, 4-5, 11, 13-
14, 16, 43, 124, 194, 200, 222, 242
Payton-Reid, Lt. Col., 174, 184
Peel Marshes, Battle of, 191
Ploszewski, Maj. W., 139
Polish Military Units; *1st Armored
Division*, 213, 238; *1st Independent
Parachute Brigade*, 6, 8, 19-20, 22,
28-29, 34, 38, 42, 134-135, 137,
139-140, 146-147, 154-156, 159-
160, 165, 198, 213-214, 235
Poppe, Gen. (-), 51, 64, 89, 130, 152
Pott, Maj. John, 112
Powell, Maj. Geoffrey, 67, 112, 129,

131, 160, 185
Pyle, Ernie, xiii

Queripel, Capt. Lionel, 112

Ramsay, Admiral Sir Bertram, 9
Rauter, Gen. Hanns Albin, 32, 57, 205-
206
"Red Lion Route," 221
"Red Ball Express," xiii, 10
Redman, Capt. T.F., 209
Reinhard, Gen. Hans, 53, 152, 169
Reinhhold, SS-Capt. Leo H., 94
Reynolds, Michael, 204
Richmond, Sgt. Leroy, 119
Ridgeway, Lt. Gen. Matthew, 8, 28-29,
105, 124, 171
Ritchie, Lt. Gen. Sir Neil, 14, 22, 25,
130, 149, 208
Roberts, Maj. Gen. Philip, 15, 45
Robinson, Sgt. Peter, 120-122, 125
Roeree, Lt. Col. Theodoor, 204
Roestel, SS-Lt. Col. Franz, 147, 153,
204
Rommel, Field Marshal Erwin, 16, 49
Roosevelt, President Franklin D., 5
Ruhr Valley, xiv-xv, 6-8, 11, 24, 26-27,
51
Rundstedt, Field Marshal Gerd von, xv,
44, 55, 211
Ryan, Cornelius, 27, 68, 127, 134,
160, 204, 227

Saar Valley, 7, 11
Scheldt Estuary, 10-12, 22, 27, 34, 44,
51, 218
Scherbening, Lt. Gen., 74, 91, 117
Seyss-Inquhart, Arthur, 205
Shoerener, Field-Marshal (-), 204
Silvester, Maj. Gen. Lindsay
McDonald, 208
Simpson, Lt. Dennis, 128
Sims, Pvt. James, 193
Sink, Lt. Col. Robert, 17, 64, 148, 181,
208

Skalka, Dr. Egon, 177-178
Smith, Maj. Gen. Edmund Hakewill, 135
Smith, Gen. Walter Bedell, 59, 196, 199
Smyth, Lt. Col. (-), 112, 129, 173
Sobocinski, Capt. W., 139
Son River bridge, 2, 29, 35-36, 39, 54, 61, 64, 67-69, 85, 89, 90, 104-105, 119, 129-130, 181, 194-195, 197-198, 212, 226
Sonnenstahl, SS-Lt. Col., 106, 117
Sosabowski, Maj. Gen. S.F., xvii, 6, 113, 144, 200, 237-239; a new plan, 140; air operations, 227; argument over tactics, 159; bad communications, 145; clashes with Ivor Thomas, 15; crossing the river, 146, 154; forms parachute brigade, 235; insults and humiliation, 165; meets with Horrocks on D+7, 236; Mook rail bridge, 26; night crossing the river, 155, 158-167; not impressed with British efforts, 236; Operation Comet, 20, 43; parachute drop, 138-139; plan to drop near Driel-Heveadorp Ferry, 134-135; Polish drop, 41; post war, 207, 240; thought British were overconfident, 31; Urquhart's failing, 171
Spindler, SS-Lt. Col. Ludwig, 49, 82-83, 84, 109-111
St. Oedenrode, 35, 64, 88, 104, 141, 158, 169, 181
Stadler, SS-Major Gen. Silvester, 1, 203
Stainforth, Lt. Peter, 79, 99, 128, 178
Stearley, Brig. Gen. Ralph, 231
Steveninck, Col. De Ruyter van, 29
Stevens, Lt. Col. R., 140, 159, 165-166, 236
Stoors, Lt. David, 140
Stopka, Maj. John P., 87
Storrs, Lt. David, 146
Strong, Kenneth, 199
Student, "Luftwaffe" Colonel-General Kurt, 44, 46, 52, 54, 147, 149, 157, 211
Supreme Headquarters Allied Expeditionary Force (SHAEF), xiii-xvi, 4, 6-7, 11, 27, 53, 58, 192, 196, 217, 221-223

Tate, Lt. Bob, 184
Tathem-Warter, Maj. Digby, 75, 77-78, 101, 128, 208
Taylor, Lt. Col. George, 138, 144, 146, 148, 153, 236
Taylor, Maj. Gen. Maxwell, 17, 35, 152-153, 170, 172, 226; American buildup, 104; arrives in Eindhoven, 89; assessment, 197, 243; D+3, 104; D+4, 141; D+6, 153; D+7, 63; D-Day, 62-63, 69; intellectual, 16; meeting with Dempsey, 36, 69; post war, 206; Ridgeway arrives, 105
Tedder, Air Marshal Sir Authur, 27
ter Horst, Kate, 177
Tettau, Maj. Gen. Baron Hans von, 53, 55-57, 95-96, 112, 131, 157, 161, 172, 175-176, 205, 214-215
Thomas, Maj. Gen. Ivor, 15, 123, 158-160, 162, 164-165, 238
Thompson, Lt. John S., 70
Tieke, Wilhelm, 82
Tilly, Lt. Col. Gerald, 160-161, 166
Tucker, Maj. Michael L., 184, 186-187, 206
Tucker, Lt. Col. Reuben, 17, 106, 115-116, 120, 122, 124, 140, 155, 227
Turnhout Canal, 23-24, 90, 103

Uden, 35, 88, 141, 148, 151-152, 171, 214
"Ultra", 21, 27, 50, 52, 54, 56, 58-60, 83, 228
United States Military Units, First Army, xiii, 4, 8-9, 11, 21, 27-28, 44, 191, 213; Second Tactical Air Force, 231; Third Army, xiii, 4, 11, 14, 194, 196, 222-223; Sixth Army,

xiii, 4; *7th Armored Division*, 182, 208, 215; *Eighth Air Force*, 33, 231; *Ninth Air Force*, 33; *Ninth Army*, 4, 204, 213; *Ninth Troop Carrier Command*, 38; *Twelfth Army Group*, 4; *17th Airborne Division*, 10; *26th Infantry Division*, 221; *29th Infantry Division*, 221; *82nd Airborne Division*, xii, 3, 6, 17, 20, 28, 30, 59, 91-92, 105, 130, 171, 182, 194, 228, 243; air operations, 232; artillery, 106; assault crossing of the Waal, 115; assessment of the campaign, 198; capture of Grave bridge, 70; capture of the Honinghutie bridge, 213; casualties, 206; crossing the river, 155, 157; D+1, 91; D+4, 140; D+6, 154; D+12, 26, 215; D-Day, 70, 197; D-Day a qualified success, 85; drop plan, 226-227; Grave bridge, 29; Groesbeek Heights, 37; landings, 70; Maas-Waal Canal bridge, 29; Nijmegen bridge, 29, 39, 91, 117; post battle, 206; pride in achievement, 127; route of advance, 36; route to target, 34; *101st Airborne Division*, xii, 2-3, 6, 12, 16-17, 22, 28, 53-54, 66, 69, 130, 169, 189, 204, 221, 226; air operations, 232; airborne landings, 63; artillery arrives on D+6, 153; assessment of the campaign, 198; D+1, 88; D+2, 103; D+3, 131; D+4, 141; D+5, 147, 149; D+6, 151-152, 171, 214; D+9, 170, 181; D-Day, 65, 68; D-Day a qualified success, 85; drop plan, 36; Eindhoven bridge, 29; Nijmegen Bridge, 121; occupies Eindhoven, 213; post battle, 206; route of advance, 34-35; seven different drop zones, 40; Son River bridge, 29, 90; *501st Parachute Infantry Regiment*, 63-64, 130, 141, 147- 148, 152;

502nd Parachute Infantry Regiment, 61-62, 64, 87-88, 104, 141, 148, 157; *504th Parachute Infantry Regiment*, 17, 37, 105-106, 115, 117-118, 120, 227; *505th Parachute Infantry Regiment*, 37, 71, 74, 92, 116, 120; *506th Parachute Infantry Regiment*, 17, 63-64, 68, 89, 141, 148, 152; *508th Parachute Infantry Regiment*, 37, 71, 72, 105; captures Beek, 106; D-Day, 74; Groesbeek Heights, 74; Honinghutie, 71; Nijmegen bridge, 72, 92, 116-117; *878th Aviation Engineer Battalion*, 19, 34; *Glider Infantry Regiment*, 106; *IX Troop Carrier Command*, 19, 33, 225; *XII Corps*, 182; *XIX Corps*, 182, 215; *XVIII Airborne Corps*, 8, 28, 230

Urquhart, Maj. Brian, 12, 17, 32, 58-59, 199-200, 207, 244

Urquhart, Gen. Roy, 6, 15-16, 112, 140, 175, 239; 43rd Division, 161; admires Sosabowski, 235; air operations, 226-228, 230; arrives at Hackett's HQ, 112; assessment of Bittrich, 47; assessment of the campaign, 201; bad communications, 132-133, 143, 146; Browning's "...a bridge to far..." quote, 22; compliments artillery, 174; crossing the river, 154; cut off from his support, 85; D+1, 95; D+3, 127, 131; D+4, 132, 173; D+5, 143, 145-146; D+6, 138; D+7, 165; D+8, 182-183; D-Day, 81; destuction of the 11th Parachute Battalion, 110; did not know about *Ultra*, 59-60; Driel-Heveadorp Ferry, 38, 135; Eric Down, 171; escapes Arnhem, 185, 187; failure of Gen. Thomas, 194; finally returns to HQ, 97; Fourth Parachute Brigade retreats, 113; Hackett reports, 129; inside the British perimeter, 176-177, 179;

leadership and tactics, 42; little chance of relieving Frost, 114; looks for Lathbury, 81; lost battle for two airborne lifts, 39; meets with Lathbury, 76-77; message to Horrocks, 134; night crossing of the river, 160-162; northern most landings at Arnhem, 37; Operation *Comet*, 20; paralysis in British command, 95; plans to replace 1st Airborne, 153; post war, 207; reconnaissance jeeps fail to arrive, 80; should have pushed Browning harder, 40; Sosabowski expected to take Arnham Bridge, 41; supply situation, 231

Valburg, 143, 146, 154, 163, 184, 236
Valkenswaard, 66-69, 90, 105, 121, 143, 193-194, 198
Vandaleur, Lt. Col. J.O.E., 2, 31, 66-67, 105
Vandervoort, Lt. Col. Ben., 105, 108, 115, 119-121
Veghel, 25, 29, 35, 63-64, 88, 130, 147, 151-152, 158, 169, 214
Victoria Cross, Grayburn, Lt. Jack, 127; Queripel, Capt. Lionel, 112

Waizenegger, Lt. Col. (-), 51
Walch, Gordon, 58

Wallis, Maj. David (-), 101
Walther, Col. (-), 65-66, 153
Walton, Brigadier Ben, 122-123, 154, 159, 161, 166
Warrack, Col. Graeme, 177-178, 205, 209
Warren, Lt. Col. Shields, 71-72
Webster, Pfc. Daniel K., 2-3
Weert, 25, 103-104, 130, 142, 149, 214
West Wall, xi, 44, 46, 51, 204
Wierzbowski, Lt. Edward L., 62, 68, 87-89, 149
Wignall, Maj. F.E.B., 68
Wilhelmina Canal, 2, 25, 35-36, 61, 65, 87, 104, 129, 141, 149
Williams, Maj. Gen. Paul L., 19, 33-34, 39, 207, 221, 225
Wilmot, Chester, 197, 226
Wings of the Wind, 79
Wolters, Lt. Cdr. Arnoldus, 177-178
Wrottesley, Capt. The Hon. Richard, 143, 145, 154

Zangen, Lt. Gen. Gustav von, 44-46, 54, 169
Zuid-Willemsvaart Canal, 25, 29, 35, 63-64, 104, 130, 141- 142, 149, 151, 157, 181
Zuyder Zee, 27, 51
Zwolanski, Capt. L., 140